Behind the Scenes!!

2

STORY AND ART BY **BISCO HATORI**

Behind the Scenes!! 02

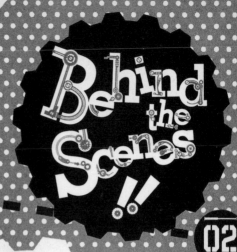

CONTENTS

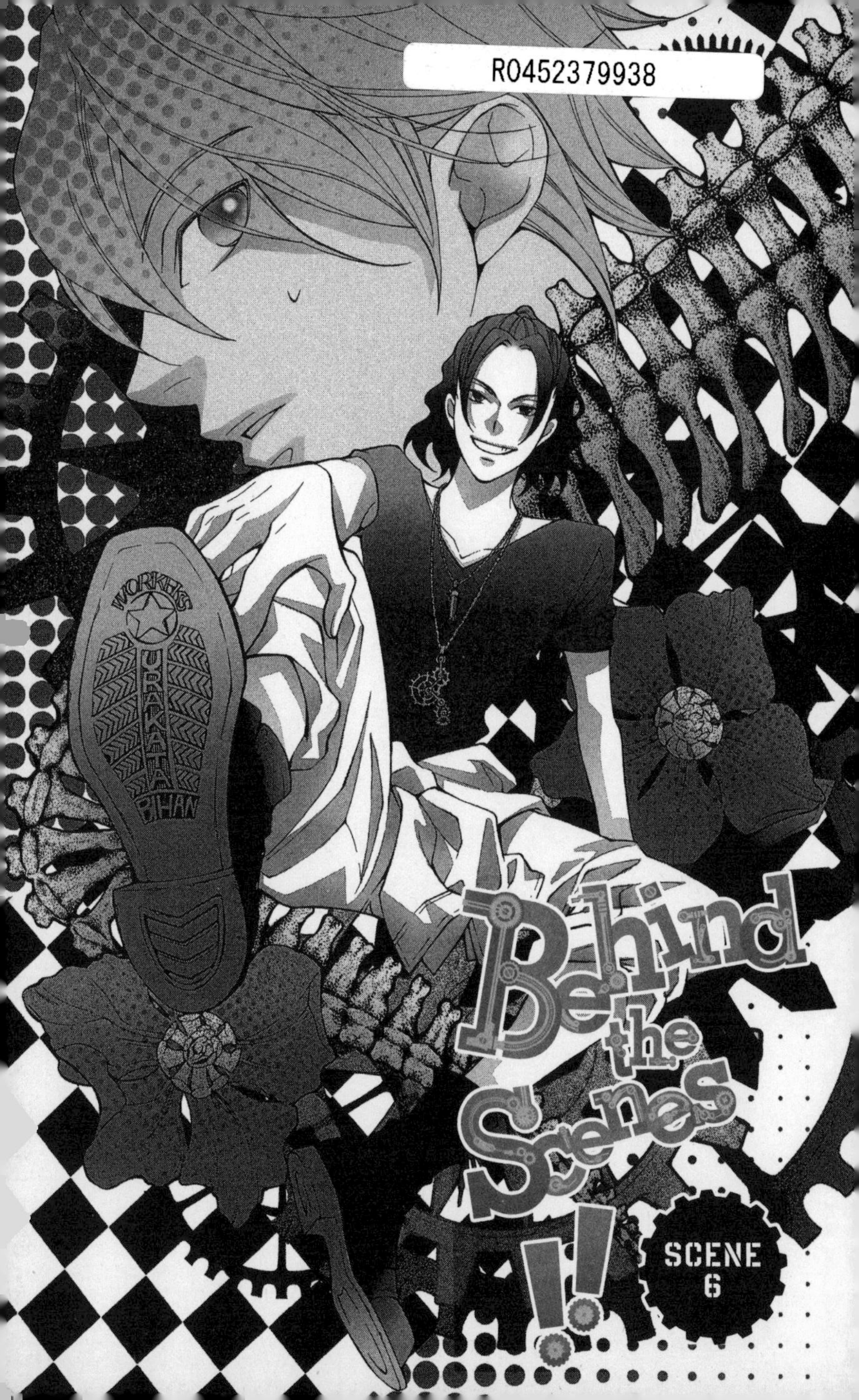
WORKERS
URAKATA
BIHAN
Behind the Scenes!!
SCENE 6

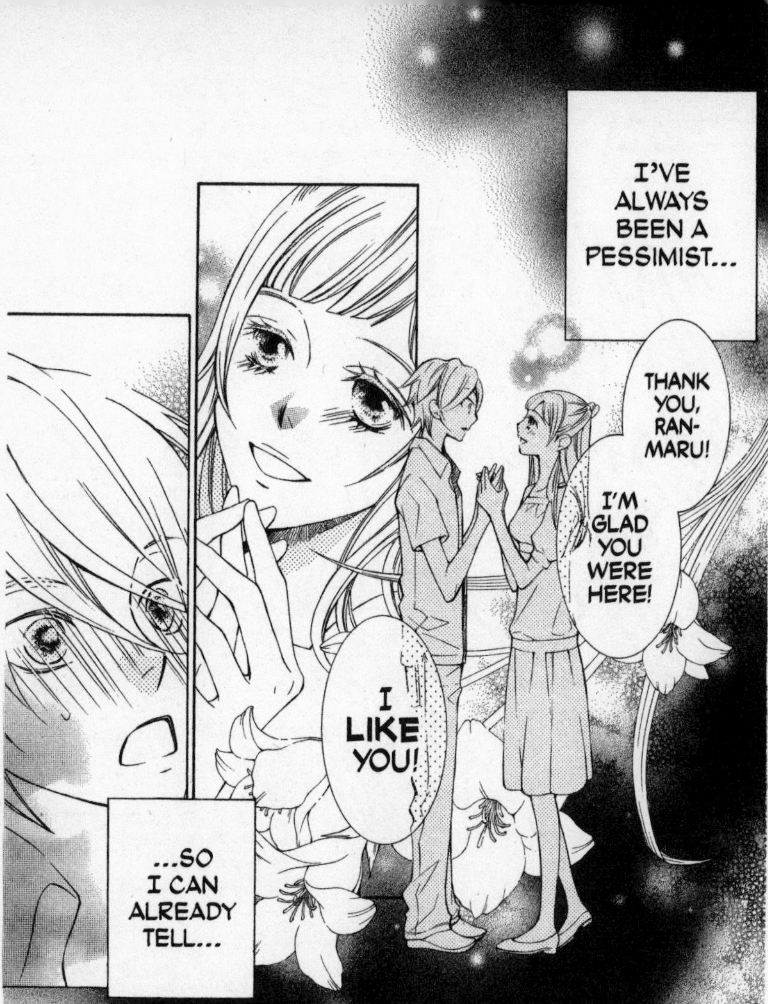
I'VE ALWAYS BEEN A PESSIMIST...
THANK YOU, RAN-MARU!
I'M GLAD YOU WERE HERE!
I LIKE YOU!
...SO I CAN ALREADY TELL...

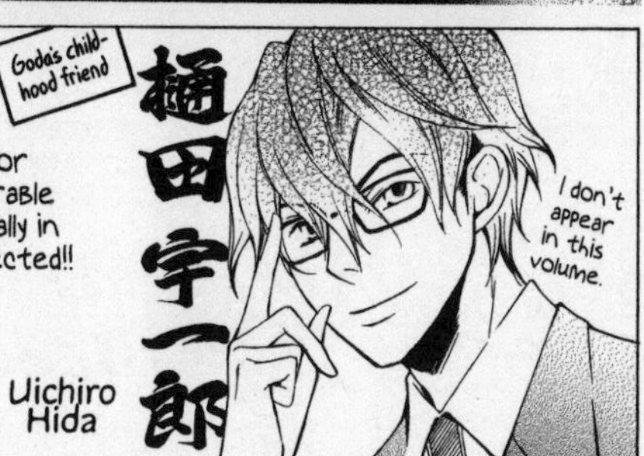
Goda's child-hood friend
樋田宇一郎
I don't appear in this volume.

I named this character after director Peter Weir (in an almost indecipherable way). I love actor Jim Carrey, especially in *The Truman Show*, which Weir directed!!

Uichiro will show up again.

Uichiro Hida

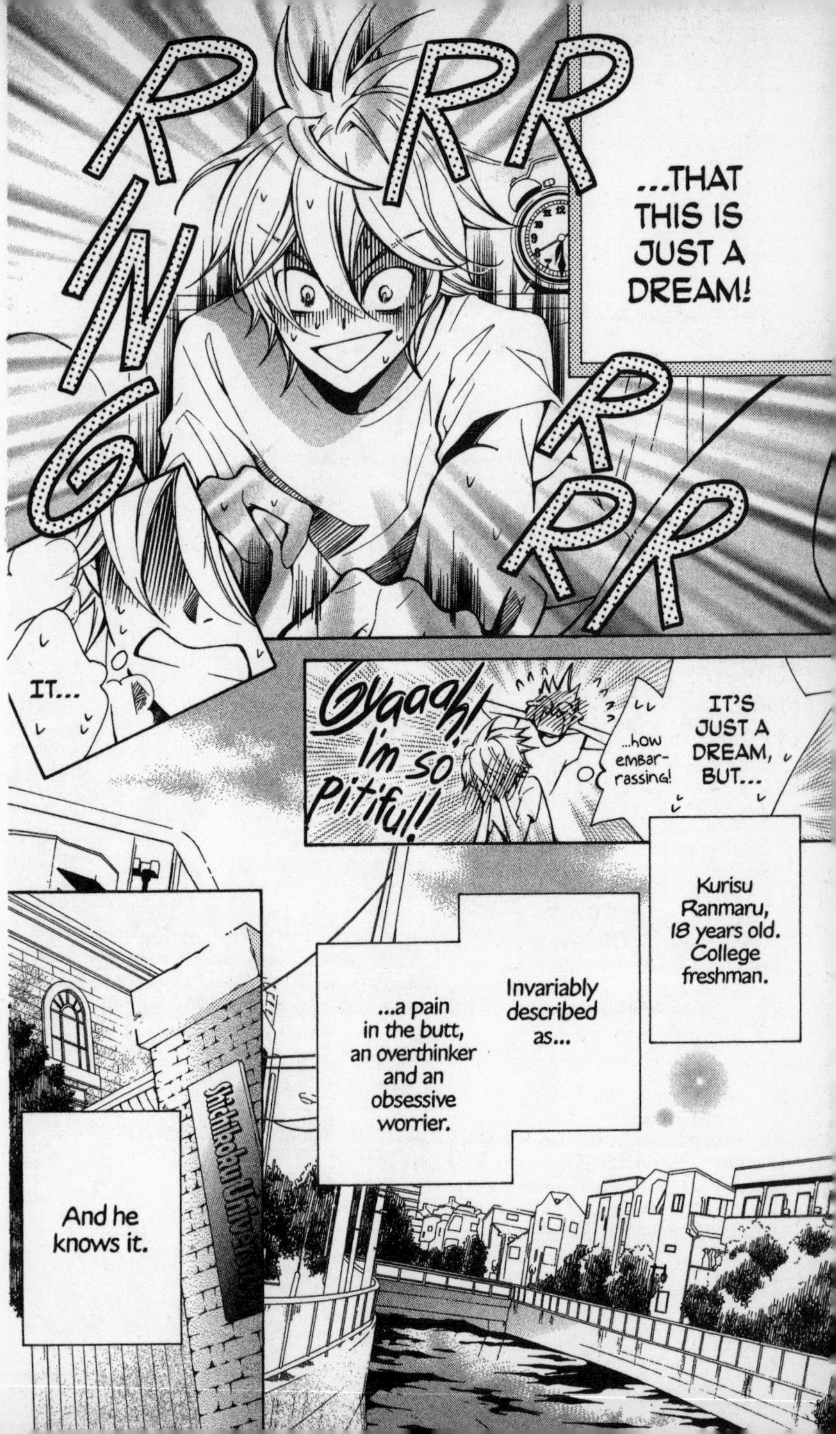
RRR
RING
...THAT THIS IS JUST A DREAM!
RRR
IT...
IT'S JUST A DREAM, BUT...
...how embarrassing!
Gyaagh! I'm so pitiful!
Kurisu Ranmaru, 18 years old. College freshman.
Invariably described as...
...a pain in the butt, an overthinker and an obsessive worrier.
And he knows it.

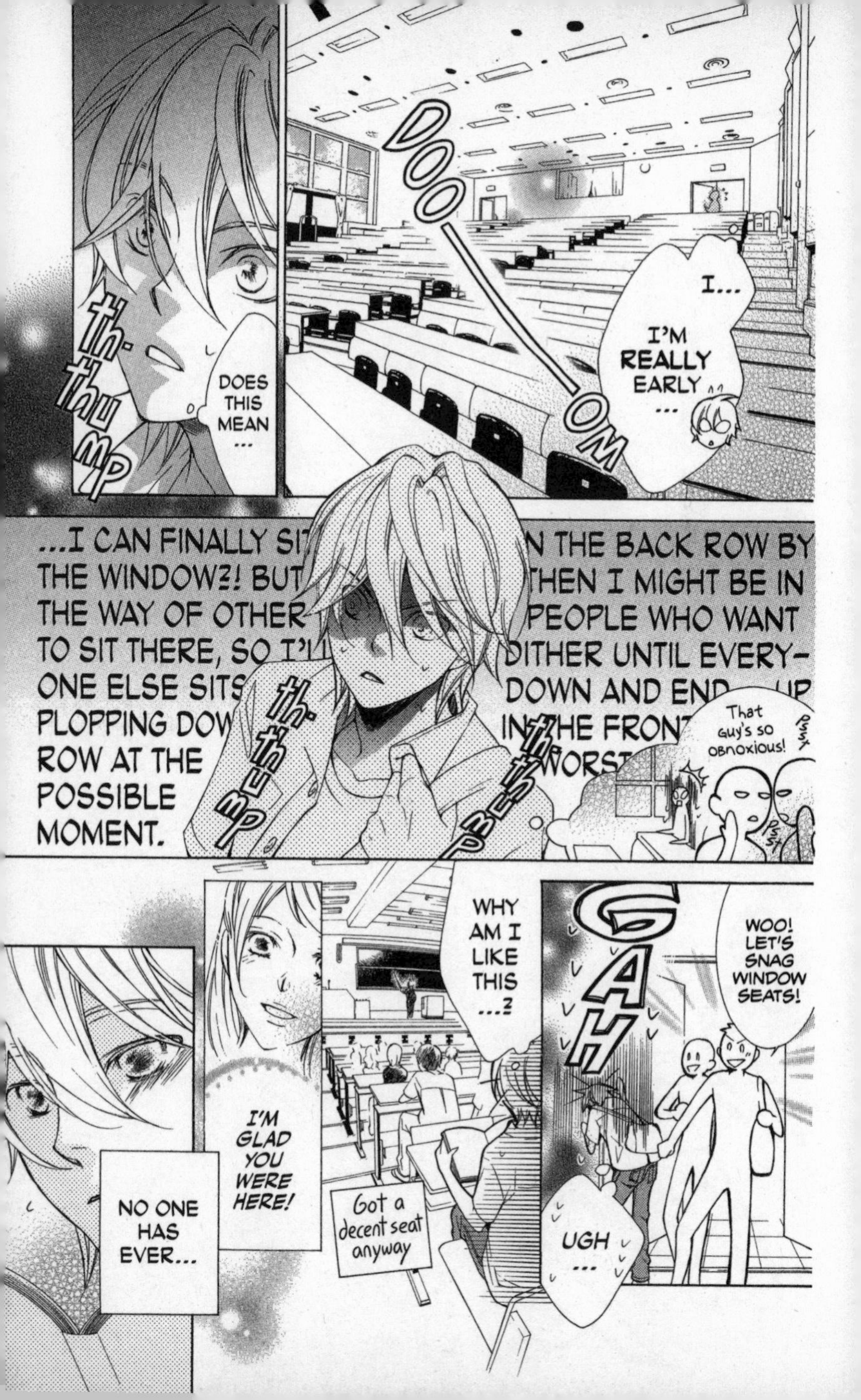
DOOOOM
I...
I'M REALLY EARLY...
DOES THIS MEAN...
th-thump
...I CAN FINALLY SIT
N THE BACK ROW BY
THE WINDOW?! BUT
THEN I MIGHT BE IN
THE WAY OF OTHER
PEOPLE WHO WANT
TO SIT THERE, SO I'L
DITHER UNTIL EVERY-
ONE ELSE SITS
DOWN AND END
UP
PLOPPING DOW
IN THE FRONT
ROW AT THE
WORST
POSSIBLE MOMENT.
That Guy's so obnoxious!
Psst
Psst
WOO! LET'S SNAG WINDOW SEATS!
GAAH
UGH...
WHY AM I LIKE THIS...?
Got a decent seat anyway
I'M GLAD YOU WERE HERE!
NO ONE HAS EVER...

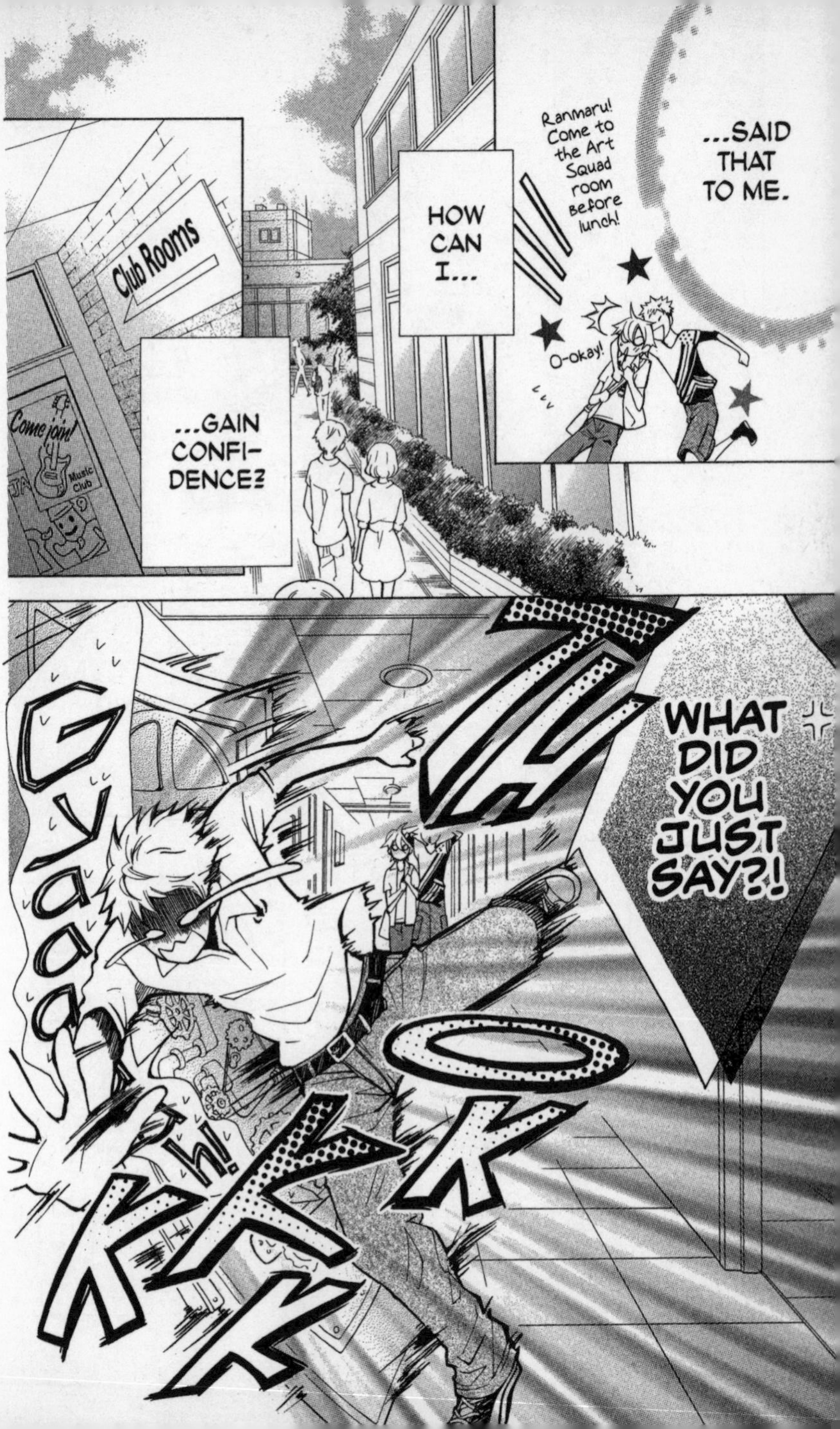

...SAID THAT TO ME.
Ranmaru! Come to the Art Squad room before lunch!
O-okay!
HOW CAN I...
...GAIN CONFIDENCE?
Club Rooms
Come join!
Music Club
WHAT DID YOU JUST SAY?!
Gyaaaah!

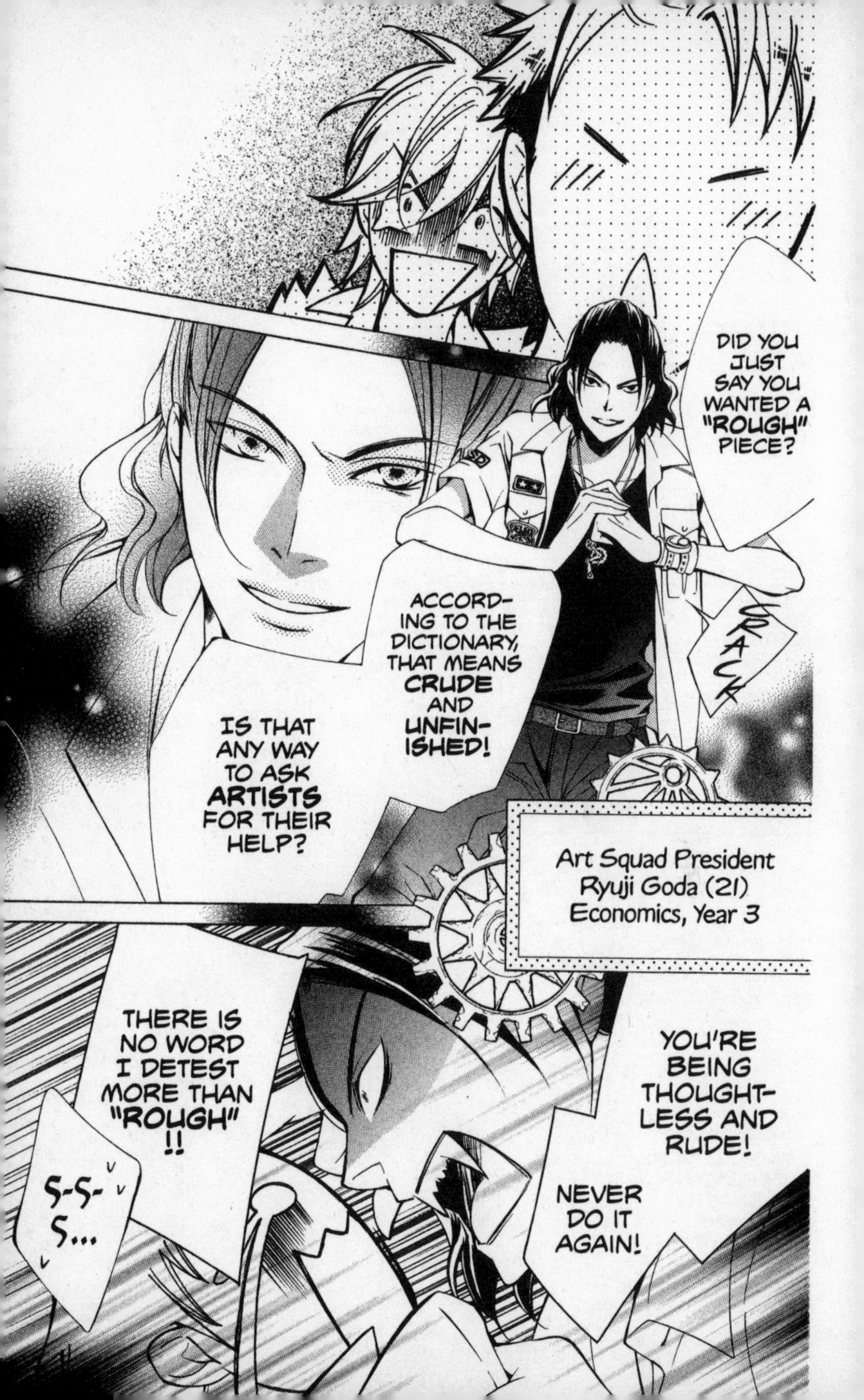
DID YOU JUST SAY YOU WANTED A "ROUGH" PIECE?
CRACK
ACCORDING TO THE DICTIONARY, THAT MEANS CRUDE AND UNFINISHED!
IS THAT ANY WAY TO ASK ARTISTS FOR THEIR HELP?
Art Squad President Ryuji Goda (21) Economics, Year 3
YOU'RE BEING THOUGHTLESS AND RUDE!
NEVER DO IT AGAIN!
THERE IS NO WORD I DETEST MORE THAN "ROUGH"!!
S-S-S...

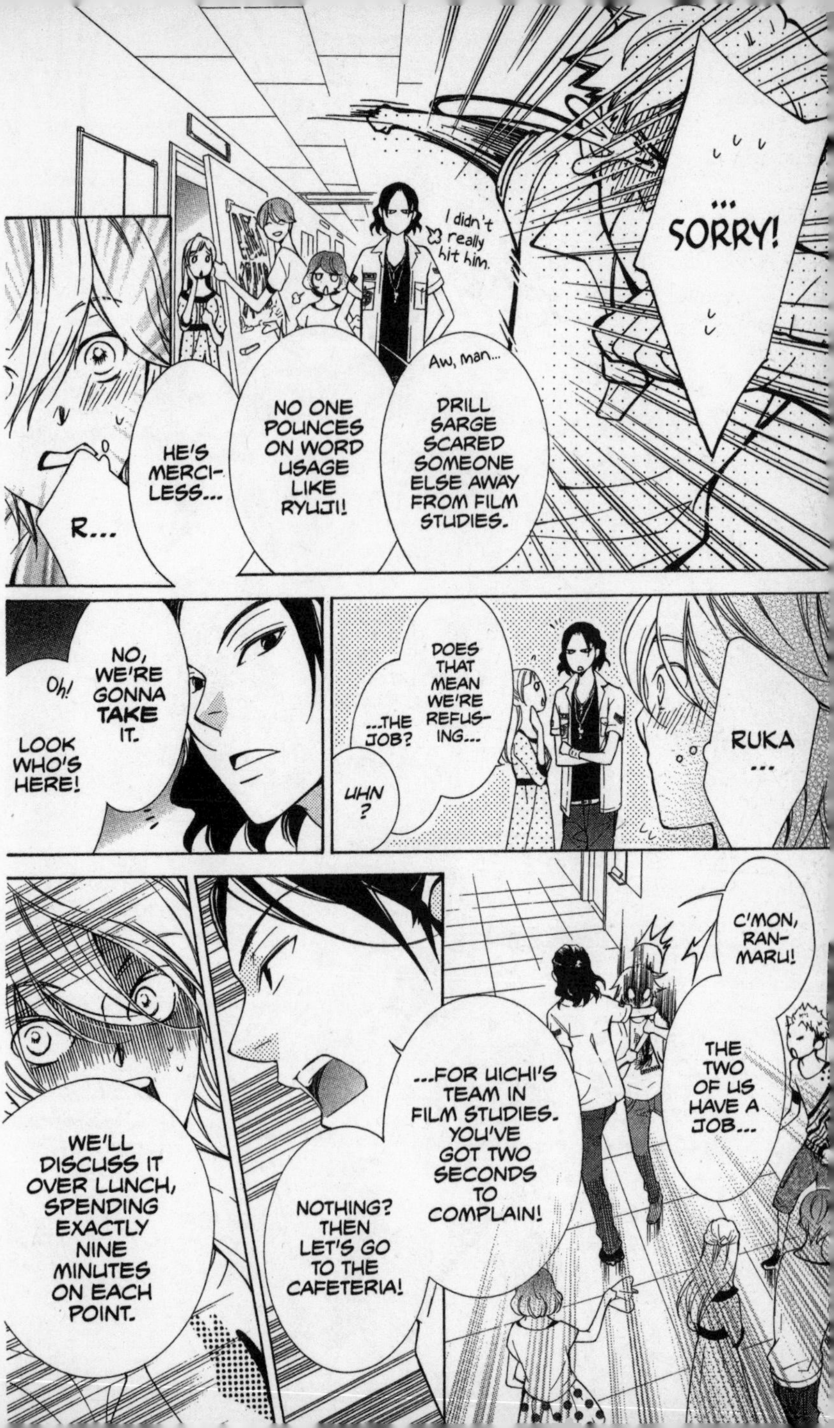
...SORRY!
I didn't really hit him.
Aw, man...
DRILL SARGE SCARED SOMEONE ELSE AWAY FROM FILM STUDIES.
NO ONE POUNCES ON WORD USAGE LIKE RYUJI!
HE'S MERCILESS...
R...
RUKA...
DOES THAT MEAN WE'RE REFUSING...
...THE JOB?
UHN?
NO, WE'RE GONNA TAKE IT.
Oh!
LOOK WHO'S HERE!
C'MON, RANMARU!
THE TWO OF US HAVE A JOB...
...FOR UICHI'S TEAM IN FILM STUDIES. YOU'VE GOT TWO SECONDS TO COMPLAIN!
NOTHING? THEN LET'S GO TO THE CAFETERIA!
WE'LL DISCUSS IT OVER LUNCH, SPENDING EXACTLY NINE MINUTES ON EACH POINT.

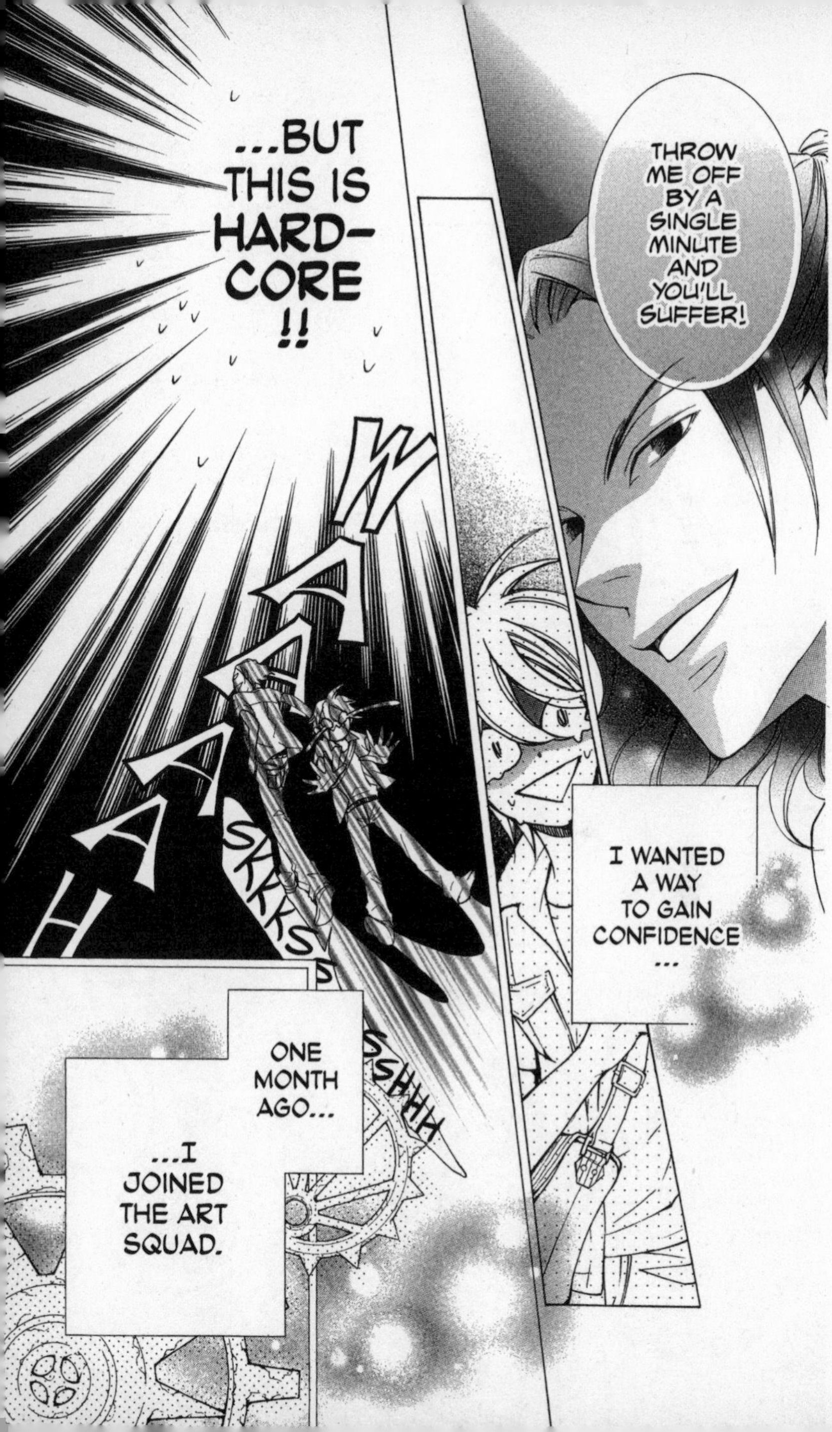
THROW ME OFF BY A SINGLE MINUTE AND YOU'LL SUFFER!
I WANTED A WAY TO GAIN CONFIDENCE...
...BUT THIS IS HARD-CORE!!
WAAAAH
SKKKSSSSHHH
ONE MONTH AGO...
...I JOINED THE ART SQUAD.

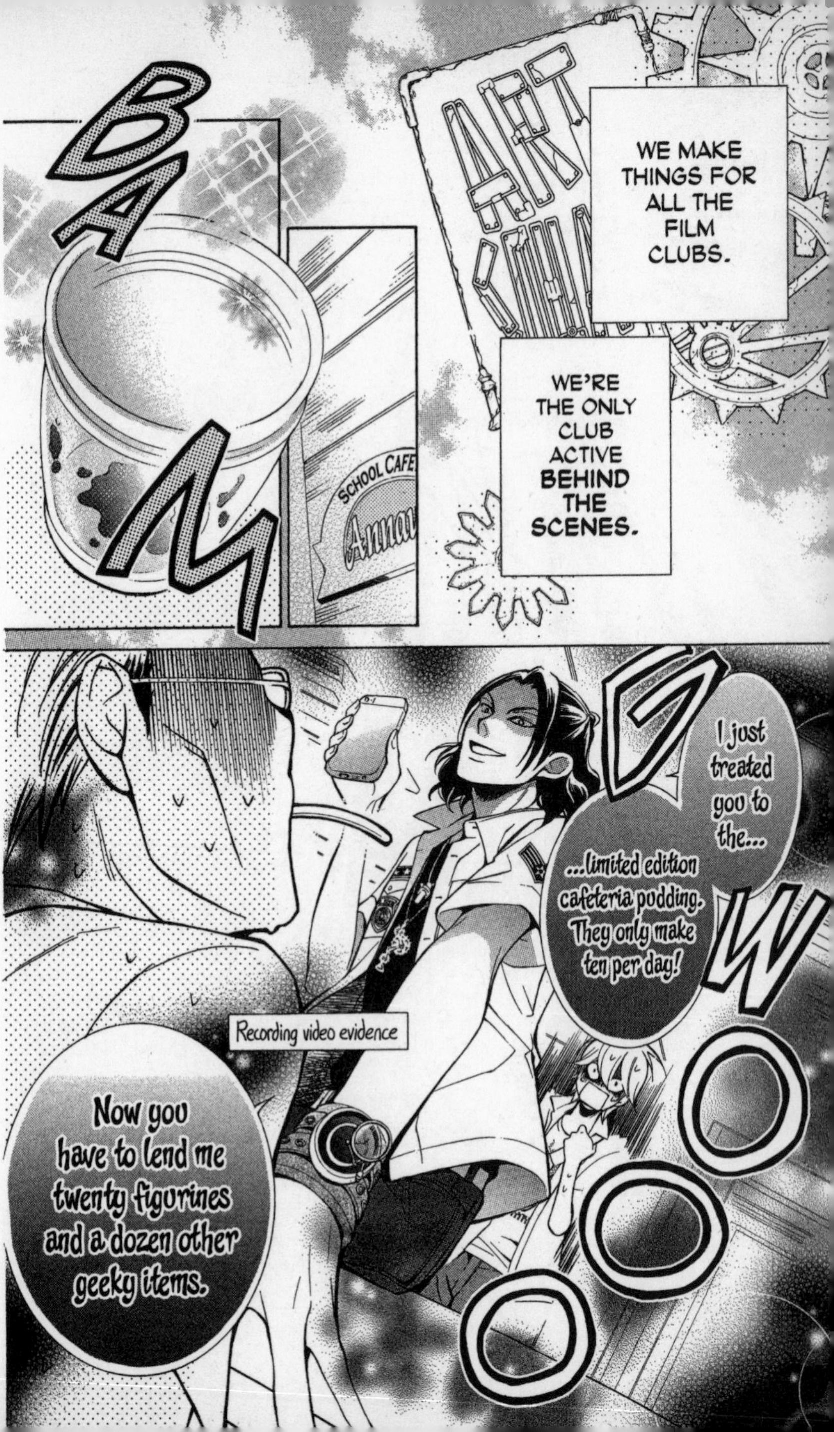
WE MAKE THINGS FOR ALL THE FILM CLUBS.
WE'RE THE ONLY CLUB ACTIVE BEHIND THE SCENES.
SCHOOL CAFE
BAM
I just treated you to the...
...limited edition cafeteria pudding. They only make ten per day!
Recording video evidence
Now you have to lend me twenty figurines and a dozen other geeky items.

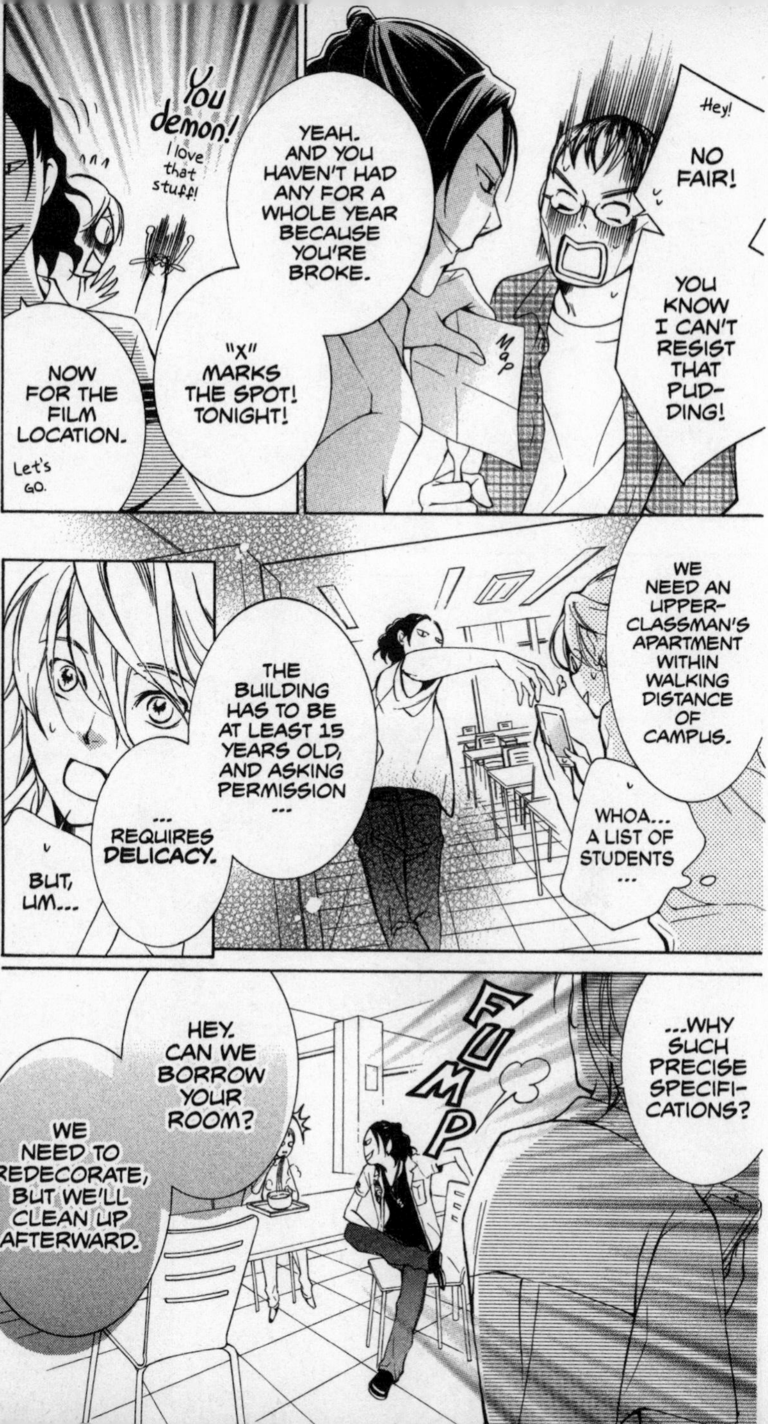
Hey!
NO FAIR!
YOU KNOW I CAN'T RESIST THAT PUD-DING!
Map
YEAH. AND YOU HAVEN'T HAD ANY FOR A WHOLE YEAR BECAUSE YOU'RE BROKE.
You demon!
I love that stuff!
"X" MARKS THE SPOT! TONIGHT!
NOW FOR THE FILM LOCATION.
Let's GO.
WE NEED AN UPPER-CLASSMAN'S APARTMENT WITHIN WALKING DISTANCE OF CAMPUS.
WHOA... A LIST OF STUDENTS...
THE BUILDING HAS TO BE AT LEAST 15 YEARS OLD, AND ASKING PERMISSION...
...REQUIRES DELICACY.
BUT, UM...
...WHY SUCH PRECISE SPECIFI-CATIONS?
FUMP
HEY. CAN WE BORROW YOUR ROOM?
WE NEED TO REDECORATE, BUT WE'LL CLEAN UP AFTERWARD.

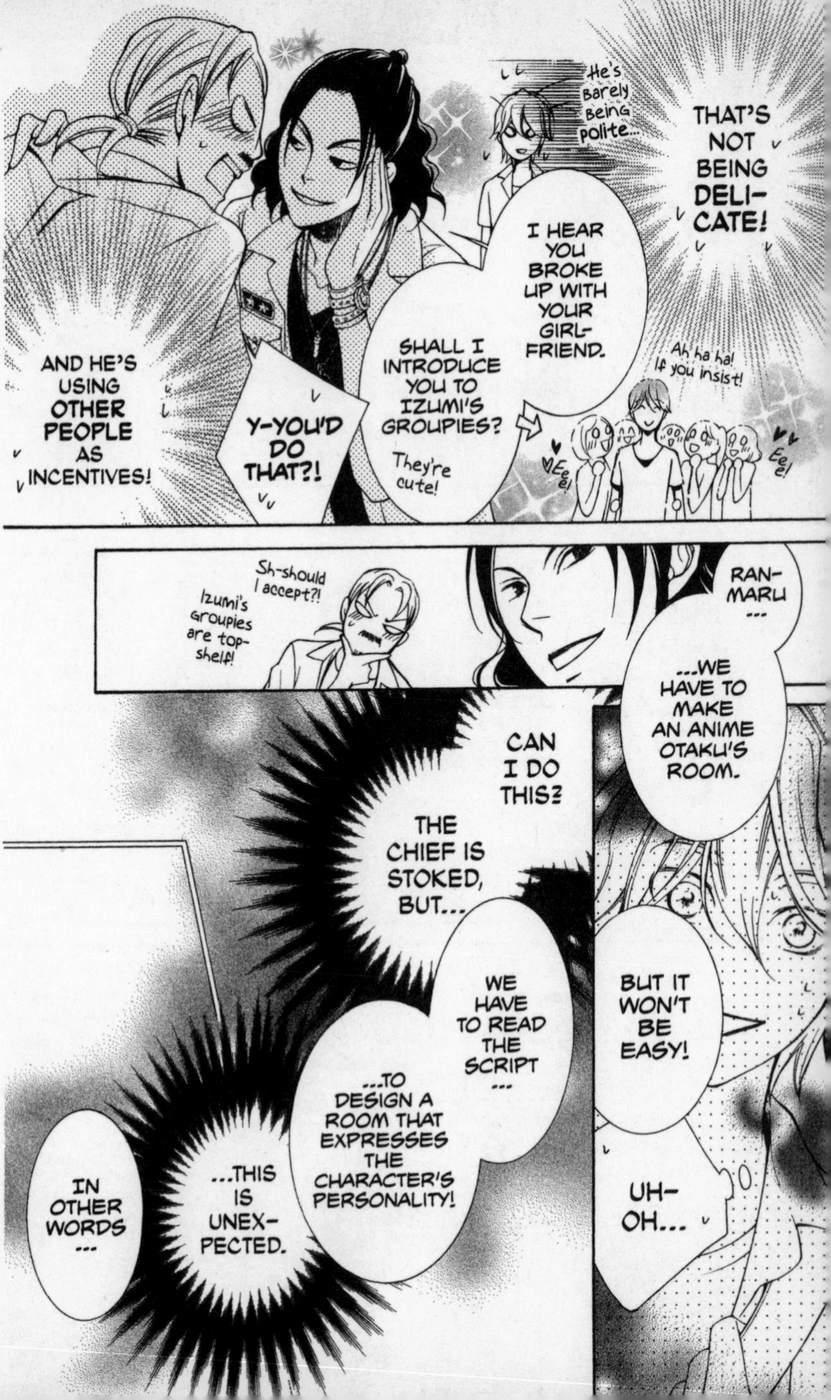
THAT'S NOT BEING DELICATE!
He's barely being polite...
I HEAR YOU BROKE UP WITH YOUR GIRLFRIEND.
Ah ha ha! If you insist!
Eee!
Eee!
SHALL I INTRODUCE YOU TO IZUMI'S GROUPIES?
They're cute!
Y-YOU'D DO THAT?!
AND HE'S USING OTHER PEOPLE AS INCENTIVES!
RANMARU...
Sh-should I accept?!
Izumi's groupies are top-shelf!
...WE HAVE TO MAKE AN ANIME OTAKU'S ROOM.
BUT IT WON'T BE EASY!
UH-OH...
CAN I DO THIS?
THE CHIEF IS STOKED, BUT...
WE HAVE TO READ THE SCRIPT...
...TO DESIGN A ROOM THAT EXPRESSES THE CHARACTER'S PERSONALITY!
...THIS IS UNEXPECTED.
IN OTHER WORDS...

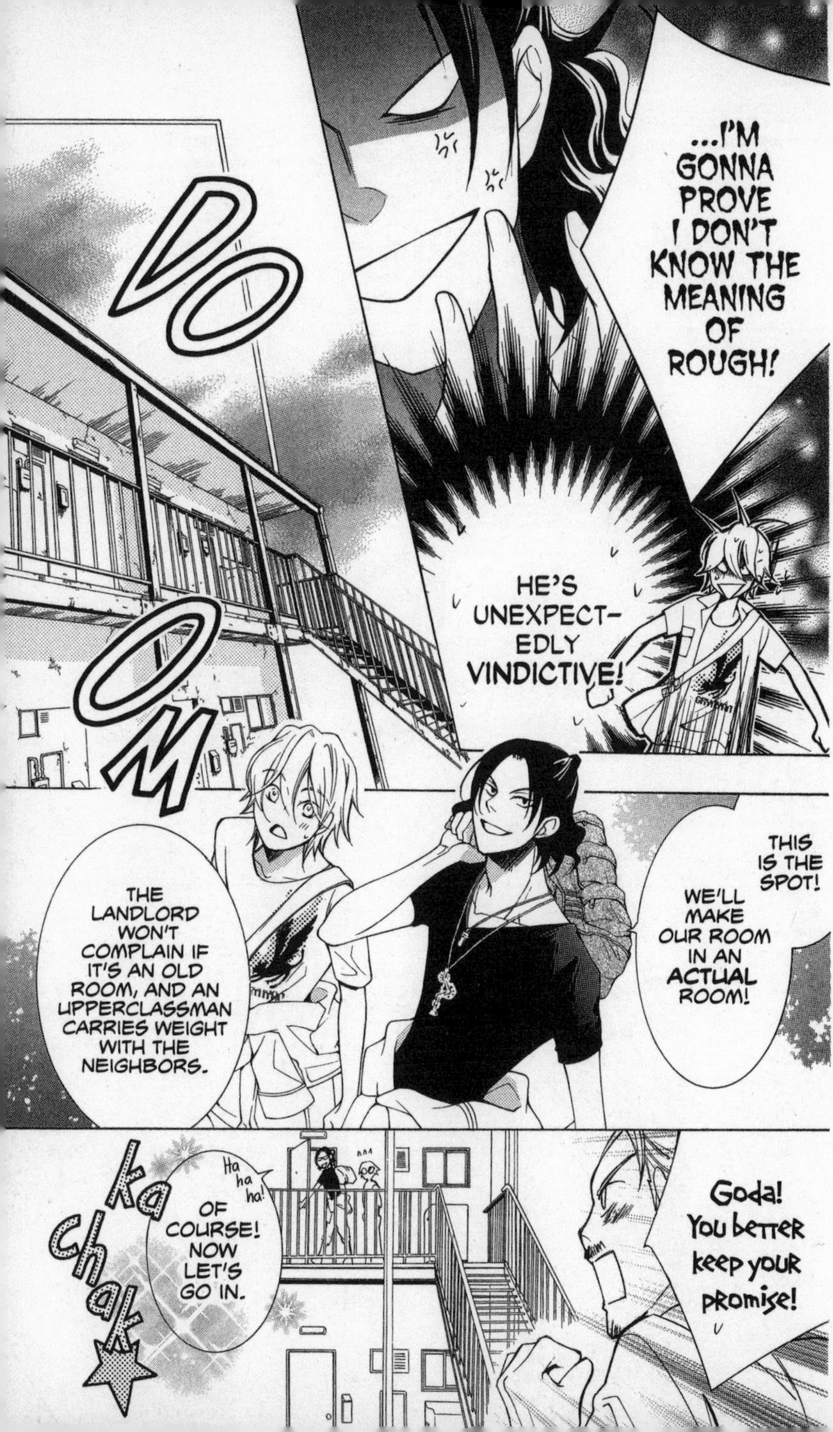
...I'M GONNA PROVE I DON'T KNOW THE MEANING OF ROUGH!
HE'S UNEXPECT-EDLY VINDICTIVE!
DOOOM
THIS IS THE SPOT!
WE'LL MAKE OUR ROOM IN AN ACTUAL ROOM!
THE LANDLORD WON'T COMPLAIN IF IT'S AN OLD ROOM, AND AN UPPERCLASSMAN CARRIES WEIGHT WITH THE NEIGHBORS.
Goda! You better keep your promise!
Ha ha ha!
OF COURSE! NOW LET'S GO IN.
Ka Chak

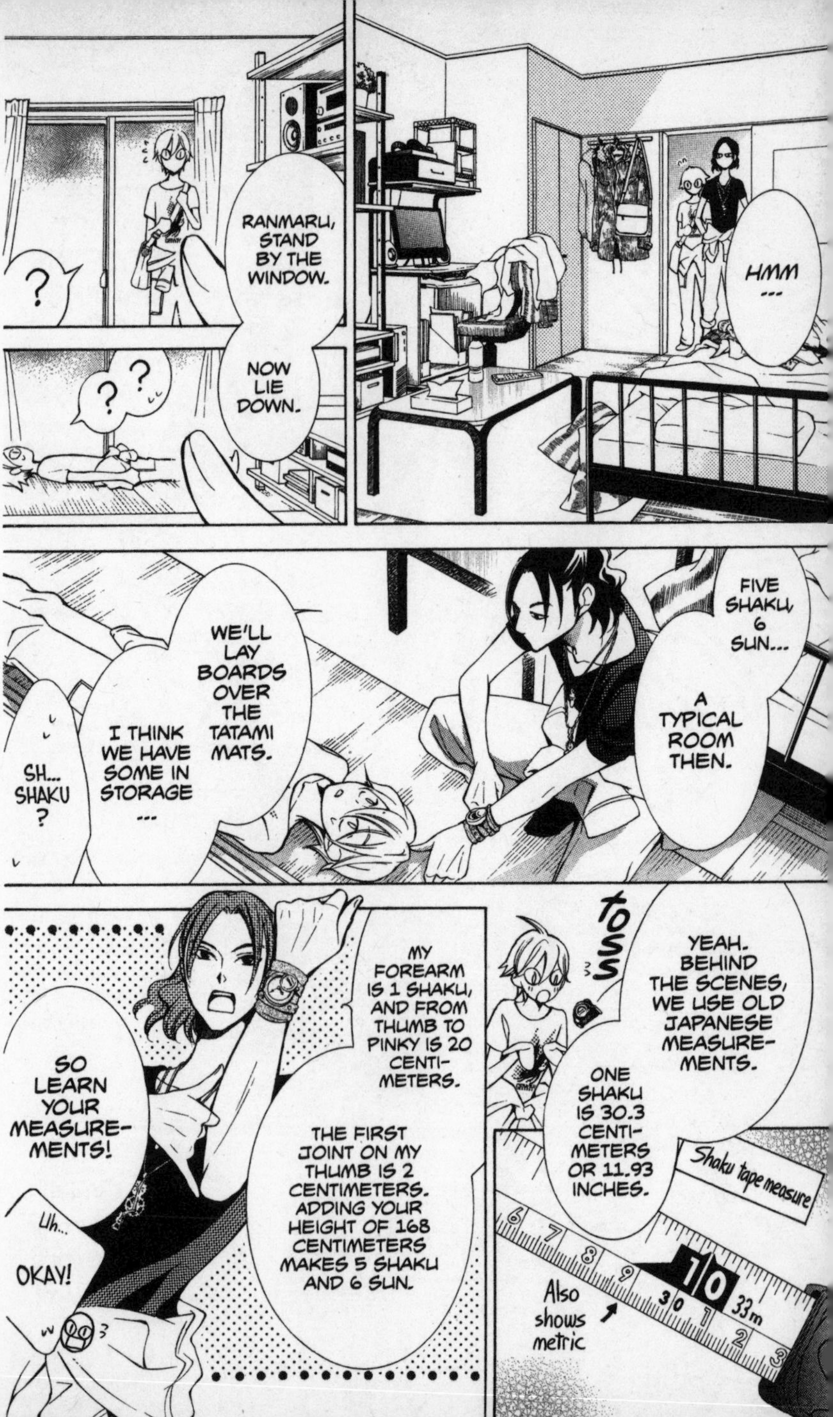
HMM...
RANMARU, STAND BY THE WINDOW.
?
NOW LIE DOWN.
? ?
FIVE SHAKU, 6 SUN...
A TYPICAL ROOM THEN.
WE'LL LAY BOARDS OVER THE TATAMI MATS.
I THINK WE HAVE SOME IN STORAGE...
SH... SHAKU?
TOSS
YEAH. BEHIND THE SCENES, WE USE OLD JAPANESE MEASUREMENTS.
ONE SHAKU IS 30.3 CENTIMETERS OR 11.93 INCHES.
Shaku tape measure
Also shows metric
MY FOREARM IS 1 SHAKU, AND FROM THUMB TO PINKY IS 20 CENTIMETERS.
THE FIRST JOINT ON MY THUMB IS 2 CENTIMETERS. ADDING YOUR HEIGHT OF 168 CENTIMETERS MAKES 5 SHAKU AND 6 SUN.
SO LEARN YOUR MEASUREMENTS!
Uh...
OKAY!

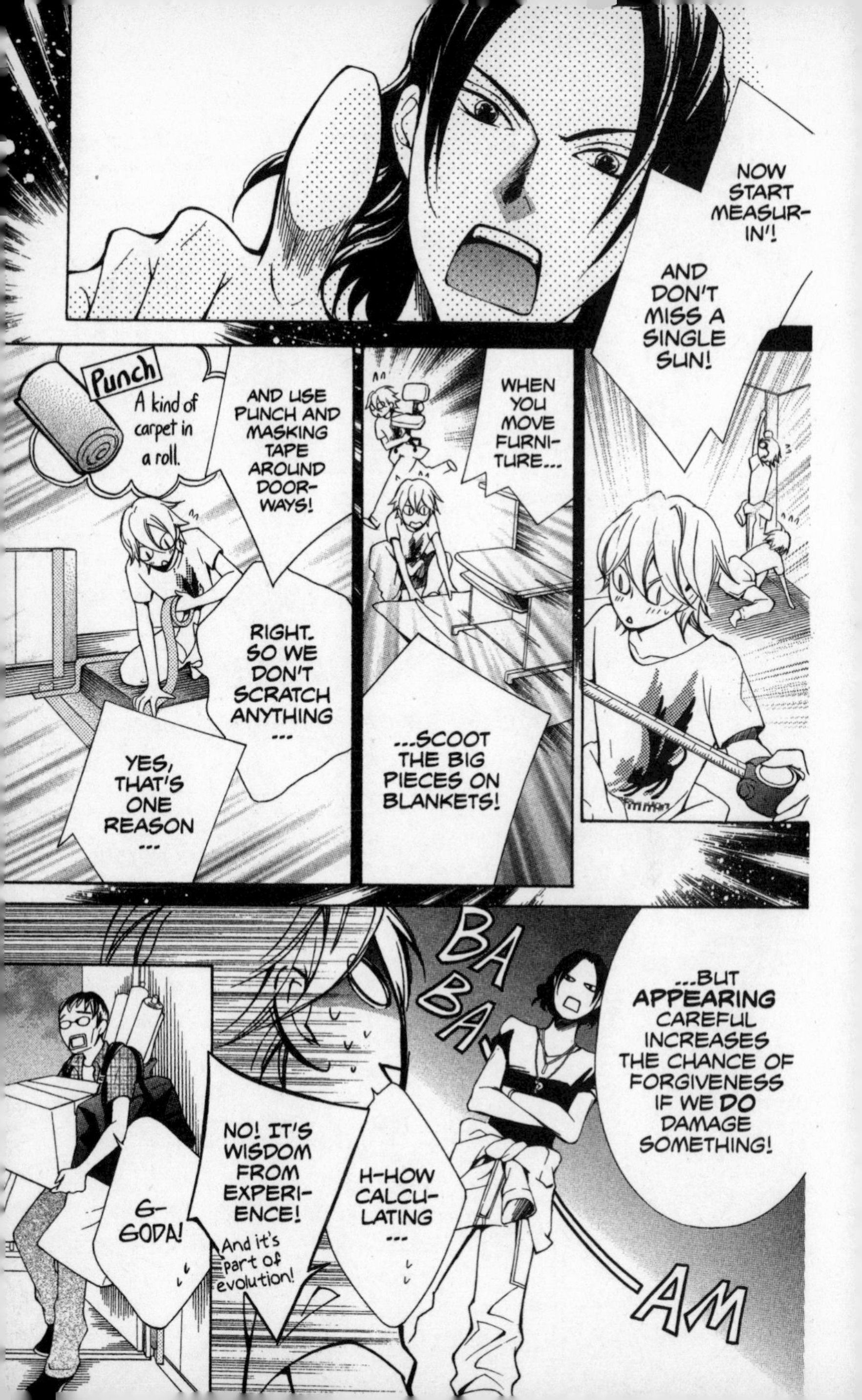
NOW START MEASURIN'!
AND DON'T MISS A SINGLE SUN!
WHEN YOU MOVE FURNITURE...
...SCOOT THE BIG PIECES ON BLANKETS!
AND USE PUNCH AND MASKING TAPE AROUND DOORWAYS!
Punch
A kind of carpet in a roll.
RIGHT. SO WE DON'T SCRATCH ANYTHING...
YES, THAT'S ONE REASON...
BABA
...BUT APPEARING CAREFUL INCREASES THE CHANCE OF FORGIVENESS IF WE DO DAMAGE SOMETHING!
AM
H-HOW CALCULATING...
NO! IT'S WISDOM FROM EXPERIENCE!
And it's part of evolution!
G-GODA!

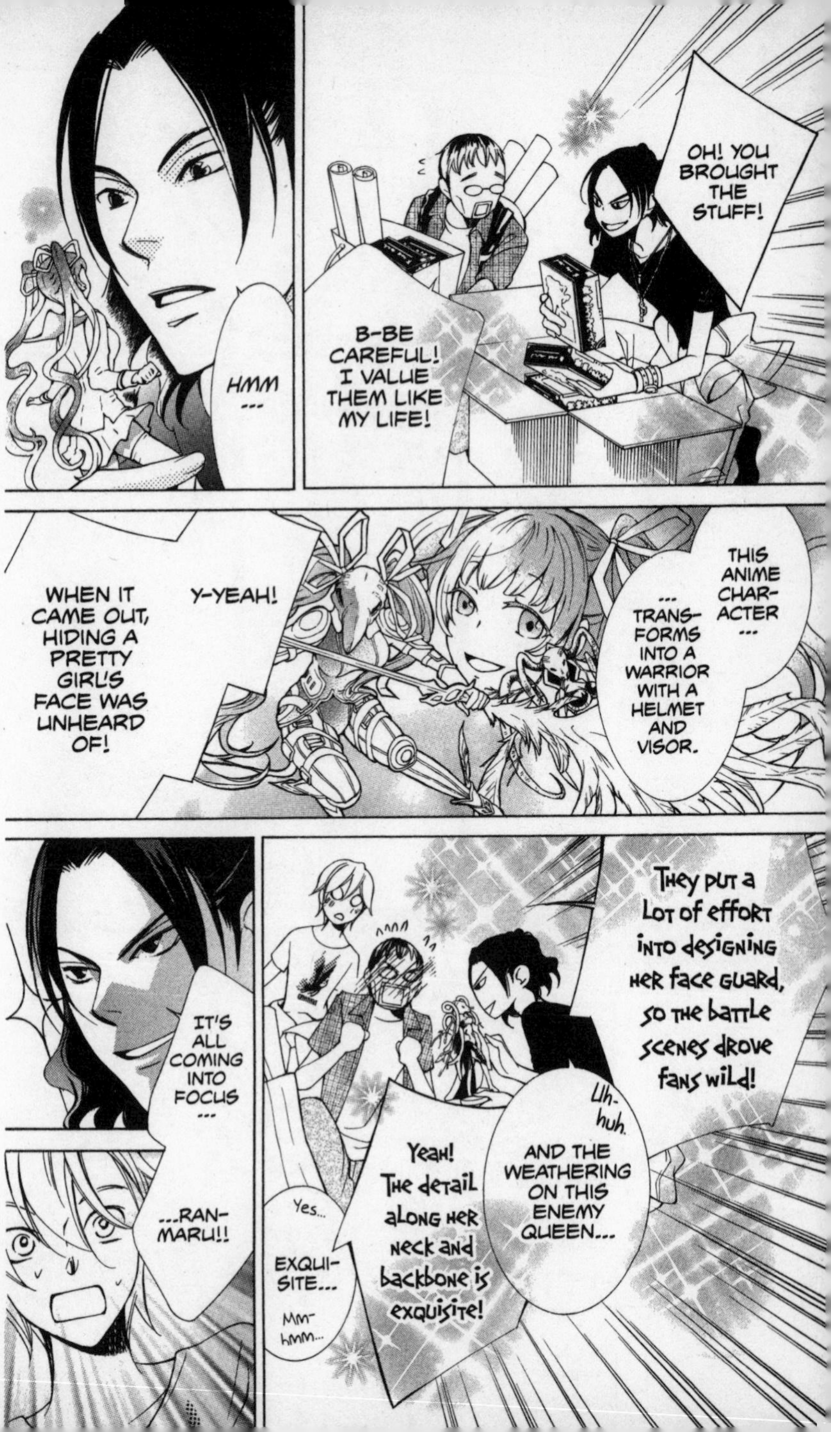
OH! YOU BROUGHT THE STUFF!
B-BE CAREFUL! I VALUE THEM LIKE MY LIFE!
HMM ---
THIS ANIME CHARACTER ---
--- TRANSFORMS INTO A WARRIOR WITH A HELMET AND VISOR.
Y-YEAH!
WHEN IT CAME OUT, HIDING A PRETTY GIRL'S FACE WAS UNHEARD OF!
They put a lot of effort into designing her face guard, so the battle scenes drove fans wild!
Uh-huh.
AND THE WEATHERING ON THIS ENEMY QUEEN...
Yeah! The detail along her neck and backbone is exquisite!
Yes...
EXQUISITE...
Mm-hmm...
IT'S ALL COMING INTO FOCUS ---
...RAN-MARU!!

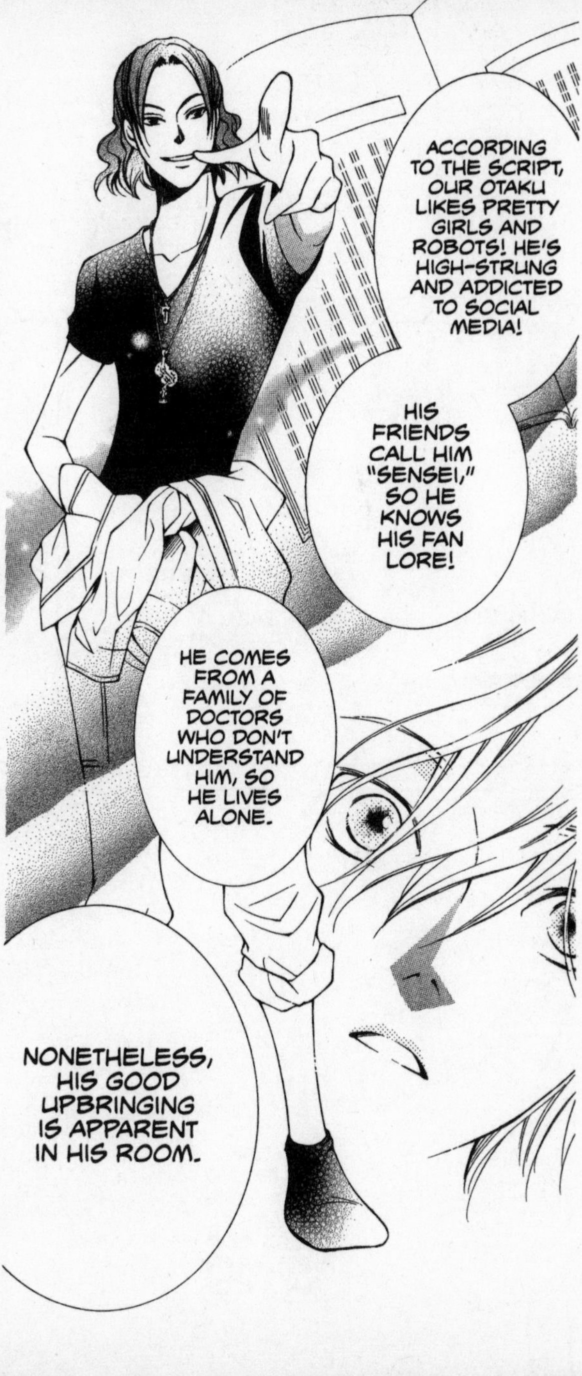
ACCORDING TO THE SCRIPT, OUR OTAKU LIKES PRETTY GIRLS AND ROBOTS! HE'S HIGH-STRUNG AND ADDICTED TO SOCIAL MEDIA!
HIS FRIENDS CALL HIM "SENSEI," SO HE KNOWS HIS FAN LORE!
HE COMES FROM A FAMILY OF DOCTORS WHO DON'T UNDERSTAND HIM, SO HE LIVES ALONE.
NONETHELESS, HIS GOOD UPBRINGING IS APPARENT IN HIS ROOM.

1

This is *Behind the Scenes!!* volume 2! Thanks for checking it out!

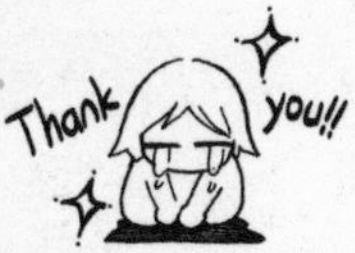
Thank you!!

If volume 1 was like hoeing a field forever and ever...

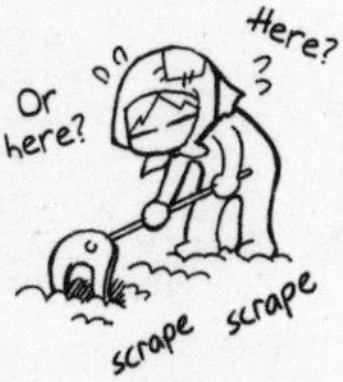
Here?
Or here?
scrape scrape

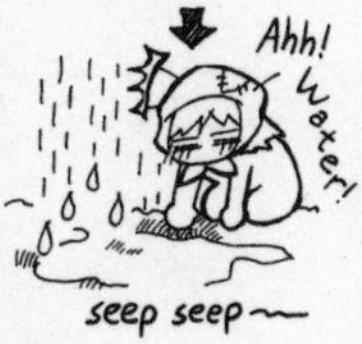
Ahh! Water!
seep seep~

...volume 2 feels like it's soaking into my body.

Read on!

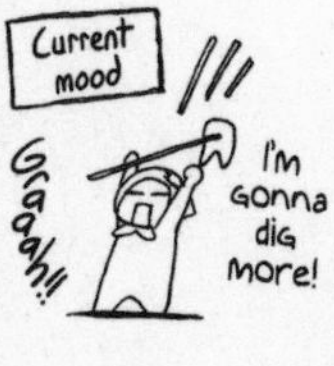
Current mood
Graaah!!
I'm gonna dig more!

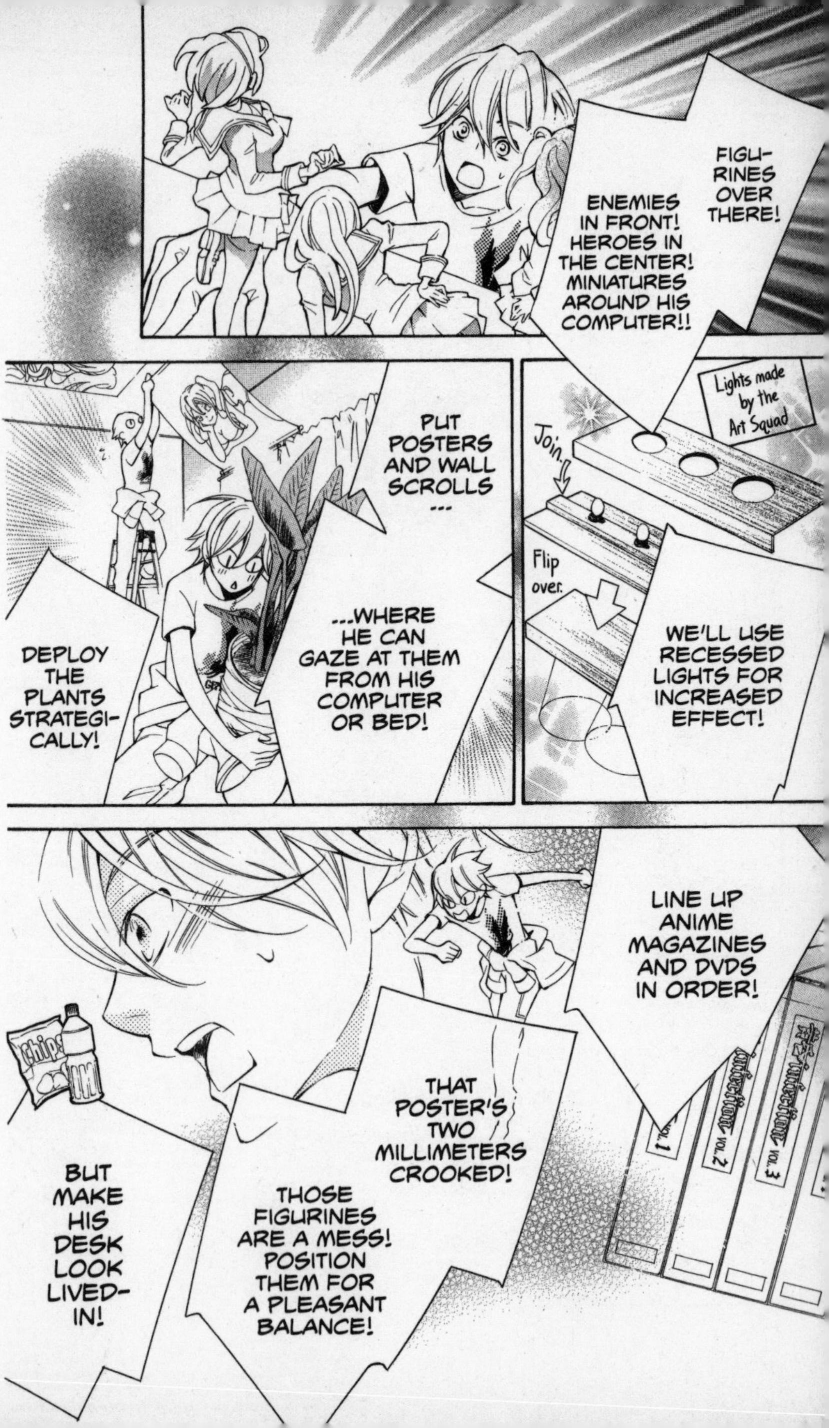
FIGU-
RINES
OVER
THERE!
ENEMIES
IN FRONT!
HEROES IN
THE CENTER!
MINIATURES
AROUND HIS
COMPUTER!!
Lights made
by the
Art Squad
Join.
Flip
over.
WE'LL USE
RECESSED
LIGHTS FOR
INCREASED
EFFECT!
PUT
POSTERS
AND WALL
SCROLLS
...
...WHERE
HE CAN
GAZE AT THEM
FROM HIS
COMPUTER
OR BED!
DEPLOY
THE
PLANTS
STRATEGI-
CALLY!
LINE UP
ANIME
MAGAZINES
AND DVDS
IN ORDER!
THAT
POSTER'S
TWO
MILLIMETERS
CROOKED!
THOSE
FIGURINES
ARE A MESS!
POSITION
THEM FOR
A PLEASANT
BALANCE!
chips
BUT
MAKE
HIS
DESK
LOOK
LIVED-
IN!

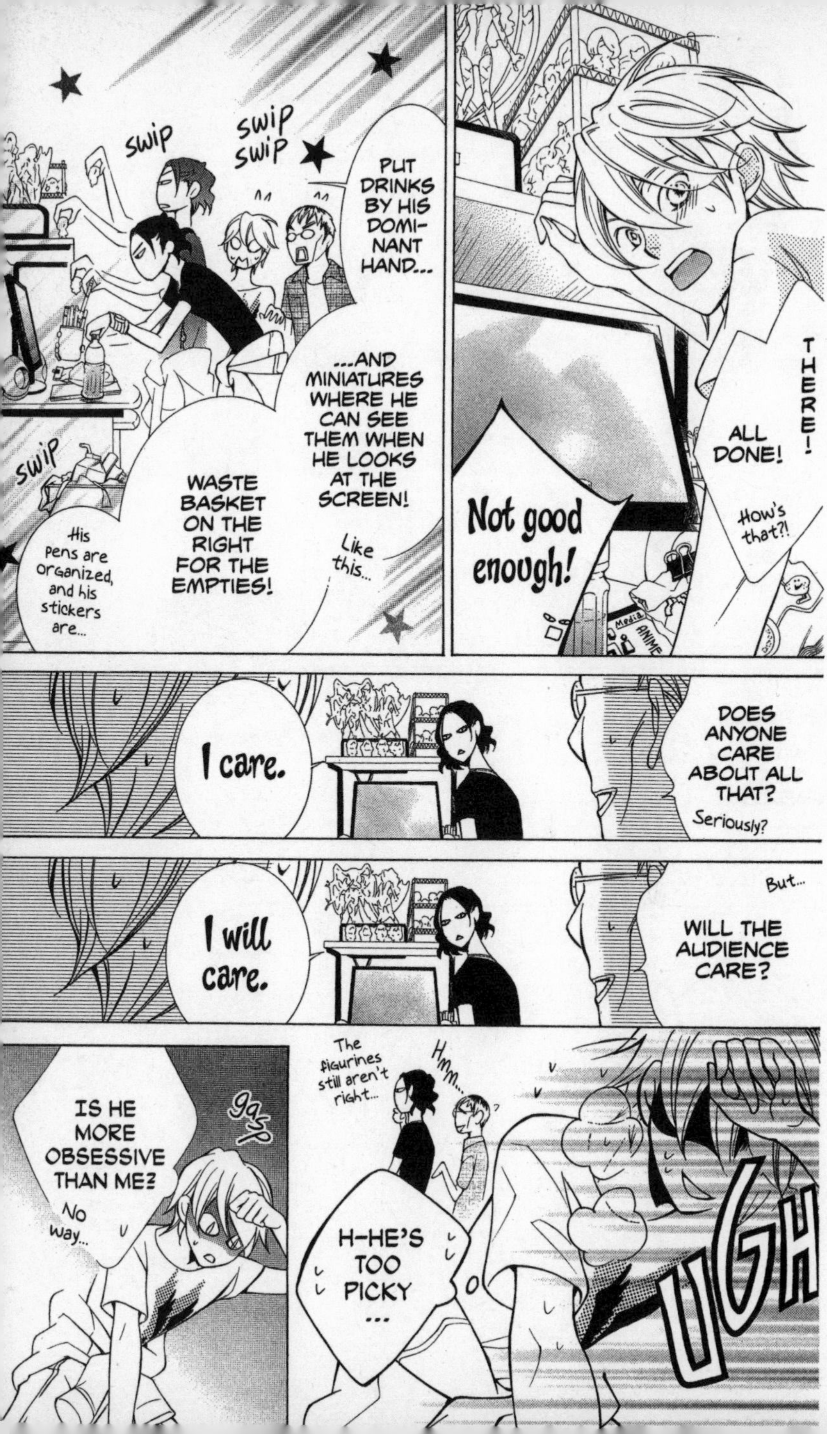
THERE!
ALL DONE!
How's that?!
Not good enough!
swip
swip swip
PUT DRINKS BY HIS DOMINANT HAND...
...AND MINIATURES WHERE HE CAN SEE THEM WHEN HE LOOKS AT THE SCREEN!
Like this...
swip
WASTE BASKET ON THE RIGHT FOR THE EMPTIES!
His pens are organized, and his stickers are...
DOES ANYONE CARE ABOUT ALL THAT?
Seriously?
I care.
But...
WILL THE AUDIENCE CARE?
I will care.
UGH
Hmm...
The figurines still aren't right...
H-HE'S TOO PICKY...
gasp
IS HE MORE OBSESSIVE THAN ME?
No way...

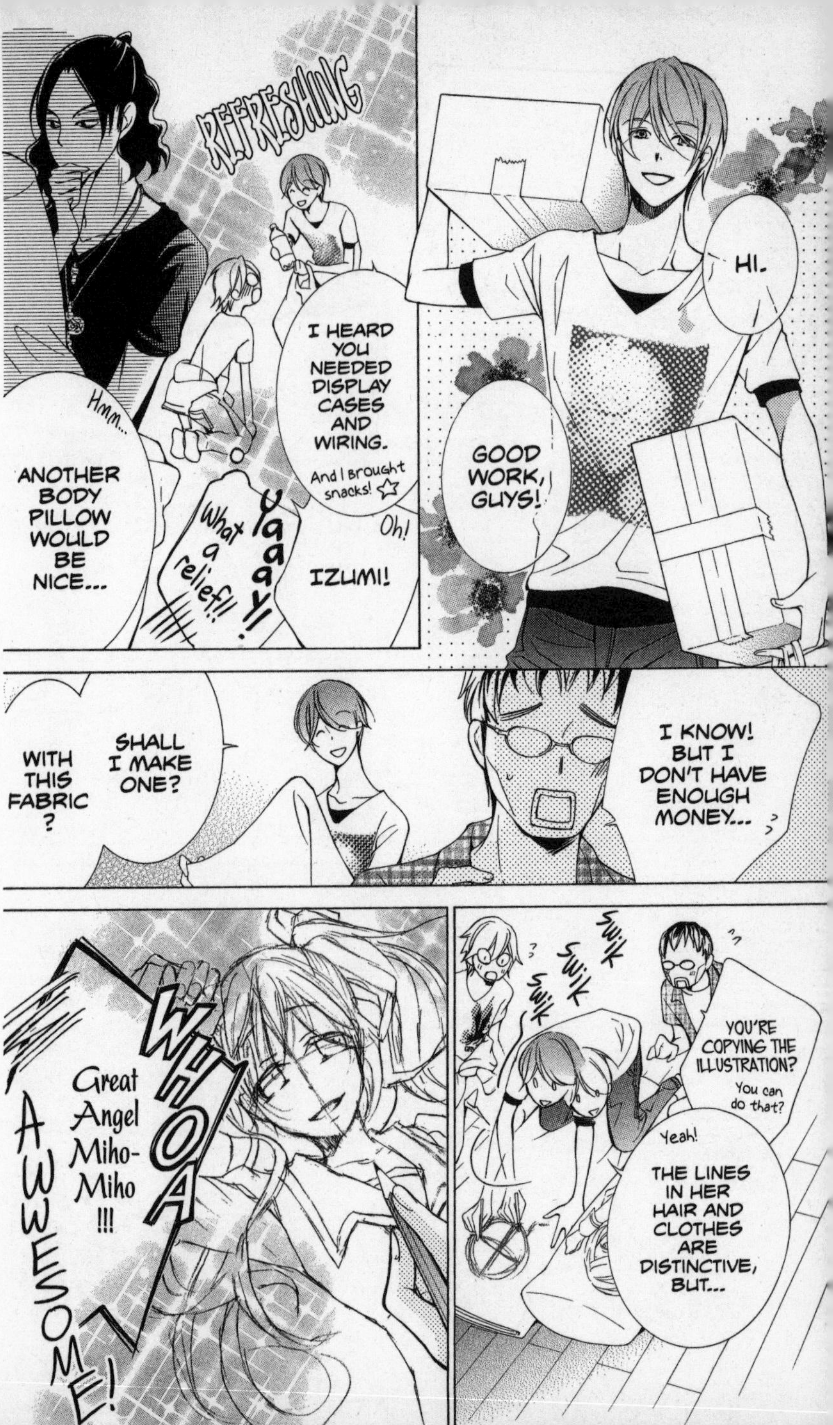
HI.
GOOD WORK, GUYS!
REFRESHING
I HEARD YOU NEEDED DISPLAY CASES AND WIRING.
And I brought snacks!
Oh!
IZUMI!
Yaaay!!
What a relief!!
Hmm...
ANOTHER BODY PILLOW WOULD BE NICE...
I KNOW! BUT I DON'T HAVE ENOUGH MONEY...
SHALL I MAKE ONE?
WITH THIS FABRIC?
swik
swik
swik
YOU'RE COPYING THE ILLUSTRATION?
You can do that?
Yeah!
THE LINES IN HER HAIR AND CLOTHES ARE DISTINCTIVE, BUT...
WHOA
Great Angel Miho-Miho!!!
AWWESOME!

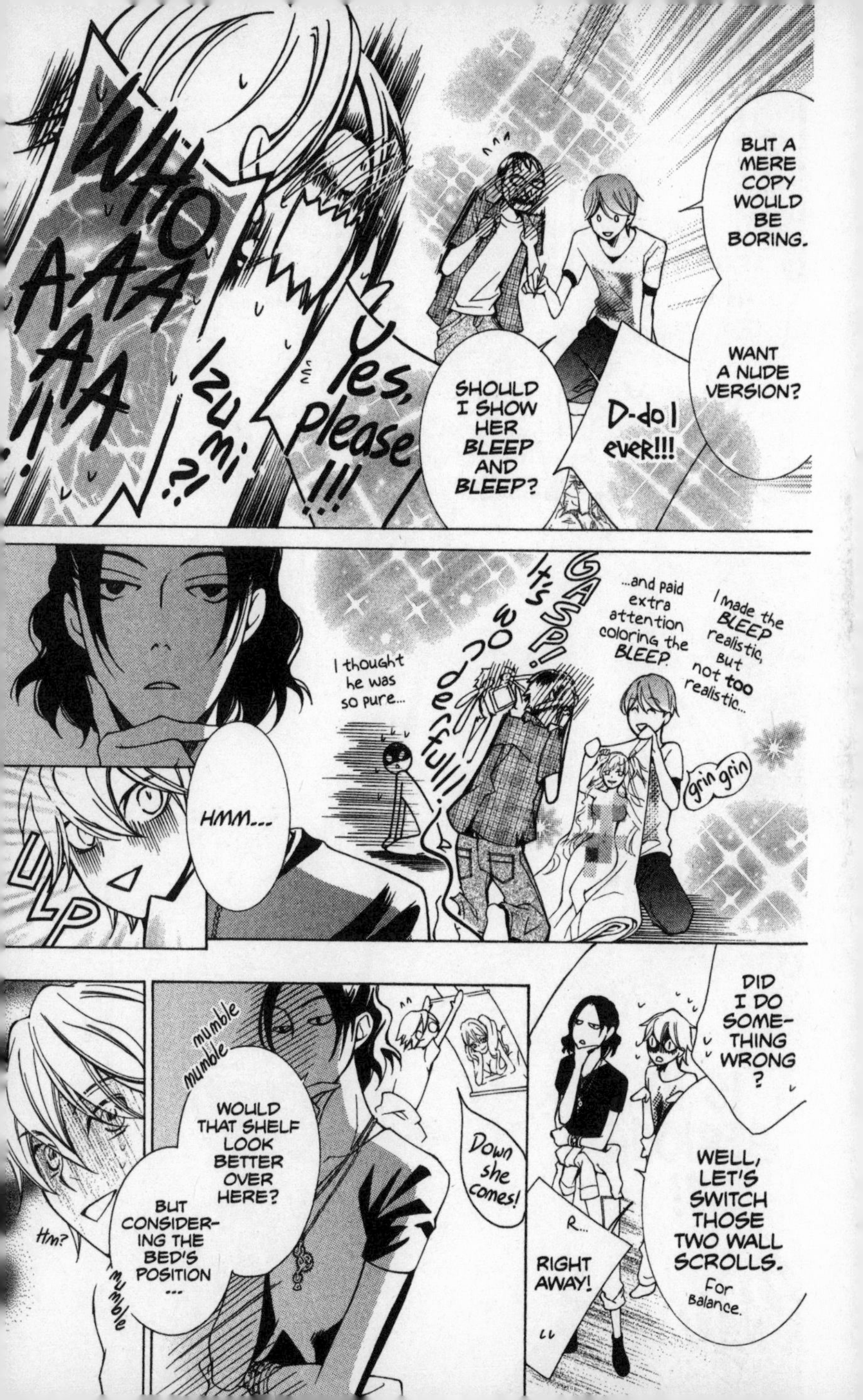
BUT A MERE COPY WOULD BE BORING.
WANT A NUDE VERSION?
D-do I ever!!!
SHOULD I SHOW HER BLEEP AND BLEEP?
Yes, please!!!
Izumi ?!
WHOAAAAAA!!
I made the BLEEP realistic, but not too realistic...
...and paid extra attention coloring the BLEEP.
GASP!
It's wonderful!!
grin grin
I thought he was so pure...
HMM...
ULP
DID I DO SOMETHING WRONG?
WELL, LET'S SWITCH THOSE TWO WALL SCROLLS.
For Balance.
R...
RIGHT AWAY!
Down she comes!
mumble mumble
WOULD THAT SHELF LOOK BETTER OVER HERE?
BUT CONSIDERING THE BED'S POSITION...
mumble
Hm?

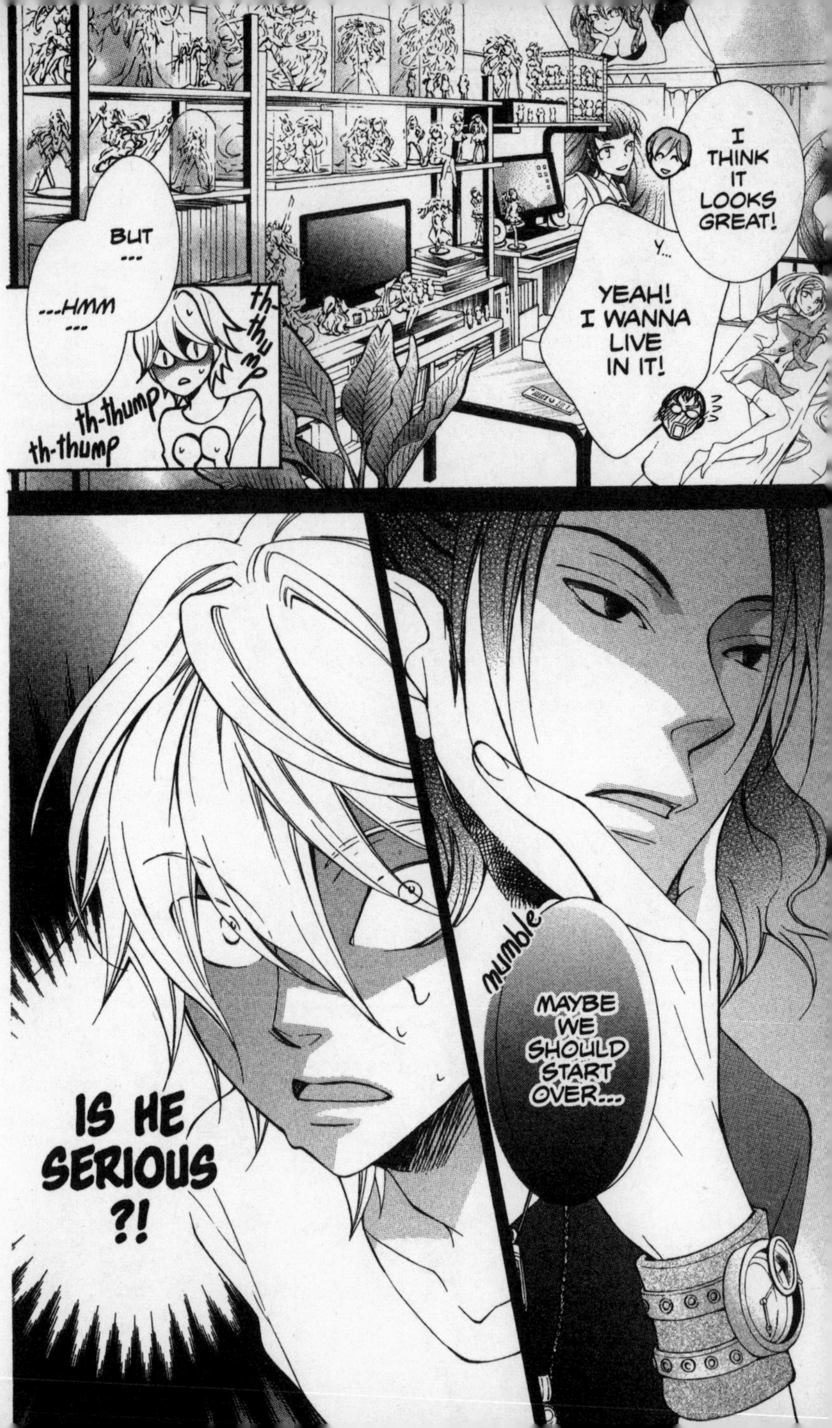
I THINK IT LOOKS GREAT!
Y... YEAH! I WANNA LIVE IN IT!
BUT --- ...HMM ---
th-thump
th-thump
th-thump
mumble
MAYBE WE SHOULD START OVER...
IS HE SERIOUS ?!

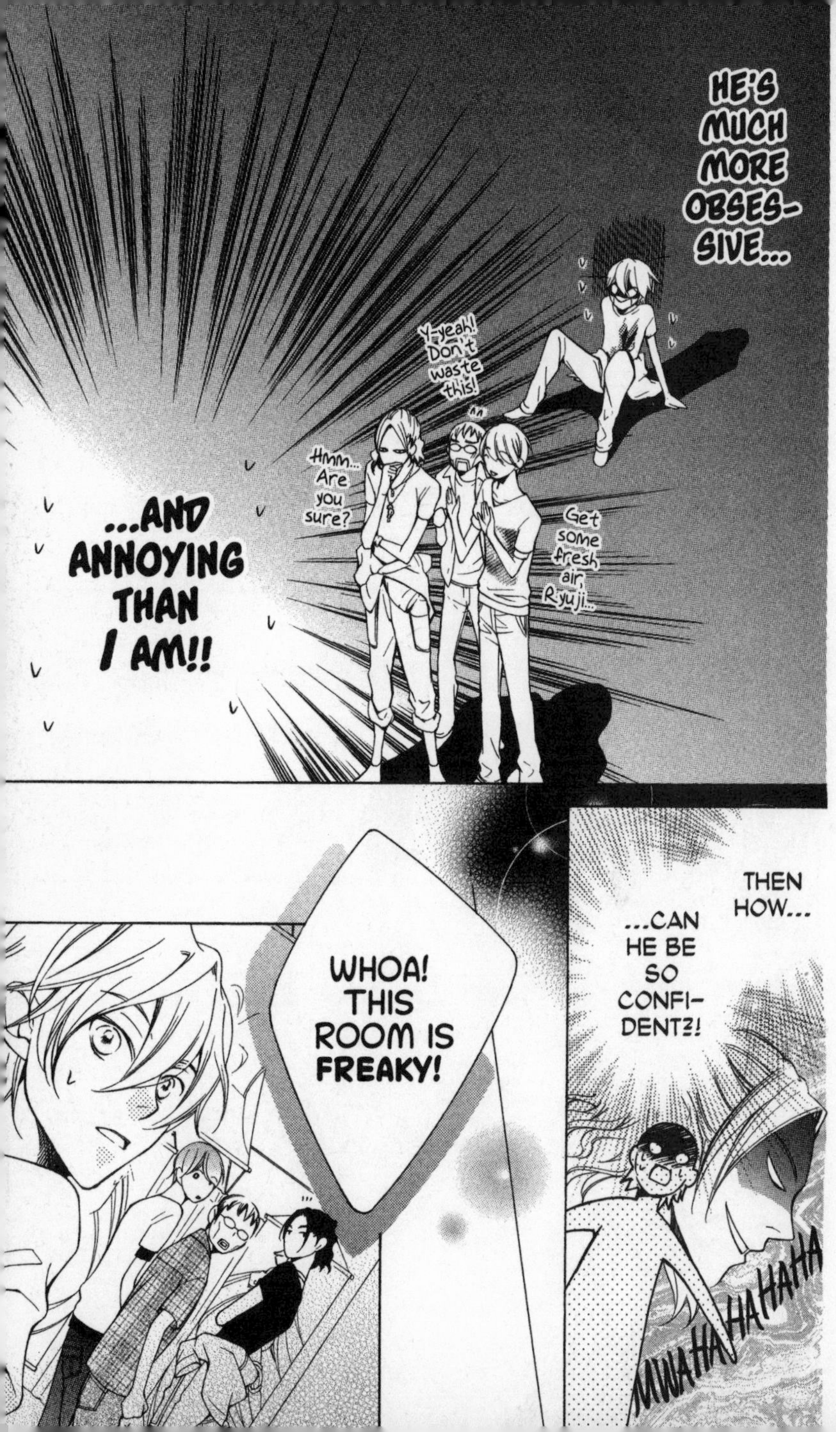
HE'S MUCH MORE OBSES-SIVE...
Y-yeah! Don't waste this!
Get some fresh air, Ryuji...
Hmm... Are you sure?
...AND ANNOYING THAN I AM!!
THEN HOW...
...CAN HE BE SO CONFI-DENT?!
MWAHAHAHAHA
WHOA! THIS ROOM IS FREAKY!

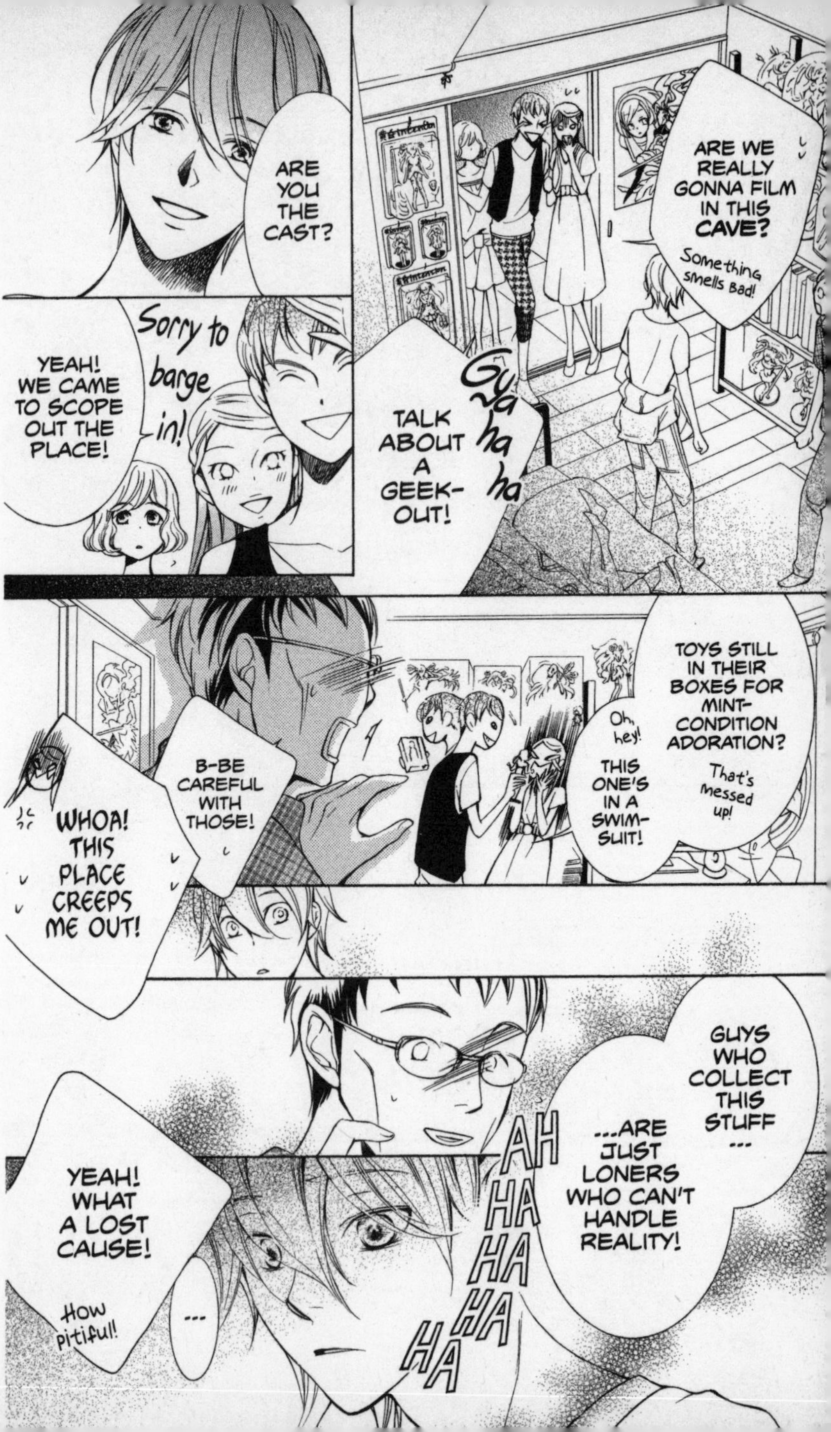
ARE WE REALLY GONNA FILM IN THIS CAVE?
Something smells Bad!
TALK ABOUT A GEEK-OUT!
Gyahaha
ARE YOU THE CAST?
Sorry to barge in!
YEAH! WE CAME TO SCOPE OUT THE PLACE!
TOYS STILL IN THEIR BOXES FOR MINT-CONDITION ADORATION?
That's messed up!
Oh, hey!
THIS ONE'S IN A SWIM-SUIT!
B-BE CAREFUL WITH THOSE!
WHOA! THIS PLACE CREEPS ME OUT!
GUYS WHO COLLECT THIS STUFF...
...ARE JUST LONERS WHO CAN'T HANDLE REALITY!
AH HA HA HA HA HA HA
YEAH! WHAT A LOST CAUSE!
How pitiful!
...

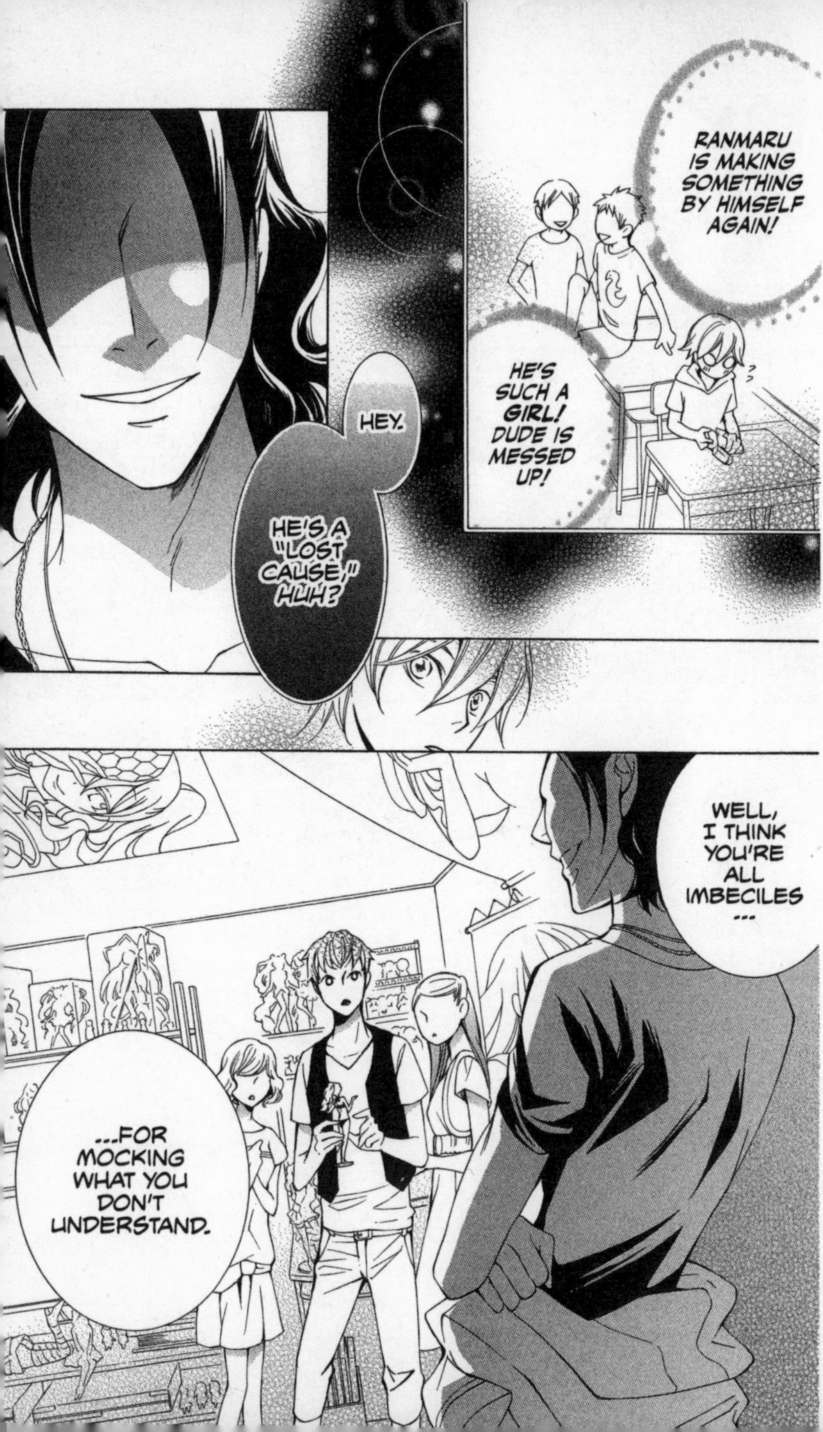
RANMARU IS MAKING SOMETHING BY HIMSELF AGAIN!
HE'S SUCH A GIRL! DUDE IS MESSED UP!
HEY.
HE'S A "LOST CAUSE," HUH?
WELL, I THINK YOU'RE ALL IMBECILES...
...FOR MOCKING WHAT YOU DON'T UNDERSTAND.

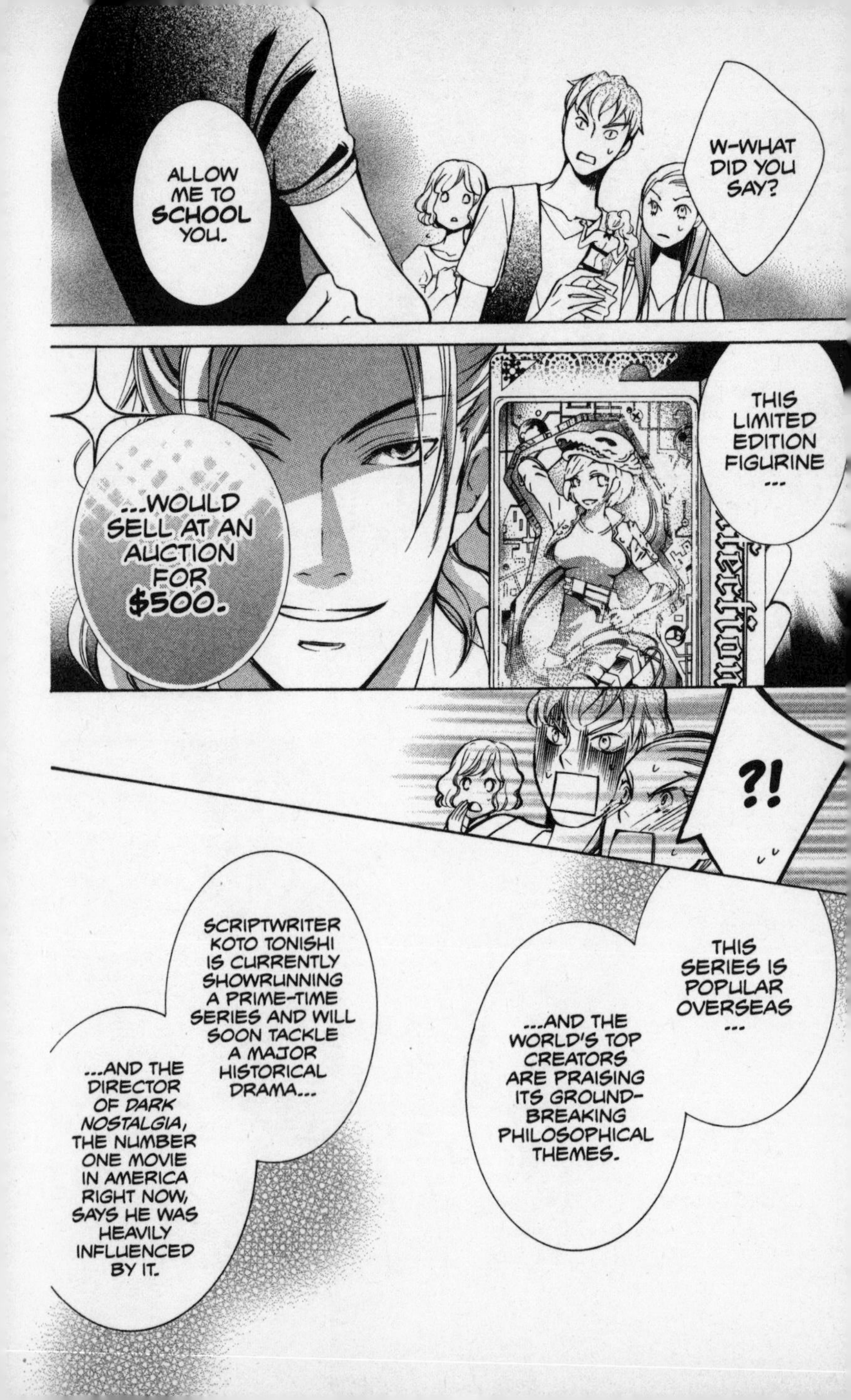
W-WHAT DID YOU SAY?
ALLOW ME TO SCHOOL YOU.
THIS LIMITED EDITION FIGURINE ---
...WOULD SELL AT AN AUCTION FOR $500.
?!
THIS SERIES IS POPULAR OVERSEAS ---
...AND THE WORLD'S TOP CREATORS ARE PRAISING ITS GROUND-BREAKING PHILOSOPHICAL THEMES.
SCRIPTWRITER KOTO TONISHI IS CURRENTLY SHOWRUNNING A PRIME-TIME SERIES AND WILL SOON TACKLE A MAJOR HISTORICAL DRAMA...
...AND THE DIRECTOR OF *DARK NOSTALGIA*, THE NUMBER ONE MOVIE IN AMERICA RIGHT NOW, SAYS HE WAS HEAVILY INFLUENCED BY IT.

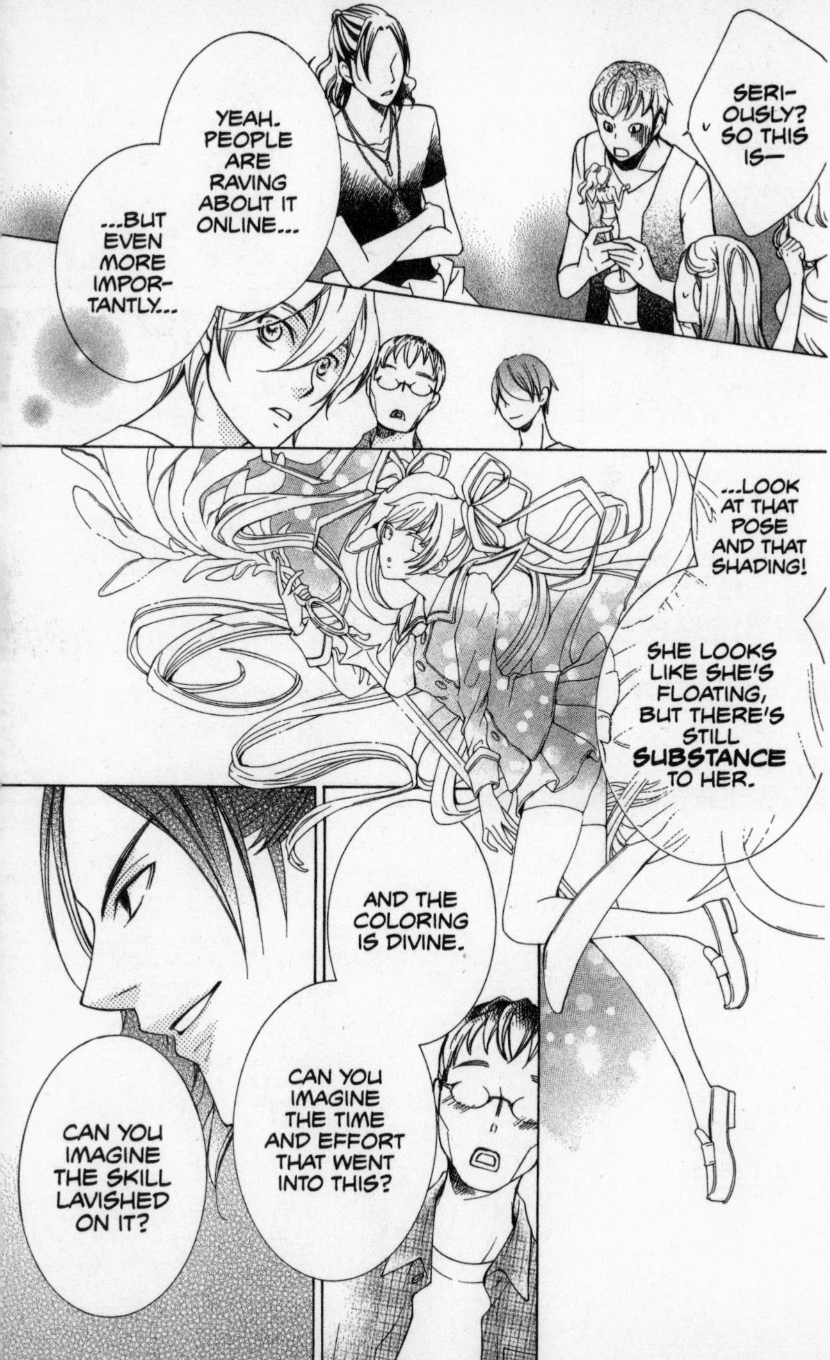
SERIOUSLY? SO THIS IS—
YEAH. PEOPLE ARE RAVING ABOUT IT ONLINE...
...BUT EVEN MORE IMPORTANTLY...
...LOOK AT THAT POSE AND THAT SHADING!
SHE LOOKS LIKE SHE'S FLOATING, BUT THERE'S STILL SUBSTANCE TO HER.
AND THE COLORING IS DIVINE.
CAN YOU IMAGINE THE TIME AND EFFORT THAT WENT INTO THIS?
CAN YOU IMAGINE THE SKILL LAVISHED ON IT?

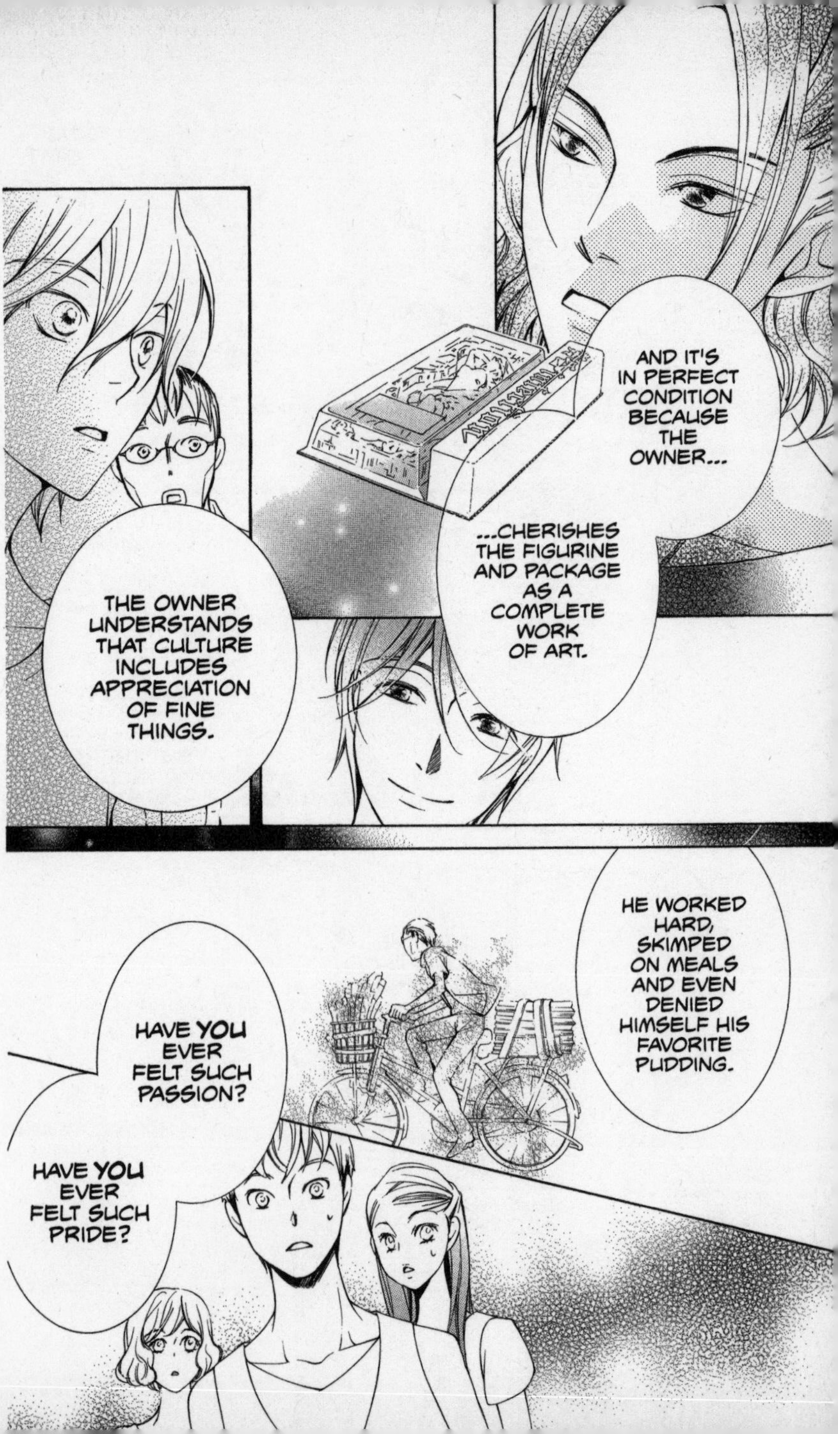
AND IT'S IN PERFECT CONDITION BECAUSE THE OWNER...
...CHERISHES THE FIGURINE AND PACKAGE AS A COMPLETE WORK OF ART.
THE OWNER UNDERSTANDS THAT CULTURE INCLUDES APPRECIATION OF FINE THINGS.
HE WORKED HARD, SKIMPED ON MEALS AND EVEN DENIED HIMSELF HIS FAVORITE PUDDING.
HAVE YOU EVER FELT SUCH PASSION?
HAVE YOU EVER FELT SUCH PRIDE?

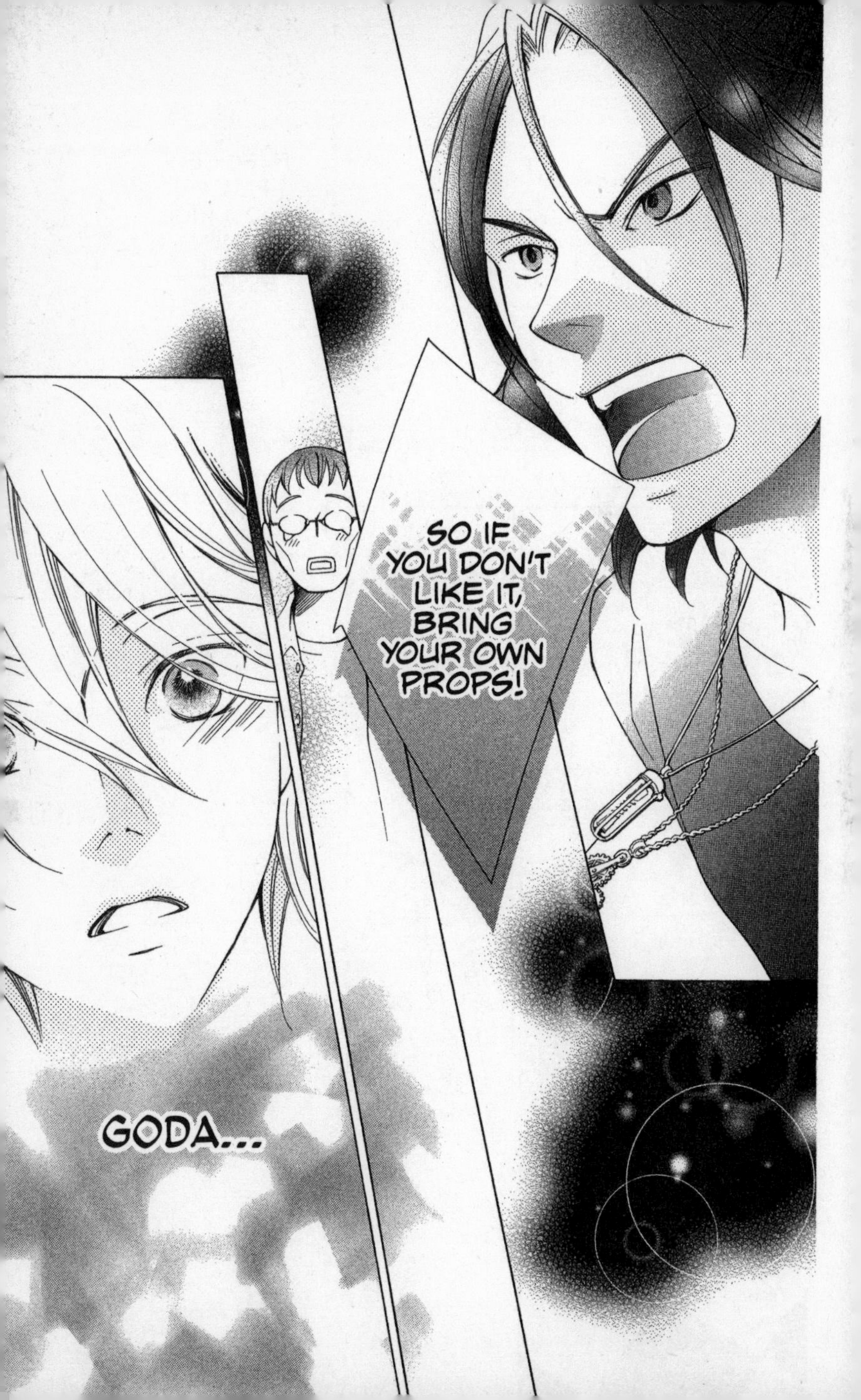
SO IF YOU DON'T LIKE IT, BRING YOUR OWN PROPS!
GODA...

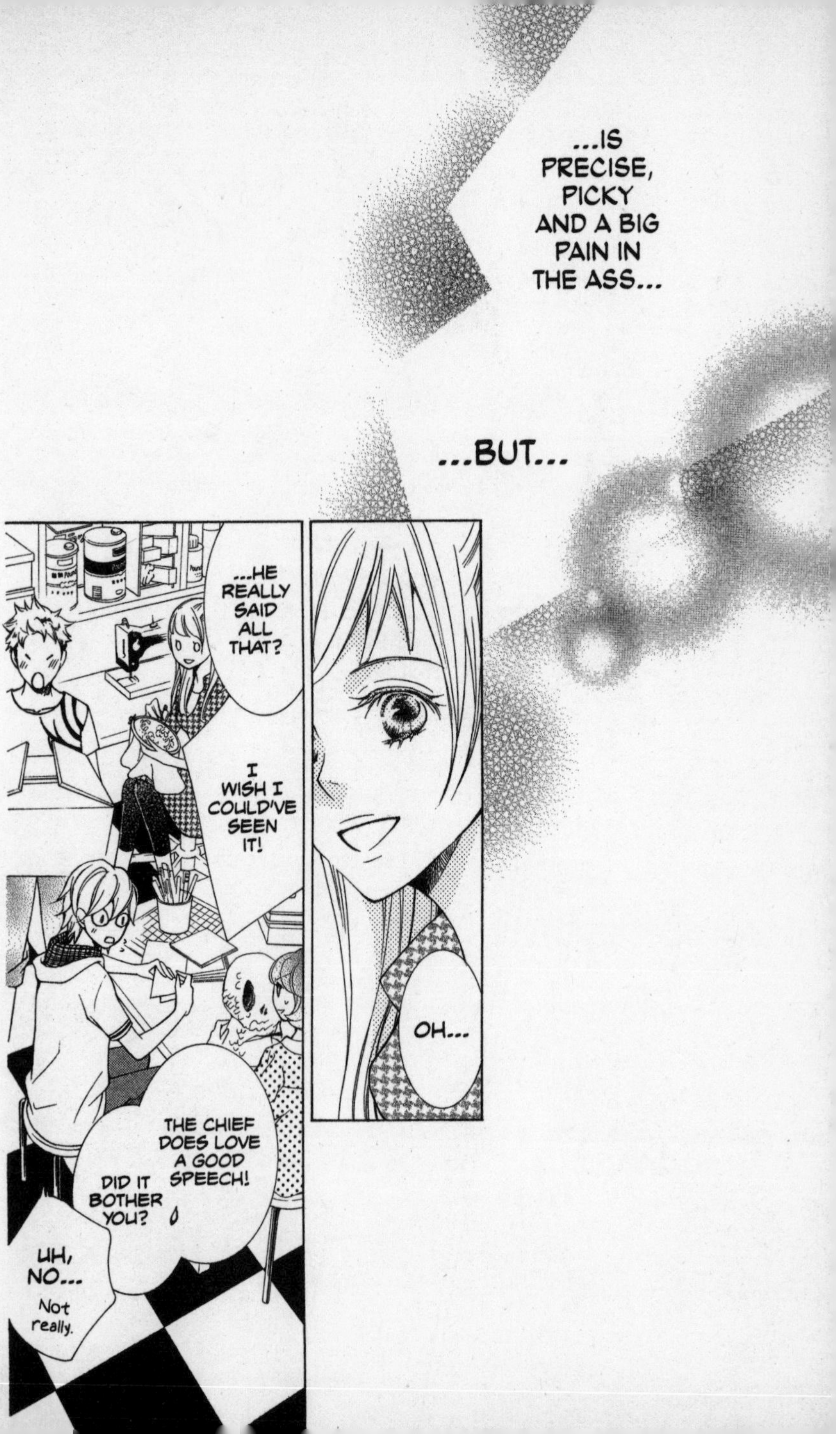
...IS PRECISE, PICKY AND A BIG PAIN IN THE ASS...
...BUT...
OH...
...HE REALLY SAID ALL THAT?
I WISH I COULD'VE SEEN IT!
THE CHIEF DOES LOVE A GOOD SPEECH!
DID IT BOTHER YOU?
UH, NO...
Not really.

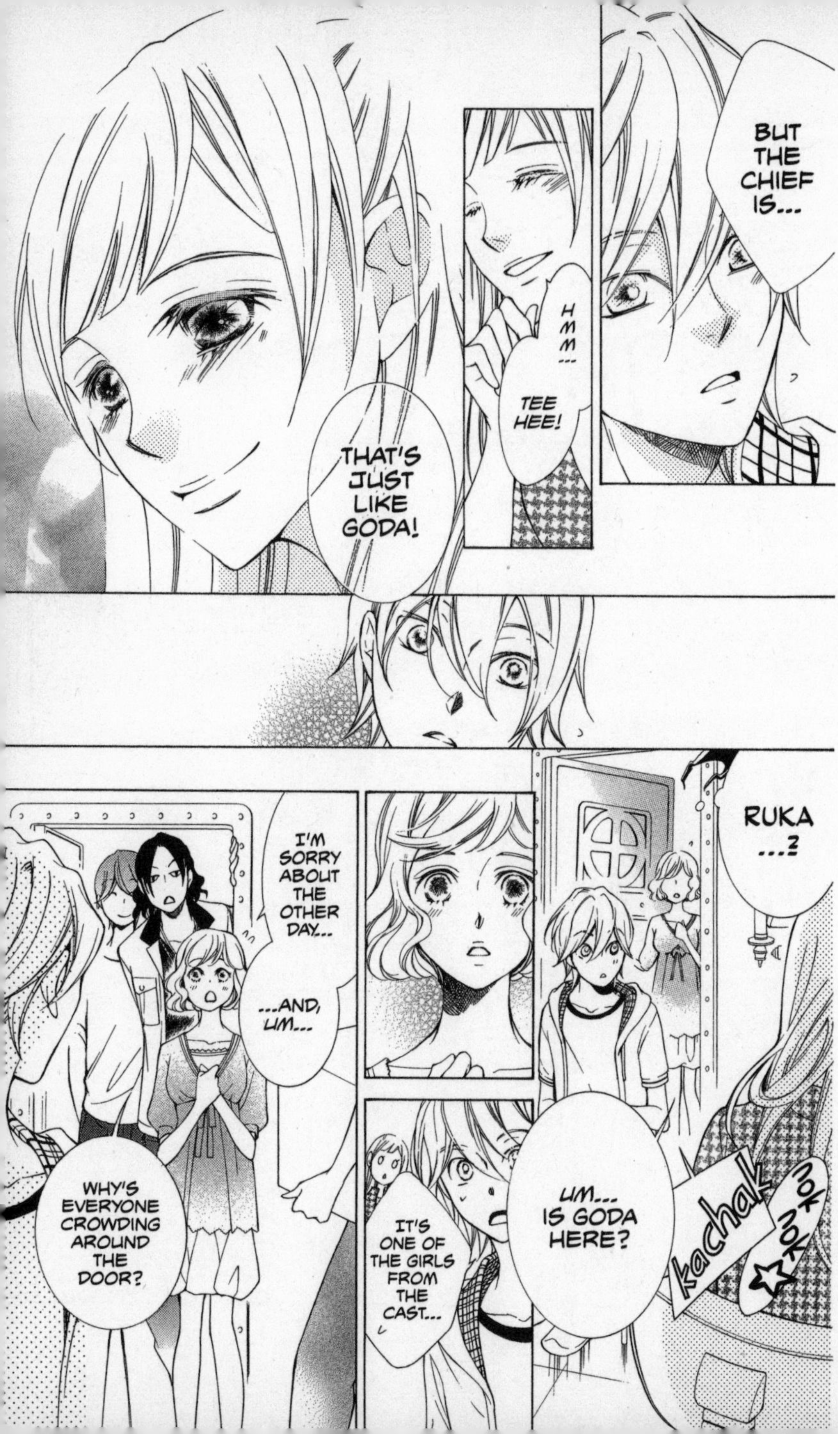
BUT THE CHIEF IS...
HMM... TEE HEE!
THAT'S JUST LIKE GODA!
RUKA ...?
nok nok
kachak
UM... IS GODA HERE?
IT'S ONE OF THE GIRLS FROM THE CAST...
I'M SORRY ABOUT THE OTHER DAY...
...AND, UM...
WHY'S EVERYONE CROWDING AROUND THE DOOR?

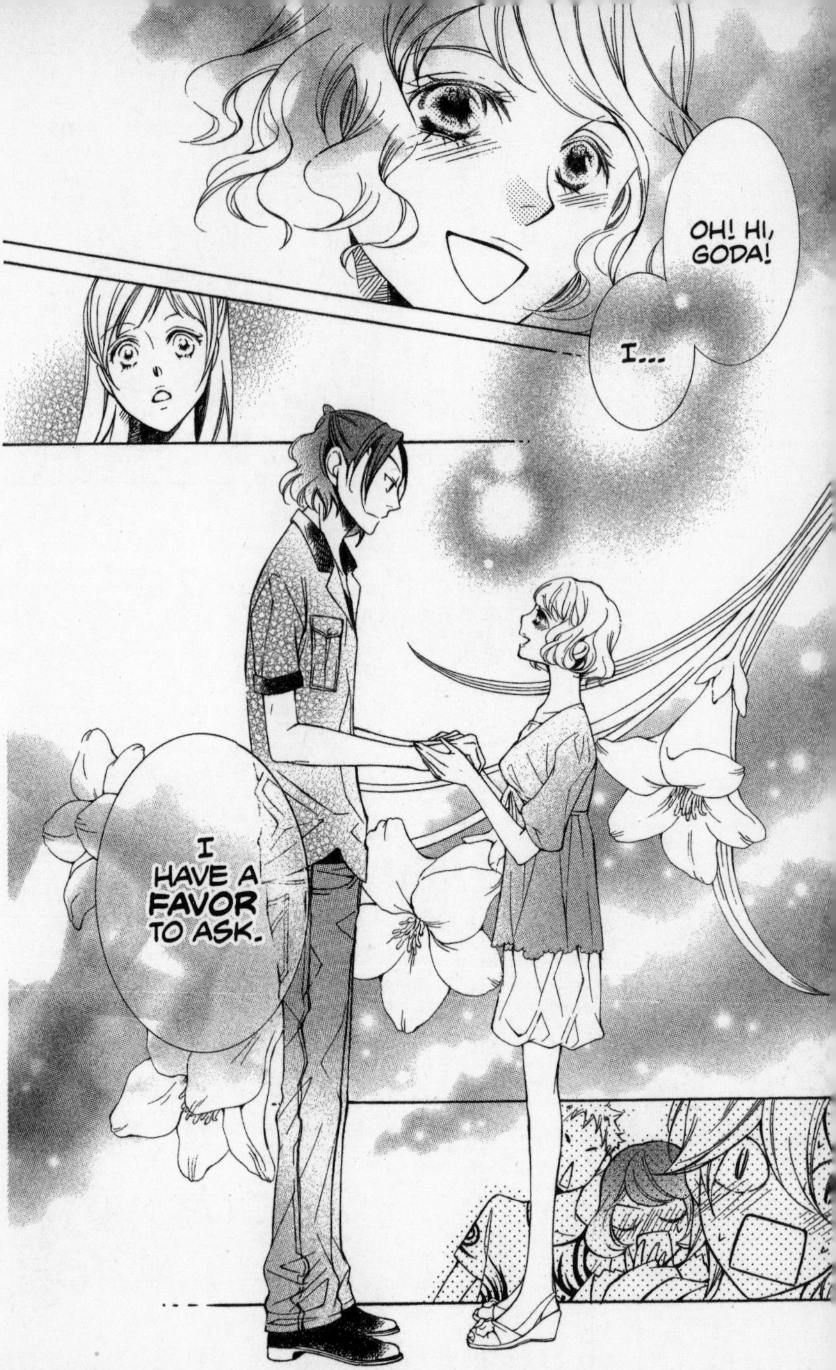
OH! HI, GODA!
I...
I HAVE A FAVOR TO ASK.

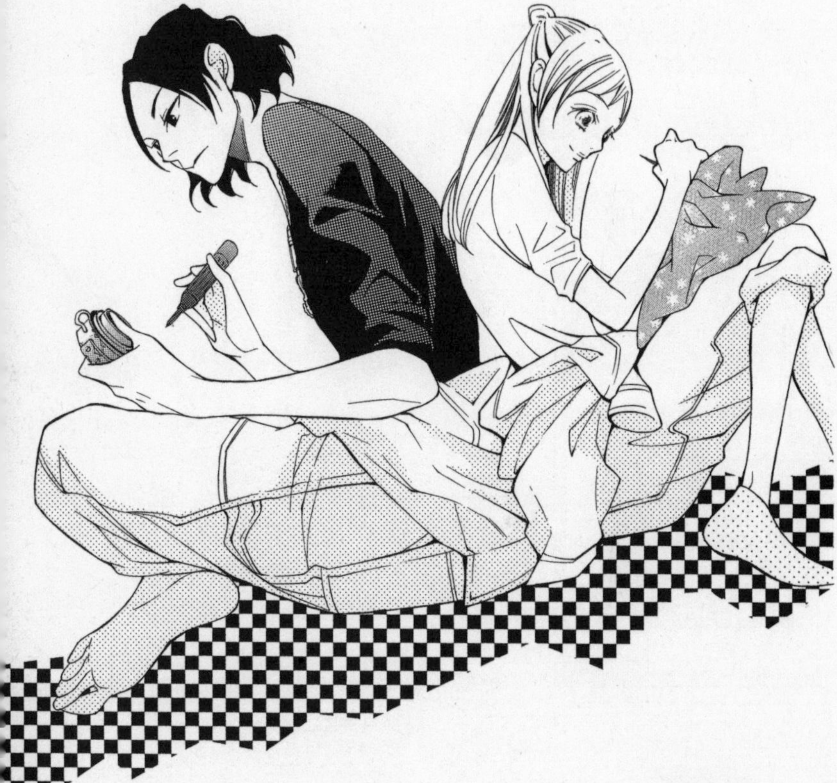

SCENE 7

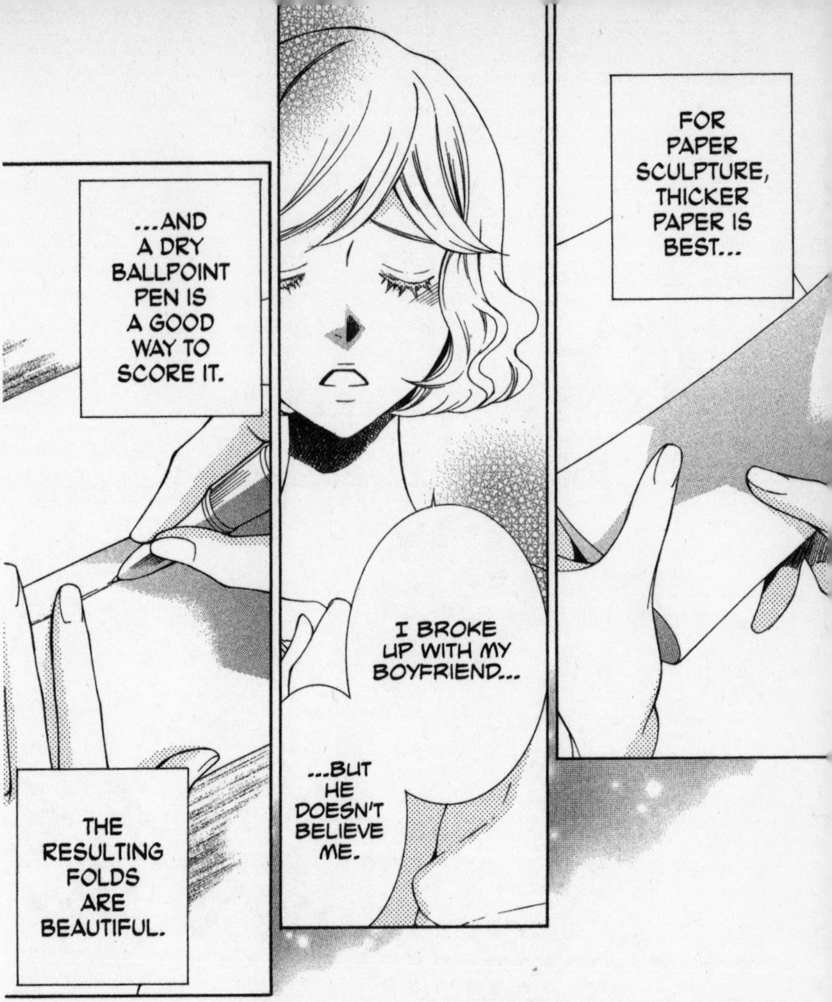
FOR PAPER SCULPTURE, THICKER PAPER IS BEST...
I BROKE UP WITH MY BOYFRIEND...
...BUT HE DOESN'T BELIEVE ME.
...AND A DRY BALLPOINT PEN IS A GOOD WAY TO SCORE IT.
THE RESULTING FOLDS ARE BEAUTIFUL.

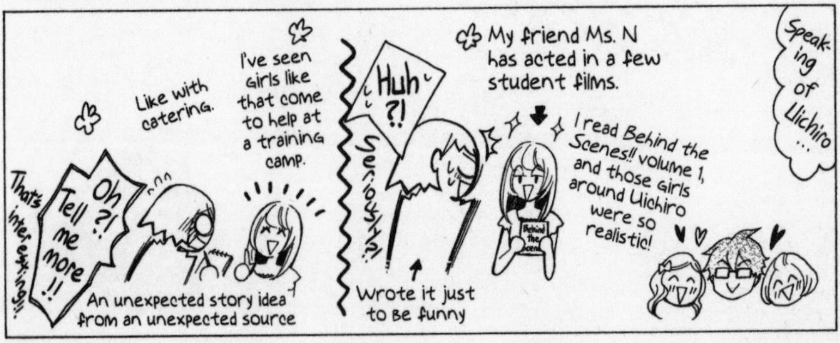
Speaking of Uichiro...
My friend Ms. N has acted in a few student films.
I read Behind the Scenes!! volume 1, and those girls around Uichiro were so realistic!
Huh?!
Seriously?!
Wrote it just to be funny
I've seen girls like that come to help at a training camp.
Like with catering.
Oh?! Tell me more!!
That's interesting!!
An unexpected story idea from an unexpected source

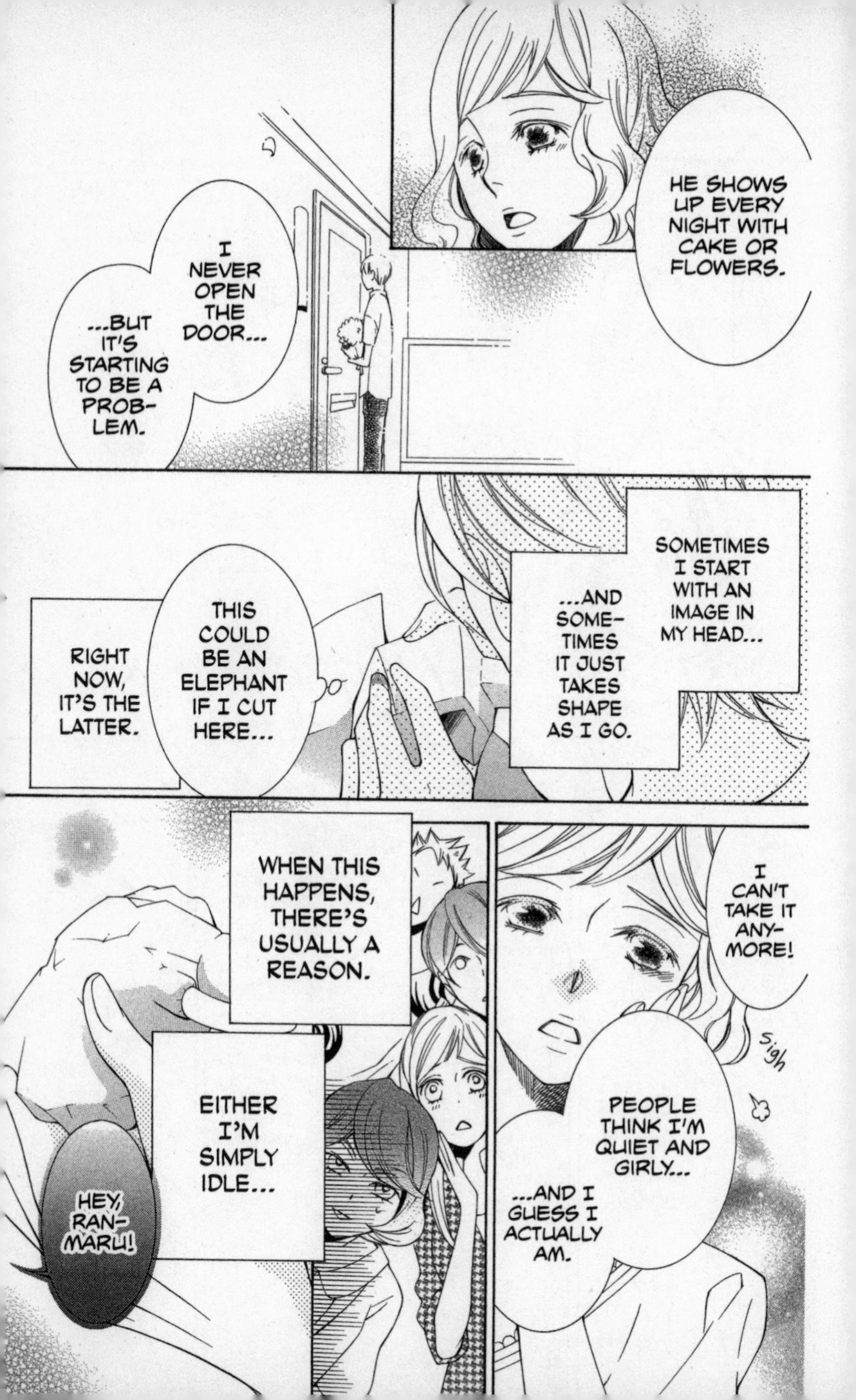
HE SHOWS UP EVERY NIGHT WITH CAKE OR FLOWERS.
I NEVER OPEN THE DOOR...
...BUT IT'S STARTING TO BE A PROBLEM.
SOMETIMES I START WITH AN IMAGE IN MY HEAD...
...AND SOMETIMES IT JUST TAKES SHAPE AS I GO.
THIS COULD BE AN ELEPHANT IF I CUT HERE...
RIGHT NOW, IT'S THE LATTER.
I CAN'T TAKE IT ANYMORE!
Sigh
PEOPLE THINK I'M QUIET AND GIRLY...
...AND I GUESS I ACTUALLY AM.
WHEN THIS HAPPENS, THERE'S USUALLY A REASON.
EITHER I'M SIMPLY IDLE...
HEY, RANMARU!

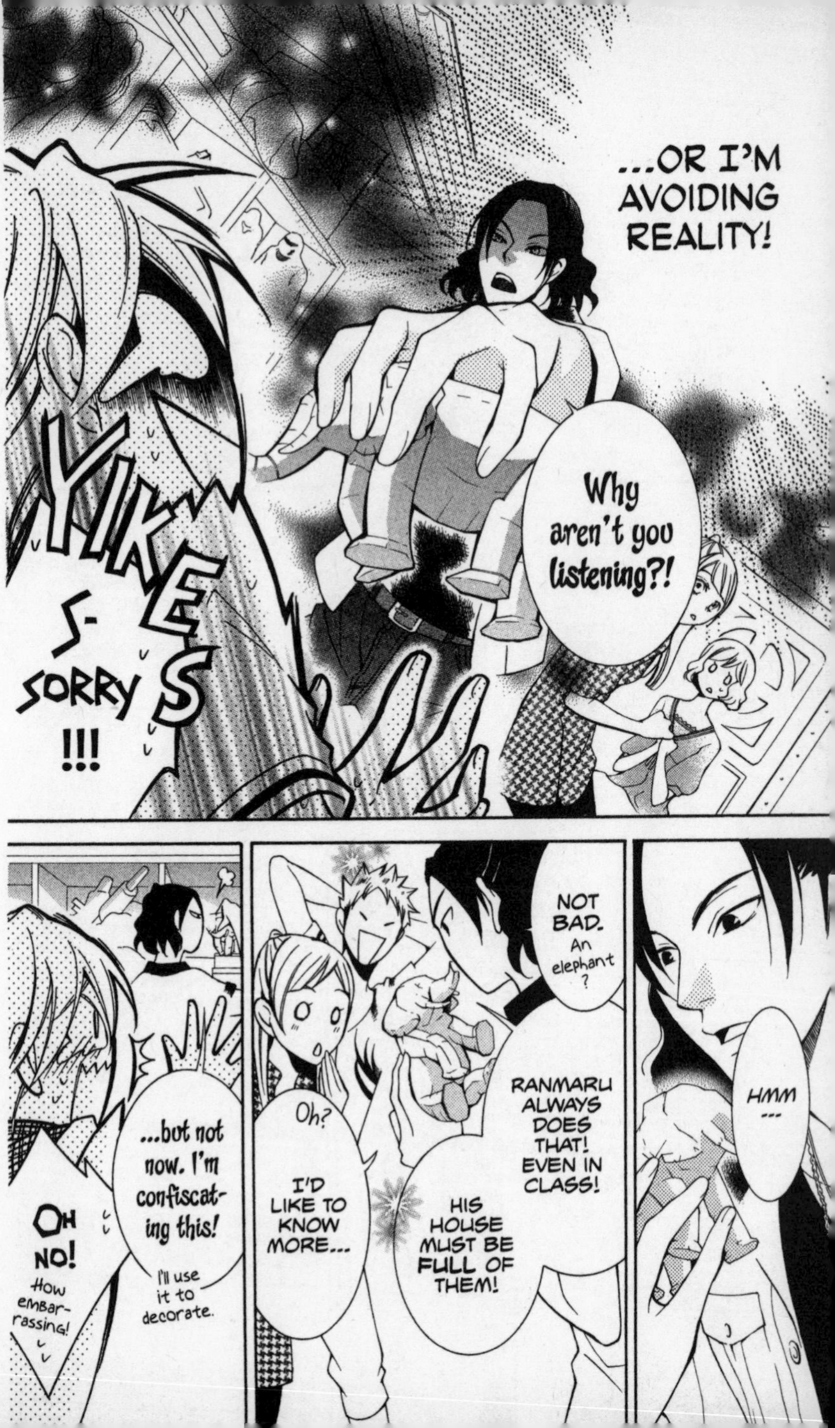
...OR I'M AVOIDING REALITY!
Why aren't you listening?!
YIKES
S-SORRY!!!
HMM...
NOT BAD. An elephant?
RANMARU ALWAYS DOES THAT! EVEN IN CLASS!
HIS HOUSE MUST BE FULL OF THEM!
Oh?
I'D LIKE TO KNOW MORE...
...but not now. I'm confiscating this!
I'll use it to decorate.
OH NO! How embarrassing!

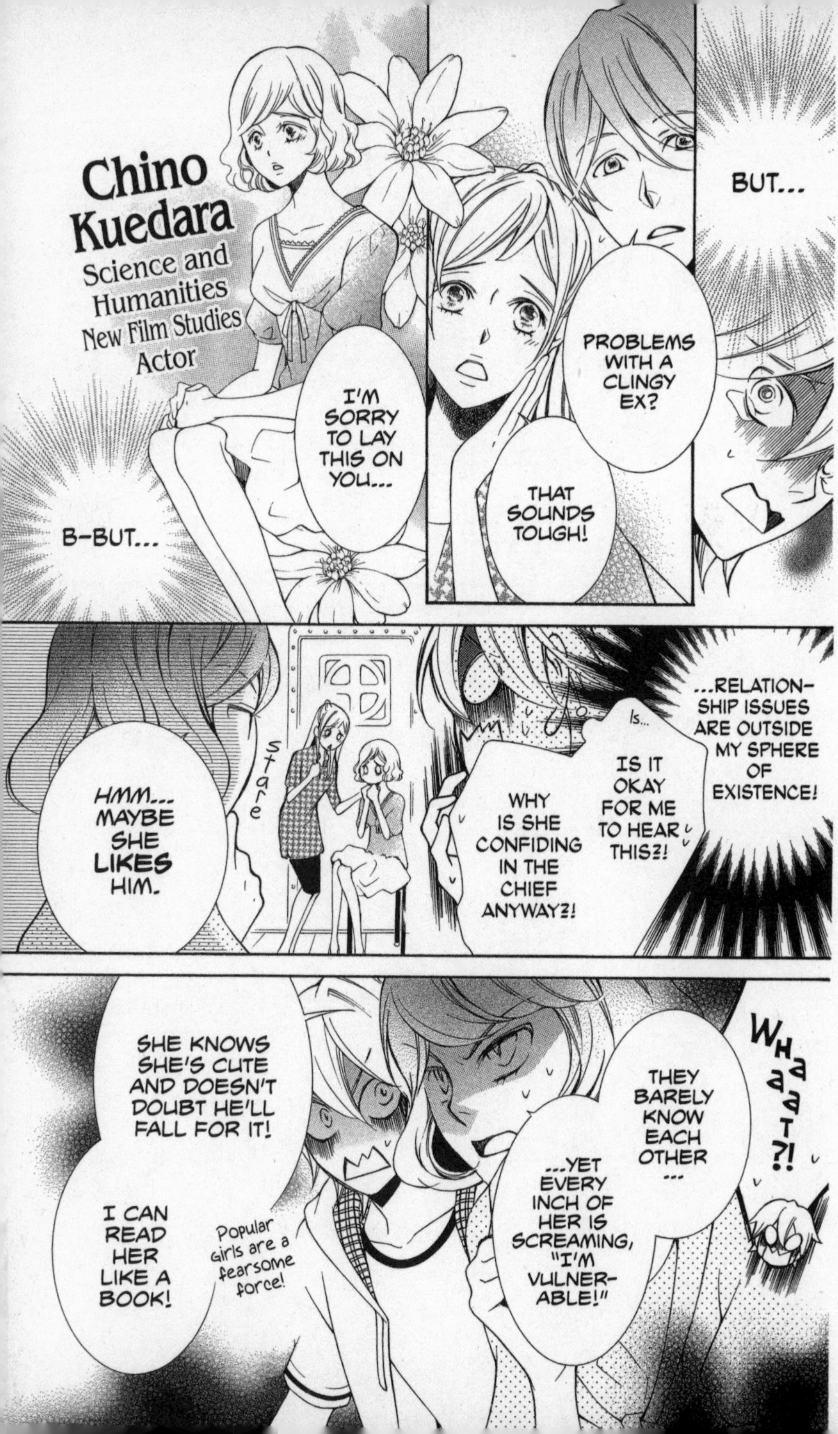
BUT...
PROBLEMS WITH A CLINGY EX?
THAT SOUNDS TOUGH!
Chino Kuedara
Science and Humanities
New Film Studies
Actor
I'M SORRY TO LAY THIS ON YOU...
B-BUT...
...RELATIONSHIP ISSUES ARE OUTSIDE MY SPHERE OF EXISTENCE!
Is...
IS IT OKAY FOR ME TO HEAR THIS?!
WHY IS SHE CONFIDING IN THE CHIEF ANYWAY?!
stare
HMM... MAYBE SHE LIKES HIM.
WHAAAT?!
THEY BARELY KNOW EACH OTHER...
...YET EVERY INCH OF HER IS SCREAMING, "I'M VULNERABLE!"
SHE KNOWS SHE'S CUTE AND DOESN'T DOUBT HE'LL FALL FOR IT!
I CAN READ HER LIKE A BOOK!
Popular girls are a fearsome force!

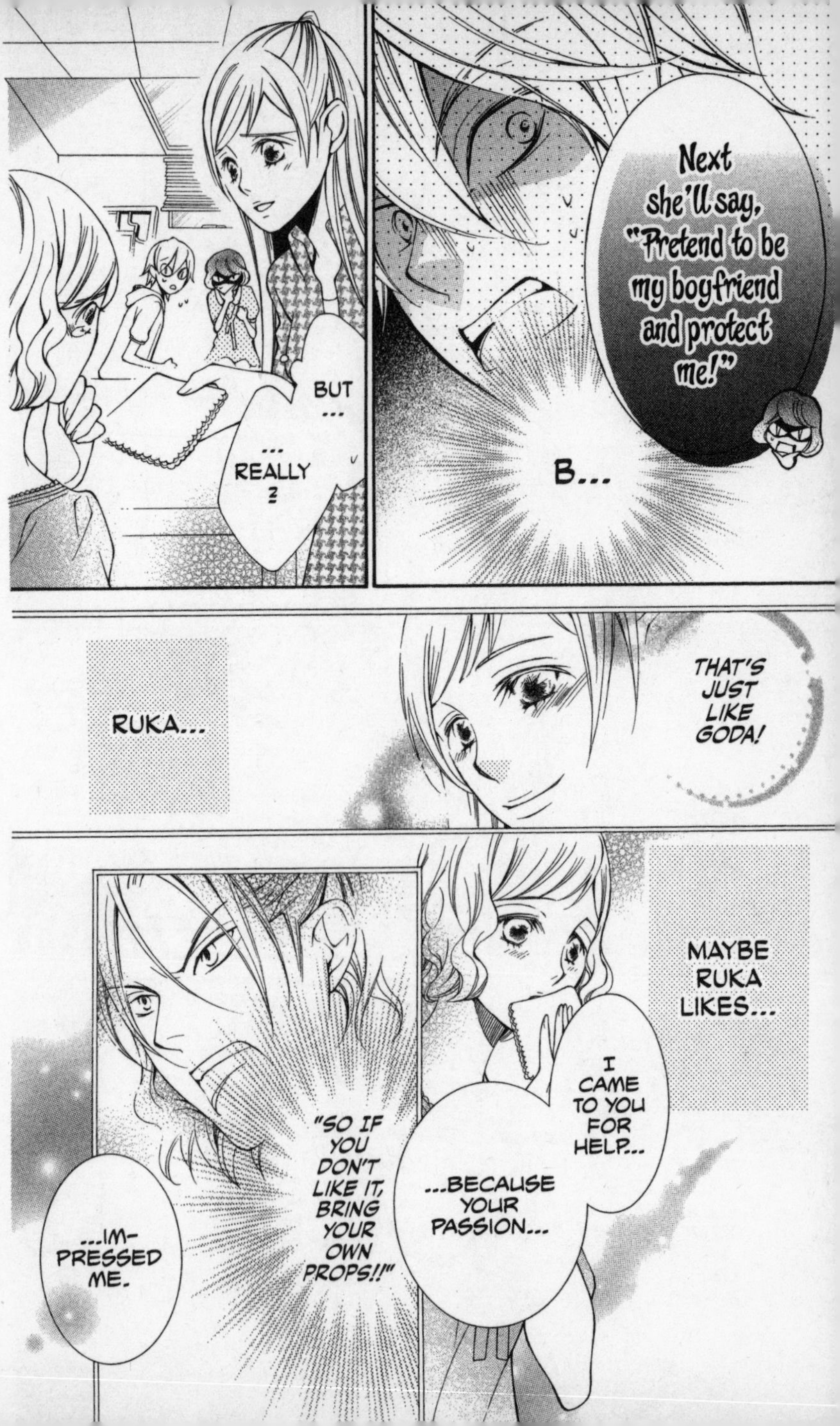

Next she'll say, "Pretend to be my boyfriend and protect me!"
B...
BUT...
...REALLY?
THAT'S JUST LIKE GODA!
RUKA...
MAYBE RUKA LIKES...
I CAME TO YOU FOR HELP...
...BECAUSE YOUR PASSION...
"SO IF YOU DON'T LIKE IT, BRING YOUR OWN PROPS!!"
...IM-PRESSED ME.

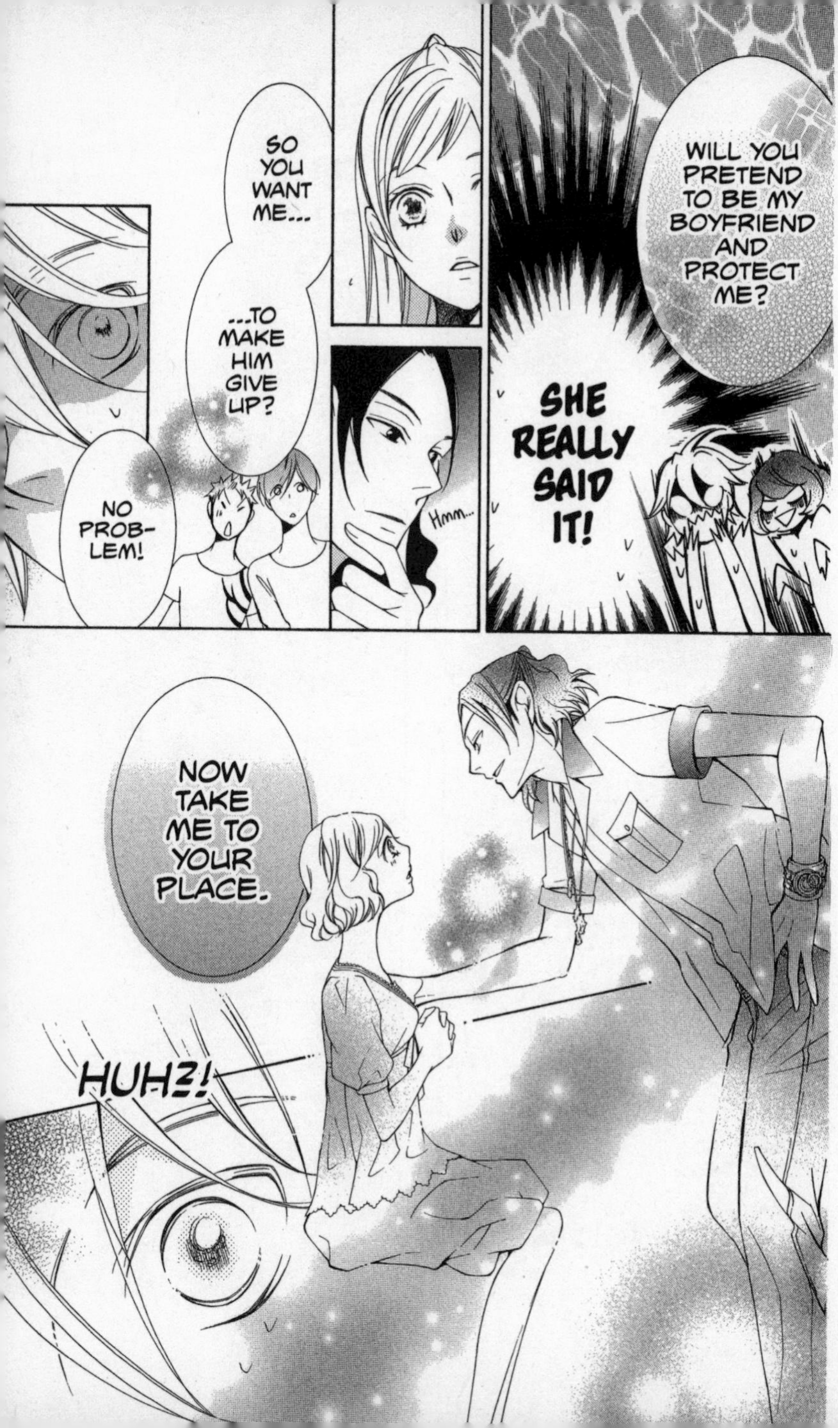
WILL YOU PRETEND TO BE MY BOYFRIEND AND PROTECT ME?
SHE REALLY SAID IT!
Hmm...
SO YOU WANT ME...
...TO MAKE HIM GIVE UP?
NO PROB-LEM!
NOW TAKE ME TO YOUR PLACE.
HUH?!

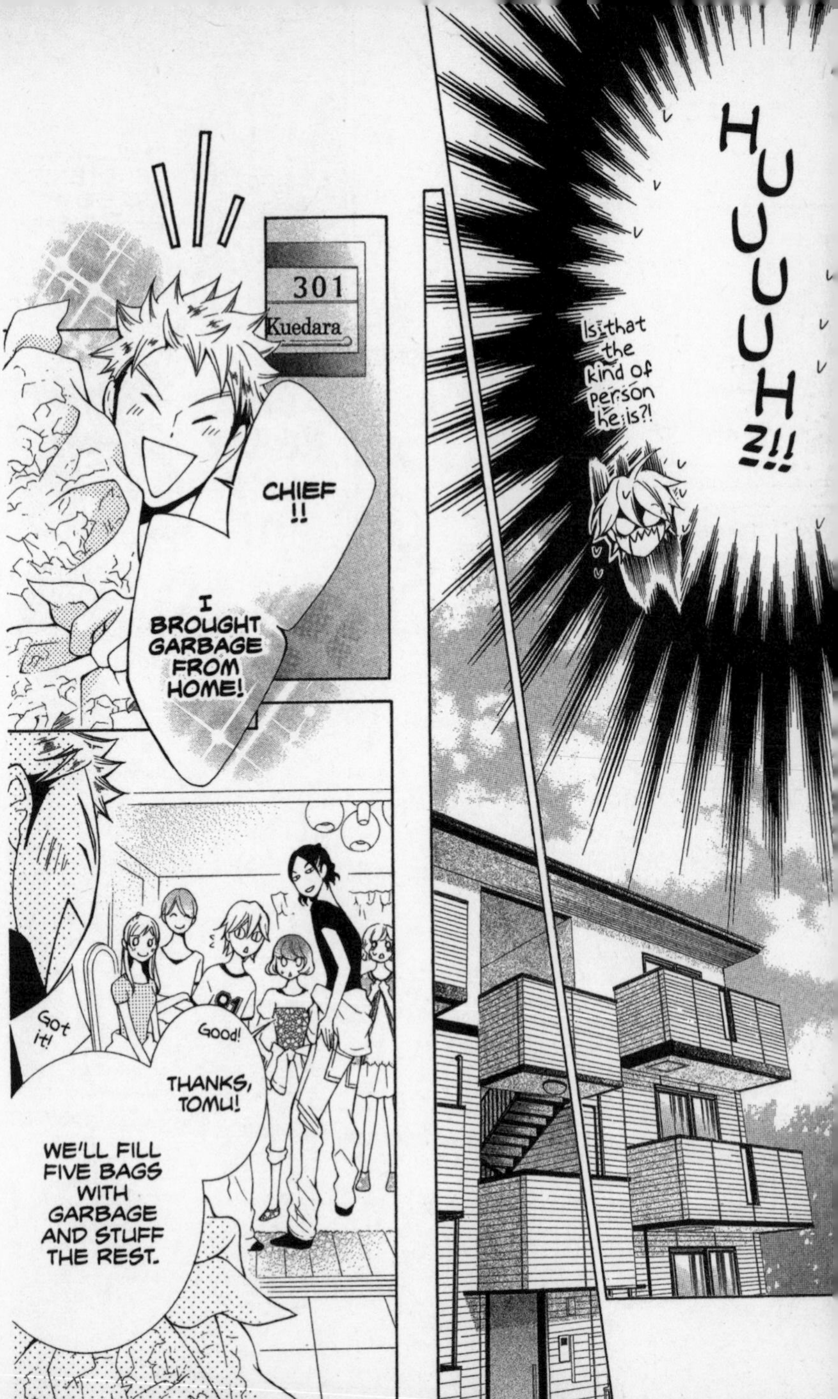
HUUUUH?!!
Is that the kind of person he is?!
301
Kuedara
CHIEF!! I BROUGHT GARBAGE FROM HOME!
Good!
THANKS, TOMU! WE'LL FILL FIVE BAGS WITH GARBAGE AND STUFF THE REST.
Got it!

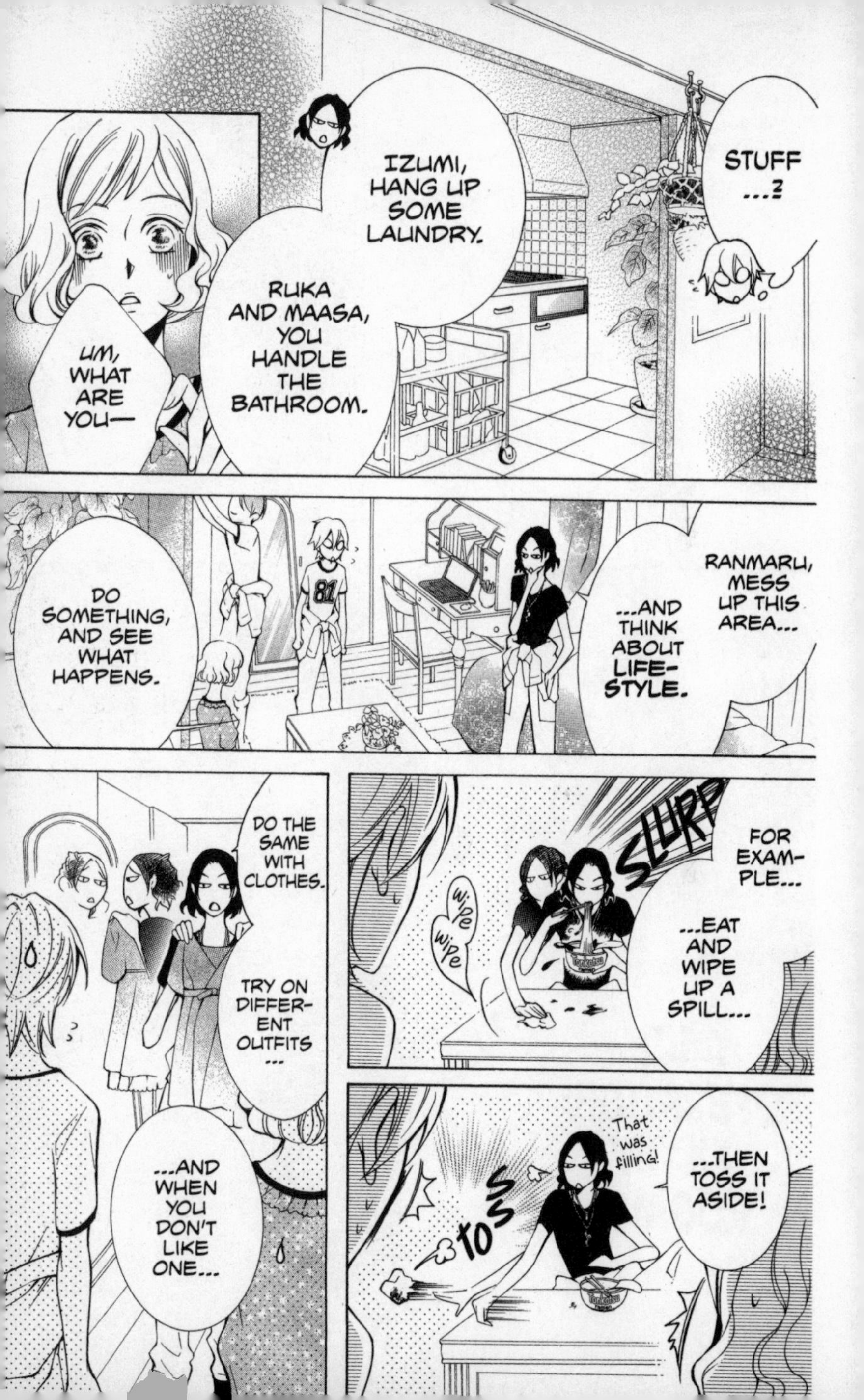
STUFF ...?
IZUMI, HANG UP SOME LAUNDRY.
RUKA AND MAASA, YOU HANDLE THE BATHROOM.
UM, WHAT ARE YOU—
RANMARU, MESS UP THIS AREA...
...AND THINK ABOUT LIFE-STYLE.
DO SOMETHING, AND SEE WHAT HAPPENS.
FOR EXAMPLE...
SLURP
...EAT AND WIPE UP A SPILL...
wipe wipe
...THEN TOSS IT ASIDE!
That was filling!
TOSS
DO THE SAME WITH CLOTHES.
TRY ON DIFFERENT OUTFITS...
...AND WHEN YOU DON'T LIKE ONE...

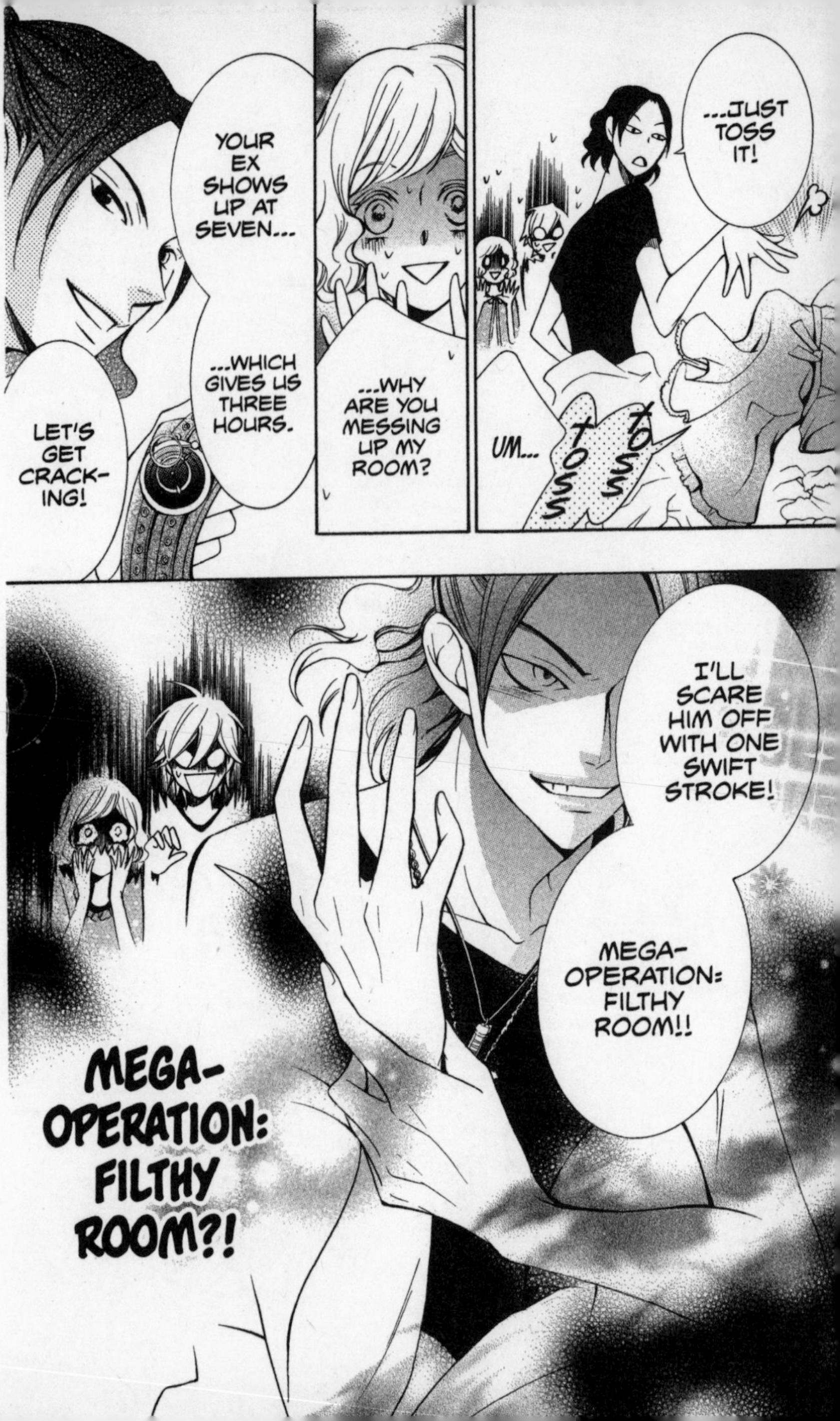
...JUST TOSS IT!
UM...
TOSS TOSS
...WHY ARE YOU MESSING UP MY ROOM?
YOUR EX SHOWS UP AT SEVEN...
...WHICH GIVES US THREE HOURS.
LET'S GET CRACKING!
I'LL SCARE HIM OFF WITH ONE SWIFT STROKE!
MEGA-OPERATION: FILTHY ROOM!!
MEGA-OPERATION: FILTHY ROOM?!

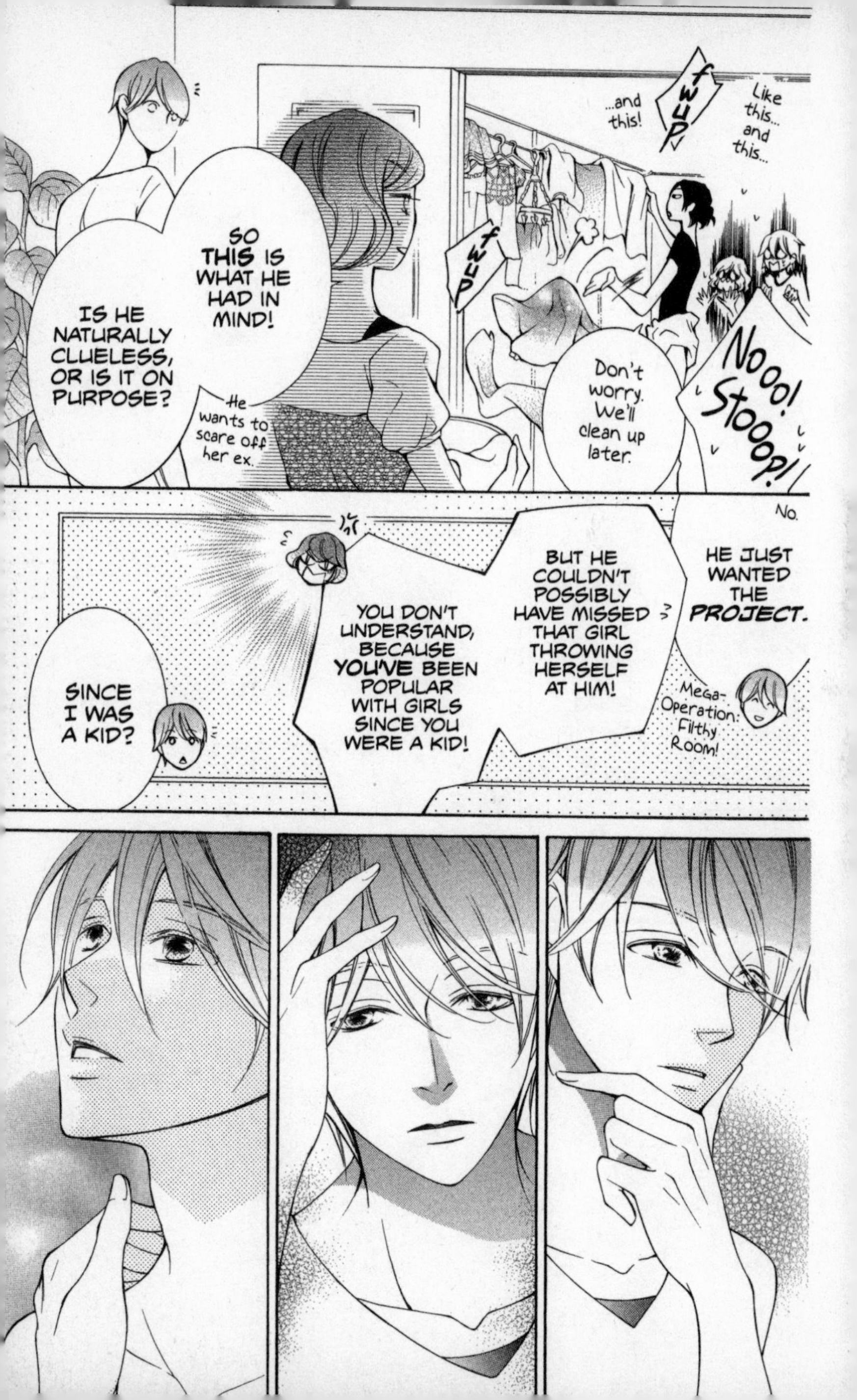

Like this... and this...
FWUP
...and this!
FWUP
Nooo! Stooop!
Don't worry. We'll clean up later.
SO THIS IS WHAT HE HAD IN MIND!
He wants to scare off her ex.
IS HE NATURALLY CLUELESS, OR IS IT ON PURPOSE?
No.
HE JUST WANTED THE PROJECT.
Mega-Operation: Filthy Room!
BUT HE COULDN'T POSSIBLY HAVE MISSED THAT GIRL THROWING HERSELF AT HIM!
YOU DON'T UNDERSTAND, BECAUSE YOU'VE BEEN POPULAR WITH GIRLS SINCE YOU WERE A KID!
SINCE I WAS A KID?

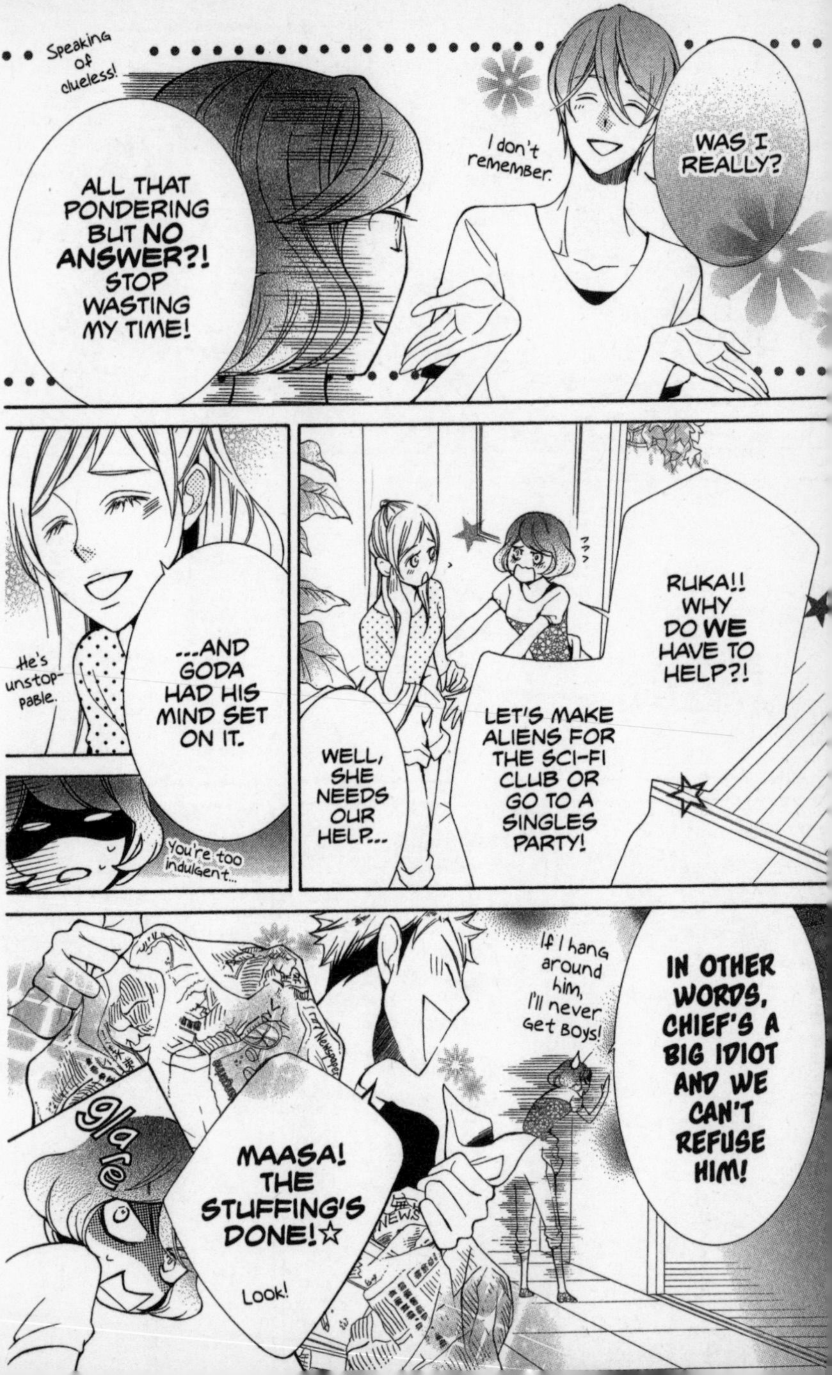
WAS I REALLY?
I don't remember.
Speaking of clueless!
ALL THAT PONDERING BUT NO ANSWER?! STOP WASTING MY TIME!
RUKA!! WHY DO WE HAVE TO HELP?!
LET'S MAKE ALIENS FOR THE SCI-FI CLUB OR GO TO A SINGLES PARTY!
WELL, SHE NEEDS OUR HELP...
...AND GODA HAD HIS MIND SET ON IT.
He's unstop-pable.
You're too indulgent...
IN OTHER WORDS, CHIEF'S A BIG IDIOT AND WE CAN'T REFUSE HIM!
If I hang around him, I'll never get boys!
MAASA! THE STUFFING'S DONE!☆
glare
Look!

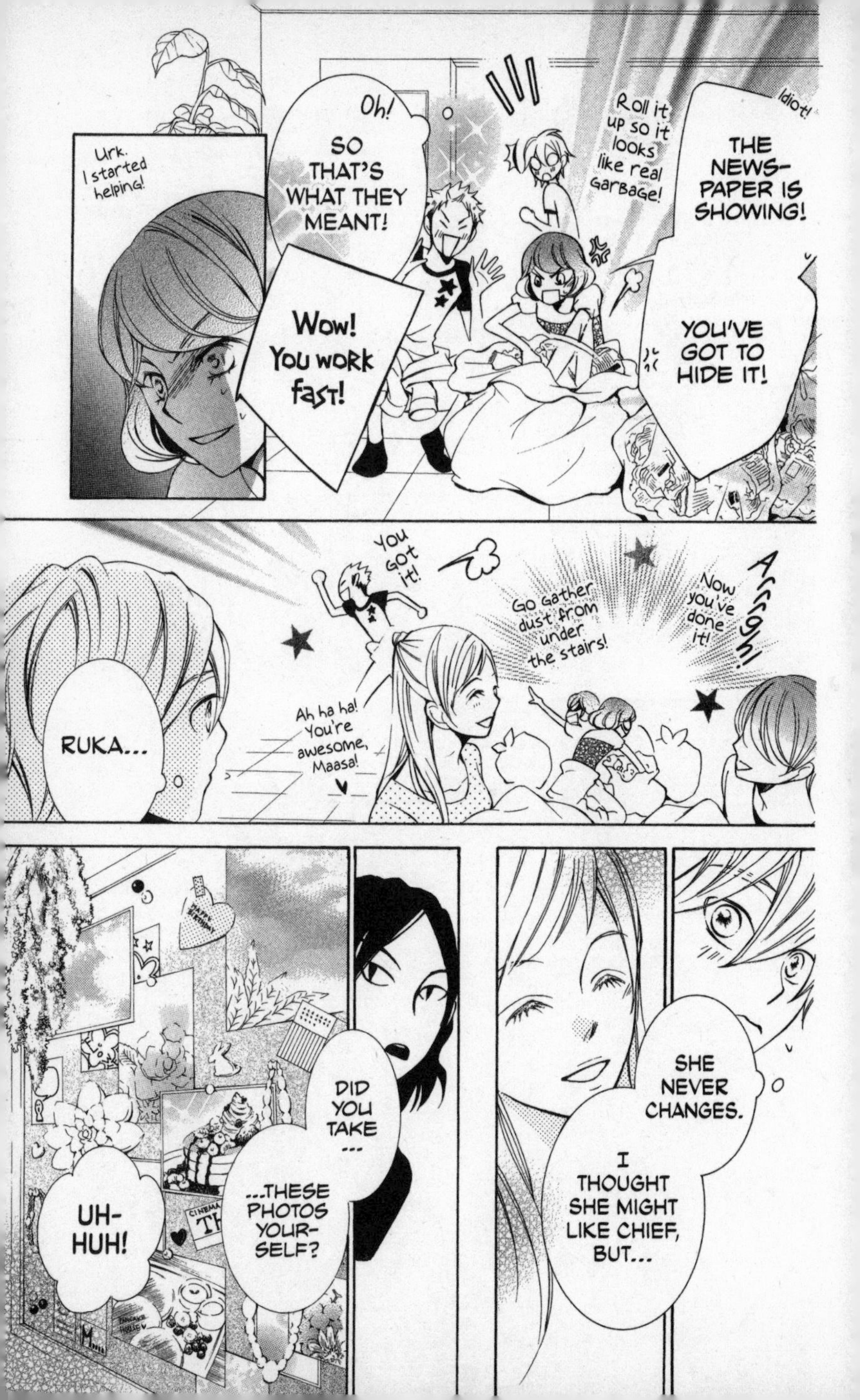
Idiot!
THE NEWS-PAPER IS SHOWING!
YOU'VE GOT TO HIDE IT!
Roll it up so it looks like real garbage!
Oh!
SO THAT'S WHAT THEY MEANT!
Wow! You work fast!
Urk. I started helping!
Arrgh!
Now you've done it!
Go gather dust from under the stairs!
You got it!
Ah ha ha! You're awesome, Maasa!
RUKA...
SHE NEVER CHANGES.
I THOUGHT SHE MIGHT LIKE CHIEF, BUT...
DID YOU TAKE...
...THESE PHOTOS YOURSELF?
UH-HUH!

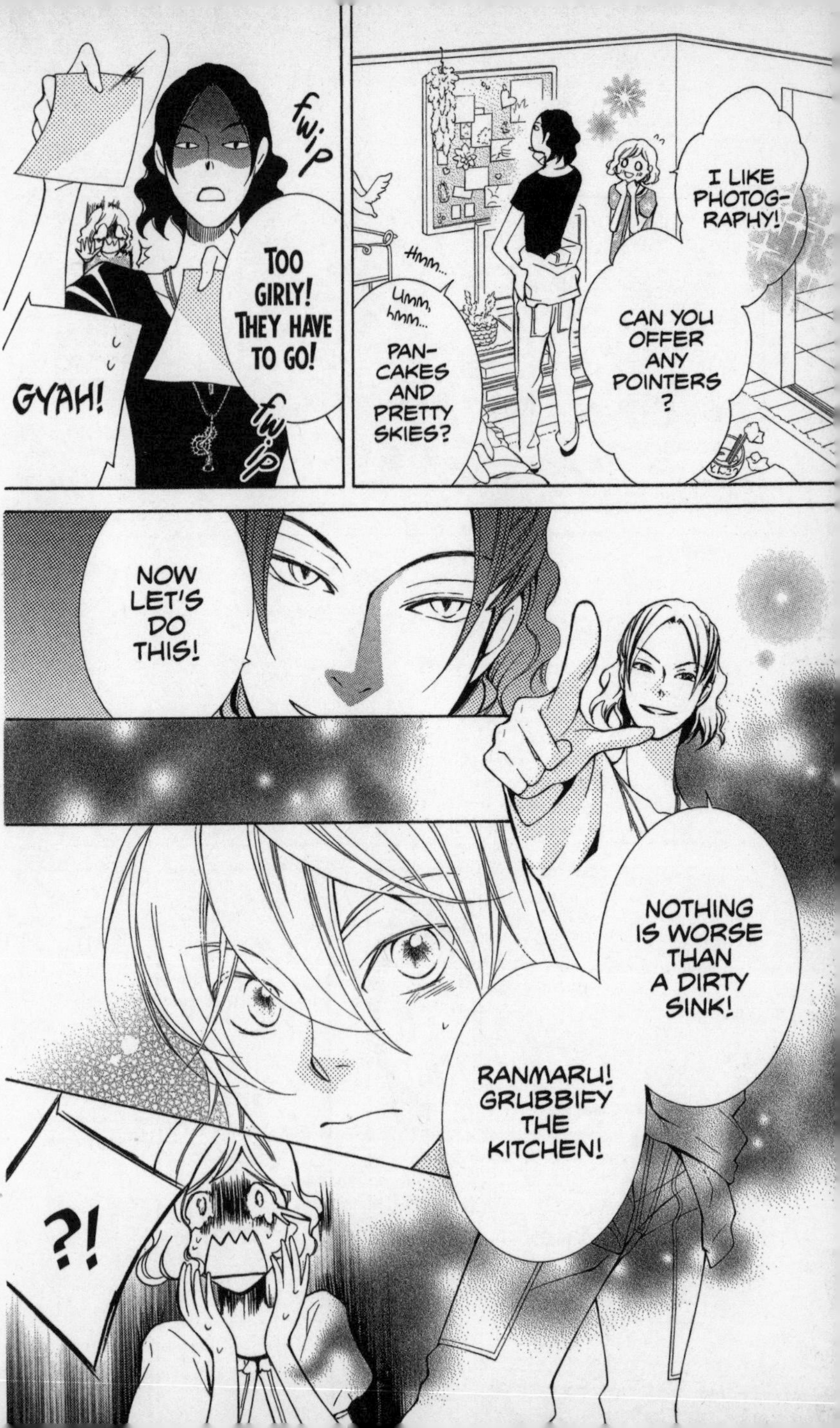
I LIKE PHOTOGRAPHY!
CAN YOU OFFER ANY POINTERS?
Hmm...
Umm, hmm...
PANCAKES AND PRETTY SKIES?
fwip
TOO GIRLY! THEY HAVE TO GO!
fwip
GYAH!
NOW LET'S DO THIS!
NOTHING IS WORSE THAN A DIRTY SINK!
RANMARU! GRUBBIFY THE KITCHEN!
?!

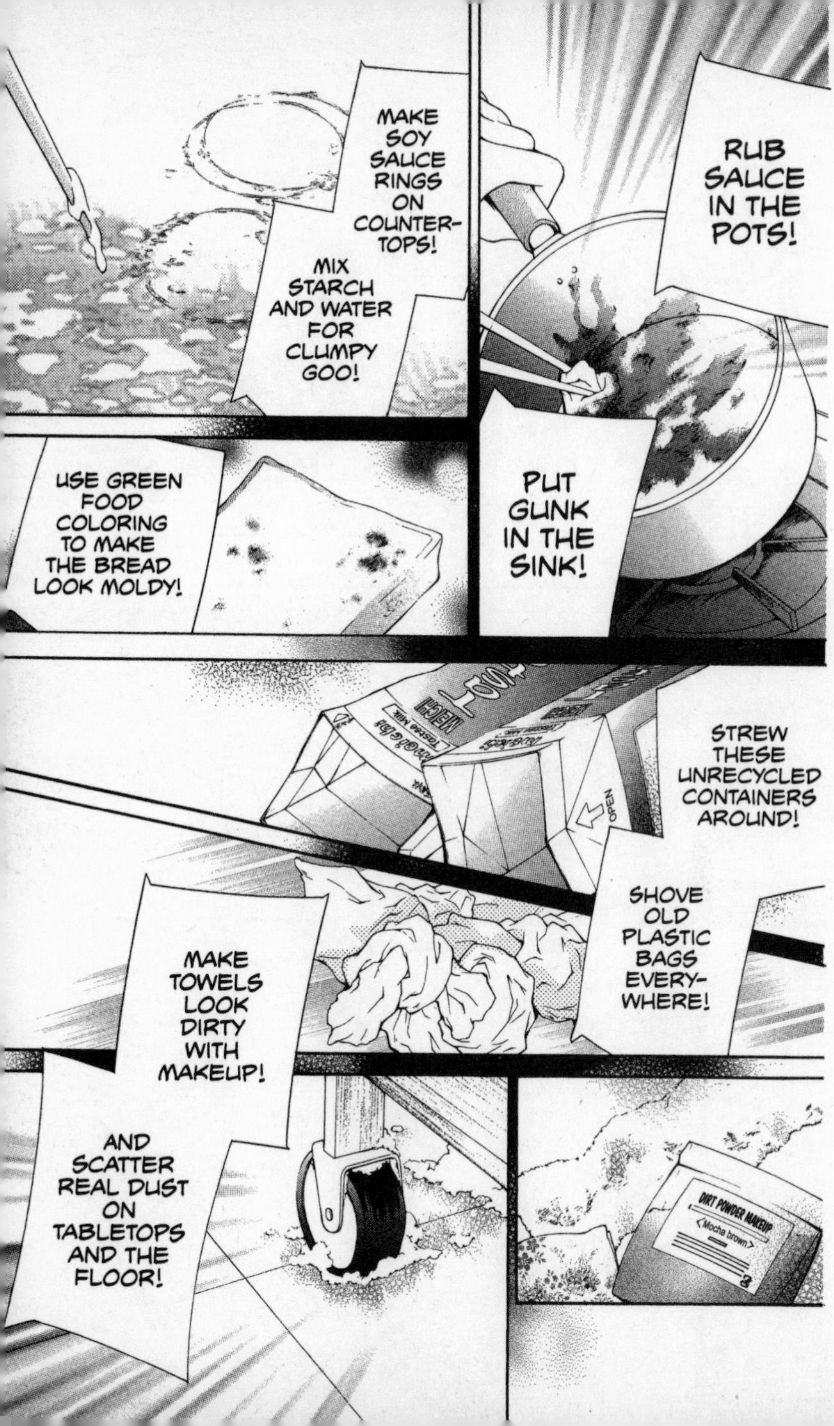
RUB SAUCE IN THE POTS!
MAKE SOY SAUCE RINGS ON COUNTER-TOPS!
MIX STARCH AND WATER FOR CLUMPY GOO!
PUT GUNK IN THE SINK!
USE GREEN FOOD COLORING TO MAKE THE BREAD LOOK MOLDY!
STREW THESE UNRECYCLED CONTAINERS AROUND!
OPEN
SHOVE OLD PLASTIC BAGS EVERY-WHERE!
MAKE TOWELS LOOK DIRTY WITH MAKEUP!
DIRT POWDER MAKEUP
<Mocha brown>
AND SCATTER REAL DUST ON TABLETOPS AND THE FLOOR!

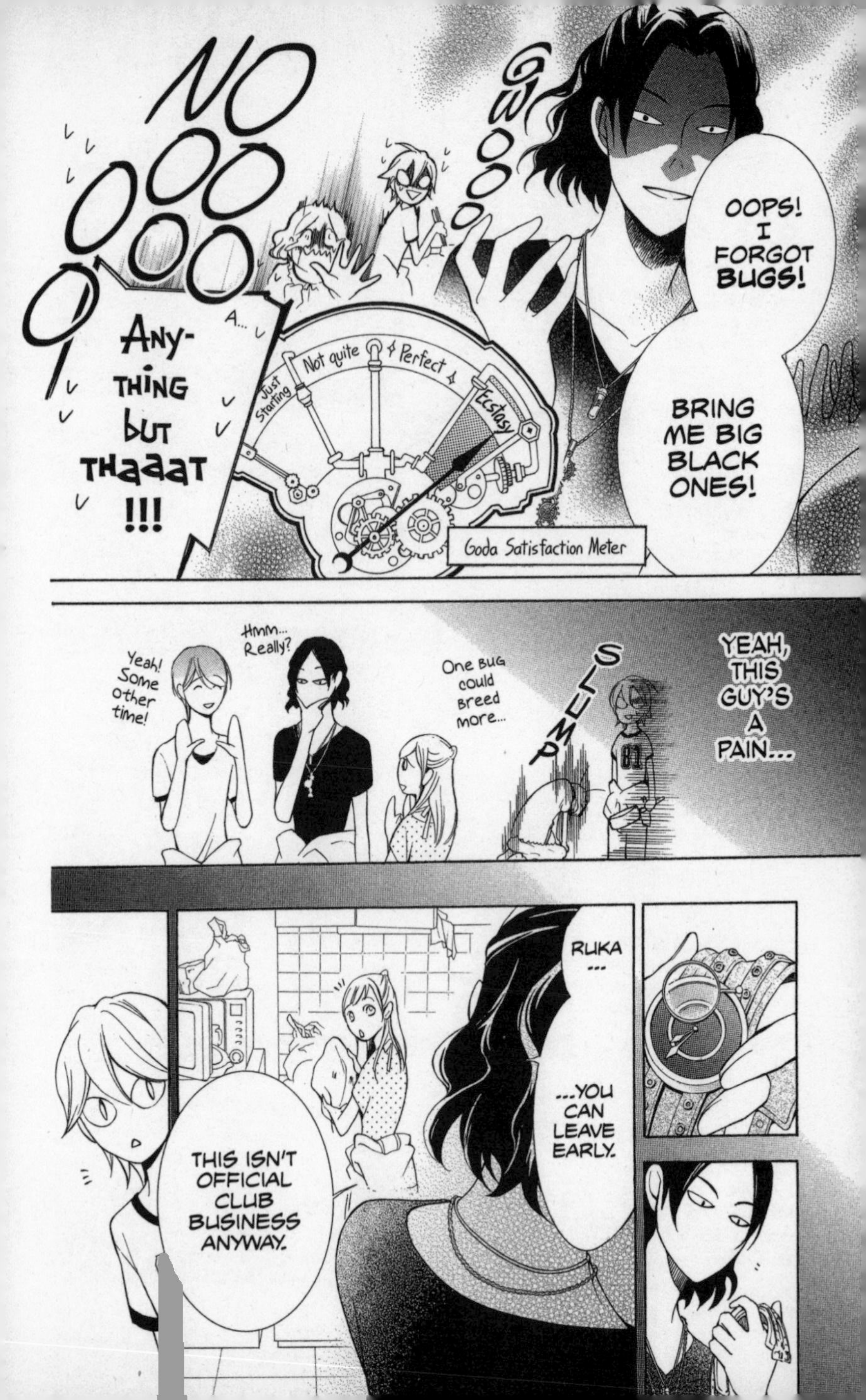
OOPS! I FORGOT BUGS!
BRING ME BIG BLACK ONES!
GWOOOO
NOOOOOOOO
A...
ANY-THING BUT THAAAT!!!
Just Starting
Not quite
Perfect
Ecstasy
Goda Satisfaction Meter
YEAH, THIS GUY'S A PAIN...
SLUMP
One bug could breed more...
Hmm... Really?
Yeah! Some other time!
RUKA...
...YOU CAN LEAVE EARLY.
THIS ISN'T OFFICIAL CLUB BUSINESS ANYWAY.

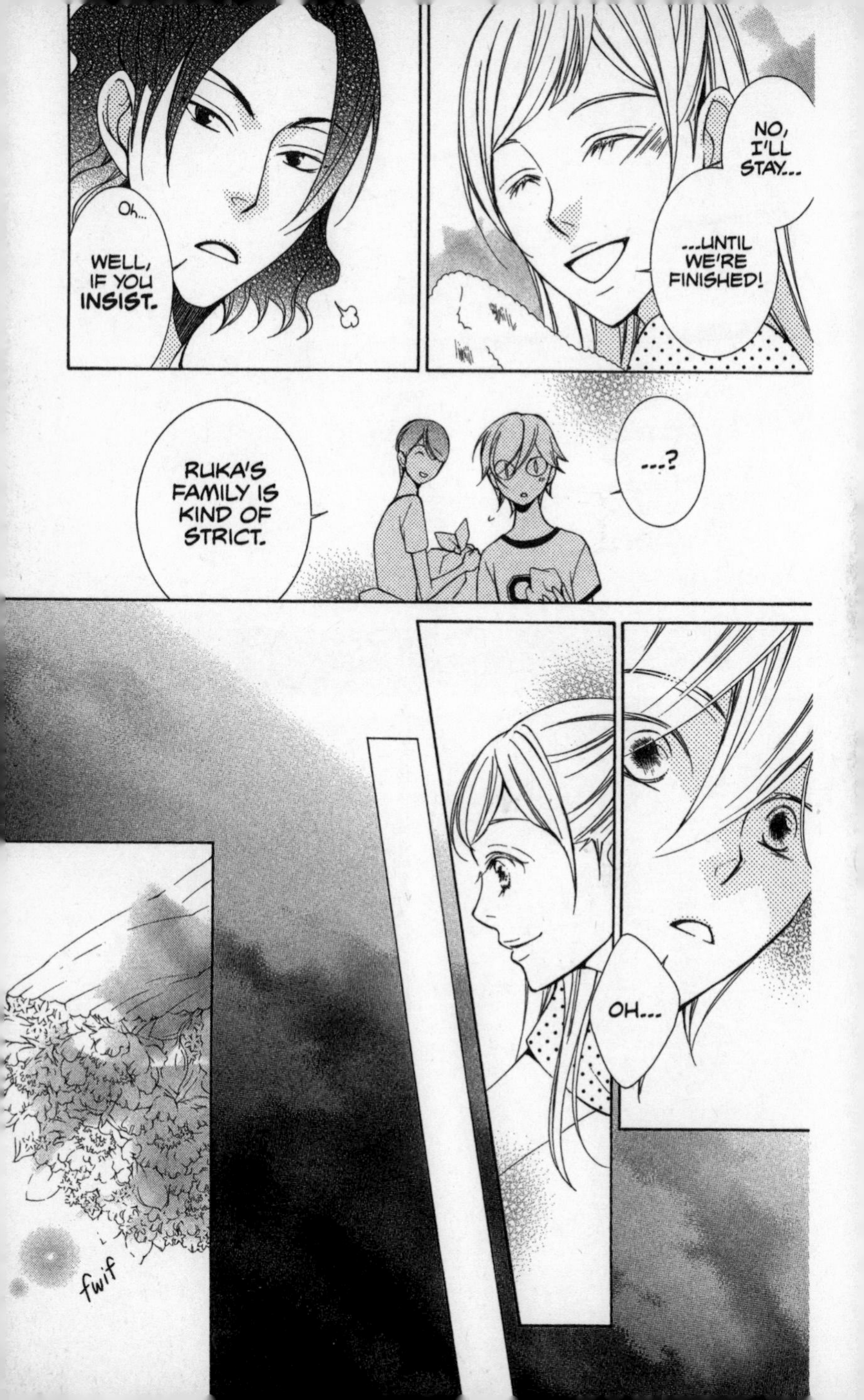
NO, I'LL STAY...
...UNTIL WE'RE FINISHED!
Oh...
WELL, IF YOU INSIST.
...?
RUKA'S FAMILY IS KIND OF STRICT.
OH...
fwif

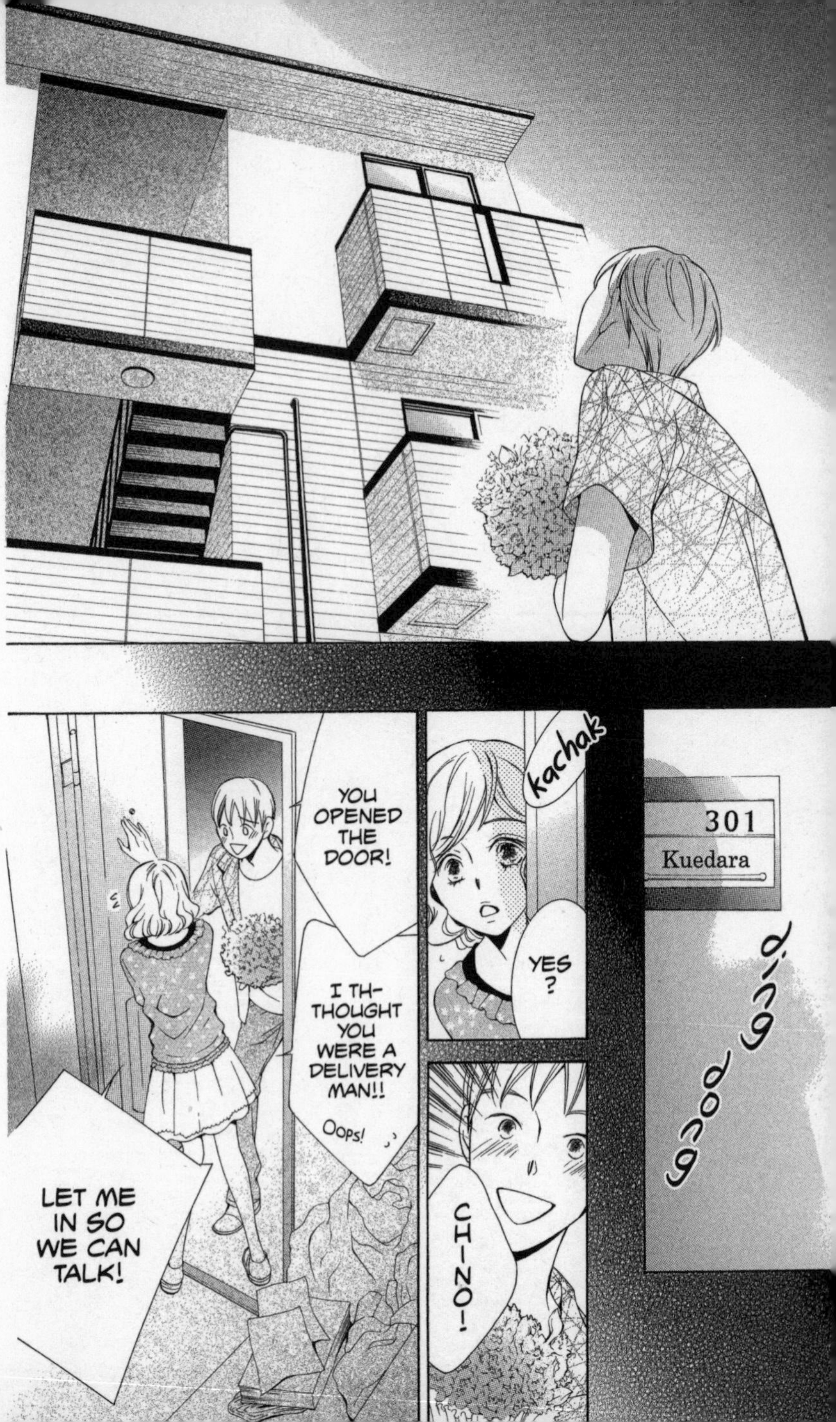
301
Kuedara
ding dong
kachak
YES?
CHINO-!
YOU OPENED THE DOOR!
I TH-THOUGHT YOU WERE A DELIVERY MAN!!
Oops!
LET ME IN SO WE CAN TALK!

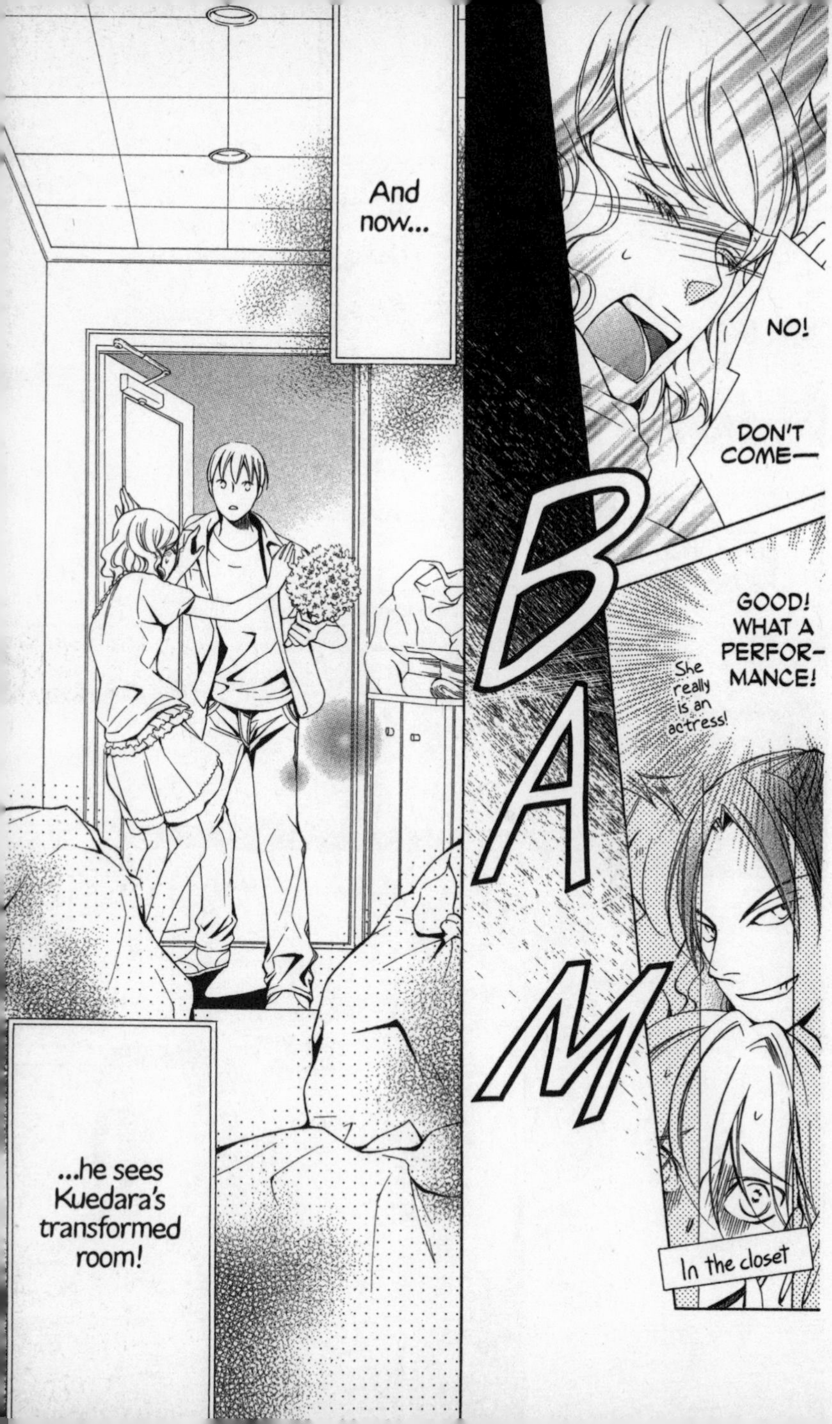
NO!
DON'T COME—
BAM
GOOD! WHAT A PERFORMANCE!
She really is an actress!
In the closet
And now...
...he sees Kuedara's transformed room!

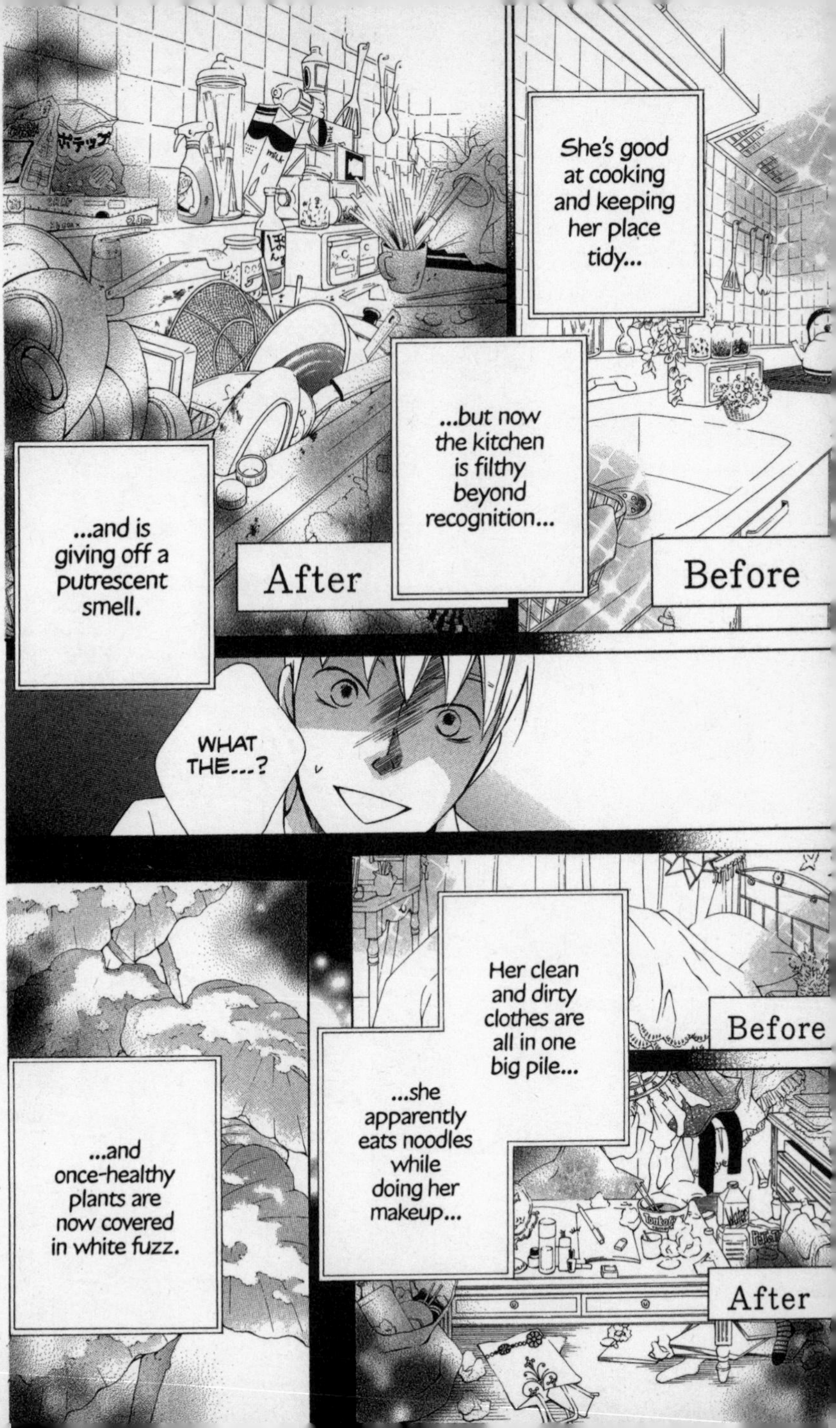
Before
She's good at cooking and keeping her place tidy...
After
...but now the kitchen is filthy beyond recognition...
...and is giving off a putrescent smell.
WHAT THE...?
Before
Her clean and dirty clothes are all in one big pile...
After
...she apparently eats noodles while doing her makeup...
...and once-healthy plants are now covered in white fuzz.

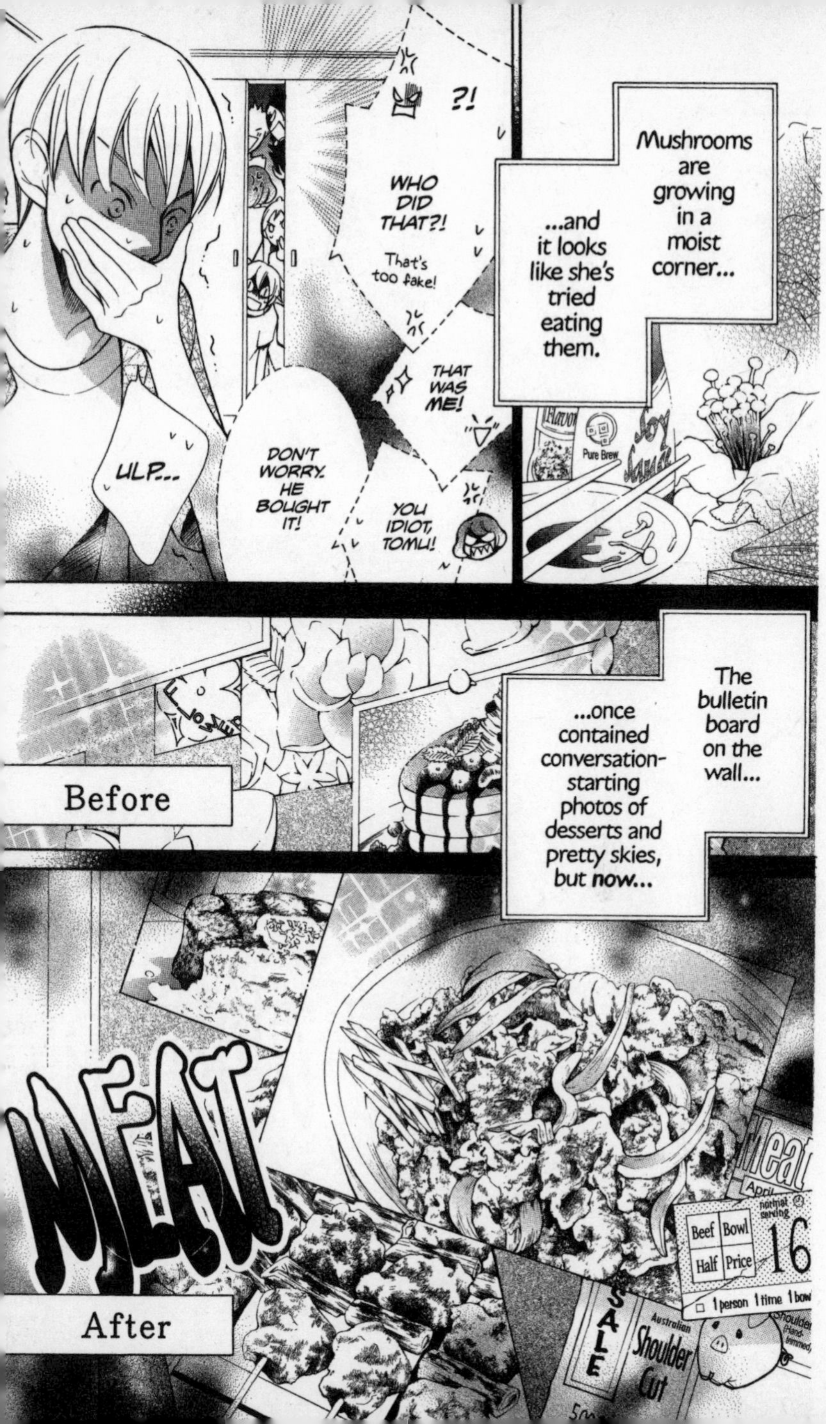
Mushrooms are growing in a moist corner...
...and it looks like she's tried eating them.
Flavor
Pure Brew
Soy Sauce
?!
WHO DID THAT?!
That's too fake!
THAT WAS ME!
YOU IDIOT, TOMU!
DON'T WORRY. HE BOUGHT IT!
ULP...
The bulletin board on the wall...
...once contained conversation-starting photos of desserts and pretty skies, but now...
Before
MEAT
After
Meat
April
normal serving
Beef Bowl
Half Price
16
1 person 1 time 1 bow
SALE
Australian
Shoulder Cut
Shoulder
(Hand-trimmed)

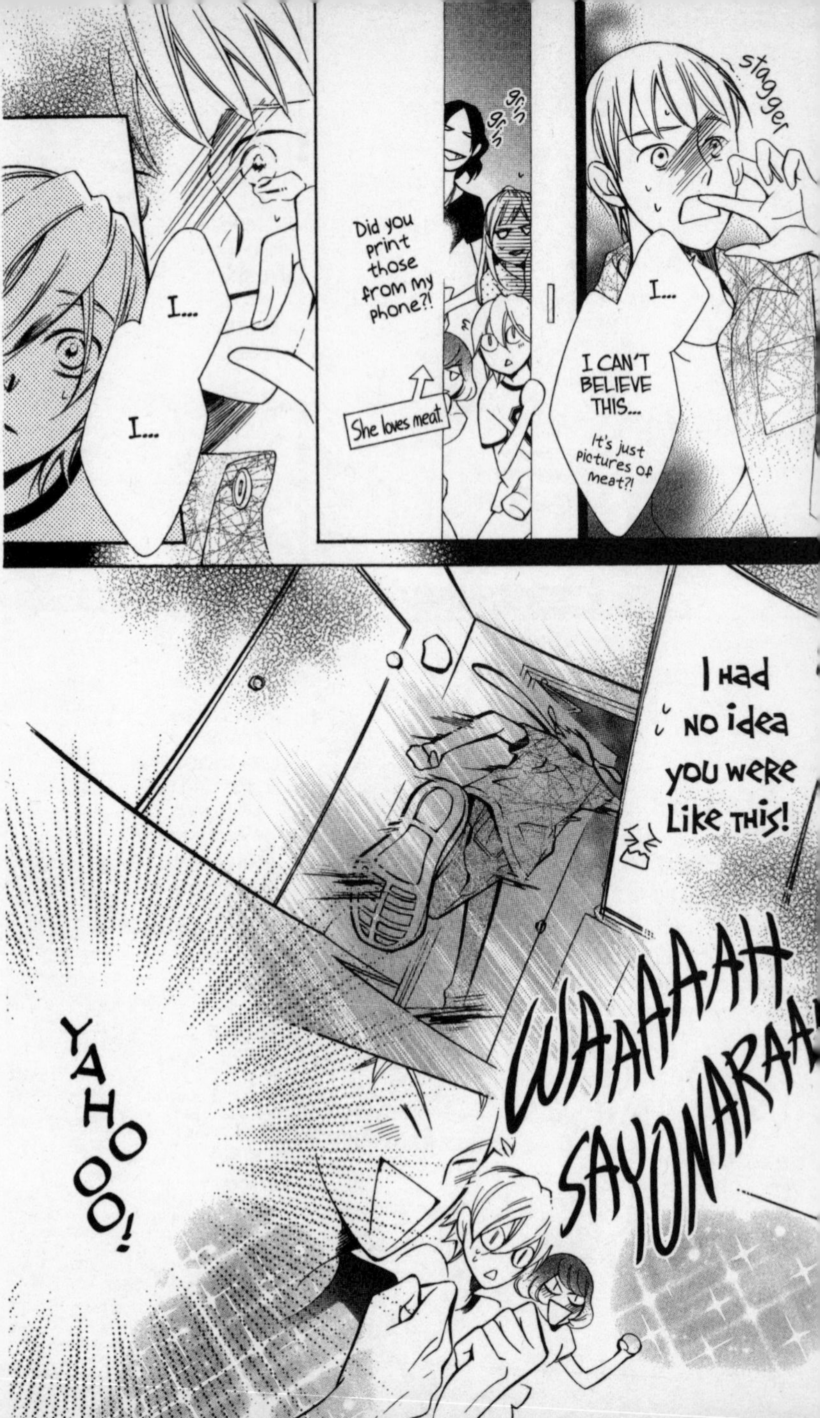
stagger
I...
I CAN'T BELIEVE THIS...
It's just pictures of meat?!
grin grin
Did you print those from my phone?!
She loves meat.
I...
I...
I had no idea you were like this!
WAAAAH SAYONARAA
YAHOOO!

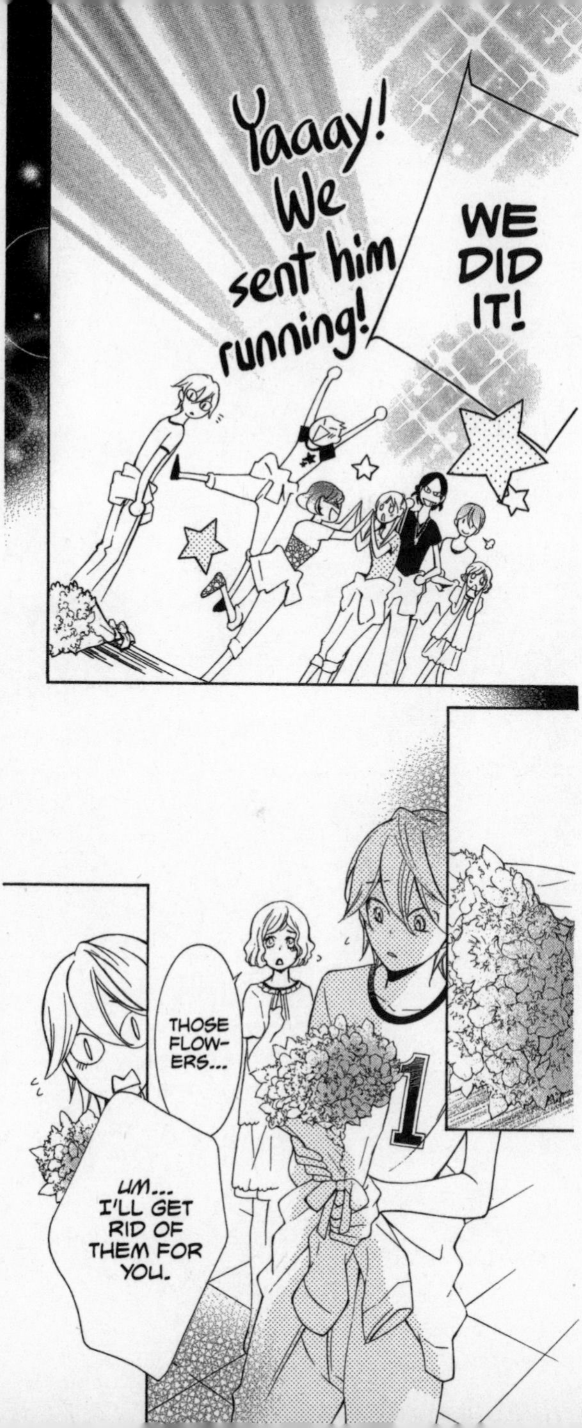
WE DID IT!
Yaaay! We sent him running!
THOSE FLOWERS...
UM... I'LL GET RID OF THEM FOR YOU.

2

When volume 1 went on sale, I held an autograph event.

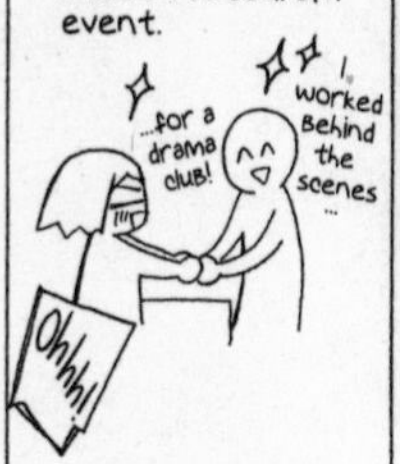
I... worked behind the scenes...
...for a drama club!
Ohhh!

Many fans shared stories about working behind the scenes!

Thank you to everyone who braved the cold weather to come to Book 1st in Shinjuku!!

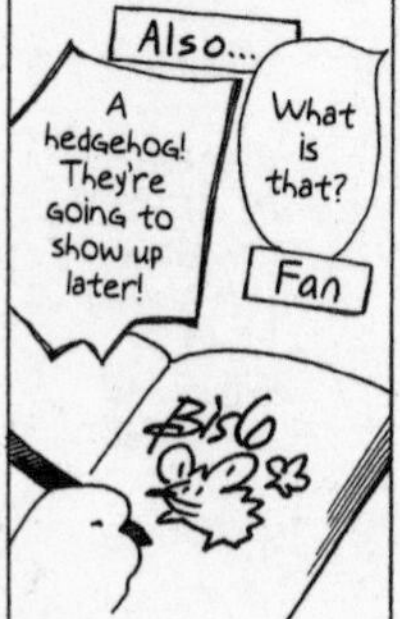
Also...
What is that?
Fan
A hedgehog! They're going to show up later!

...Or not. Sorry.

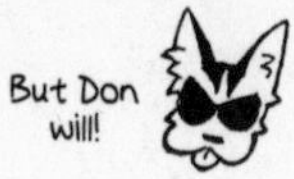
But Don will!

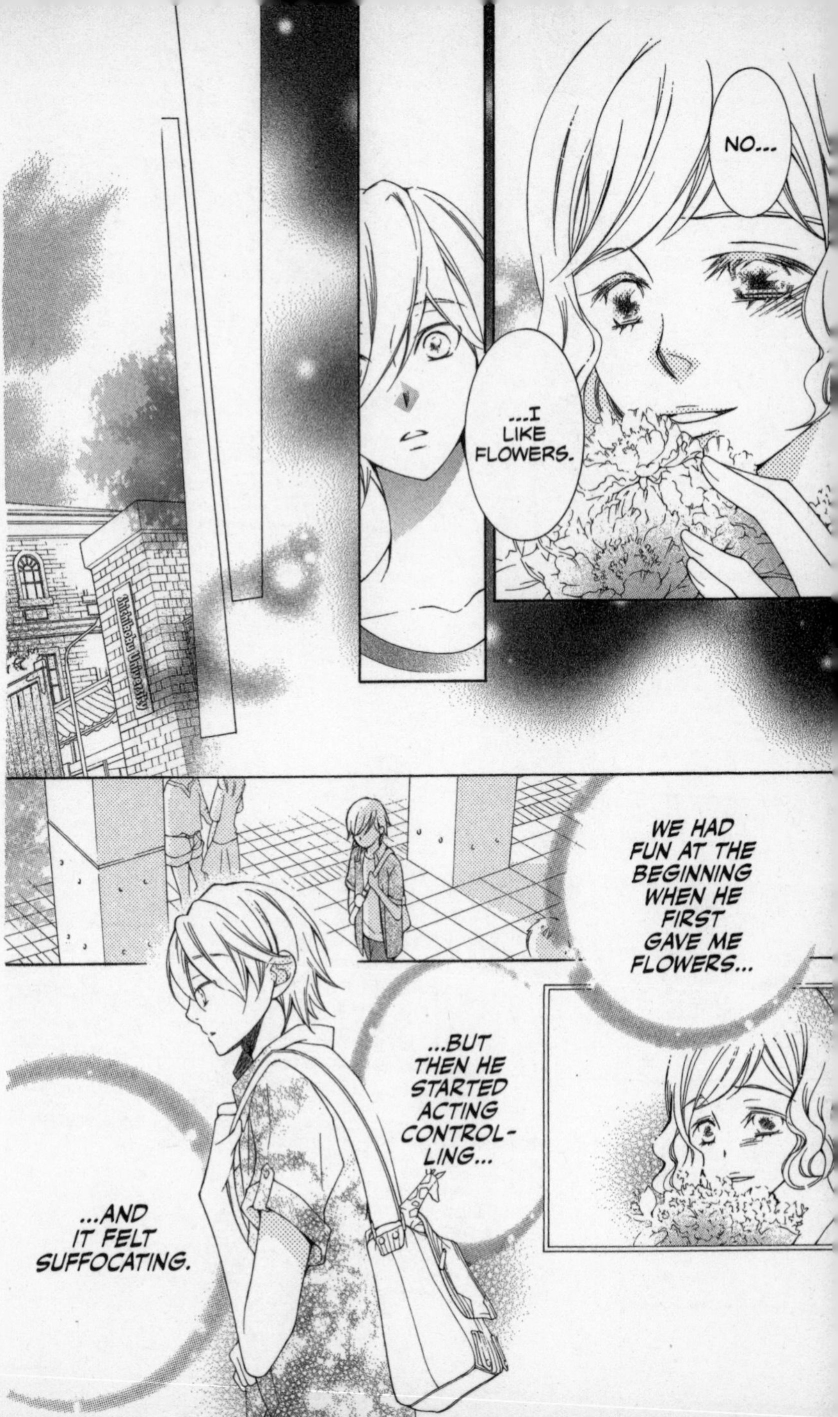
NO...
...I LIKE FLOWERS.
WE HAD FUN AT THE BEGINNING WHEN HE FIRST GAVE ME FLOWERS...
...BUT THEN HE STARTED ACTING CONTROL-LING...
...AND IT FELT SUFFOCATING.

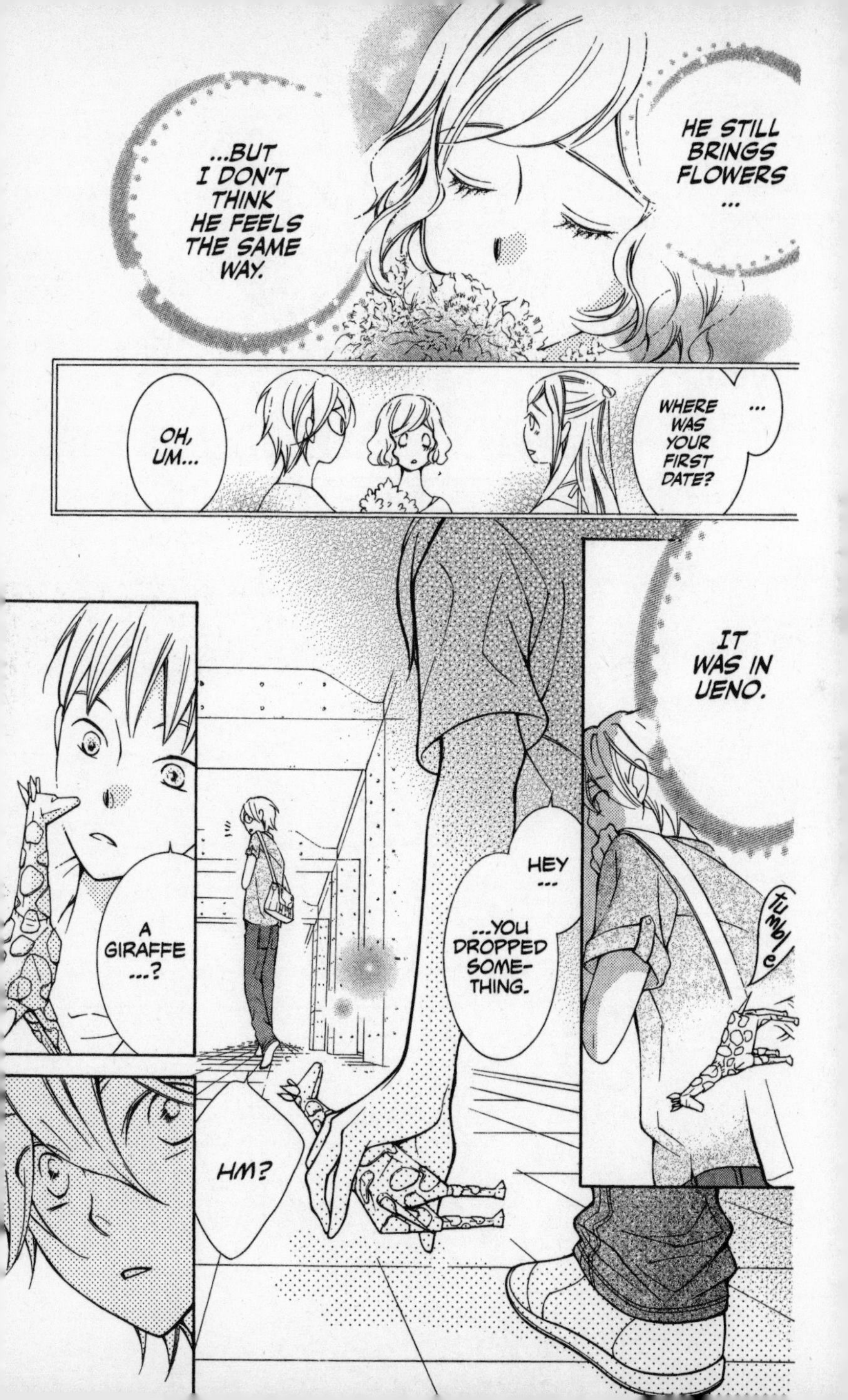
HE STILL BRINGS FLOWERS ...
...BUT I DON'T THINK HE FEELS THE SAME WAY.
WHERE WAS YOUR FIRST DATE? ...
OH, UM...
IT WAS IN UENO.
tumble
HEY ---
...YOU DROPPED SOME-THING.
A GIRAFFE ...?
HM?

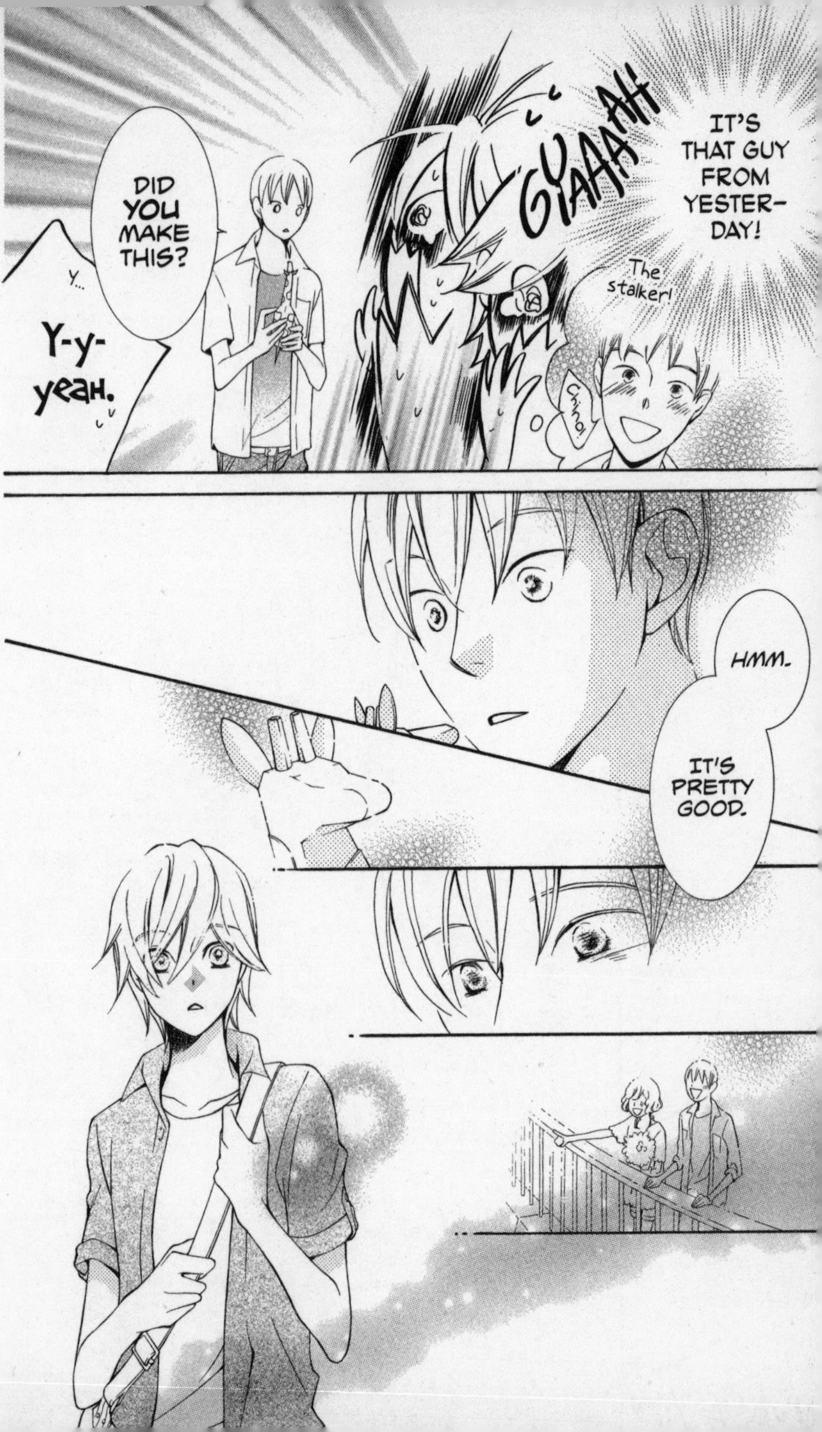
IT'S THAT GUY FROM YESTER-DAY!
GUAAAH
The stalker!
Chino!
DID YOU MAKE THIS?
Y...
Y-y-yeah.
HMM.
IT'S PRETTY GOOD.

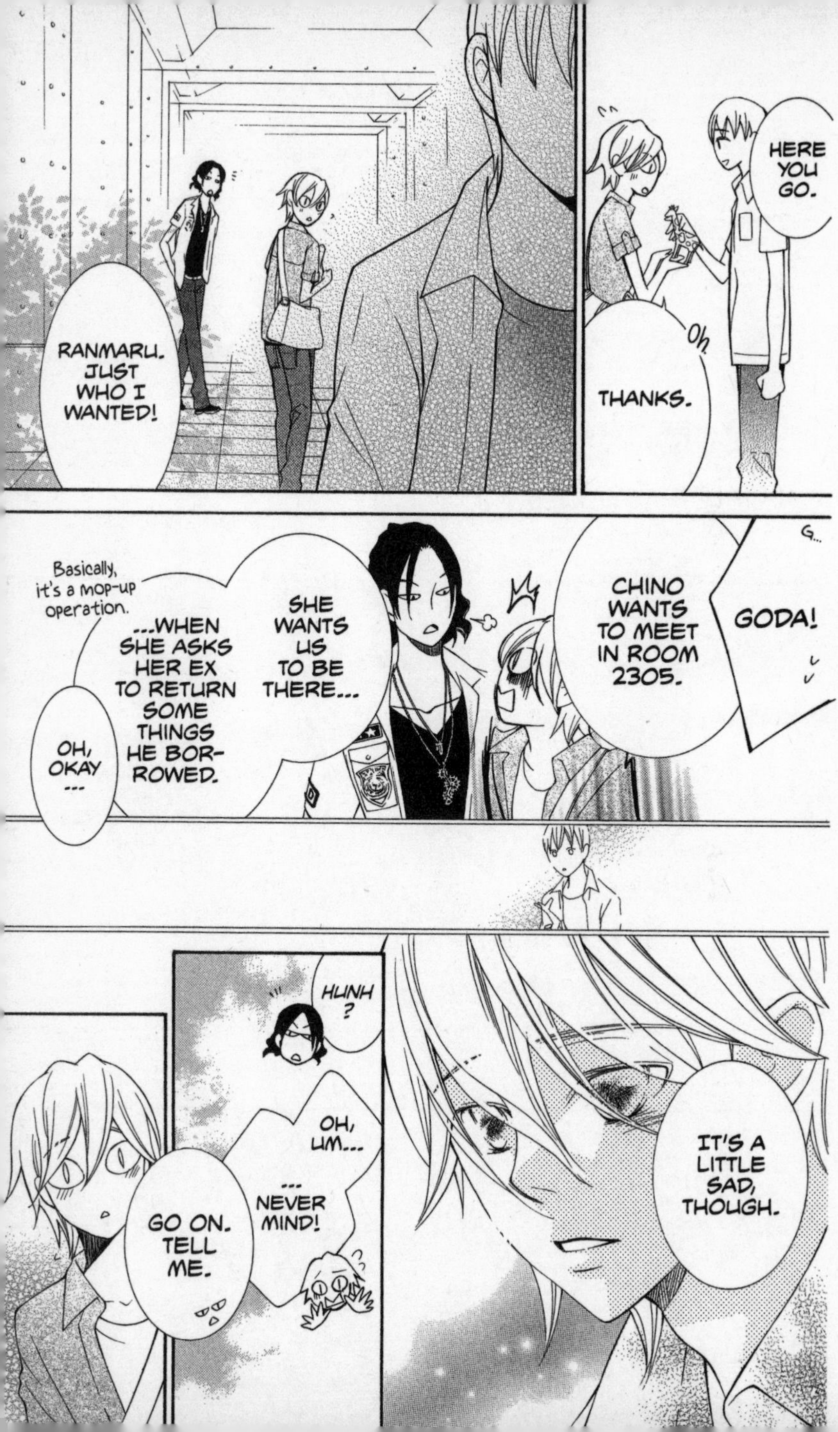
HERE YOU GO.
Oh
THANKS.
RANMARU. JUST WHO I WANTED!
G...
GODA!
CHINO WANTS TO MEET IN ROOM 2305.
SHE WANTS US TO BE THERE...
...WHEN SHE ASKS HER EX TO RETURN SOME THINGS HE BOR-ROWED.
Basically, it's a mop-up operation.
OH, OKAY...
IT'S A LITTLE SAD, THOUGH.
HUNH?
OH, UM...
...NEVER MIND!
GO ON. TELL ME.

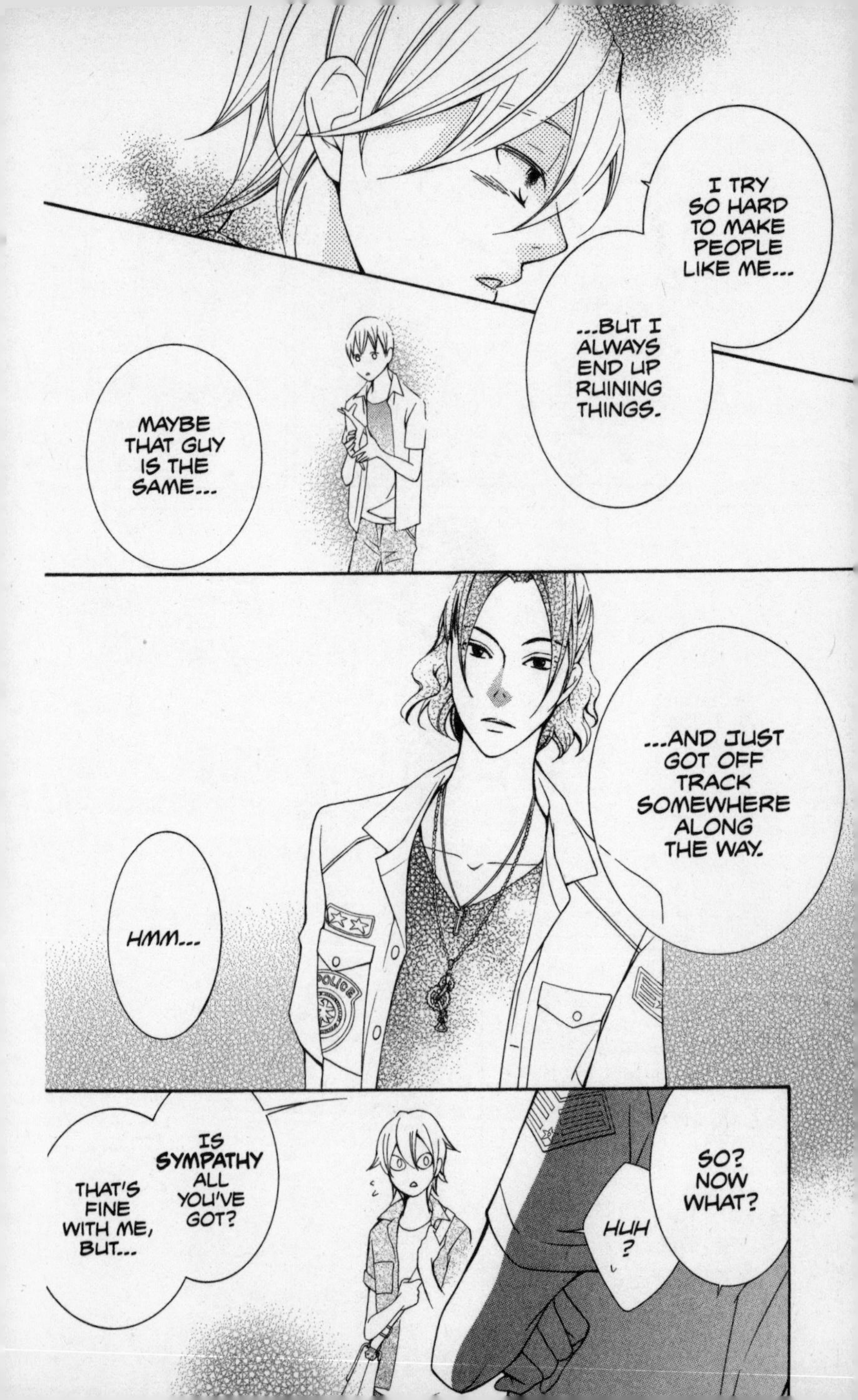
I TRY SO HARD TO MAKE PEOPLE LIKE ME...
...BUT I ALWAYS END UP RUINING THINGS.
MAYBE THAT GUY IS THE SAME...
...AND JUST GOT OFF TRACK SOMEWHERE ALONG THE WAY.
HMM...
SO? NOW WHAT?
HUH?
IS SYMPATHY ALL YOU'VE GOT?
THAT'S FINE WITH ME, BUT...

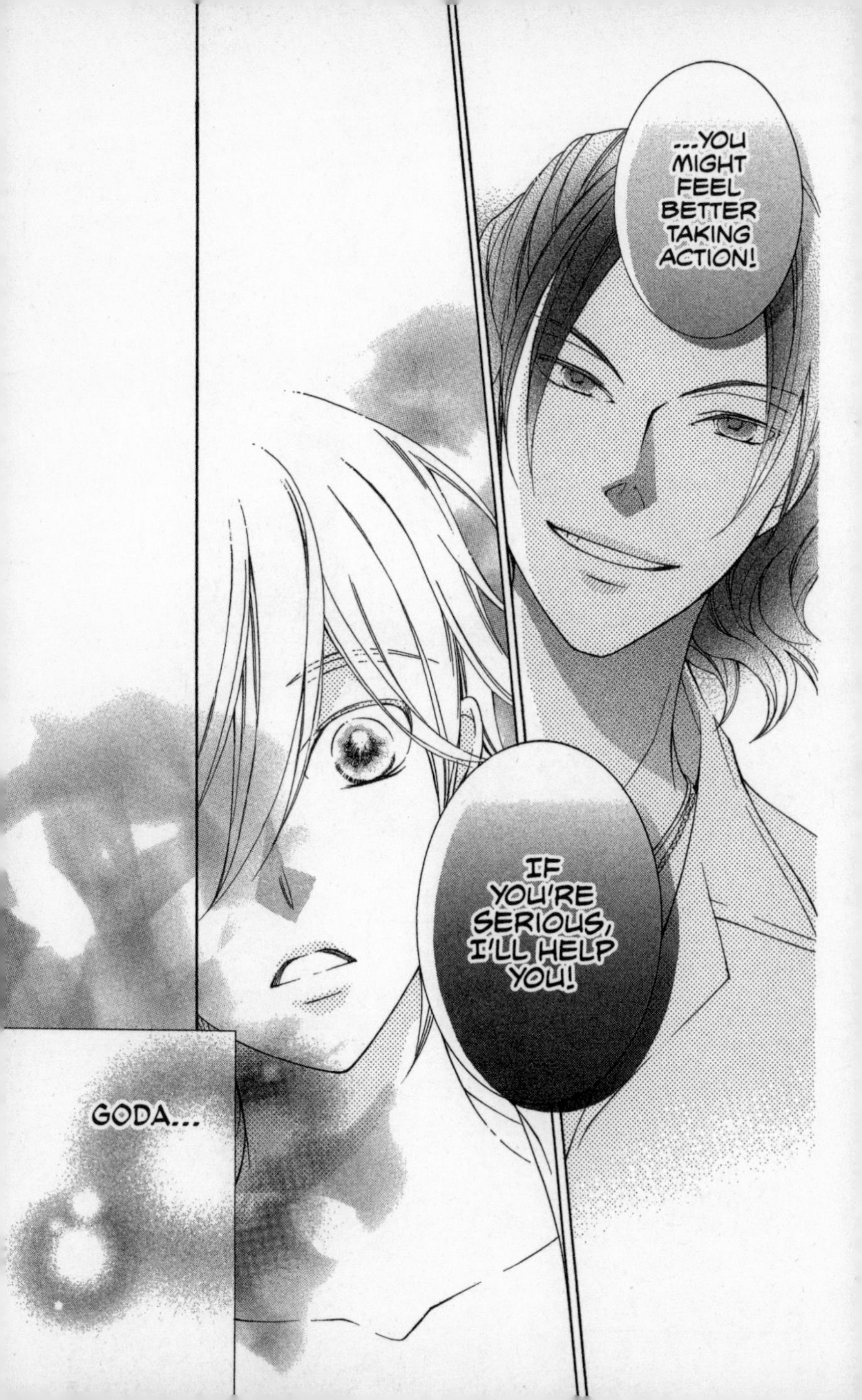
...YOU MIGHT FEEL BETTER TAKING ACTION!
IF YOU'RE SERIOUS, I'LL HELP YOU!
GODA...

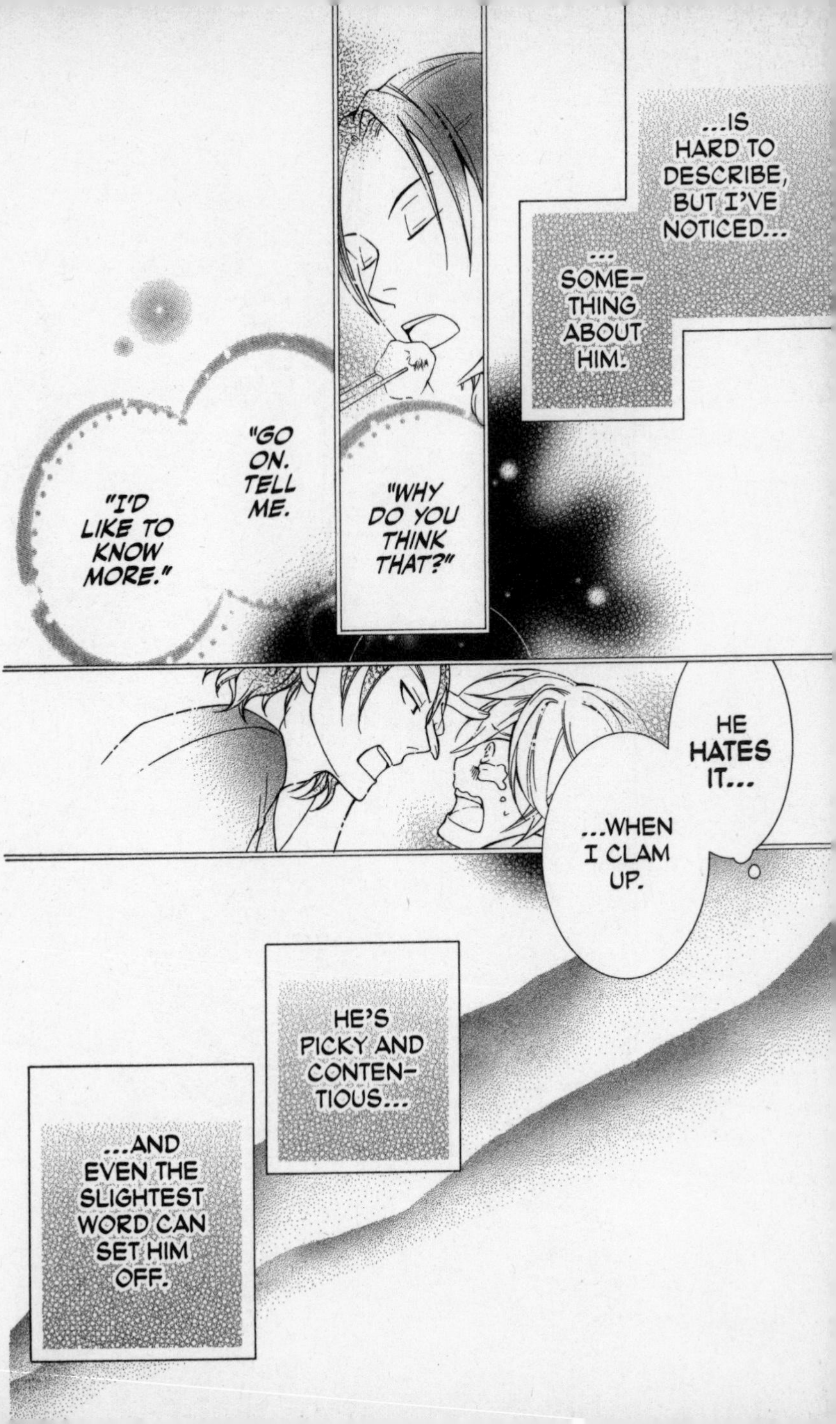
...IS HARD TO DESCRIBE, BUT I'VE NOTICED...
...SOME-THING ABOUT HIM.
"WHY DO YOU THINK THAT?"
"GO ON. TELL ME.
"I'D LIKE TO KNOW MORE."
HE HATES IT...
...WHEN I CLAM UP.
HE'S PICKY AND CONTEN-TIOUS...
...AND EVEN THE SLIGHTEST WORD CAN SET HIM OFF.

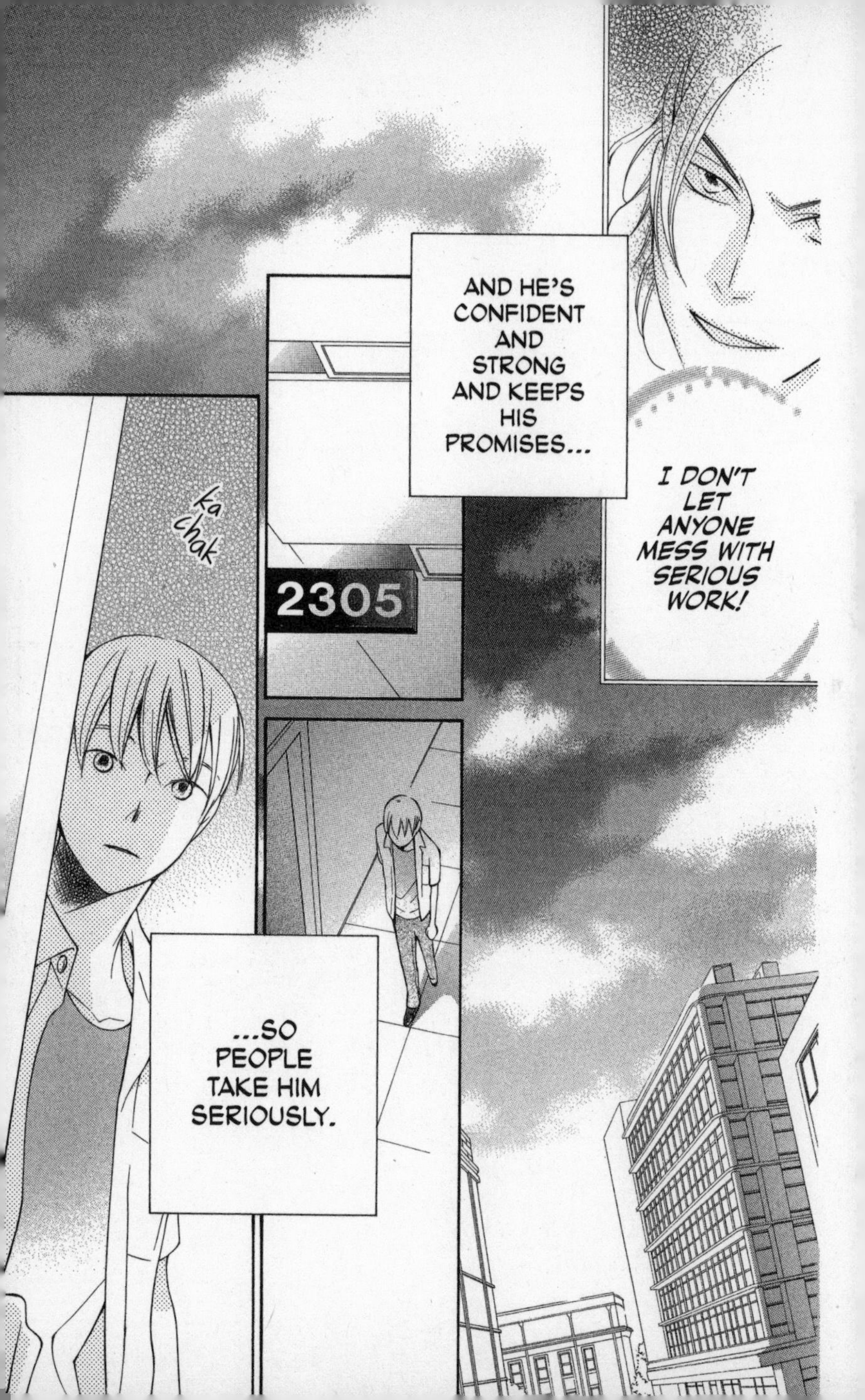
I DON'T LET ANYONE MESS WITH SERIOUS WORK!
AND HE'S CONFIDENT AND STRONG AND KEEPS HIS PROMISES...
2305
ka chak
...SO PEOPLE TAKE HIM SERIOUSLY.

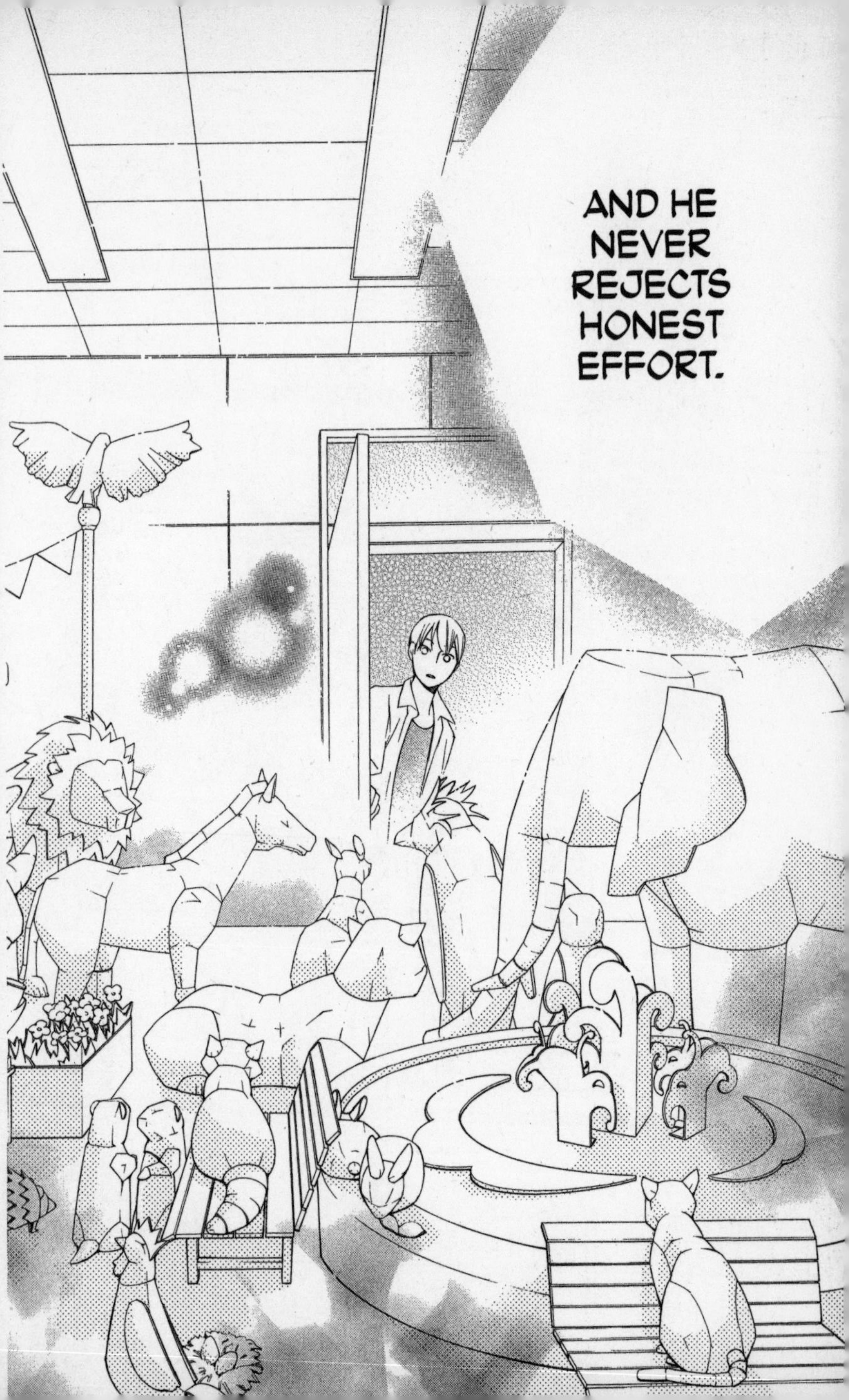
AND HE NEVER REJECTS HONEST EFFORT.

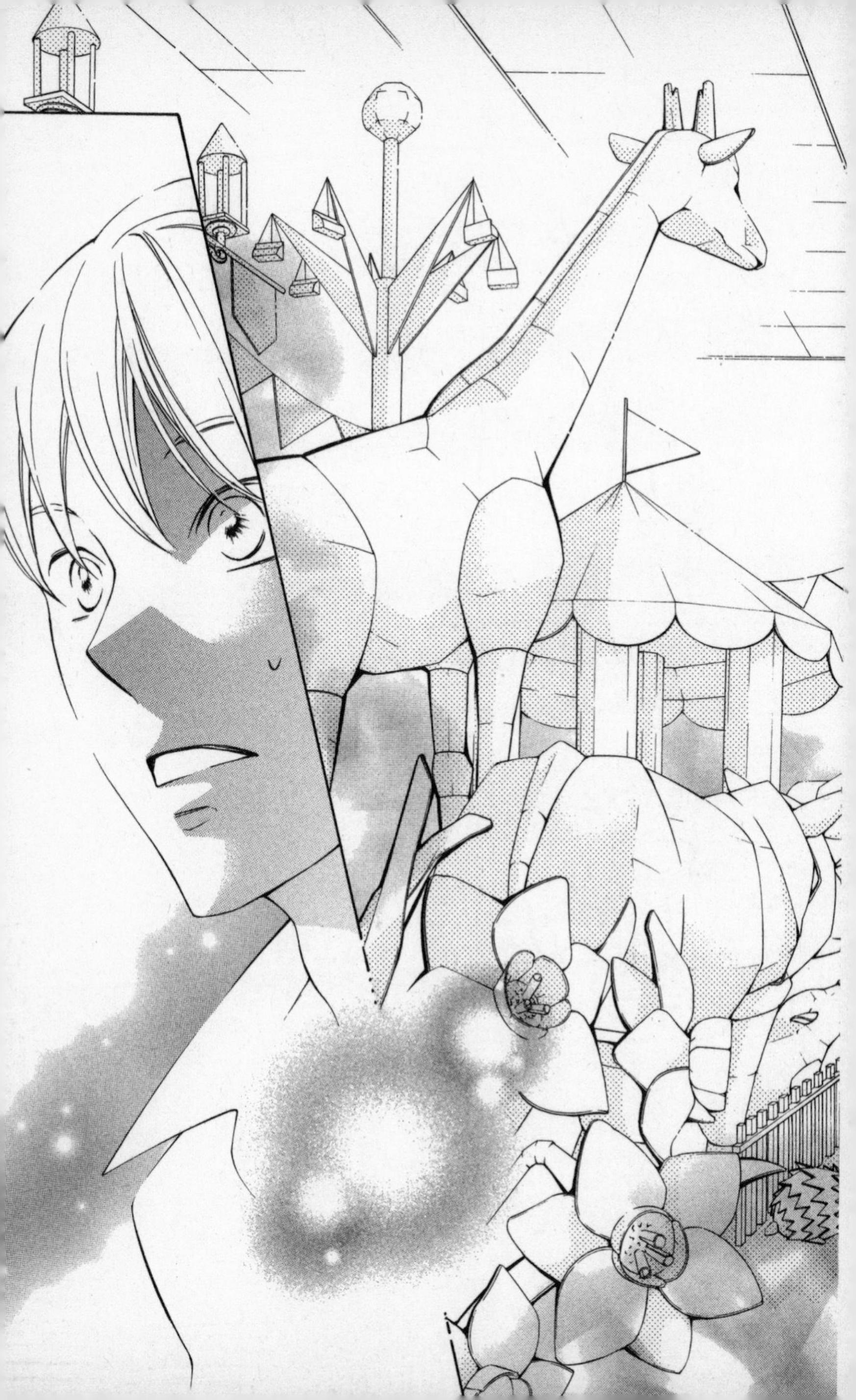

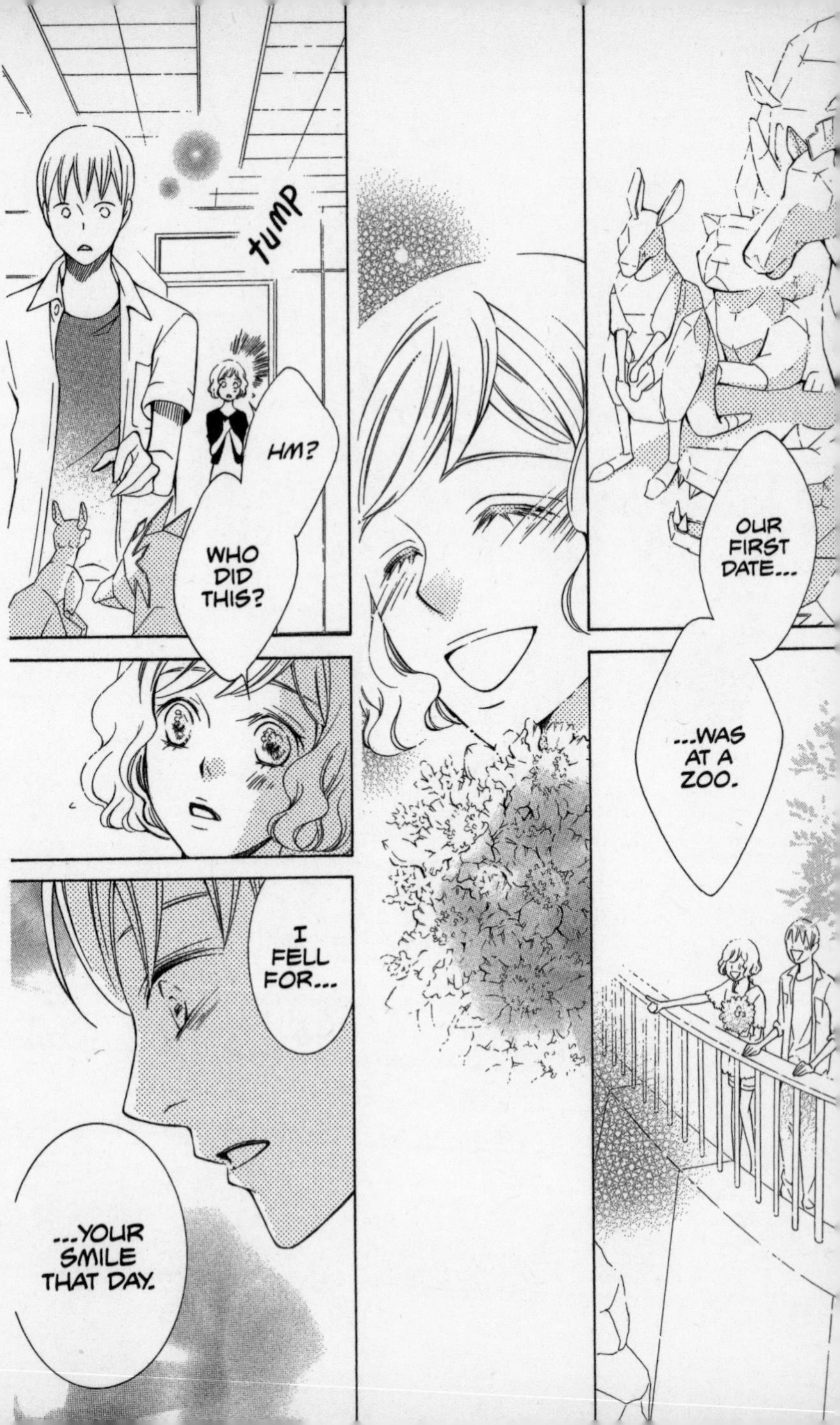
OUR FIRST DATE...
...WAS AT A ZOO.
tump
HM?
WHO DID THIS?
I FELL FOR...
...YOUR SMILE THAT DAY.

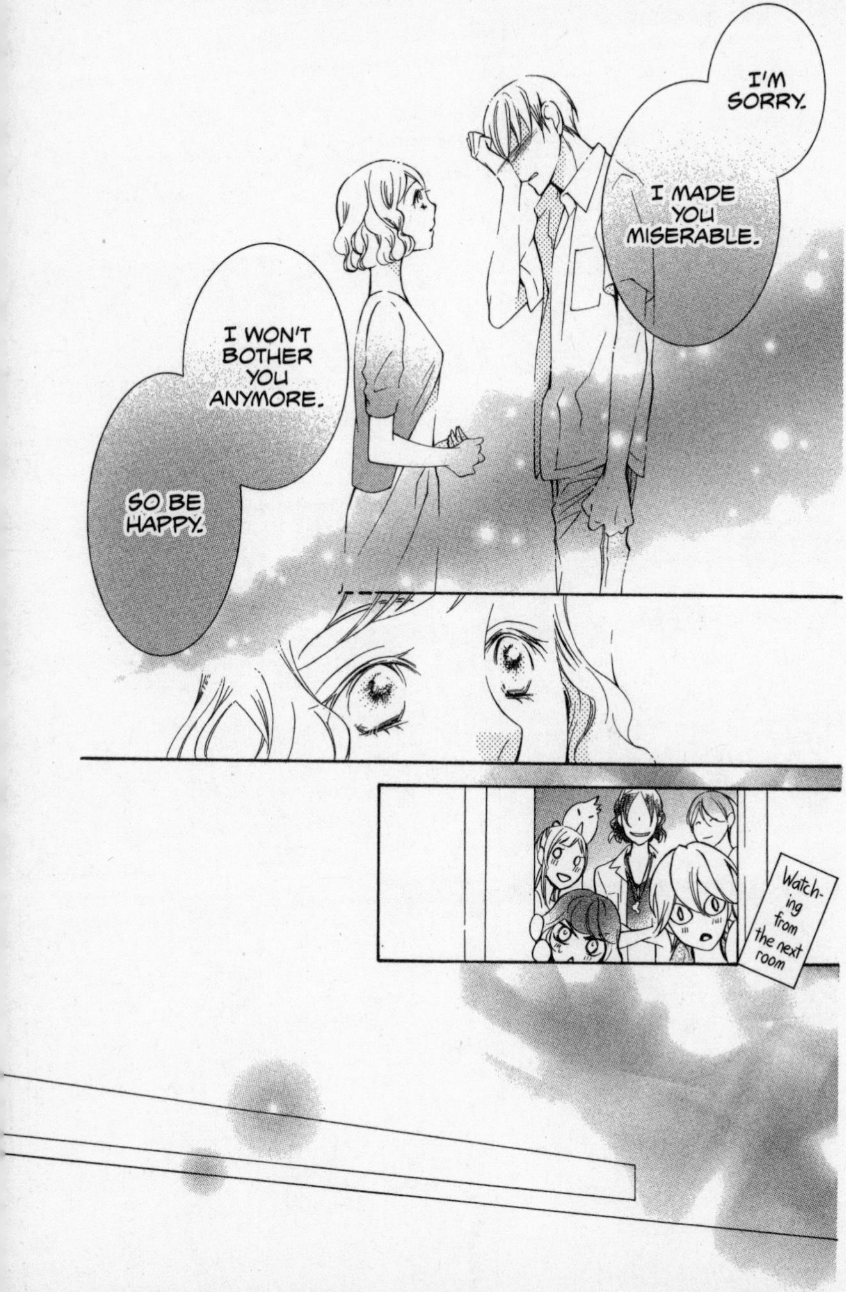
I'M SORRY.
I MADE YOU MISERABLE.
I WON'T BOTHER YOU ANYMORE.
SO BE HAPPY.
Watch-ing from the next room

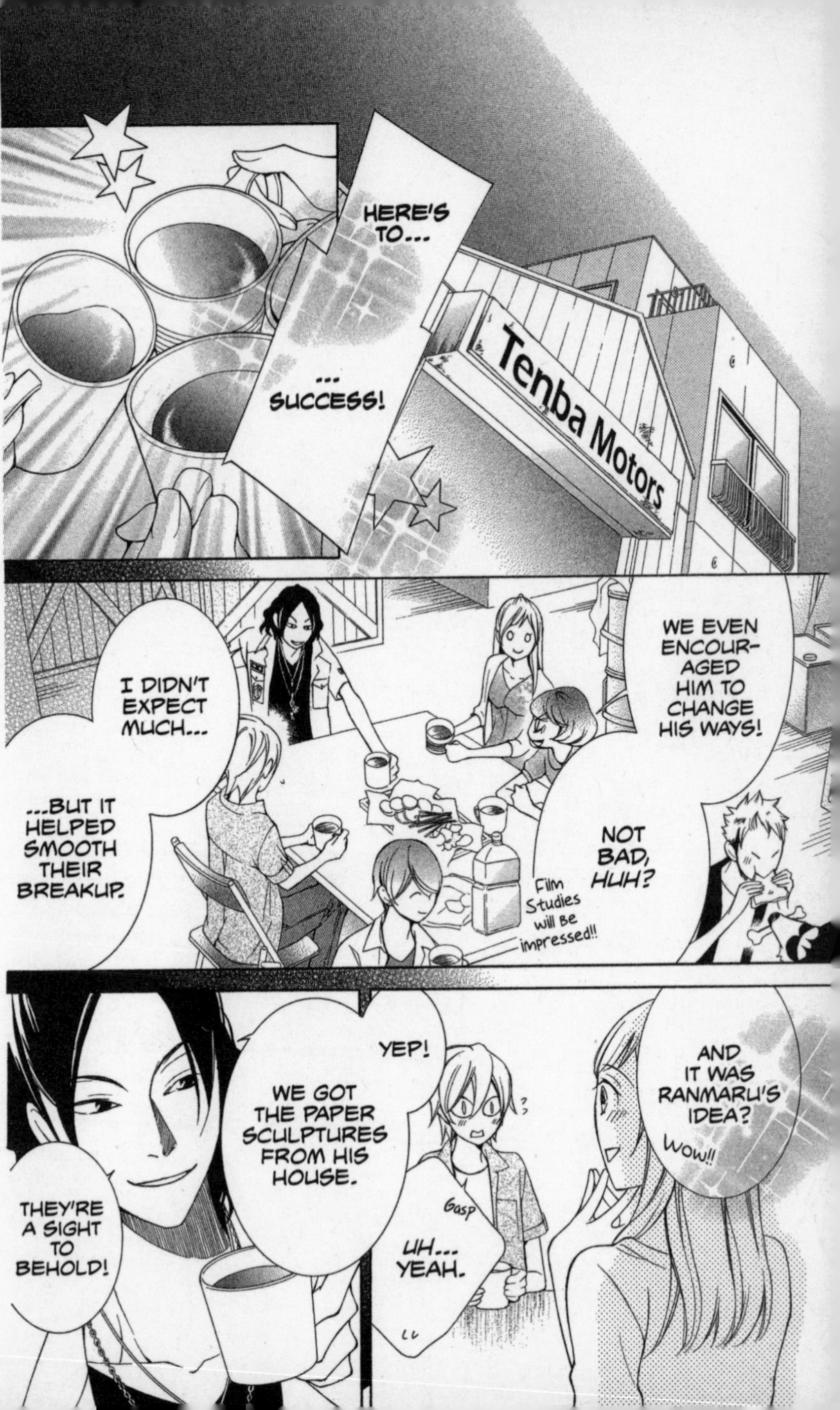
HERE'S TO...
...SUCCESS!
Tenba Motors
WE EVEN ENCOURAGED HIM TO CHANGE HIS WAYS!
NOT BAD, HUH?
Film Studies will be impressed!!
I DIDN'T EXPECT MUCH...
...BUT IT HELPED SMOOTH THEIR BREAKUP.
AND IT WAS RANMARU'S IDEA?
Wow!!
YEP!
WE GOT THE PAPER SCULPTURES FROM HIS HOUSE.
Gasp
UH... YEAH.
THEY'RE A SIGHT TO BEHOLD!

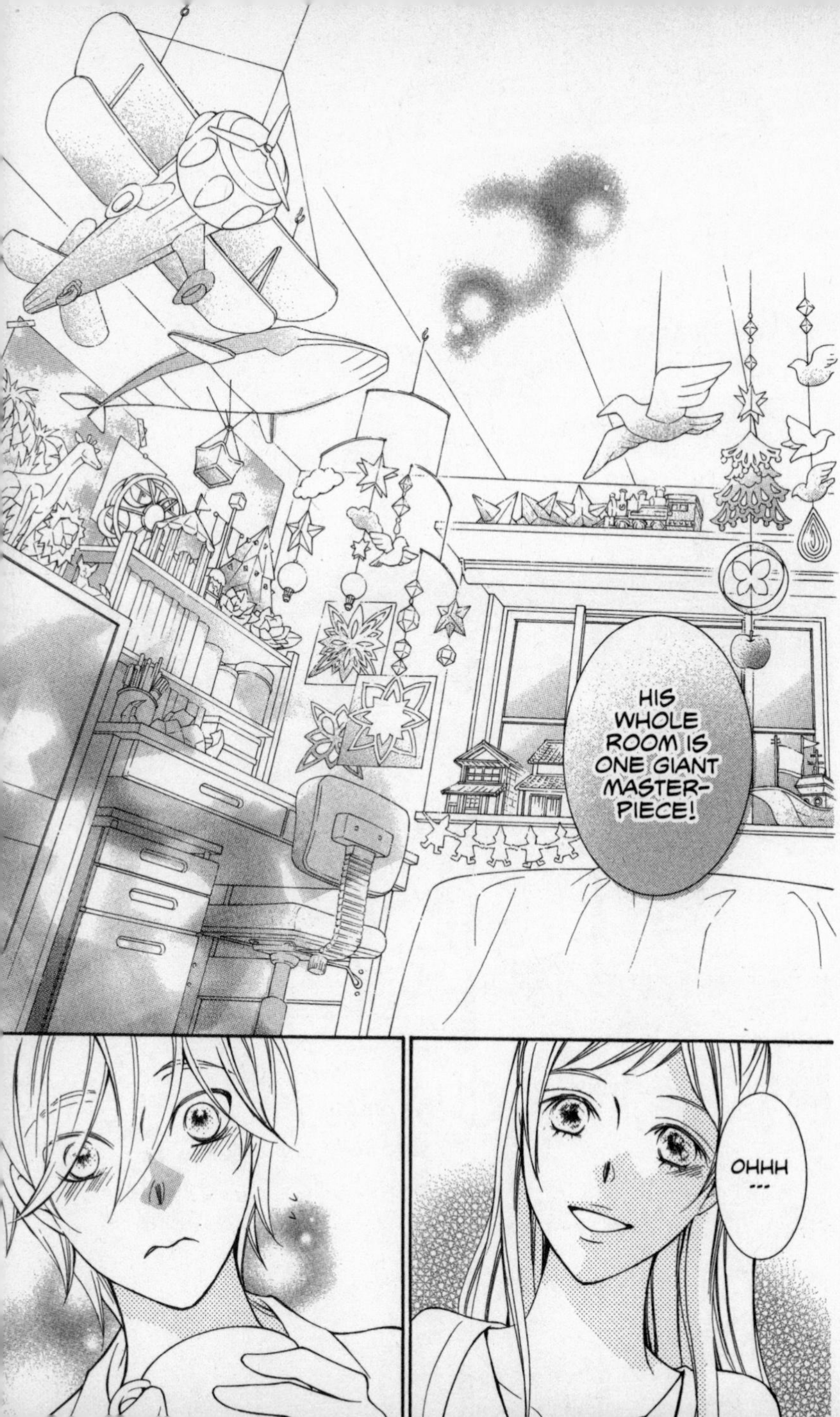
HIS WHOLE ROOM IS ONE GIANT MASTER-PIECE!
OHHH ---

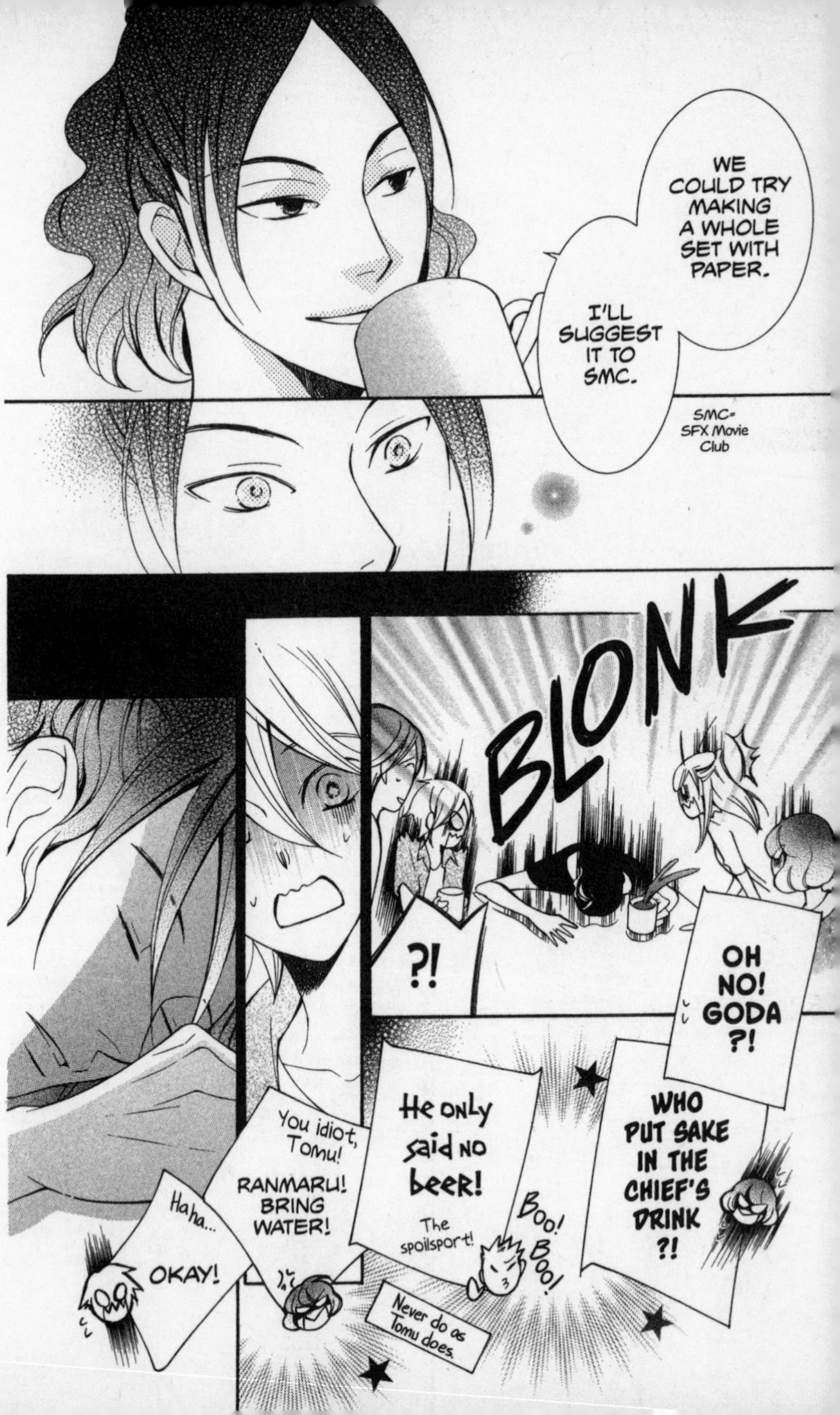
WE COULD TRY MAKING A WHOLE SET WITH PAPER.
I'LL SUGGEST IT TO SMC.
SMC= SFX Movie Club
BLONK
?!
OH NO! GODA ?!
WHO PUT SAKE IN THE CHIEF'S DRINK ?!
Boo! Boo!
He only said no beer!
The spoilsport!
You idiot, Tomu!
RANMARU! BRING WATER!
Ha ha...
OKAY!
Never do as Tomu does.

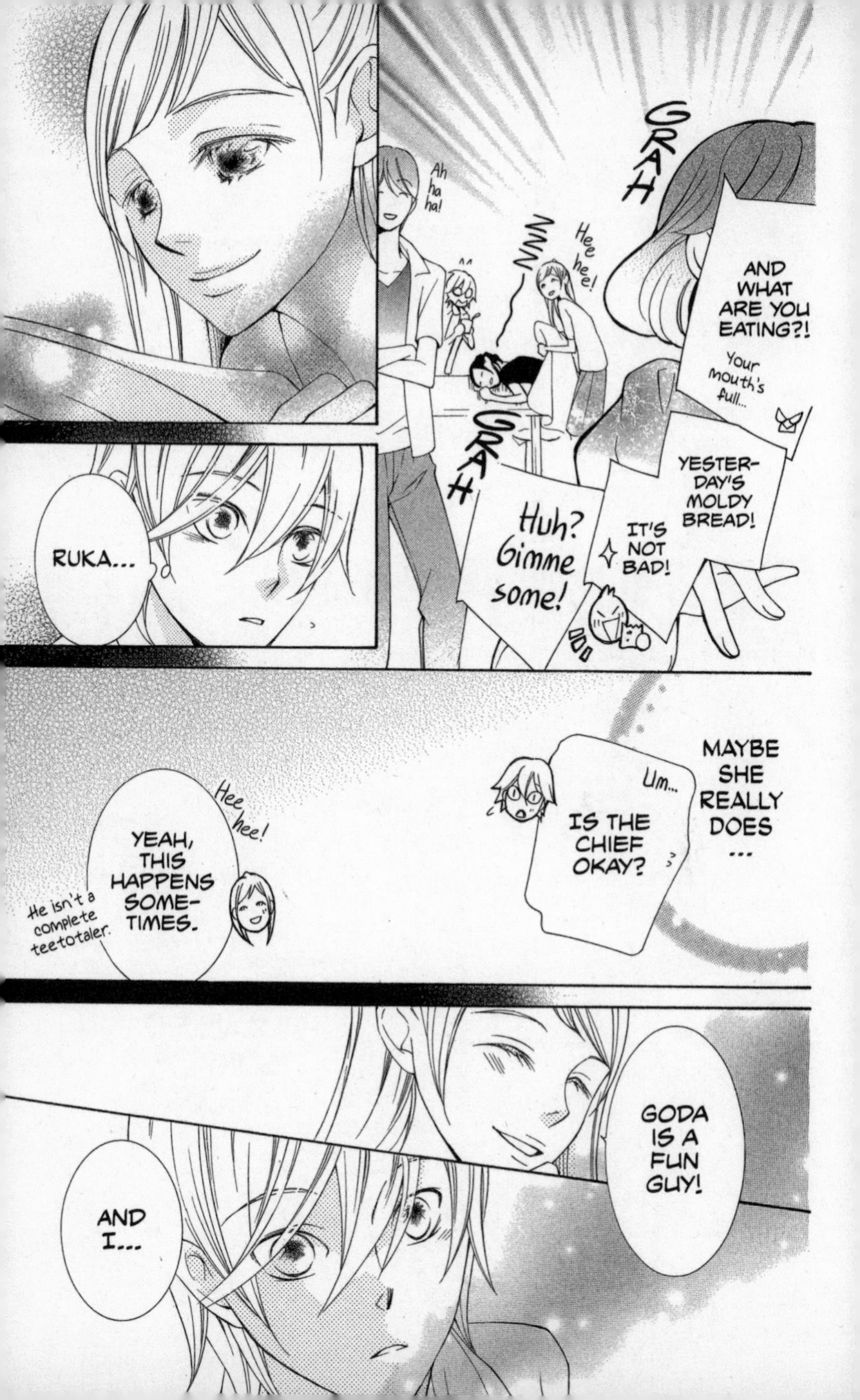
GRAH
AND WHAT ARE YOU EATING?!
Your mouth's full...
YESTER-DAY'S MOLDY BREAD!
IT'S NOT BAD!
Huh? Gimme some!
GRAH
Hee hee!
ZZZ
Ah ha ha!
RUKA...
MAYBE SHE REALLY DOES...
Um...
IS THE CHIEF OKAY?
YEAH, THIS HAPPENS SOME-TIMES.
Hee hee!
He isn't a complete teetotaler.
GODA IS A FUN GUY!
AND I...

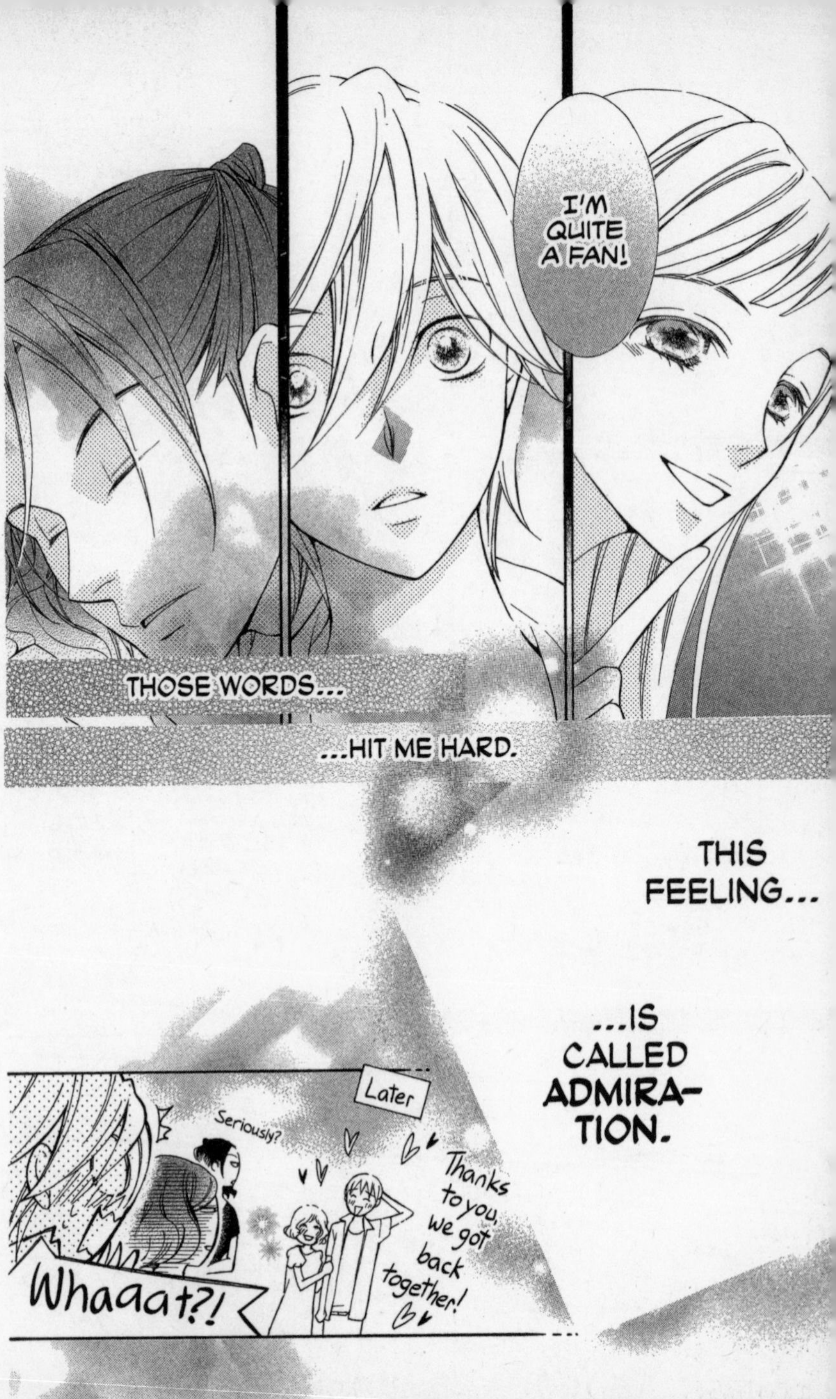
I'M QUITE A FAN!
THOSE WORDS...
...HIT ME HARD.
THIS FEELING...
...IS CALLED ADMIRA-TION.
Later
Thanks to you, we got back together!
Seriously?
Whaaat?!

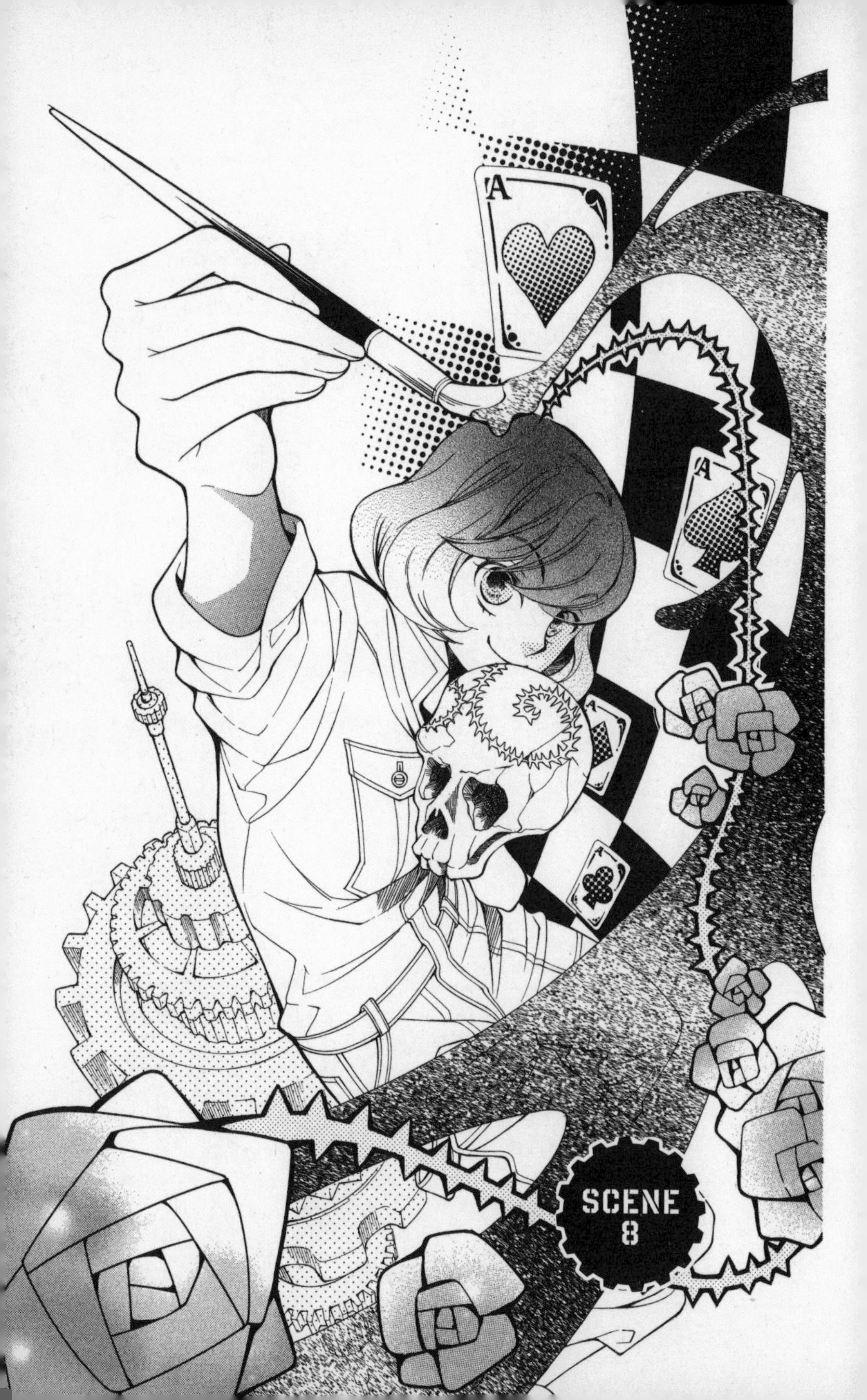
SCENE
8

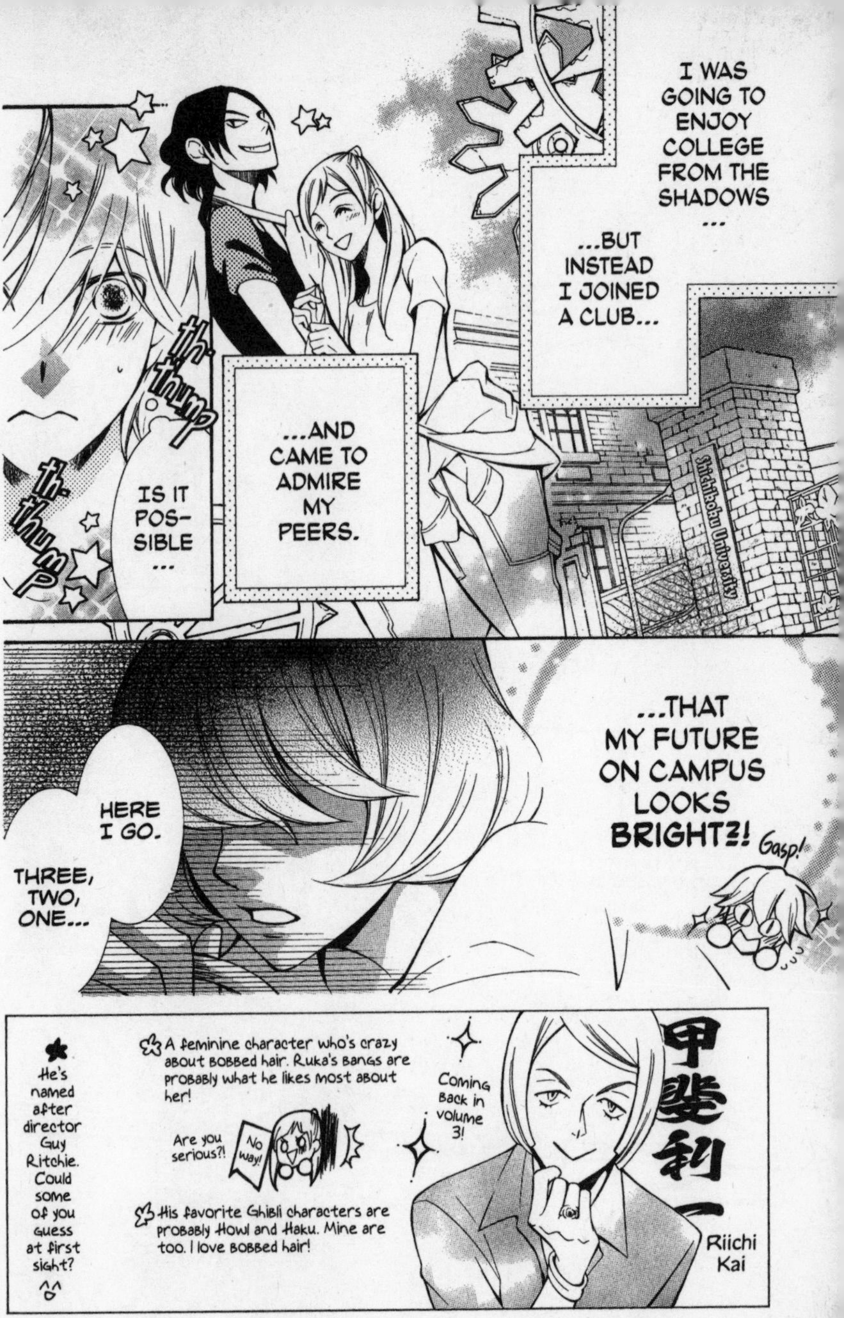
I WAS GOING TO ENJOY COLLEGE FROM THE SHADOWS...
...BUT INSTEAD I JOINED A CLUB...
Shichibuku University
...AND CAME TO ADMIRE MY PEERS.
th-thump
th-thump
IS IT POSSIBLE...
...THAT MY FUTURE ON CAMPUS LOOKS BRIGHT?!
Gasp!
HERE I GO.
THREE, TWO, ONE...
甲斐利一
Riichi Kai
Coming back in volume 3!
A feminine character who's crazy about bobbed hair. Ruka's bangs are probably what he likes most about her!
No way!
Are you serious?!
His favorite Ghibli characters are probably Howl and Haku. Mine are too. I love bobbed hair!
He's named after director Guy Ritchie. Could some of you guess at first sight?
^^

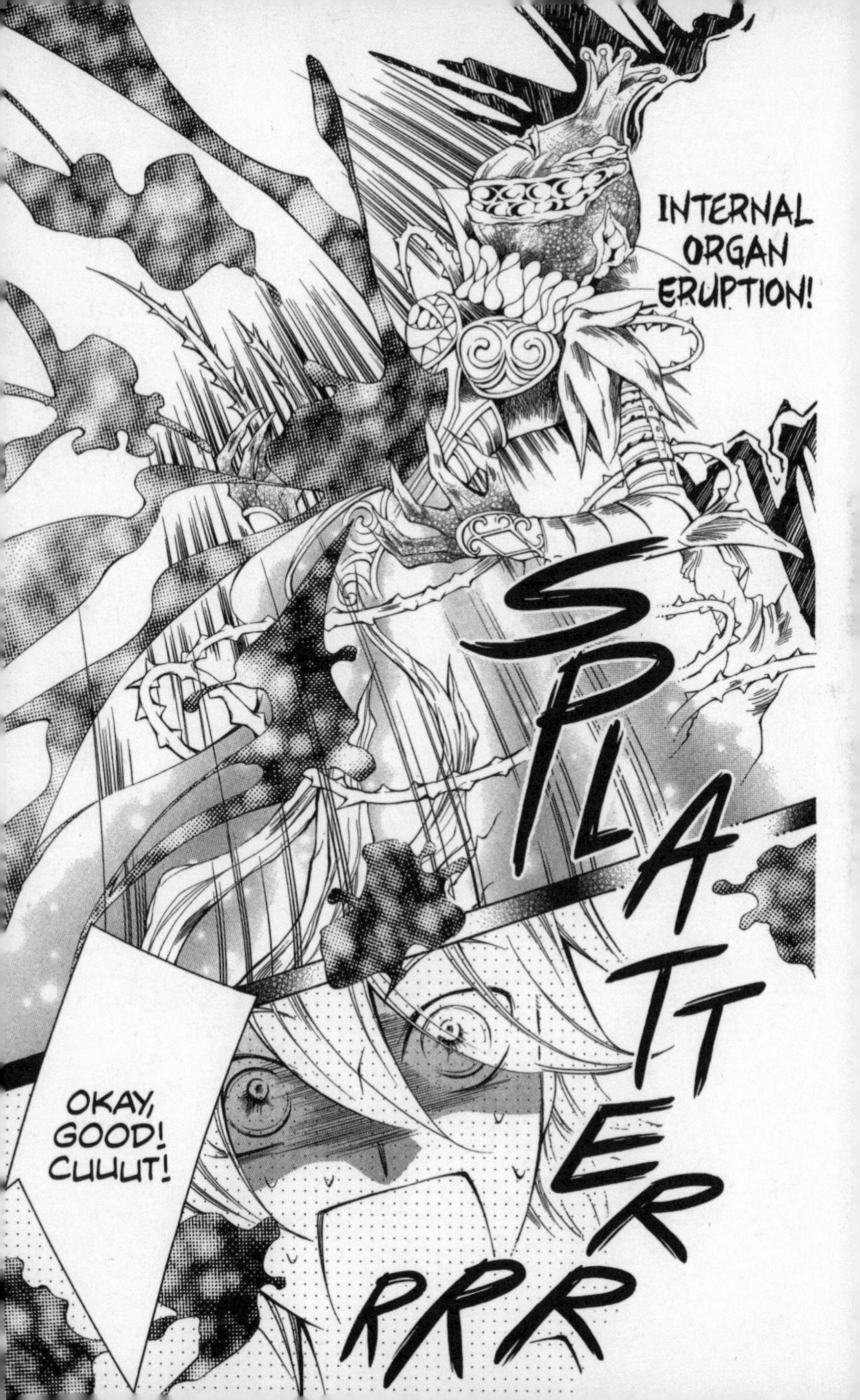
INTERNAL ORGAN ERUPTION!
SPLATTERRRR
OKAY, GOOD! CUUUT!

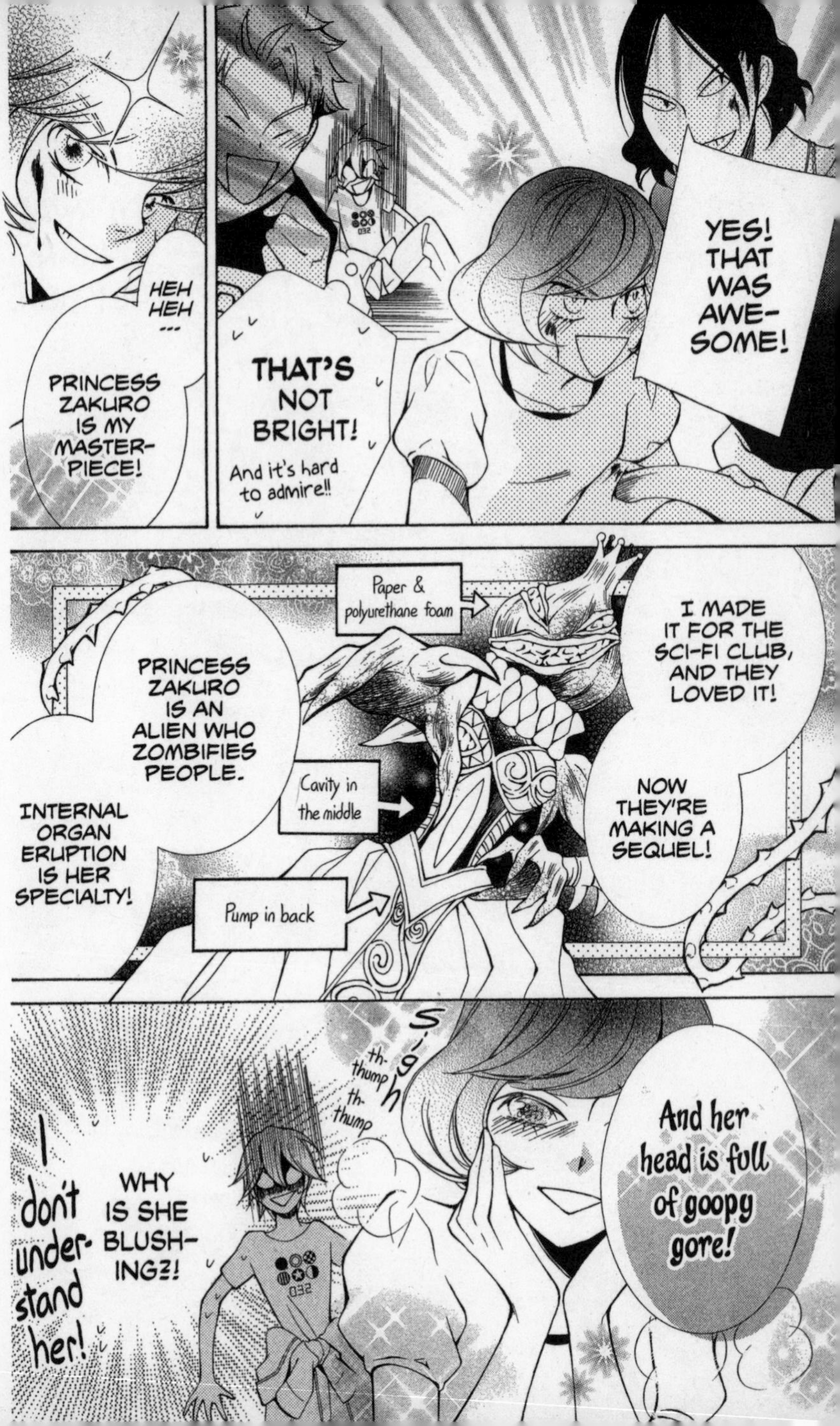
YES! THAT WAS AWE-SOME!
THAT'S NOT BRIGHT!
And it's hard to admire!!
HEH HEH ...
PRINCESS ZAKURO IS MY MASTER-PIECE!
I MADE IT FOR THE SCI-FI CLUB, AND THEY LOVED IT!
NOW THEY'RE MAKING A SEQUEL!
Paper & polyurethane foam
PRINCESS ZAKURO IS AN ALIEN WHO ZOMBIFIES PEOPLE.
Cavity in the middle
INTERNAL ORGAN ERUPTION IS HER SPECIALTY!
Pump in back
sigh
th-thump th-thump
And her head is full of goopy gore!
WHY IS SHE BLUSH-ING?!
I don't under-stand her!

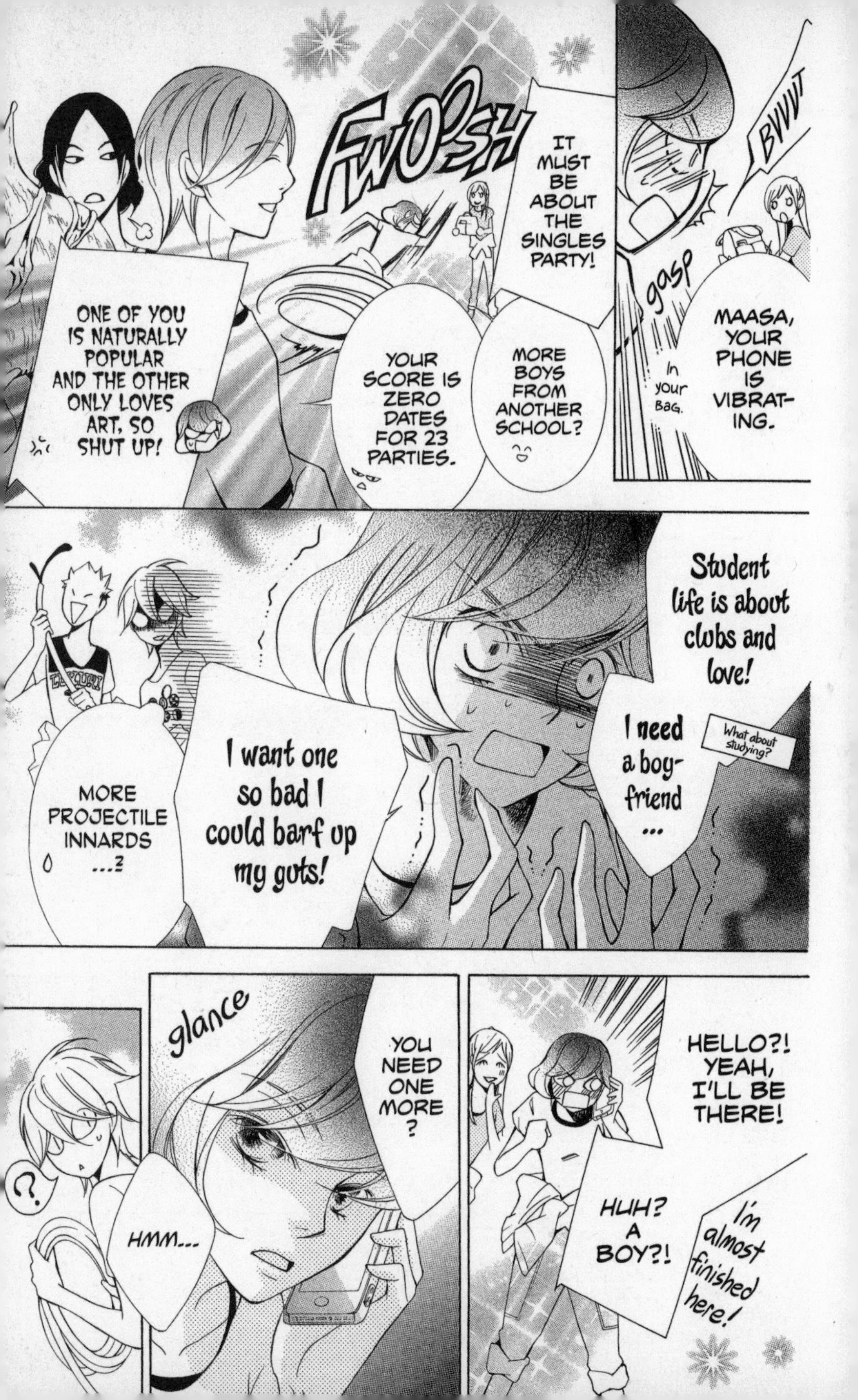
BVVVT
MAASA, YOUR PHONE IS VIBRATING.
In your Bag.
gasp
IT MUST BE ABOUT THE SINGLES PARTY!
FWOOSH
MORE BOYS FROM ANOTHER SCHOOL?
YOUR SCORE IS ZERO DATES FOR 23 PARTIES.
ONE OF YOU IS NATURALLY POPULAR AND THE OTHER ONLY LOVES ART, SO SHUT UP!
Student life is about clubs and love!
What about studying?
I need a boyfriend...
I want one so bad I could barf up my guts!
MORE PROJECTILE INNARDS...?
HELLO?! YEAH, I'LL BE THERE!
I'm almost finished here!
HUH? A BOY?!
YOU NEED ONE MORE?
glance
HMM...
?

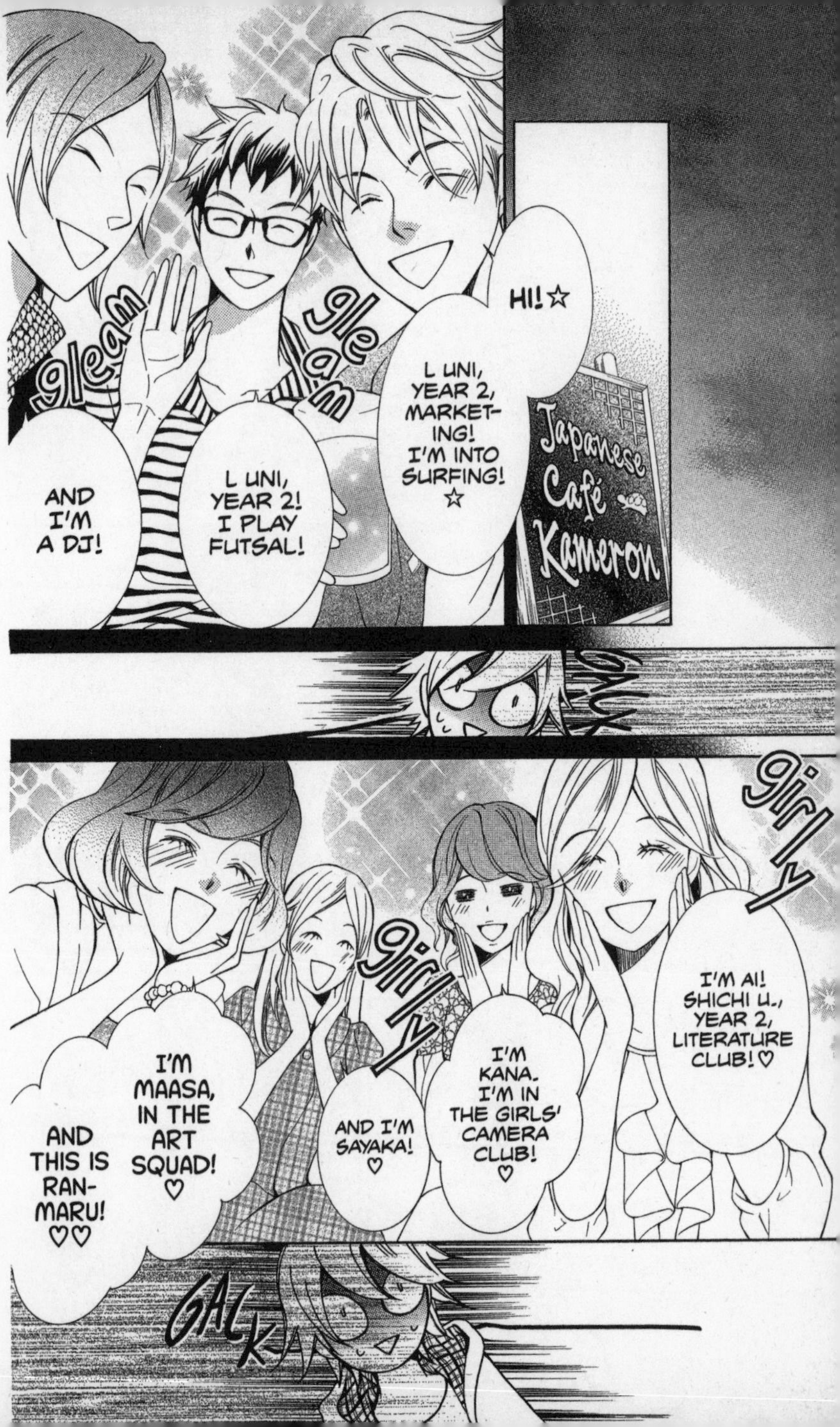

Japanese Café Kameron
HI!☆
L UNI, YEAR 2, MARKETING! I'M INTO SURFING! ☆
gleam gleam
L UNI, YEAR 2! I PLAY FUTSAL!
AND I'M A DJ!
GACK
girly girly
I'M AI! SHICHI U., YEAR 2, LITERATURE CLUB!♡
I'M KANA. I'M IN THE GIRLS' CAMERA CLUB! ♡
AND I'M SAYAKA! ♡
I'M MAASA, IN THE ART SQUAD! ♡
AND THIS IS RANMARU! ♡♡
GACK-

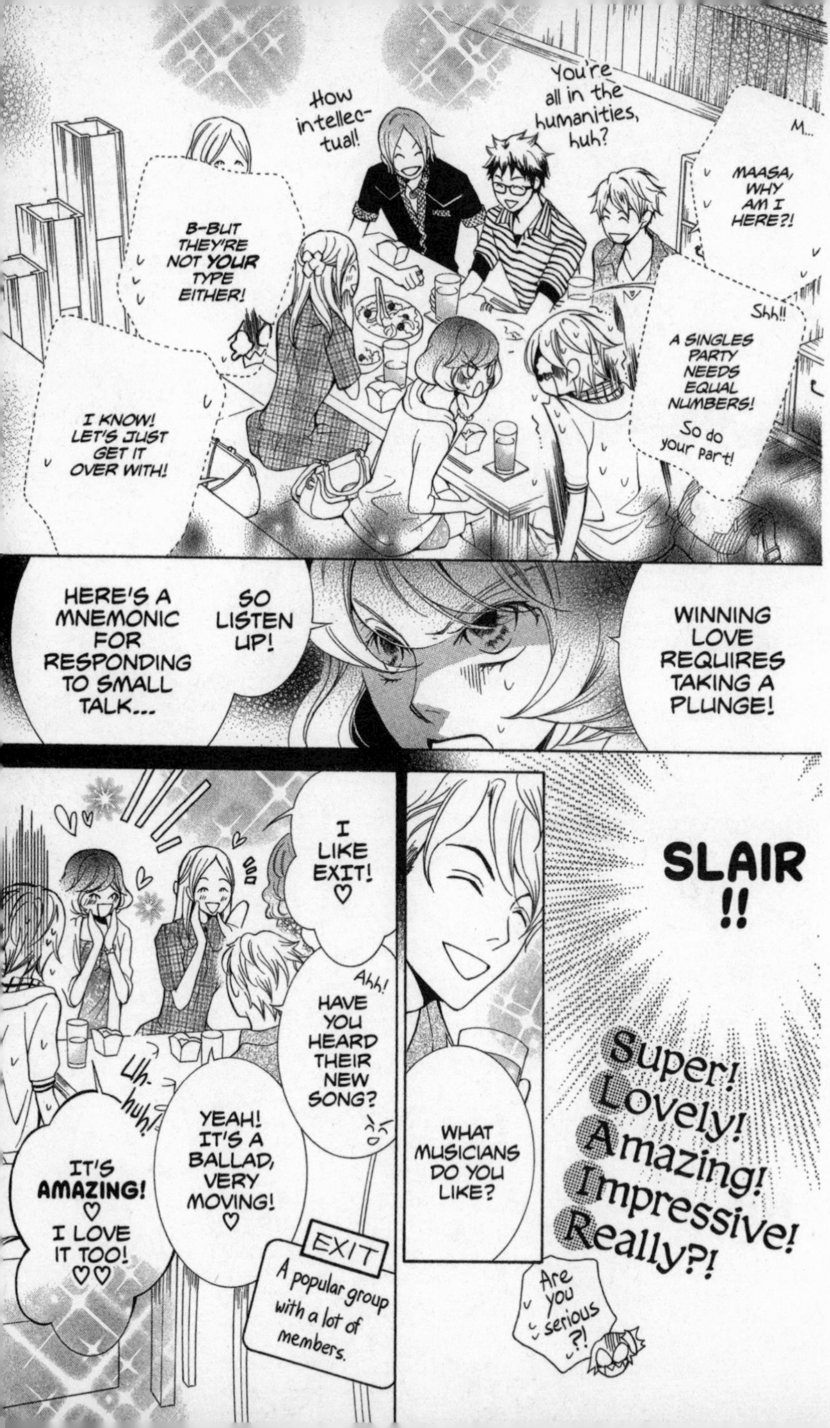
M...
MAASA, WHY AM I HERE?!
Shh!!
A SINGLES PARTY NEEDS EQUAL NUMBERS!
So do your part!
You're all in the humanities, huh?
How intellectual!
B-BUT THEY'RE NOT **YOUR** TYPE EITHER!
I KNOW! LET'S JUST GET IT OVER WITH!
WINNING LOVE REQUIRES TAKING A PLUNGE!
SO LISTEN UP!
HERE'S A MNEMONIC FOR RESPONDING TO SMALL TALK...
SLAIR!!
Super! Lovely! Amazing! Impressive! Really?!
Are you serious?!
WHAT MUSICIANS DO YOU LIKE?
I LIKE EXIT! ♡
Ahh!
HAVE YOU HEARD THEIR NEW SONG?
Uh-huh!
YEAH! IT'S A BALLAD, VERY MOVING! ♡
IT'S **AMAZING!** ♡ I LOVE IT TOO! ♡♡
EXIT
A popular group with a lot of members.

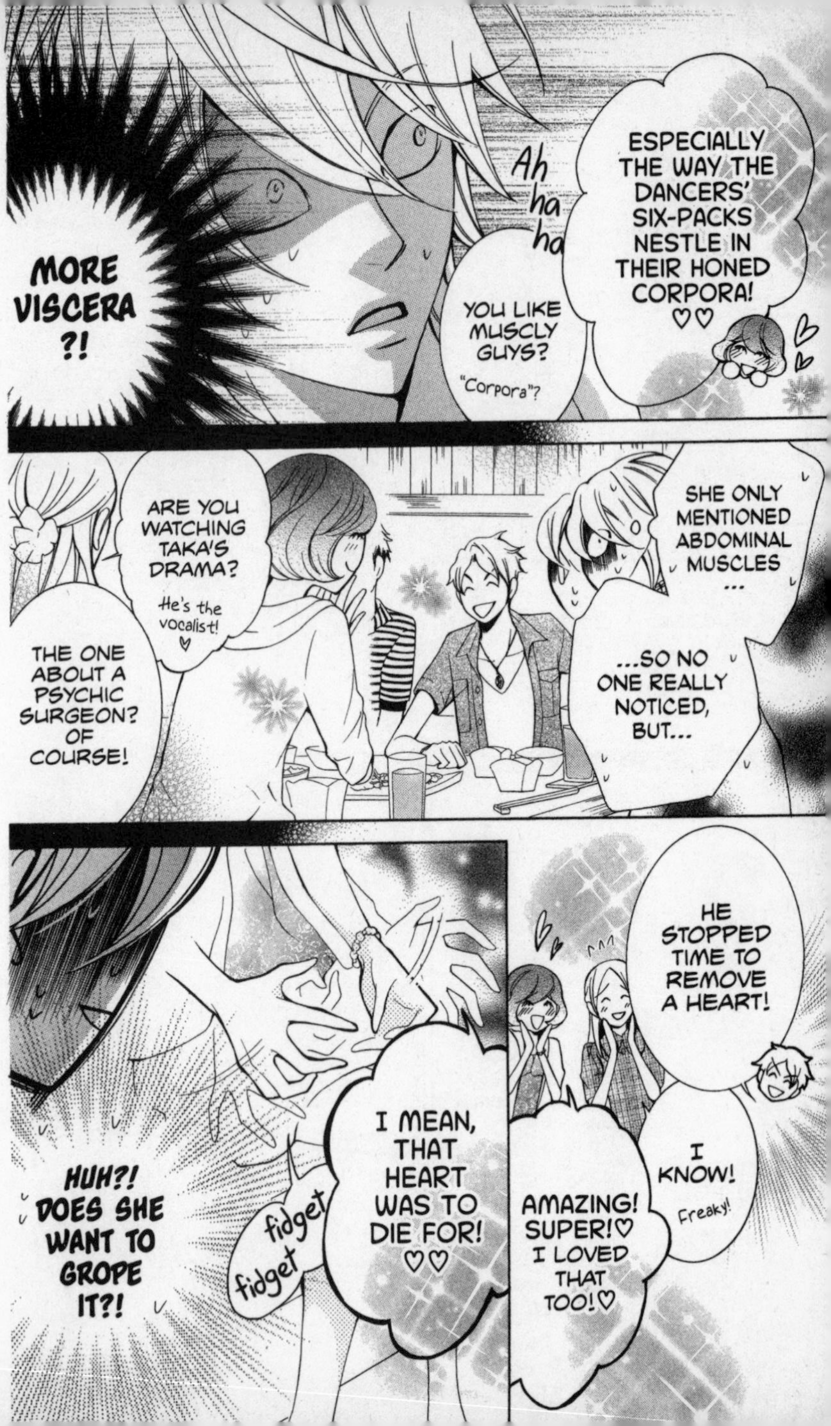
ESPECIALLY THE WAY THE DANCERS' SIX-PACKS NESTLE IN THEIR HONED CORPORA! ♡♡
Ah ha ha
YOU LIKE MUSCLY GUYS?
"Corpora"?
MORE VISCERA?!
SHE ONLY MENTIONED ABDOMINAL MUSCLES...
...SO NO ONE REALLY NOTICED, BUT...
ARE YOU WATCHING TAKA'S DRAMA?
He's the vocalist! ♡
THE ONE ABOUT A PSYCHIC SURGEON? OF COURSE!
HE STOPPED TIME TO REMOVE A HEART!
I KNOW!
Freaky!
AMAZING! SUPER!♡ I LOVED THAT TOO!♡
I MEAN, THAT HEART WAS TO DIE FOR! ♡♡
fidget fidget
HUH?! DOES SHE WANT TO GROPE IT?!

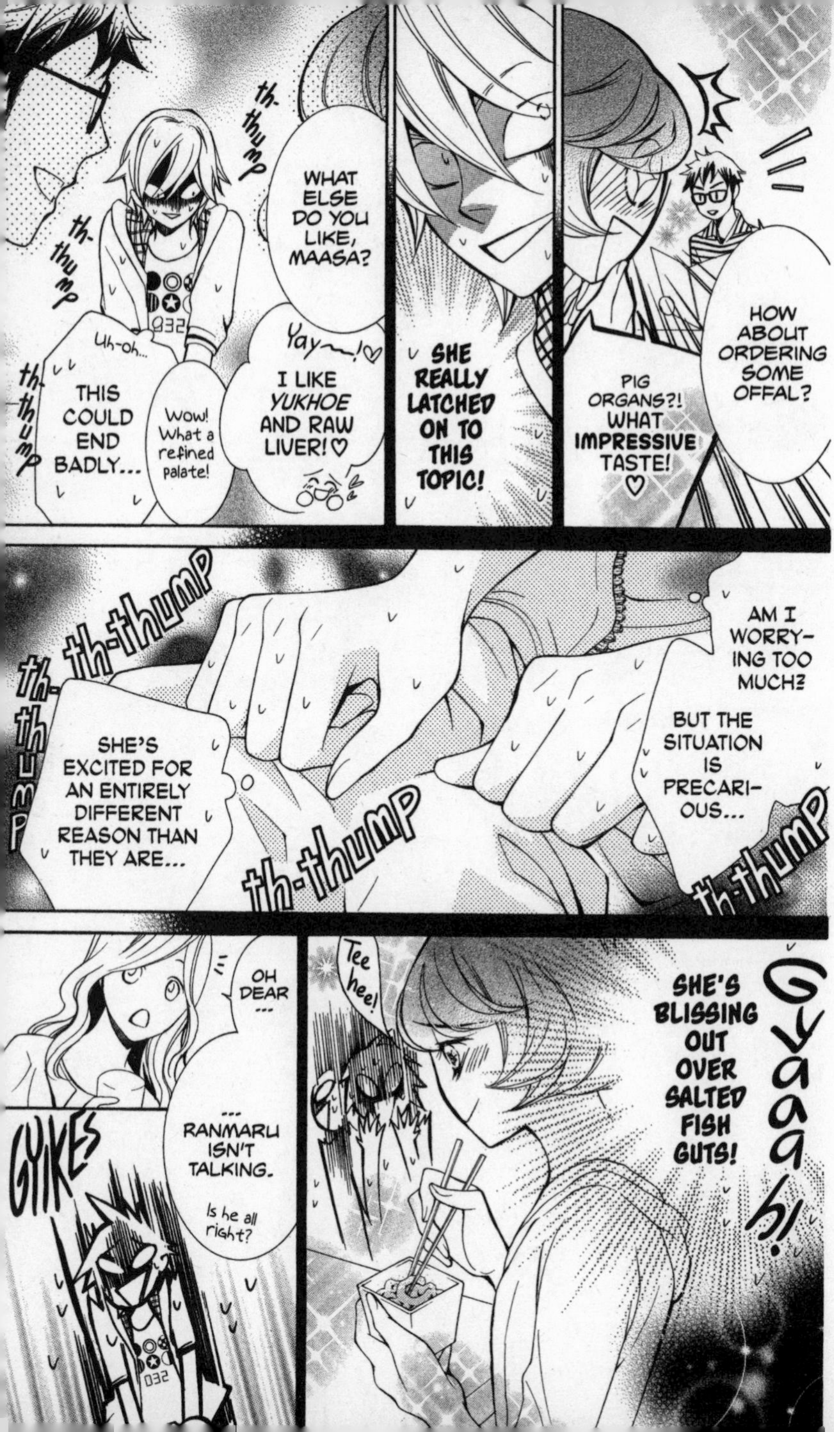
HOW ABOUT ORDERING SOME OFFAL?
PIG ORGANS?! WHAT IMPRESSIVE TASTE! ♡
SHE REALLY LATCHED ON TO THIS TOPIC!
WHAT ELSE DO YOU LIKE, MAASA?
Yay~!♡
I LIKE YUKHOE AND RAW LIVER! ♡
Wow! What a refined palate!
th-thump
th-thump
Uh-oh...
THIS COULD END BADLY...
th-thump
AM I WORRYING TOO MUCH?
BUT THE SITUATION IS PRECARIOUS...
th-thump
th-thump
th-thump
SHE'S EXCITED FOR AN ENTIRELY DIFFERENT REASON THAN THEY ARE...
th-thump
SHE'S BLISSING OUT OVER SALTED FISH GUTS!
Gyaaah!
Tee hee!
OH DEAR ...
... RANMARU ISN'T TALKING.
Is he all right?
GYIKES

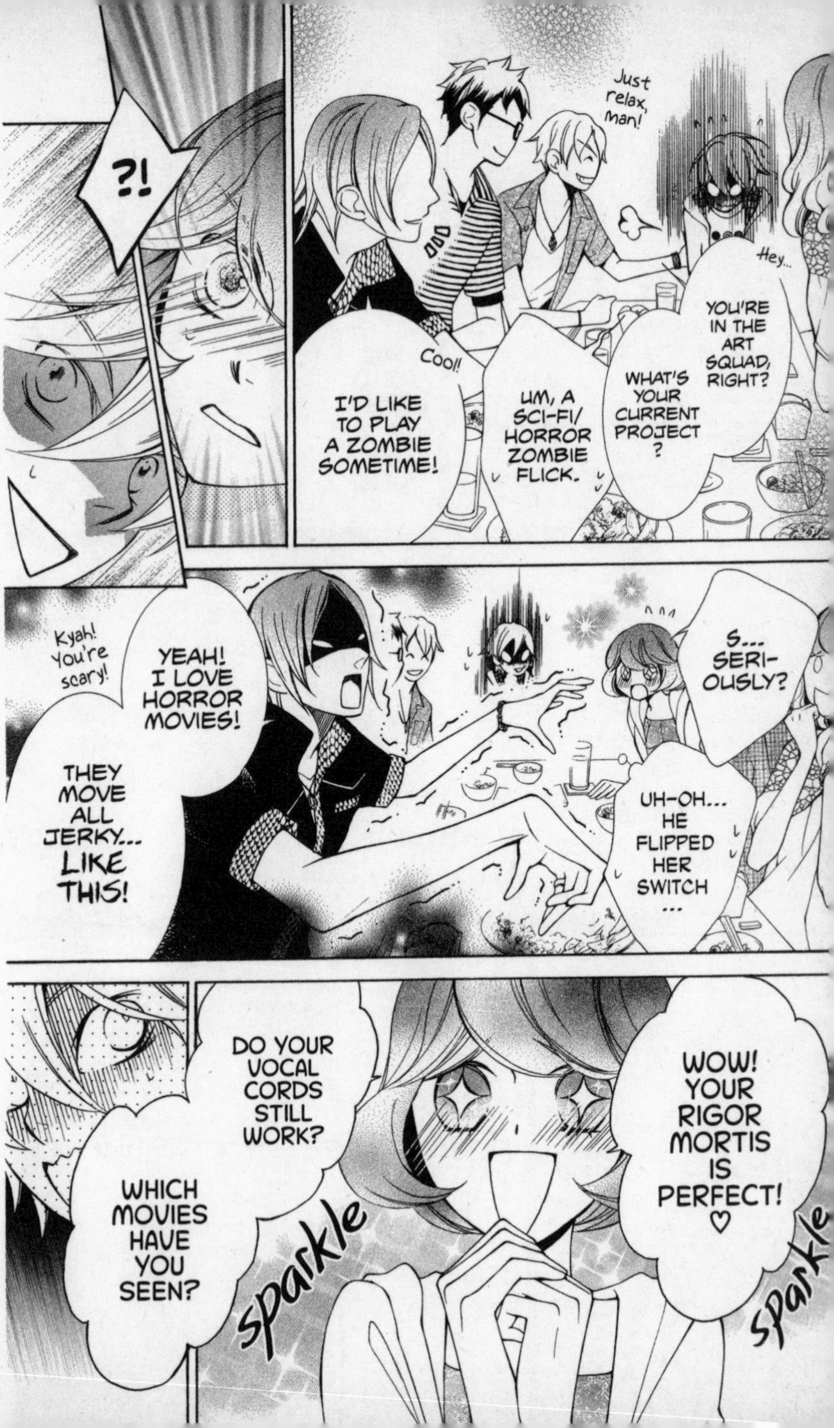
Just relax, man!
Hey...
YOU'RE IN THE ART SQUAD, RIGHT?
WHAT'S YOUR CURRENT PROJECT?
UM, A SCI-FI/HORROR ZOMBIE FLICK.
Cool!
I'D LIKE TO PLAY A ZOMBIE SOMETIME!
?!
S... SERIOUSLY?
UH-OH... HE FLIPPED HER SWITCH...
YEAH! I LOVE HORROR MOVIES!
Kyah! You're scary!
THEY MOVE ALL JERKY... LIKE THIS!
sparkle
WOW! YOUR RIGOR MORTIS IS PERFECT! ♡
DO YOUR VOCAL CORDS STILL WORK?
WHICH MOVIES HAVE YOU SEEN?
sparkle

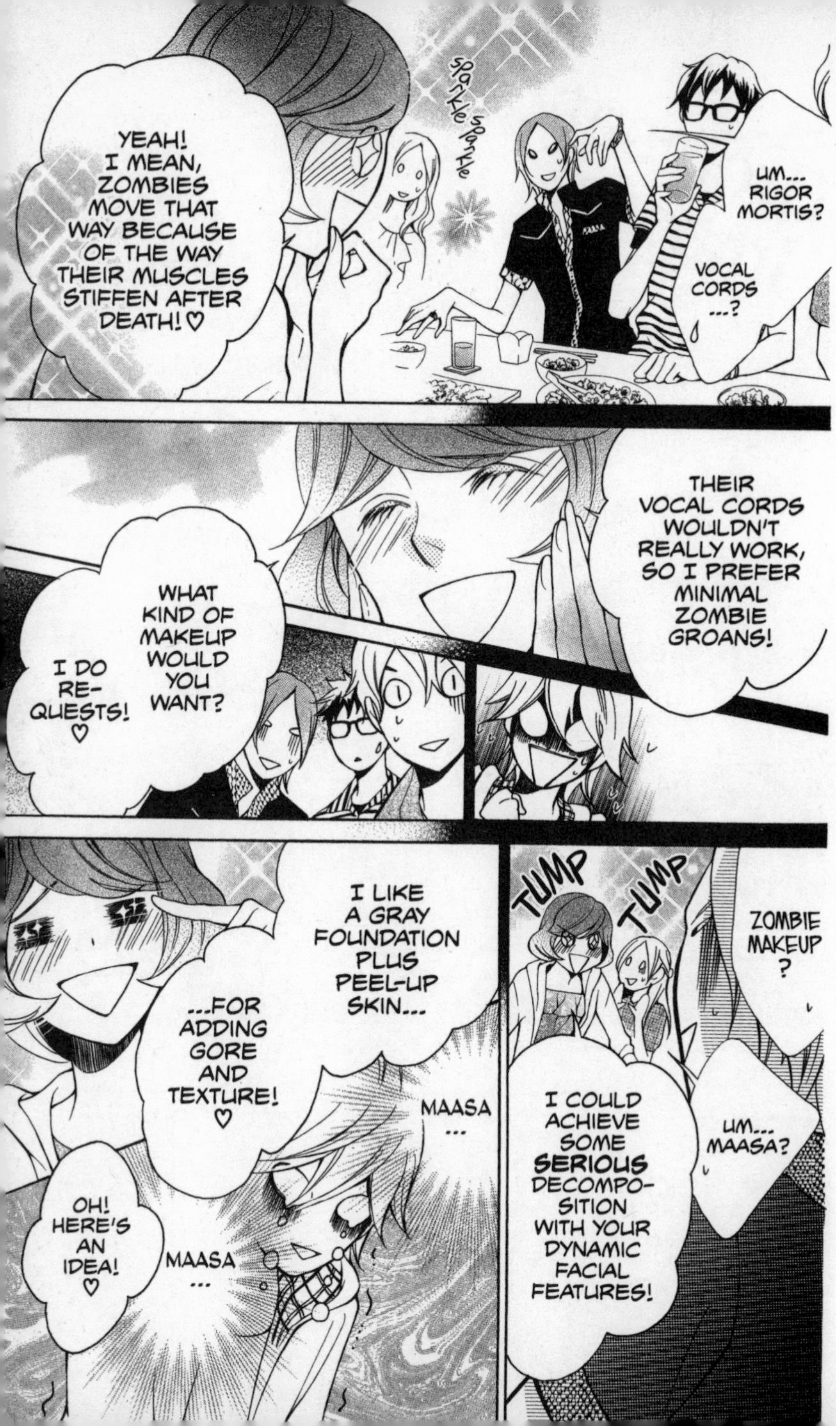
UM... RIGOR MORTIS?
VOCAL CORDS ...?
sparkle sparkle
YEAH! I MEAN, ZOMBIES MOVE THAT WAY BECAUSE OF THE WAY THEIR MUSCLES STIFFEN AFTER DEATH! ♡
THEIR VOCAL CORDS WOULDN'T REALLY WORK, SO I PREFER MINIMAL ZOMBIE GROANS!
WHAT KIND OF MAKEUP WOULD YOU WANT?
I DO RE-QUESTS! ♡
TUMP TUMP
ZOMBIE MAKEUP ?
UM... MAASA?
I COULD ACHIEVE SOME **SERIOUS** DECOMPO-SITION WITH YOUR DYNAMIC FACIAL FEATURES!
I LIKE A GRAY FOUNDATION PLUS PEEL-UP SKIN...
...FOR ADDING GORE AND TEXTURE! ♡
MAASA ...
OH! HERE'S AN IDEA! ♡
MAASA ...

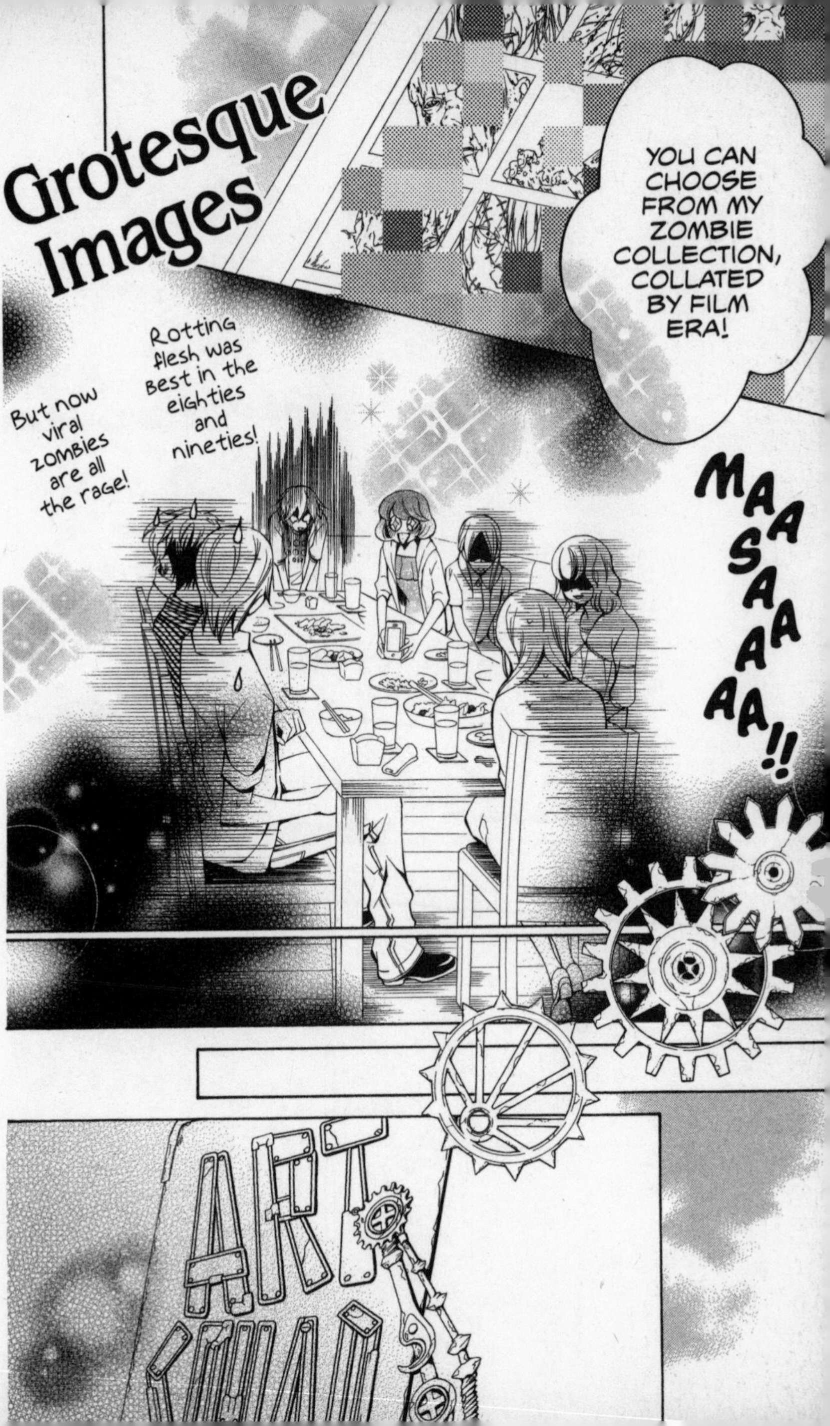
YOU CAN CHOOSE FROM MY ZOMBIE COLLECTION, COLLATED BY FILM ERA!
Grotesque Images
MAAASAAAAA!!
Rotting flesh was best in the eighties and nineties!
But now viral zombies are all the rage!
ART

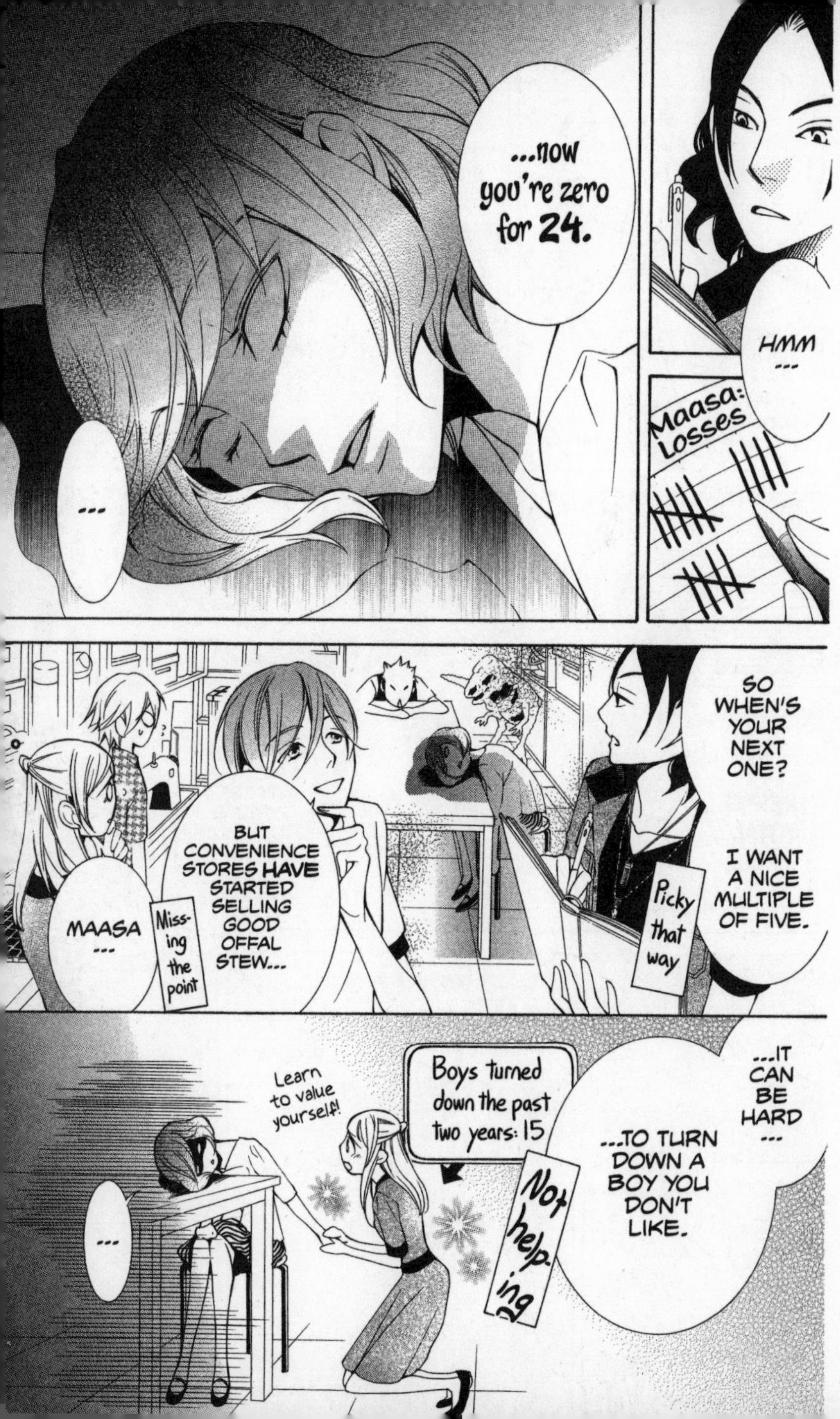
HMM ---
Maasa: Losses
...now you're zero for 24.

SO WHEN'S YOUR NEXT ONE?
I WANT A NICE MULTIPLE OF FIVE.
Picky that way
BUT CONVENIENCE STORES HAVE STARTED SELLING GOOD OFFAL STEW...
Miss-ing the point
MAASA ---
...IT CAN BE HARD ---
...TO TURN DOWN A BOY YOU DON'T LIKE.
Not help-ing
Boys turned down the past two years: 15
Learn to value yourself!

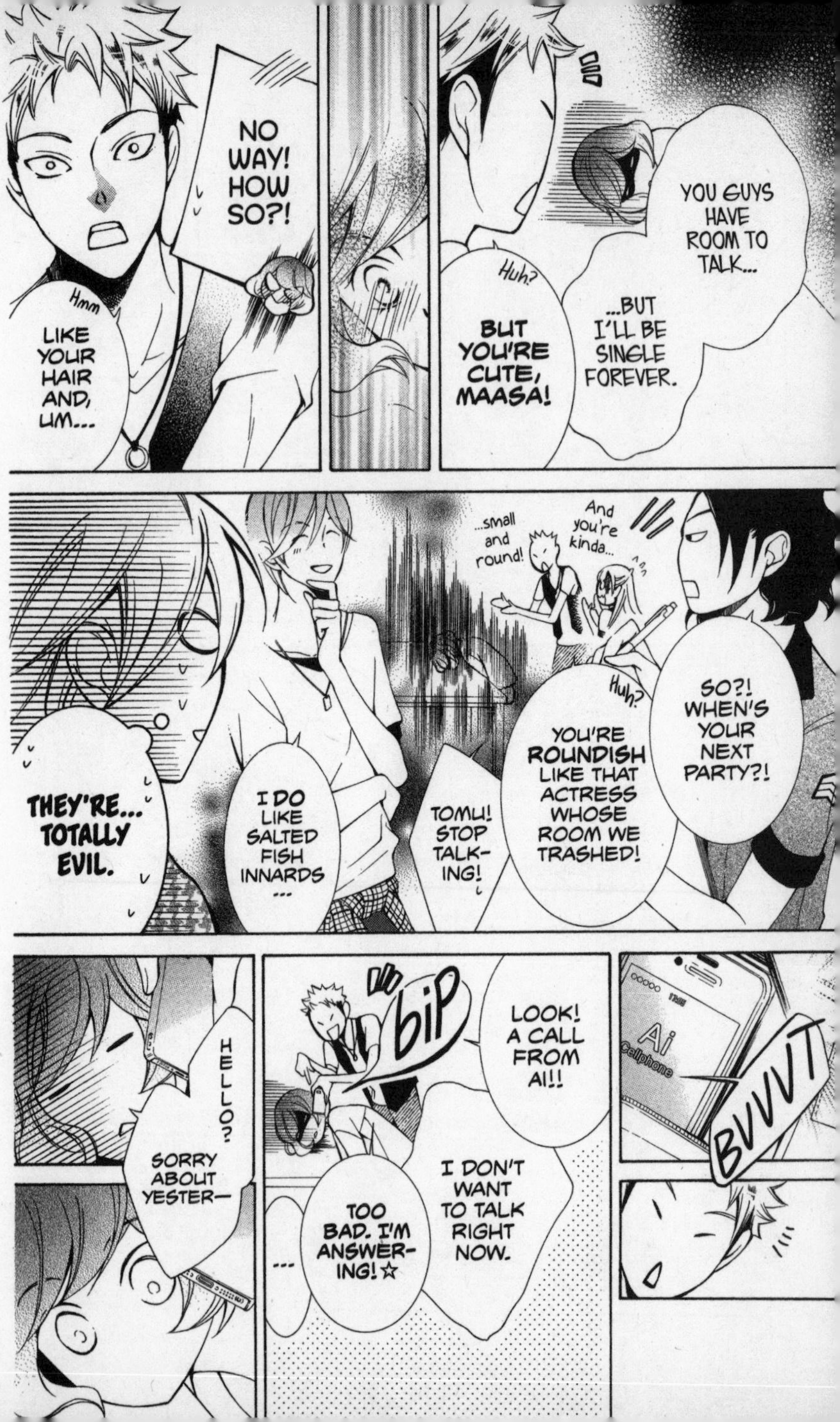
YOU GUYS HAVE ROOM TO TALK...
...BUT I'LL BE SINGLE FOREVER.
Huh?
BUT YOU'RE CUTE, MAASA!
NO WAY! HOW SO?!
Hmm
LIKE YOUR HAIR AND, UM...
SO?! WHEN'S YOUR NEXT PARTY?!
And you're kinda...
...small and round!
Huh?
YOU'RE ROUNDISH LIKE THAT ACTRESS WHOSE ROOM WE TRASHED!
TOMU! STOP TALKING!
I DO LIKE SALTED FISH INNARDS...
THEY'RE... TOTALLY EVIL.
Ai
Cellphone
BVVVT
LOOK! A CALL FROM AI!!
biP
I DON'T WANT TO TALK RIGHT NOW.
TOO BAD. I'M ANSWERING!☆
...
HELLO?
SORRY ABOUT YESTER—

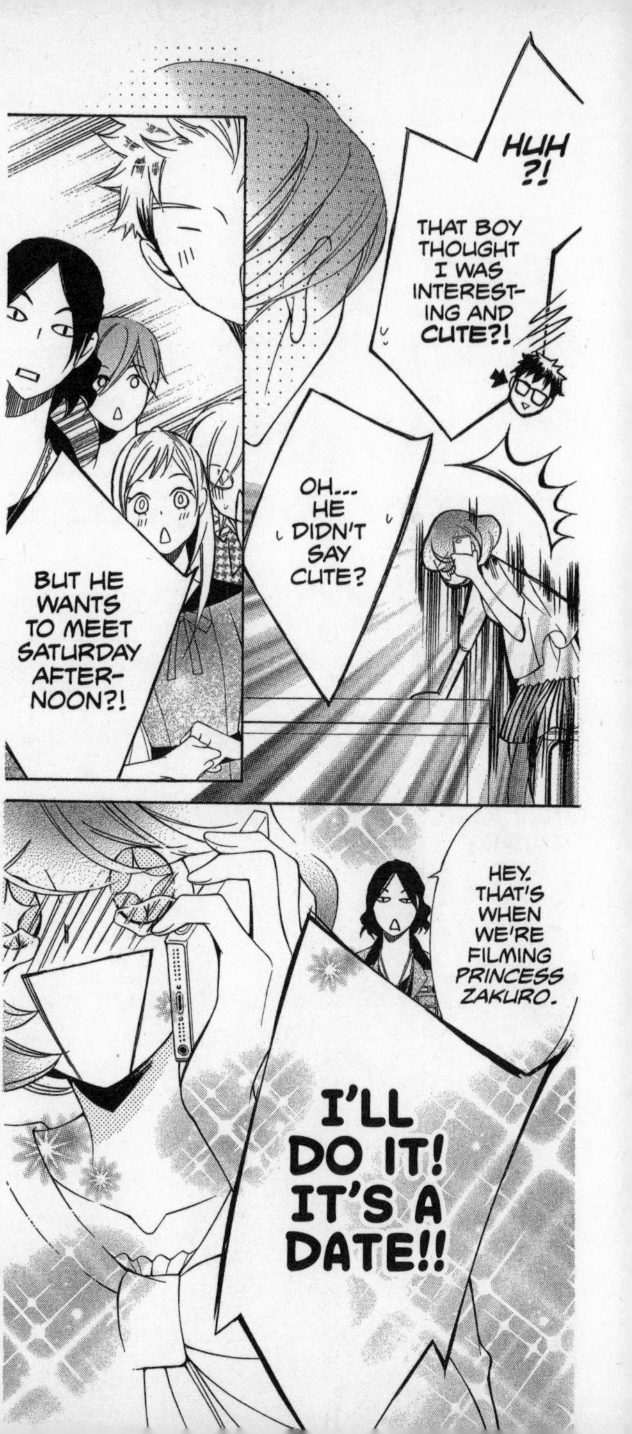
HUH ?!
THAT BOY THOUGHT I WAS INTEREST-ING AND CUTE?!
OH... HE DIDN'T SAY CUTE?
BUT HE WANTS TO MEET SATURDAY AFTER-NOON?!
HEY. THAT'S WHEN WE'RE FILMING PRINCESS ZAKURO.
I'LL DO IT! IT'S A DATE!!

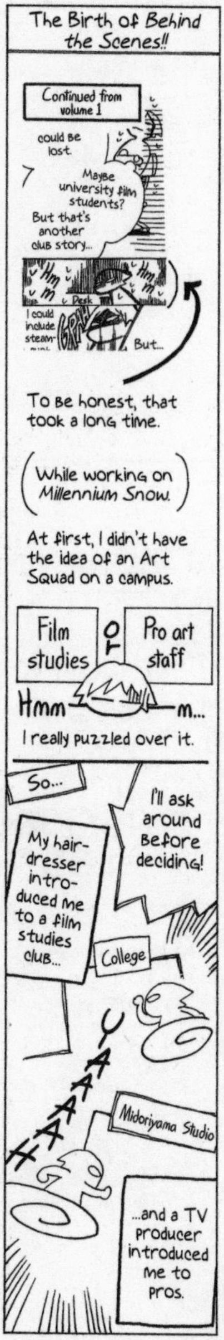
The Birth of Behind the Scenes!!
Continued from volume 1
could be lost.
Maybe university film students? But that's another club story...
Hm m Hm m
Desk
I could include steam-
But...
To be honest, that took a long time.
(While working on Millennium Snow.)
At first, I didn't have the idea of an Art Squad on a campus.
Film studies
or
Pro art staff
Hmm—m...
I really puzzled over it.
So...
I'll ask around before deciding!
My hairdresser introduced me to a film studies club...
College
YAAAAAH
Midoriyama Studio
...and a TV producer introduced me to pros.

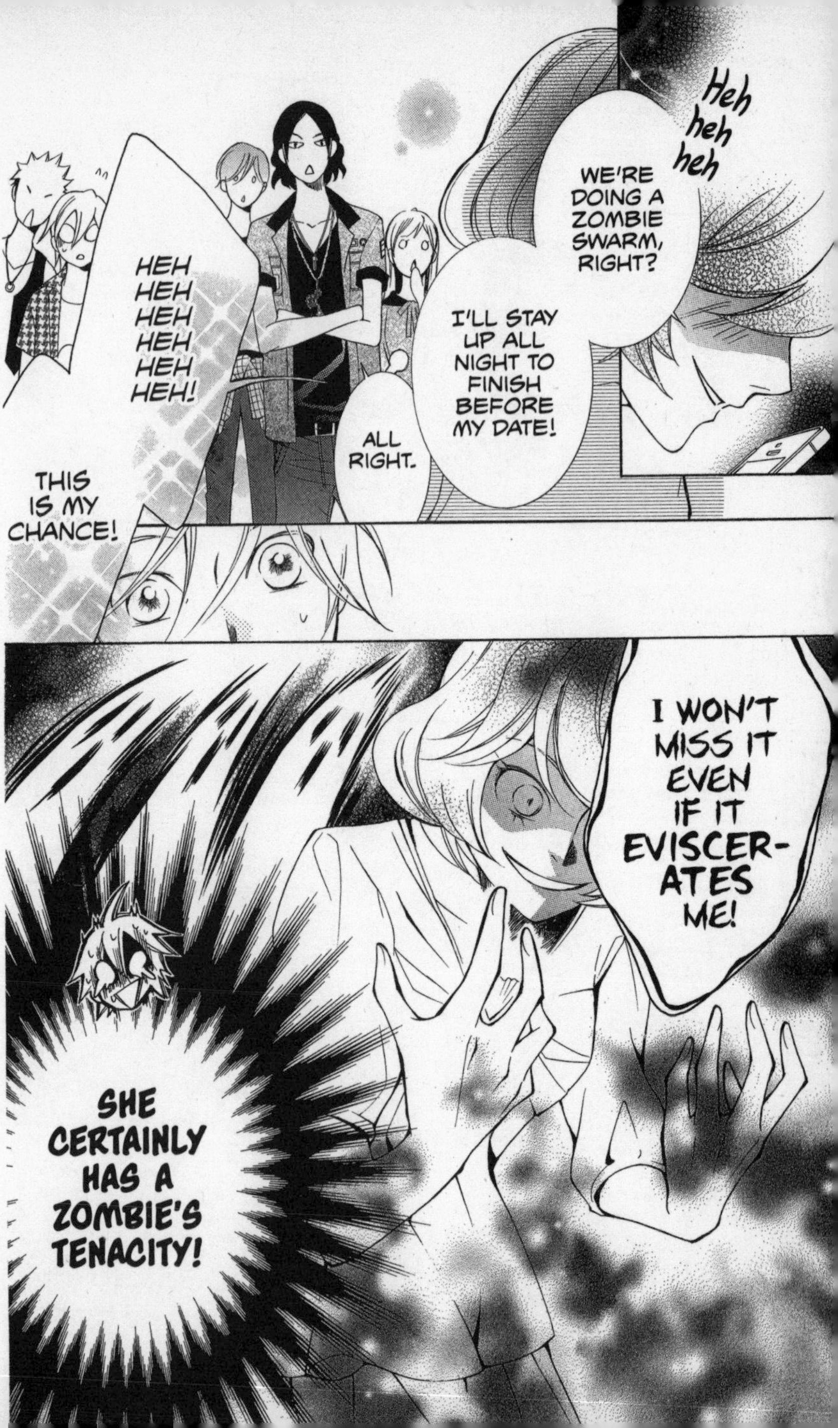
Heh heh heh
WE'RE DOING A ZOMBIE SWARM, RIGHT?
I'LL STAY UP ALL NIGHT TO FINISH BEFORE MY DATE!
ALL RIGHT.
HEH HEH HEH HEH HEH HEH!
THIS IS MY CHANCE!
I WON'T MISS IT EVEN IF IT EVISCER-ATES ME!
SHE CERTAINLY HAS A ZOMBIE'S TENACITY!

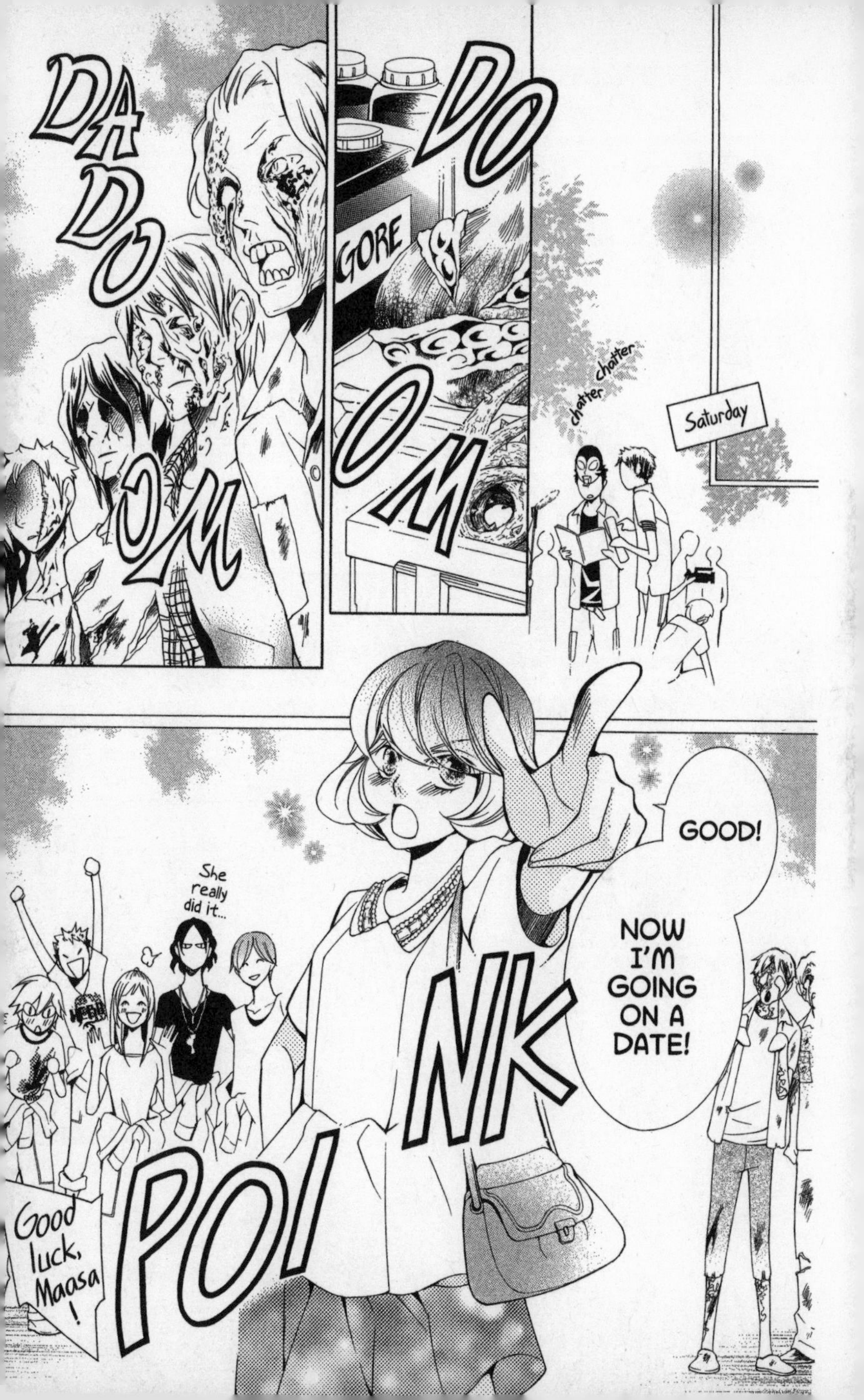
Saturday
chatter chatter
GORE
DOOM
DADOOM
GOOD!
NOW I'M GOING ON A DATE!
POINK
She really did it...
Good luck, Maasa!

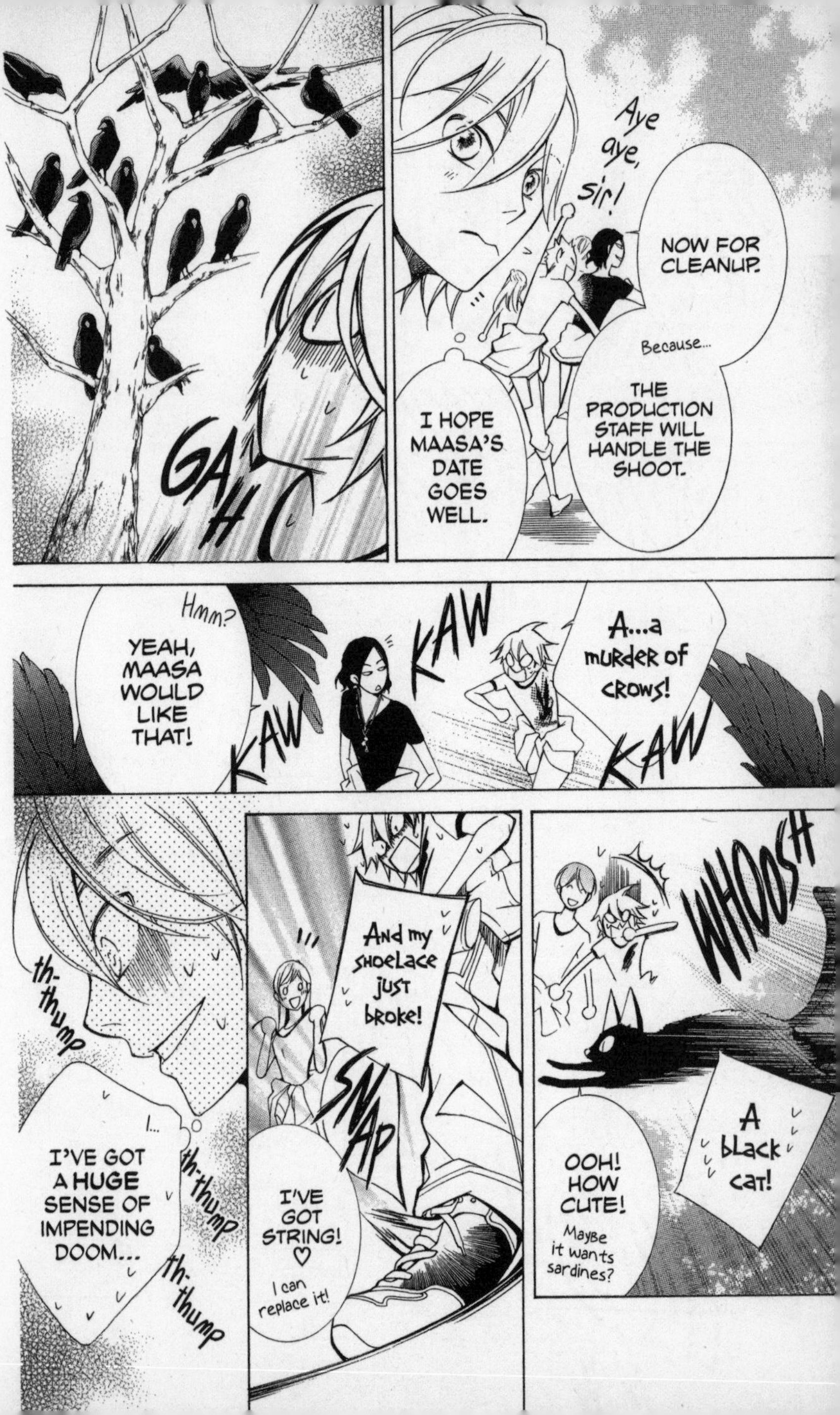
NOW FOR CLEANUP.
Aye aye, sir!
Because... THE PRODUCTION STAFF WILL HANDLE THE SHOOT.
I HOPE MAASA'S DATE GOES WELL.
GAH
A...a murder of crows!
KAW
KAW
KAW
Hmm? YEAH, MAASA WOULD LIKE THAT!
WHOOSH
A black cat!
OOH! HOW CUTE!
Maybe it wants sardines?
And my shoelace just broke!
SNAP
I'VE GOT STRING! ♡
I can replace it!
th-thump
I... I'VE GOT A HUGE SENSE OF IMPENDING DOOM...
th-thump
th-thump

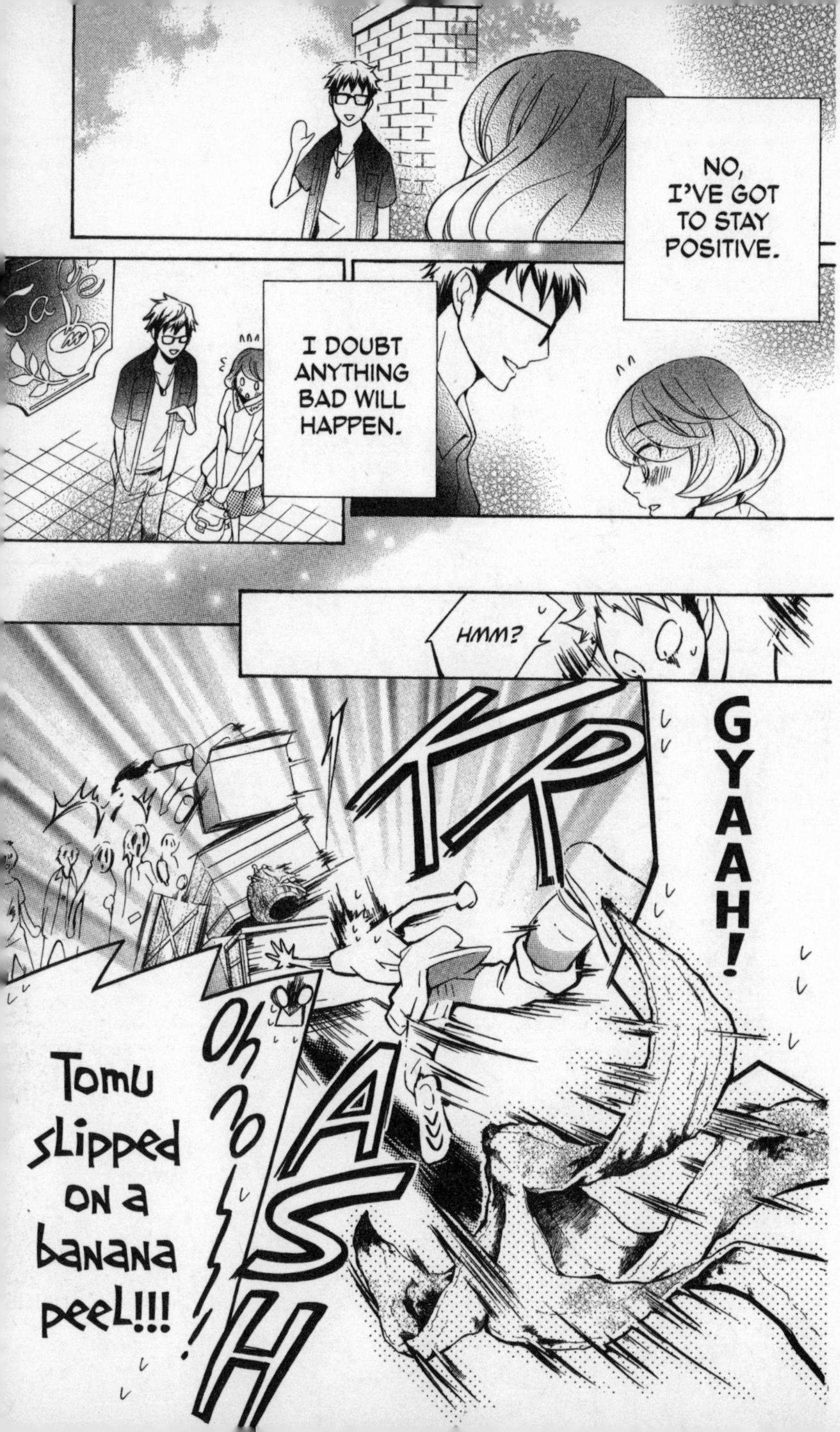
NO, I'VE GOT TO STAY POSITIVE.
I DOUBT ANYTHING BAD WILL HAPPEN.
Cafe
HMM?
GYAAH!
KRASH
Oh no...!
Tomu slipped on a banana peel!!!

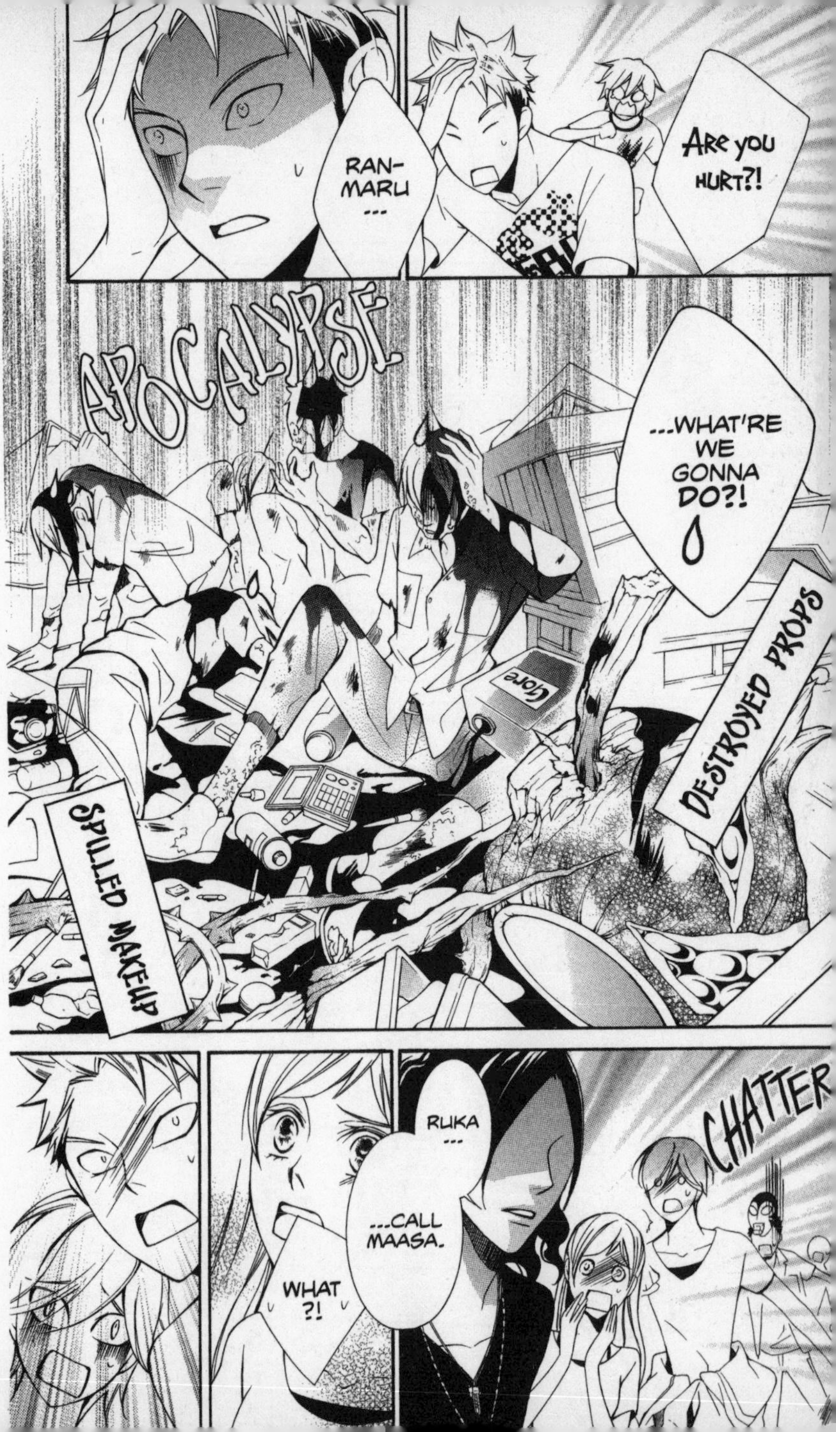
Are you HURT?!
RAN-MARU ...
...WHAT'RE WE GONNA DO?!
APOCALYPSE
DESTROYED PROPS
Gore
SPILLED MAKEUP
CHATTER
RUKA ...
...CALL MAASA.
WHAT ?!

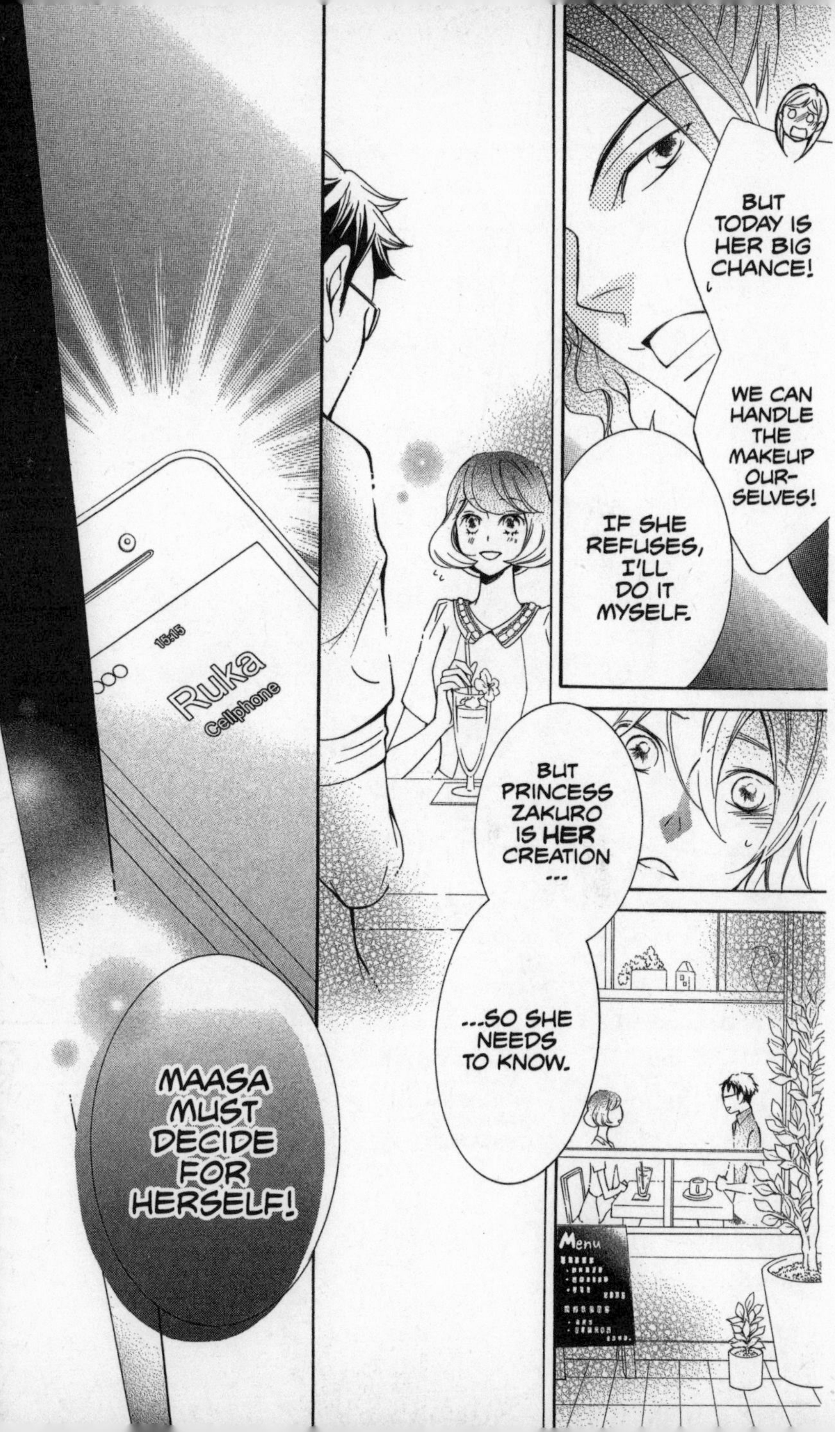
BUT TODAY IS HER BIG CHANCE!
WE CAN HANDLE THE MAKEUP OURSELVES!
IF SHE REFUSES, I'LL DO IT MYSELF.
BUT PRINCESS ZAKURO IS HER CREATION...
...SO SHE NEEDS TO KNOW.
Menu
15:15
Ruka
Cellphone
MAASA MUST DECIDE FOR HERSELF!

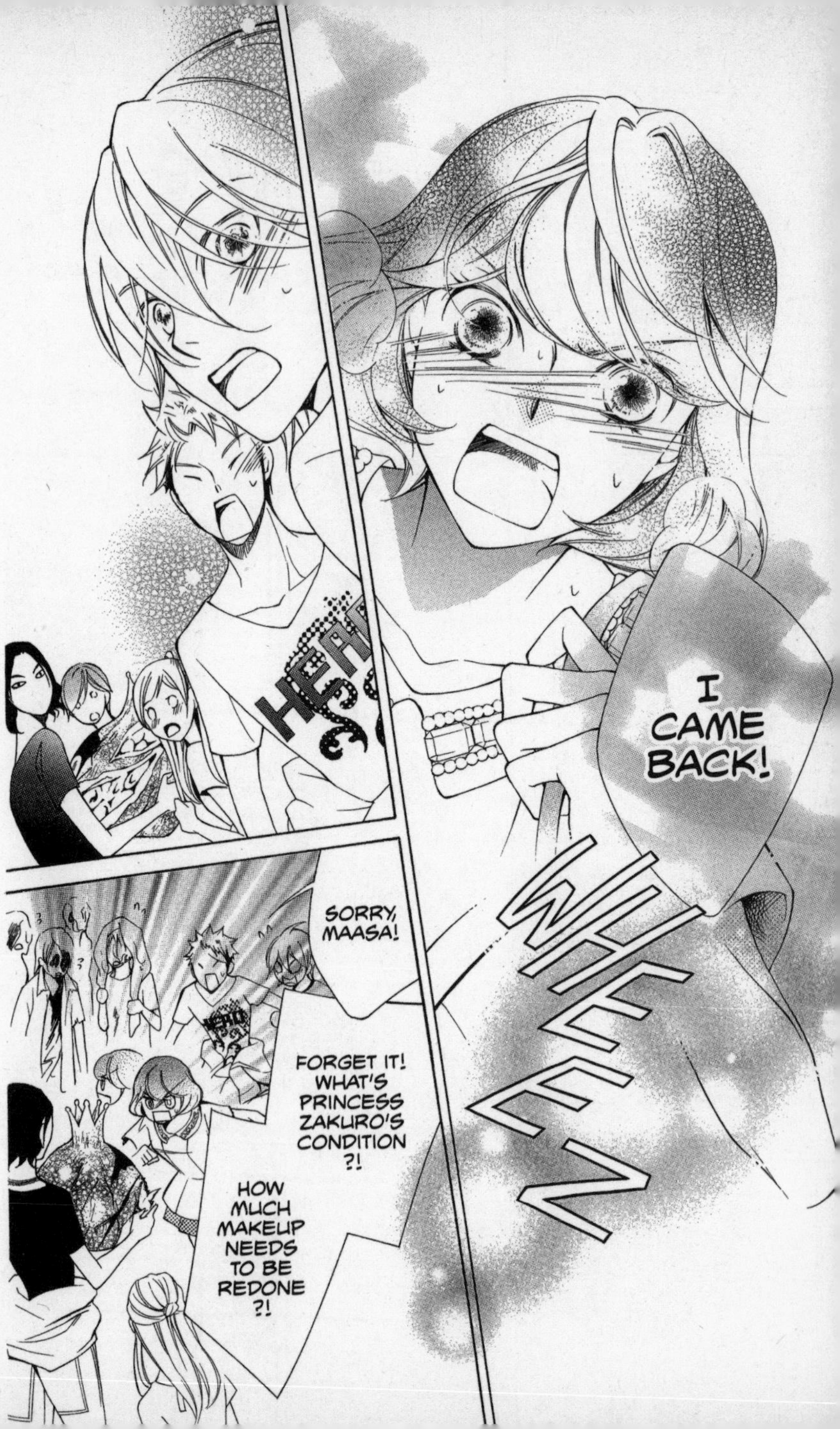
I CAME BACK!
WHEEN
SORRY, MAASA!
FORGET IT! WHAT'S PRINCESS ZAKURO'S CONDITION ?!
HOW MUCH MAKEUP NEEDS TO BE REDONE ?!

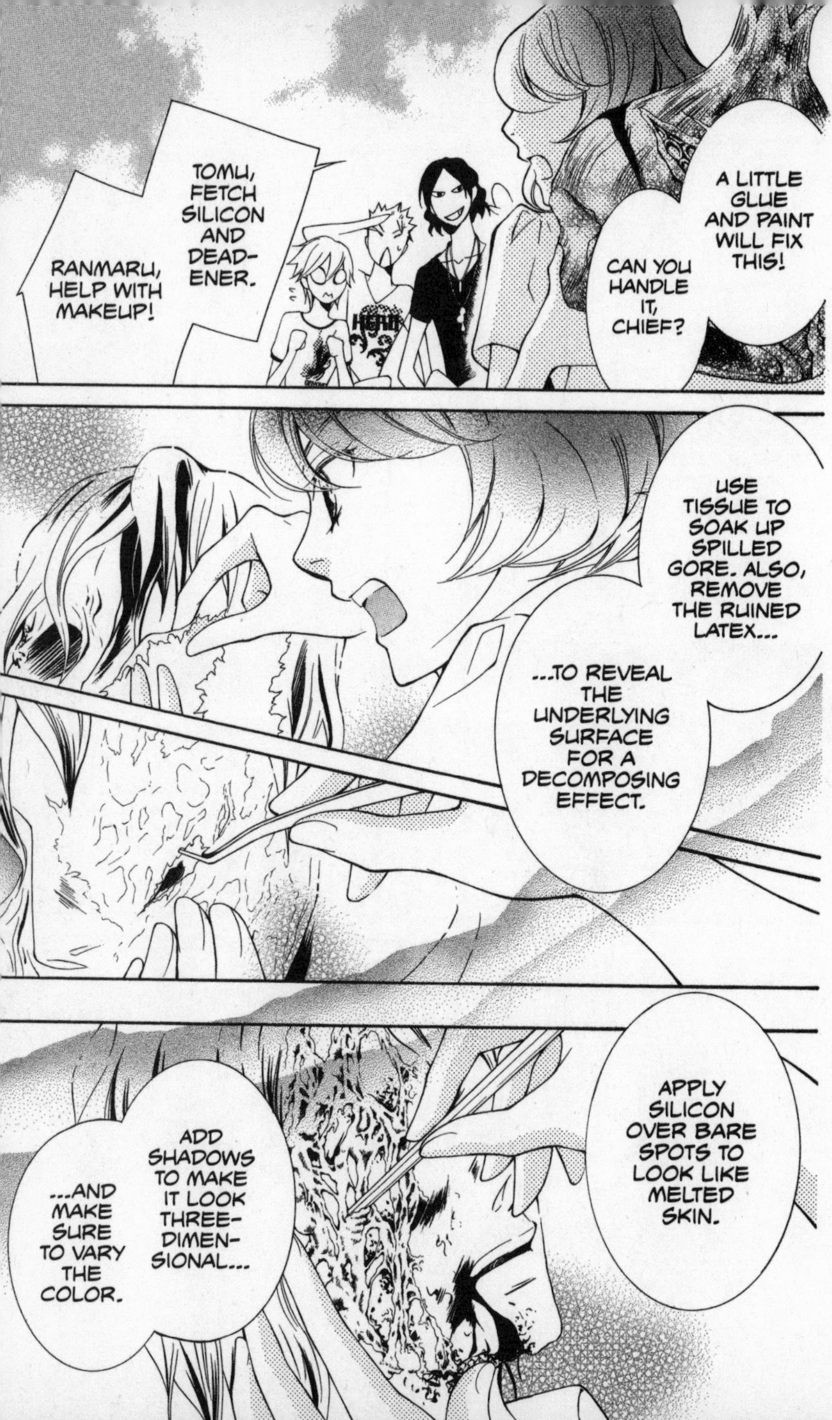
A LITTLE GLUE AND PAINT WILL FIX THIS!
CAN YOU HANDLE IT, CHIEF?
TOMU, FETCH SILICON AND DEAD-ENER.
RANMARU, HELP WITH MAKEUP!
USE TISSUE TO SOAK UP SPILLED GORE. ALSO, REMOVE THE RUINED LATEX...
...TO REVEAL THE UNDERLYING SURFACE FOR A DECOMPOSING EFFECT.
APPLY SILICON OVER BARE SPOTS TO LOOK LIKE MELTED SKIN.
ADD SHADOWS TO MAKE IT LOOK THREE-DIMEN-SIONAL...
...AND MAKE SURE TO VARY THE COLOR.

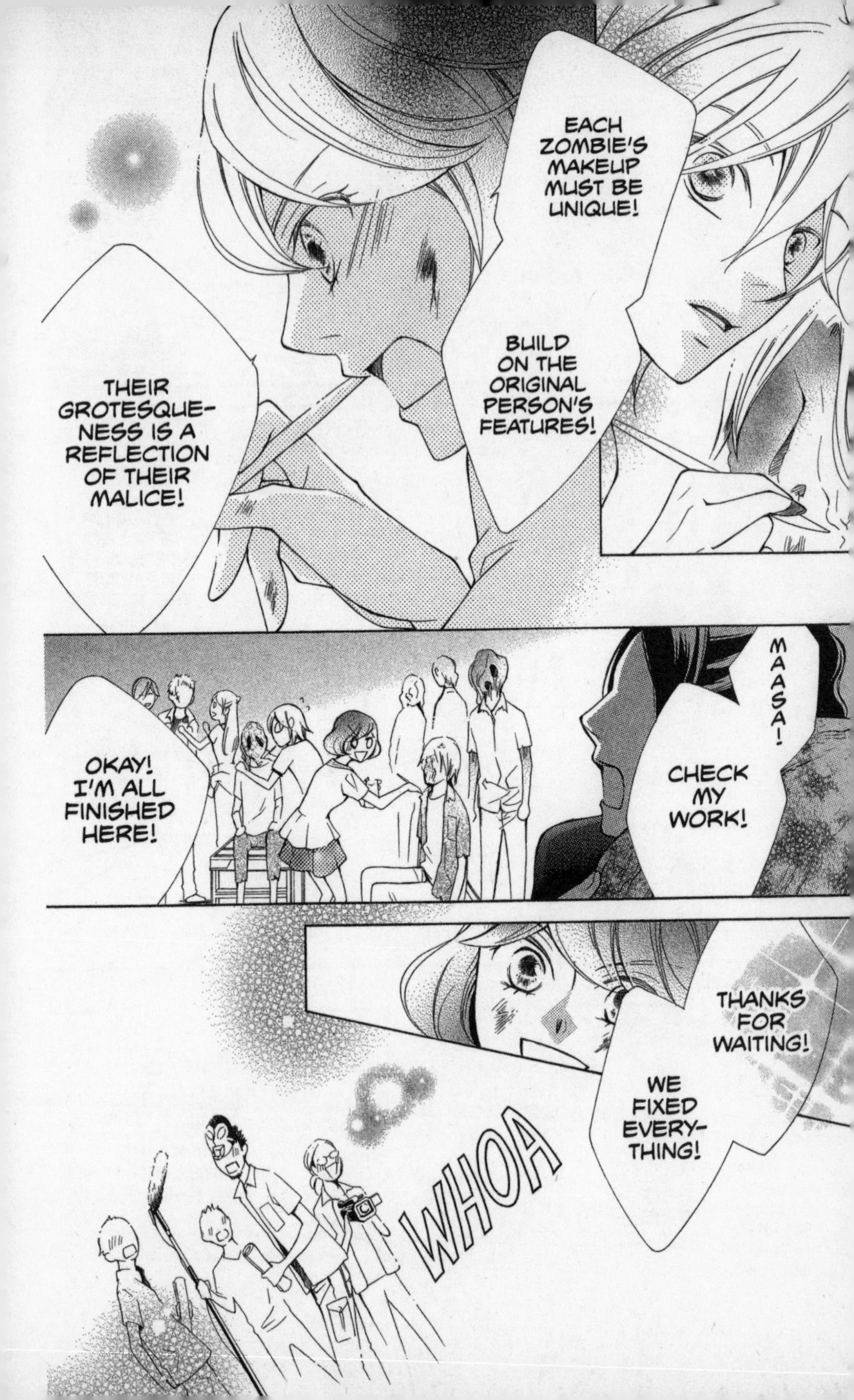
EACH ZOMBIE'S MAKEUP MUST BE UNIQUE!
BUILD ON THE ORIGINAL PERSON'S FEATURES!
THEIR GROTESQUENESS IS A REFLECTION OF THEIR MALICE!
MAASA!
CHECK MY WORK!
OKAY! I'M ALL FINISHED HERE!
THANKS FOR WAITING!
WE FIXED EVERYTHING!
WHOA

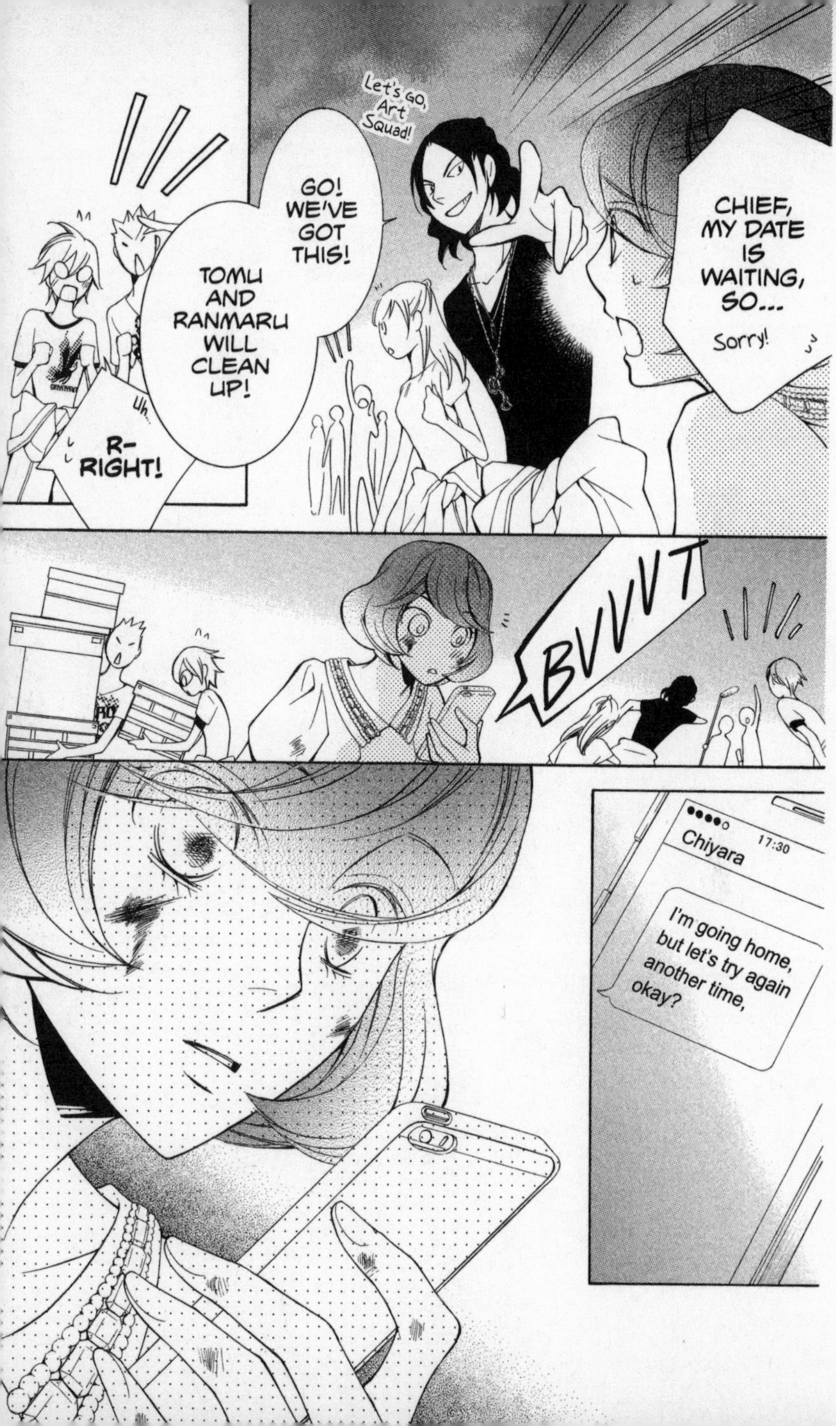
CHIEF, MY DATE IS WAITING, SO...
Sorry!
Let's go, Art Squad!
GO! WE'VE GOT THIS!
TOMU AND RANMARU WILL CLEAN UP!
Uh...
R-RIGHT!
BVVVT
Chiyara
17:30
I'm going home, but let's try again another time, okay?

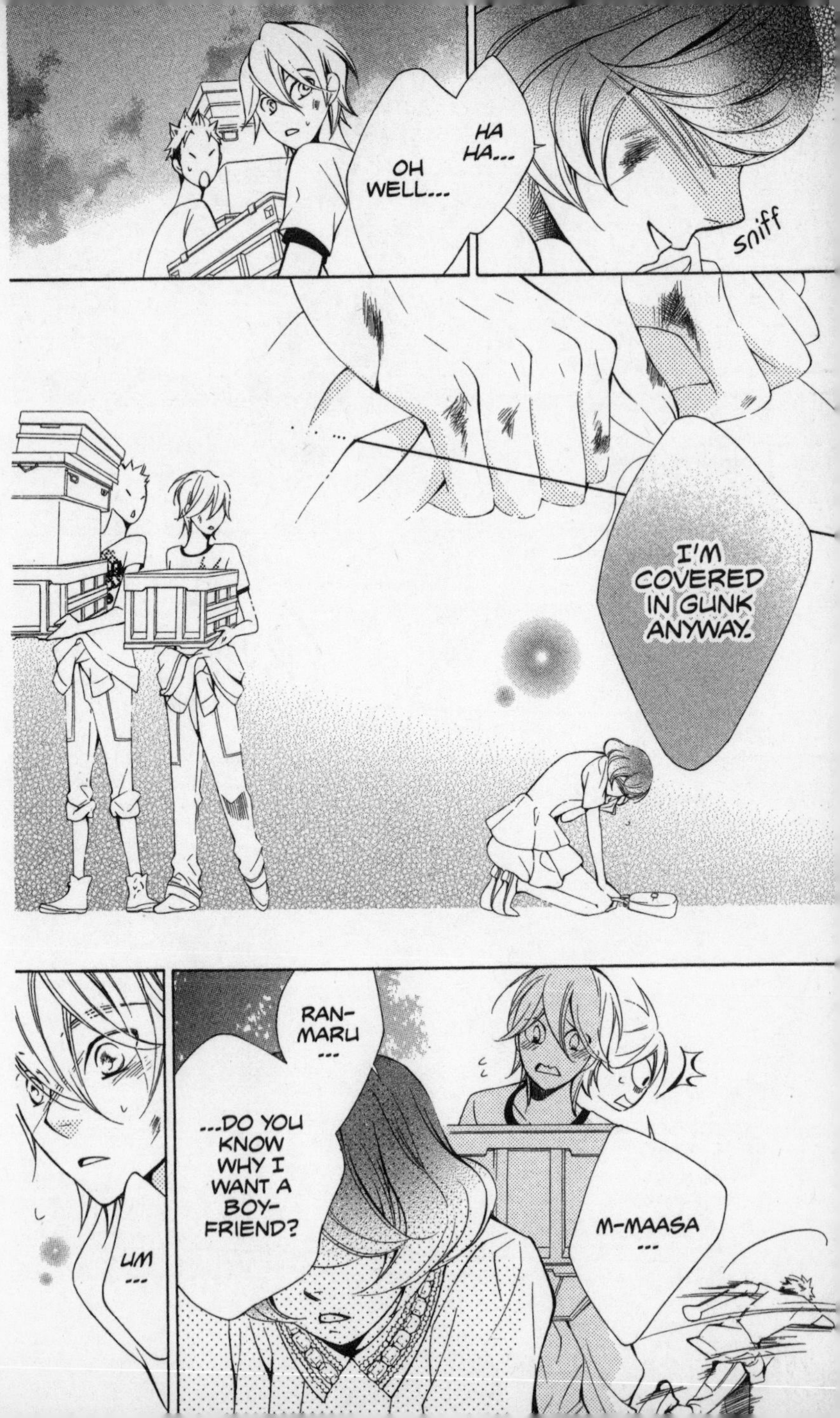

HA HA... OH WELL...
sniff
. . ...
I'M COVERED IN GUNK ANYWAY.
M-MAASA ---
RAN-MARU ---
...DO YOU KNOW WHY I WANT A BOY-FRIEND?
UM ---

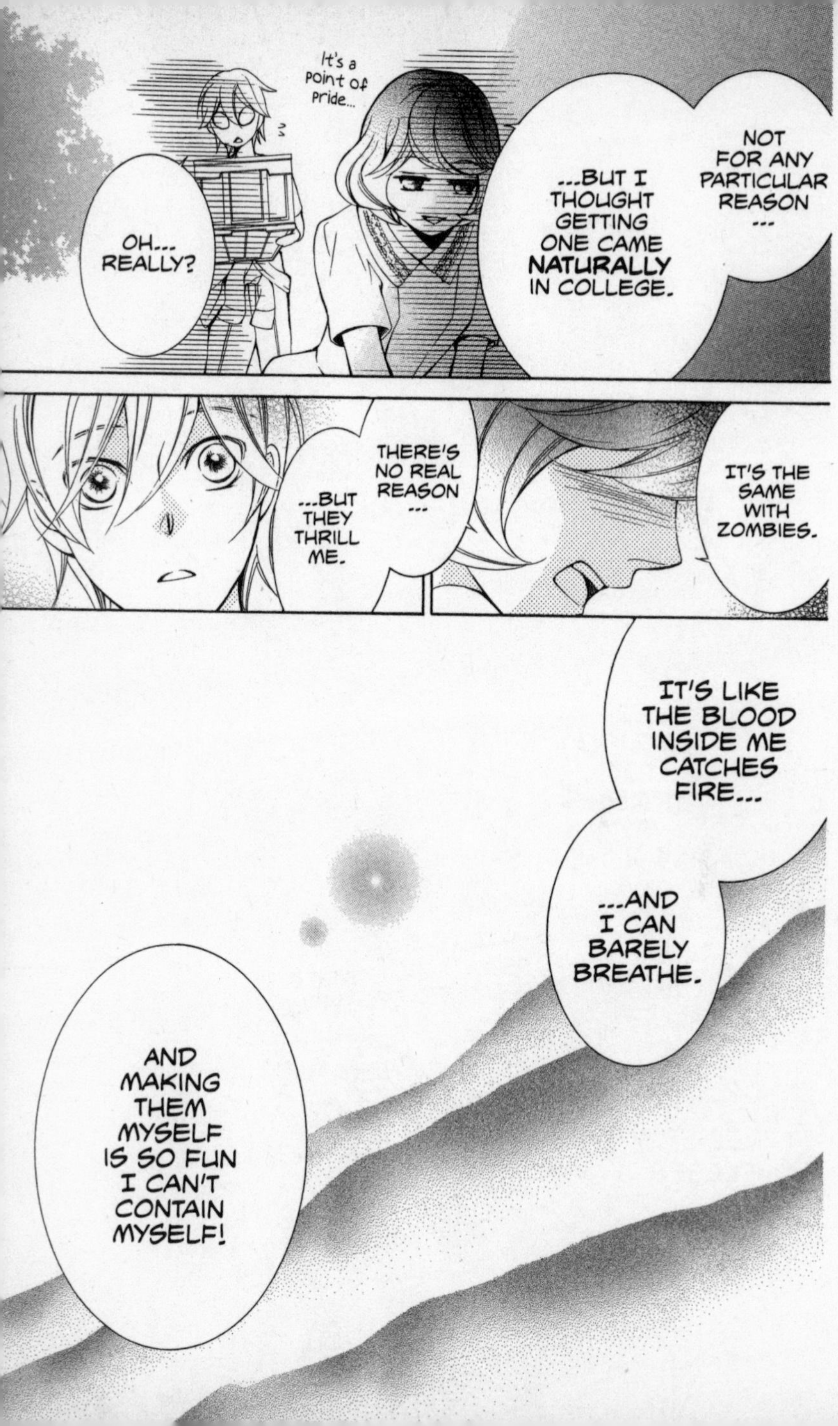
NOT FOR ANY PARTICULAR REASON...
...BUT I THOUGHT GETTING ONE CAME NATURALLY IN COLLEGE.
It's a point of pride...
OH... REALLY?
IT'S THE SAME WITH ZOMBIES.
THERE'S NO REAL REASON...
...BUT THEY THRILL ME.
IT'S LIKE THE BLOOD INSIDE ME CATCHES FIRE...
...AND I CAN BARELY BREATHE.
AND MAKING THEM MYSELF IS SO FUN I CAN'T CONTAIN MYSELF!

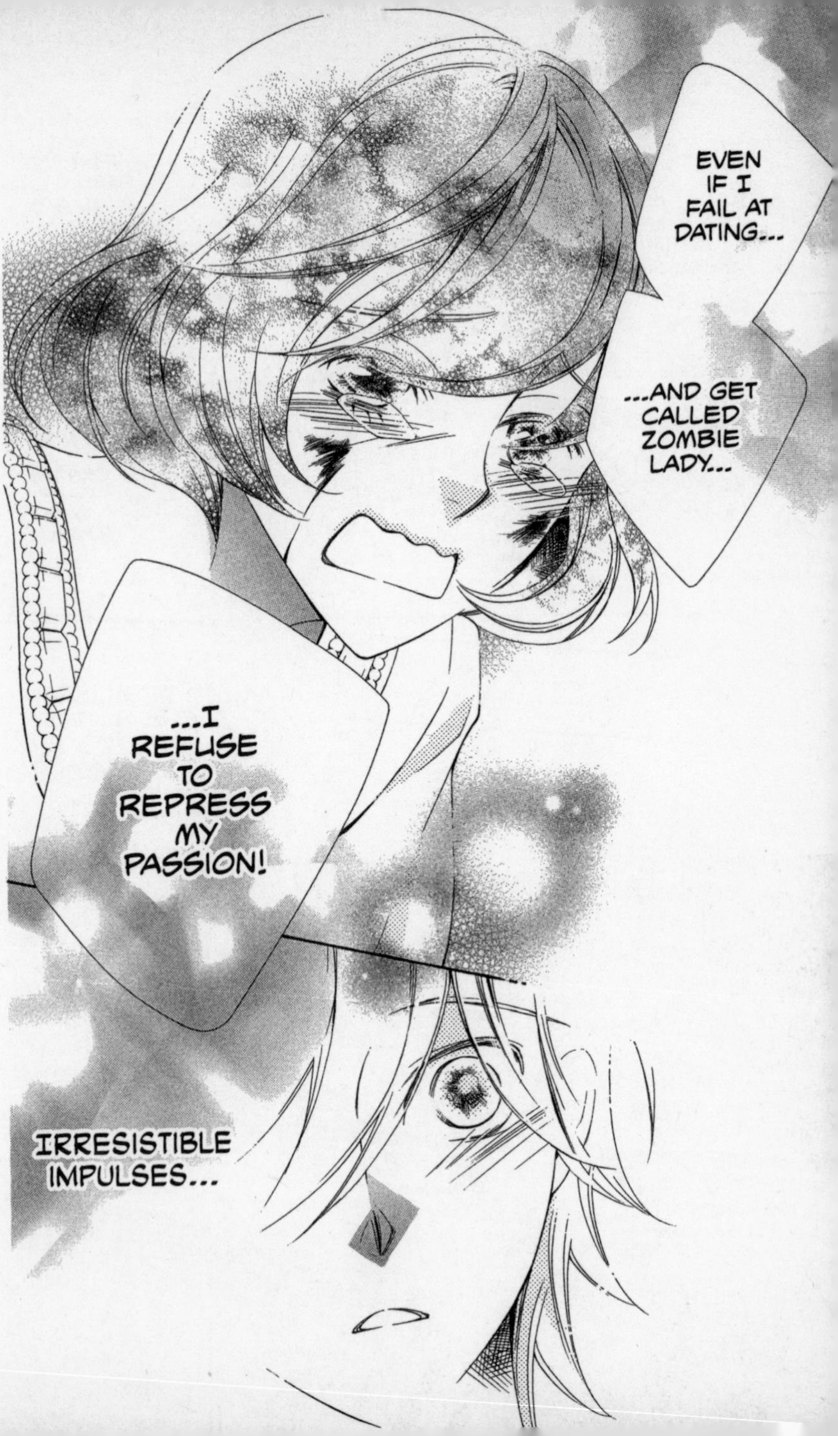
EVEN IF I FAIL AT DATING...
...AND GET CALLED ZOMBIE LADY...
...I REFUSE TO REPRESS MY PASSION!
IRRESISTIBLE IMPULSES...

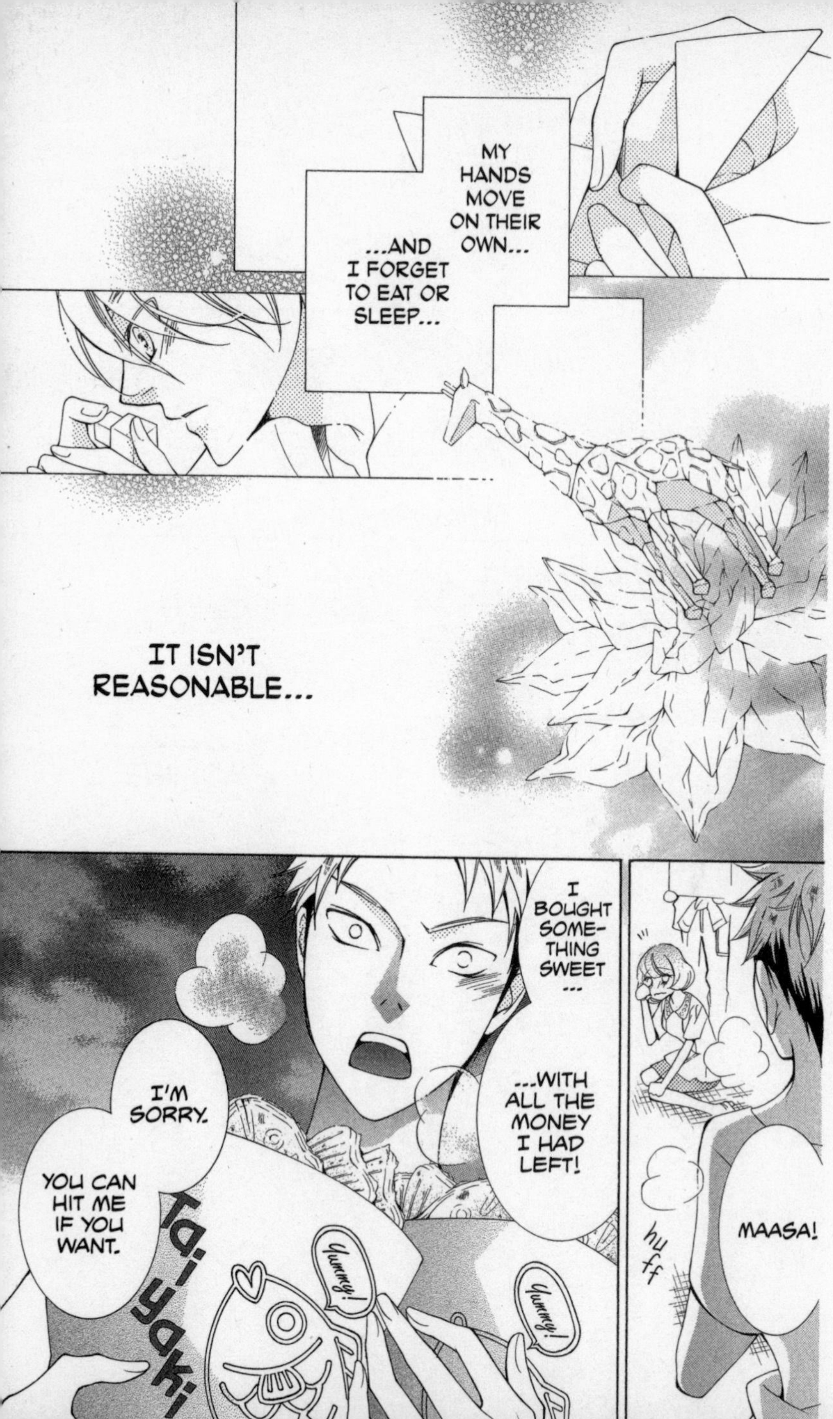
MY HANDS MOVE ON THEIR OWN...
...AND I FORGET TO EAT OR SLEEP...
IT ISN'T REASONABLE...
huff
MAASA!
I BOUGHT SOMETHING SWEET...
...WITH ALL THE MONEY I HAD LEFT!
I'M SORRY.
YOU CAN HIT ME IF YOU WANT.
Taiyaki
Yummy!
Yummy!

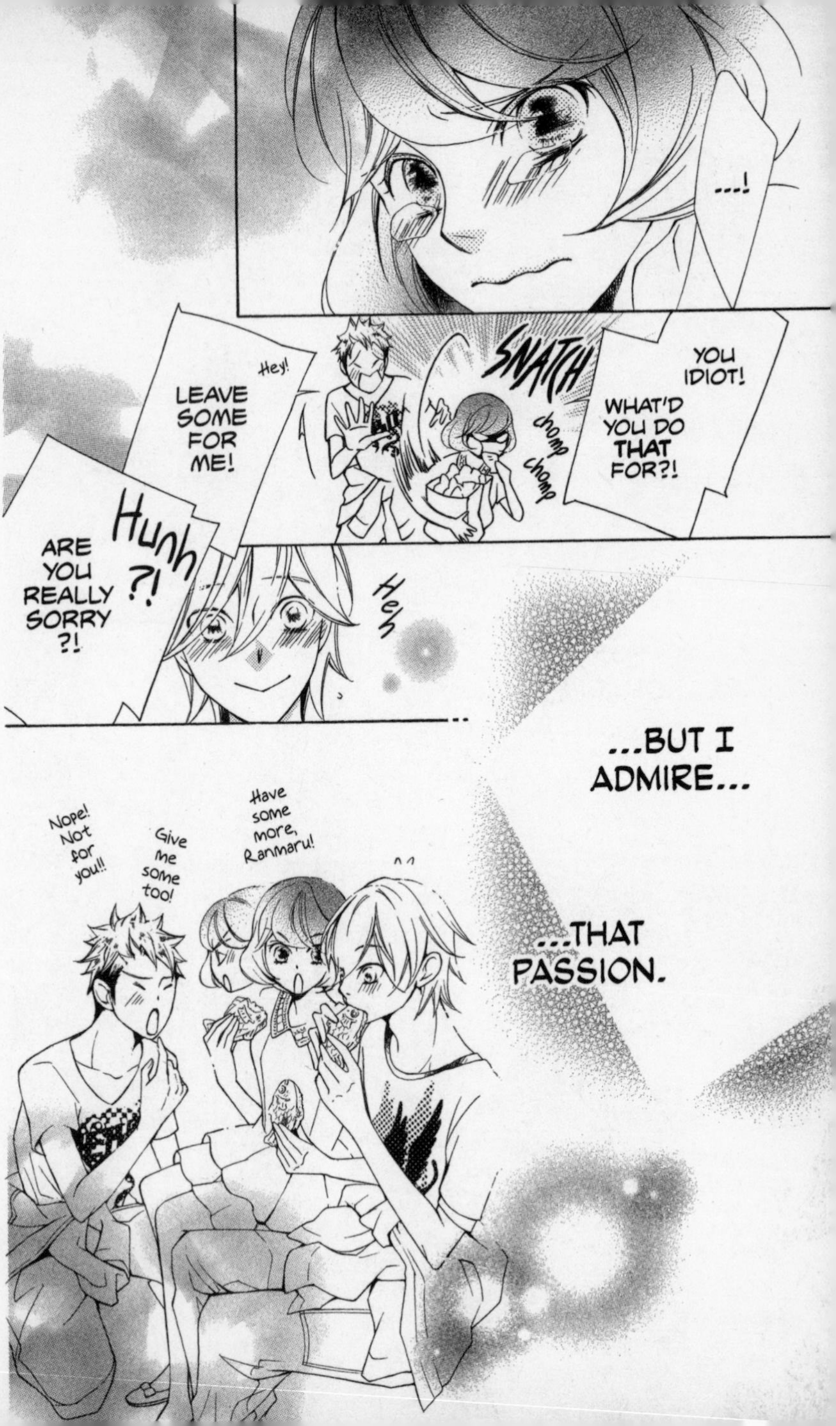
...!
YOU IDIOT! WHAT'D YOU DO THAT FOR?!
SNATCH
chomp chomp
Hey!
LEAVE SOME FOR ME!
Heh
Hunh ?!
ARE YOU REALLY SORRY ?!
...BUT I ADMIRE...
...THAT PASSION.
Have some more, Ranmaru!
Give me some too!
Nope! Not for you!!

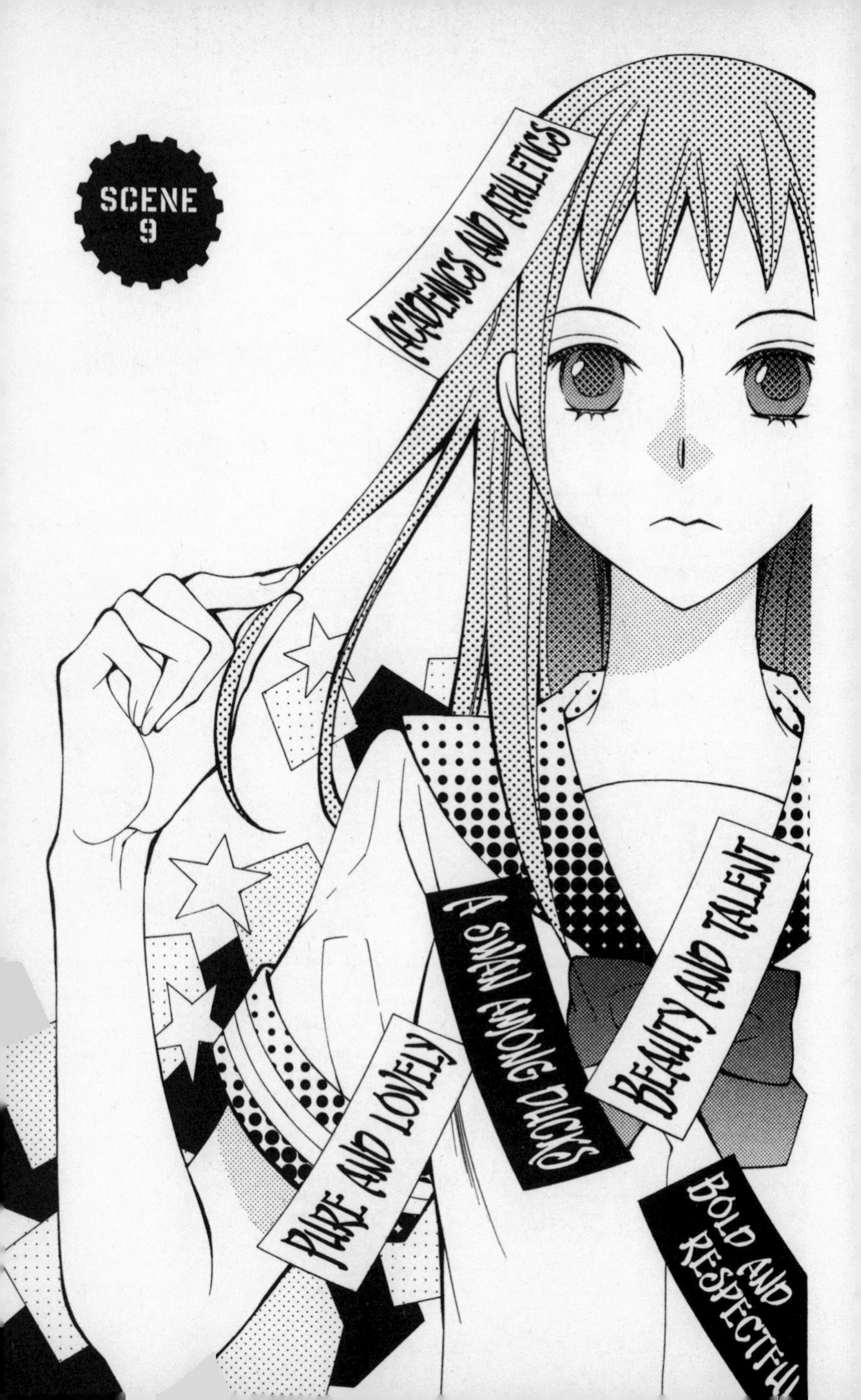
SCENE 9
ACADEMICS AND ATHLETICS
BEAUTY AND TALENT
A SWAN AMONG DUCKS
PURE AND LOVELY
BOLD AND RESPECTFUL

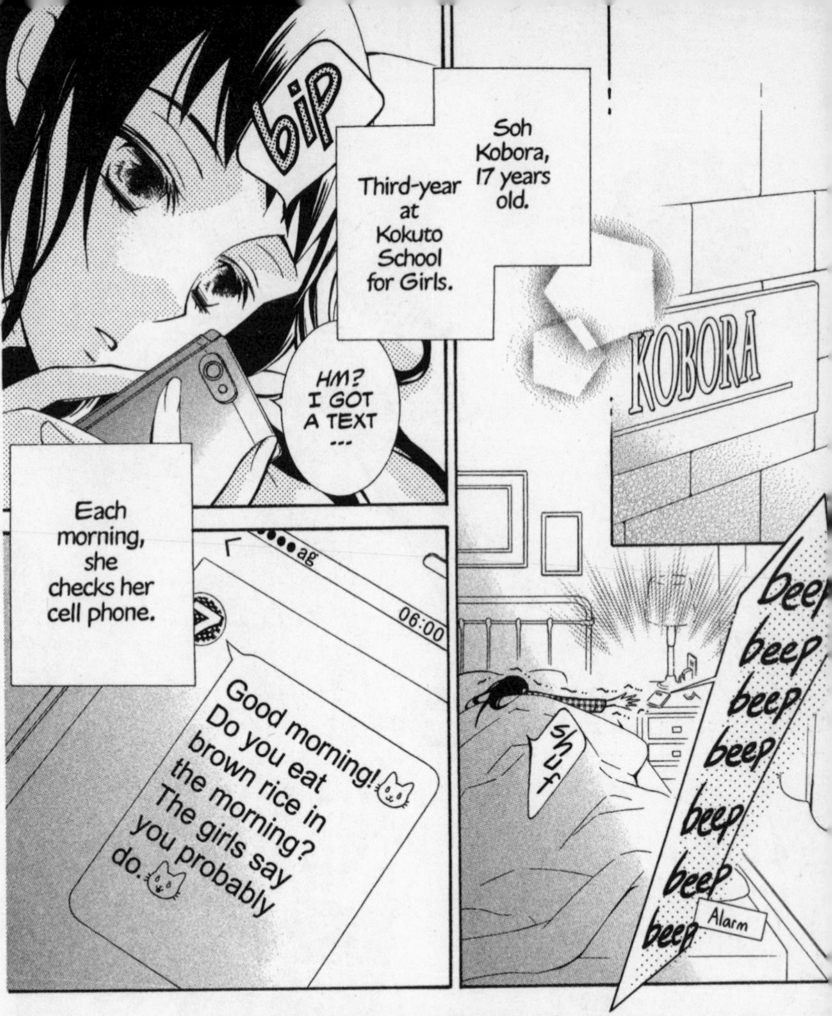
KOBORA
beep beep beep beep beep beep beep
Alarm
shuf
bip
Soh Kobora, 17 years old.
Third-year at Kokuto School for Girls.
HM? I GOT A TEXT ...
Each morning, she checks her cell phone.
06:00
Good morning! Do you eat brown rice in the morning? The girls say you probably do.

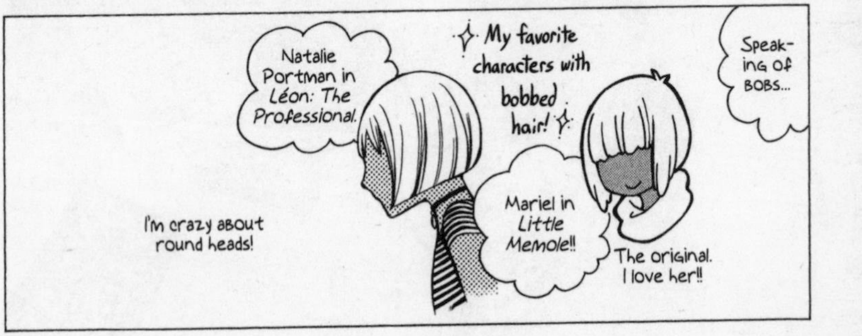
Speak-ing of BOBS...
My favorite characters with bobbed hair!
The original. I love her!!
Mariel in Little Memole!!
Natalie Portman in Léon: The Professional.
I'm crazy about round heads!

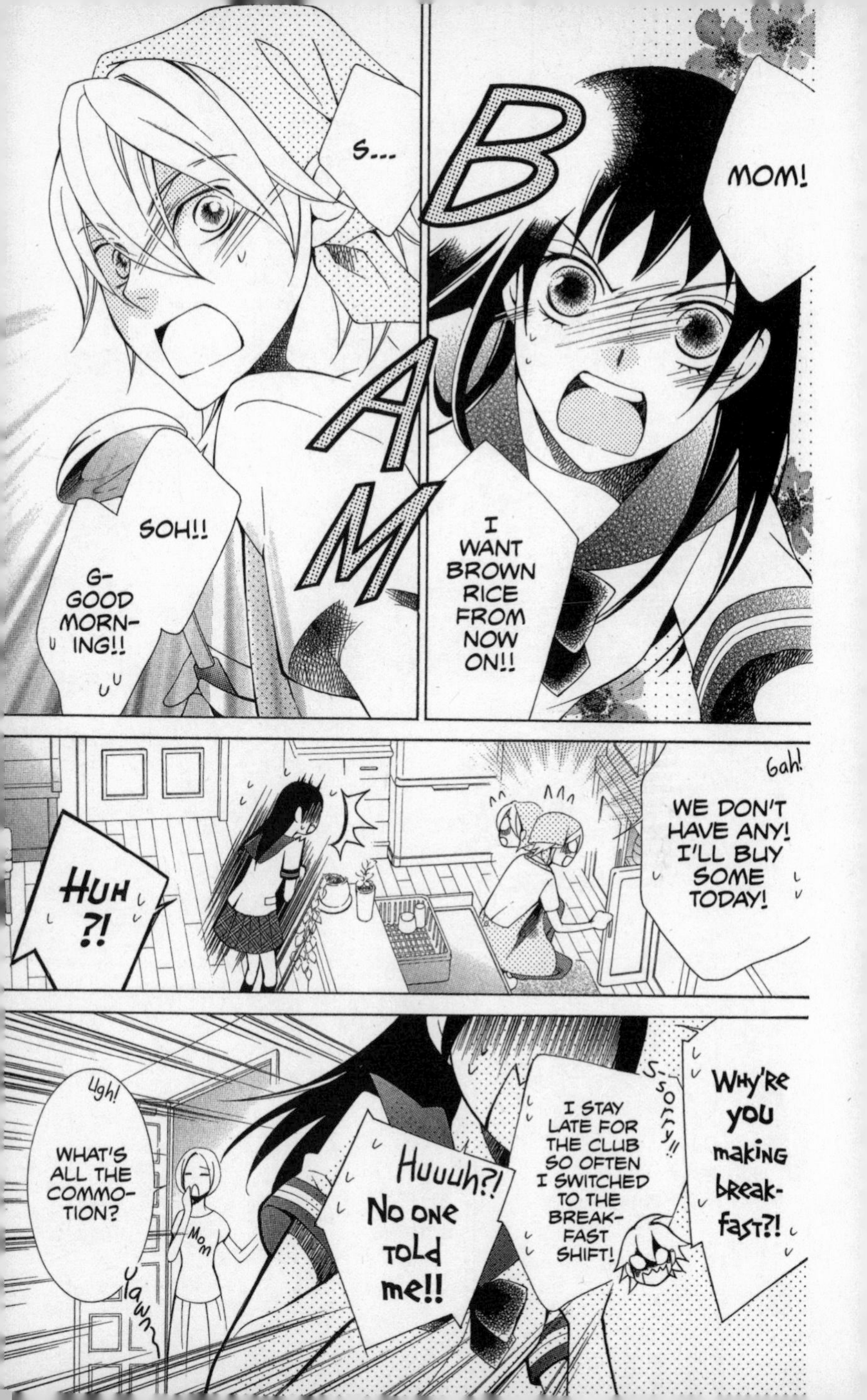
MOM!
BAM
I WANT BROWN RICE FROM NOW ON!!
S...
SOH!!
G-GOOD MORNING!!
Gah!
WE DON'T HAVE ANY! I'LL BUY SOME TODAY!
HUH?!
Why're you making break-fast?!
S-sorry!!
I STAY LATE FOR THE CLUB SO OFTEN I SWITCHED TO THE BREAK-FAST SHIFT!
Huuuh?! No one told me!!
Ugh!
WHAT'S ALL THE COMMO-TION?
Mom
Yawn

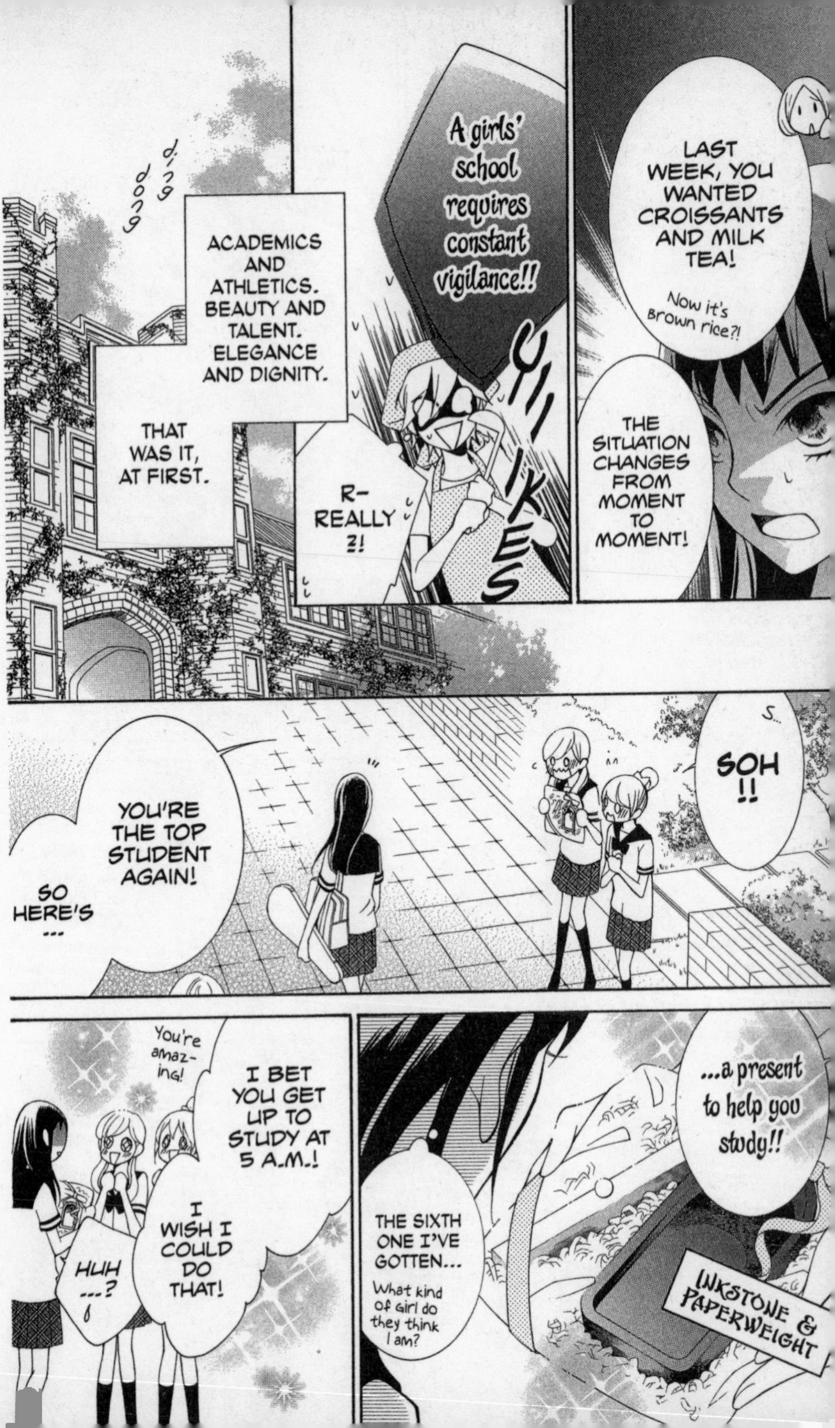
LAST WEEK, YOU WANTED CROISSANTS AND MILK TEA!
Now it's brown rice?!
THE SITUATION CHANGES FROM MOMENT TO MOMENT!
A girls' school requires constant vigilance!!
YIIIKES
R-REALLY?!
ding dong
ACADEMICS AND ATHLETICS. BEAUTY AND TALENT. ELEGANCE AND DIGNITY.
THAT WAS IT, AT FIRST.
S...
SOH!!
YOU'RE THE TOP STUDENT AGAIN!
SO HERE'S...
...a present to help you study!!
INKSTONE & PAPERWEIGHT
THE SIXTH ONE I'VE GOTTEN...
What kind of girl do they think I am?
You're amazing!
I BET YOU GET UP TO STUDY AT 5 A.M.!
I WISH I COULD DO THAT!
HUH...?

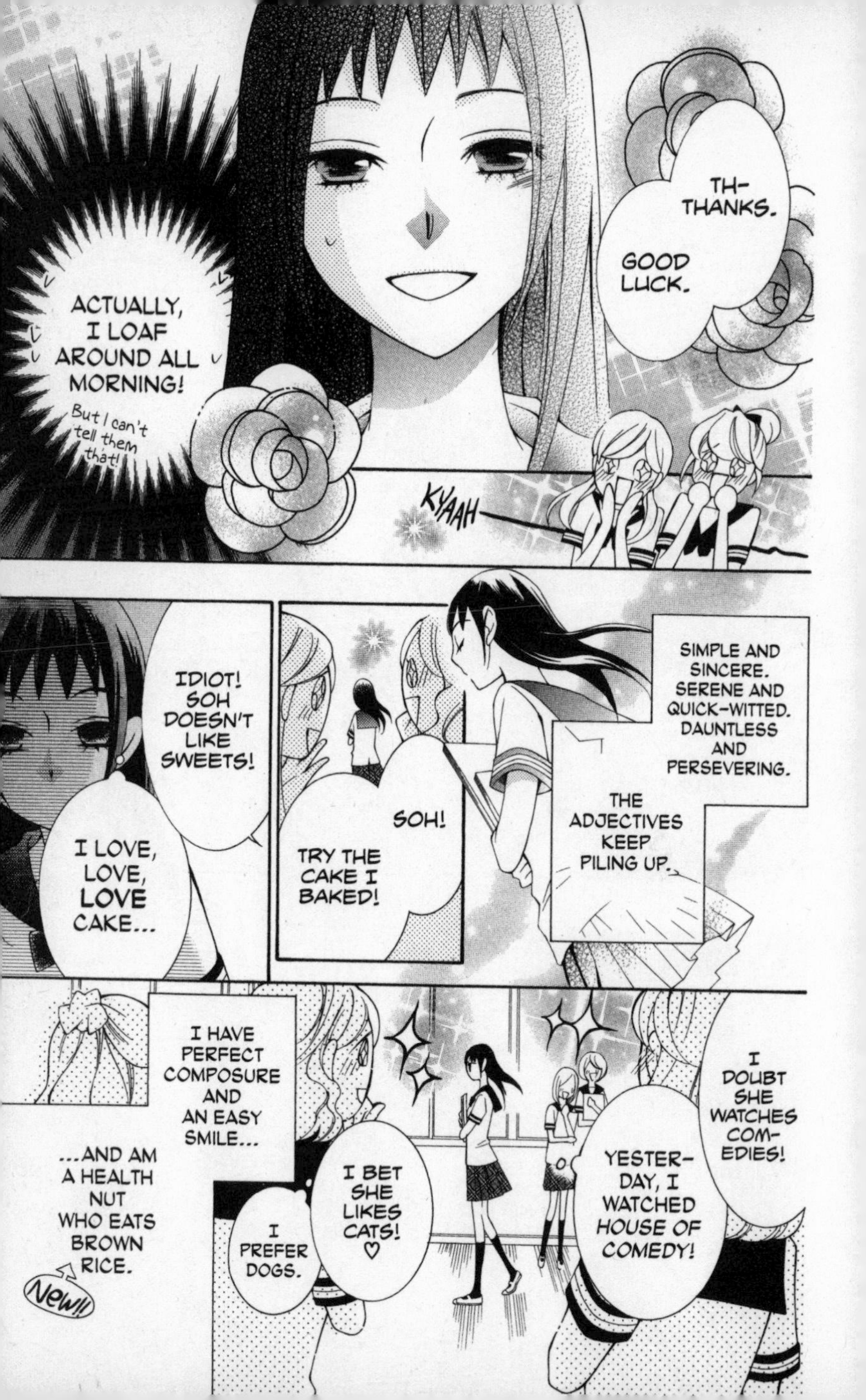
TH-THANKS.
GOOD LUCK.
KYAAH
ACTUALLY, I LOAF AROUND ALL MORNING!
But I can't tell them that!
SIMPLE AND SINCERE. SERENE AND QUICK-WITTED. DAUNTLESS AND PERSEVERING.
THE ADJECTIVES KEEP PILING UP.
SOH!
TRY THE CAKE I BAKED!
IDIOT! SOH DOESN'T LIKE SWEETS!
I LOVE, LOVE, LOVE CAKE...
I DOUBT SHE WATCHES COM-EDIES!
YESTER-DAY, I WATCHED HOUSE OF COMEDY!
I BET SHE LIKES CATS! ♡
I PREFER DOGS.
I HAVE PERFECT COMPOSURE AND AN EASY SMILE...
...AND AM A HEALTH NUT WHO EATS BROWN RICE.
New!!

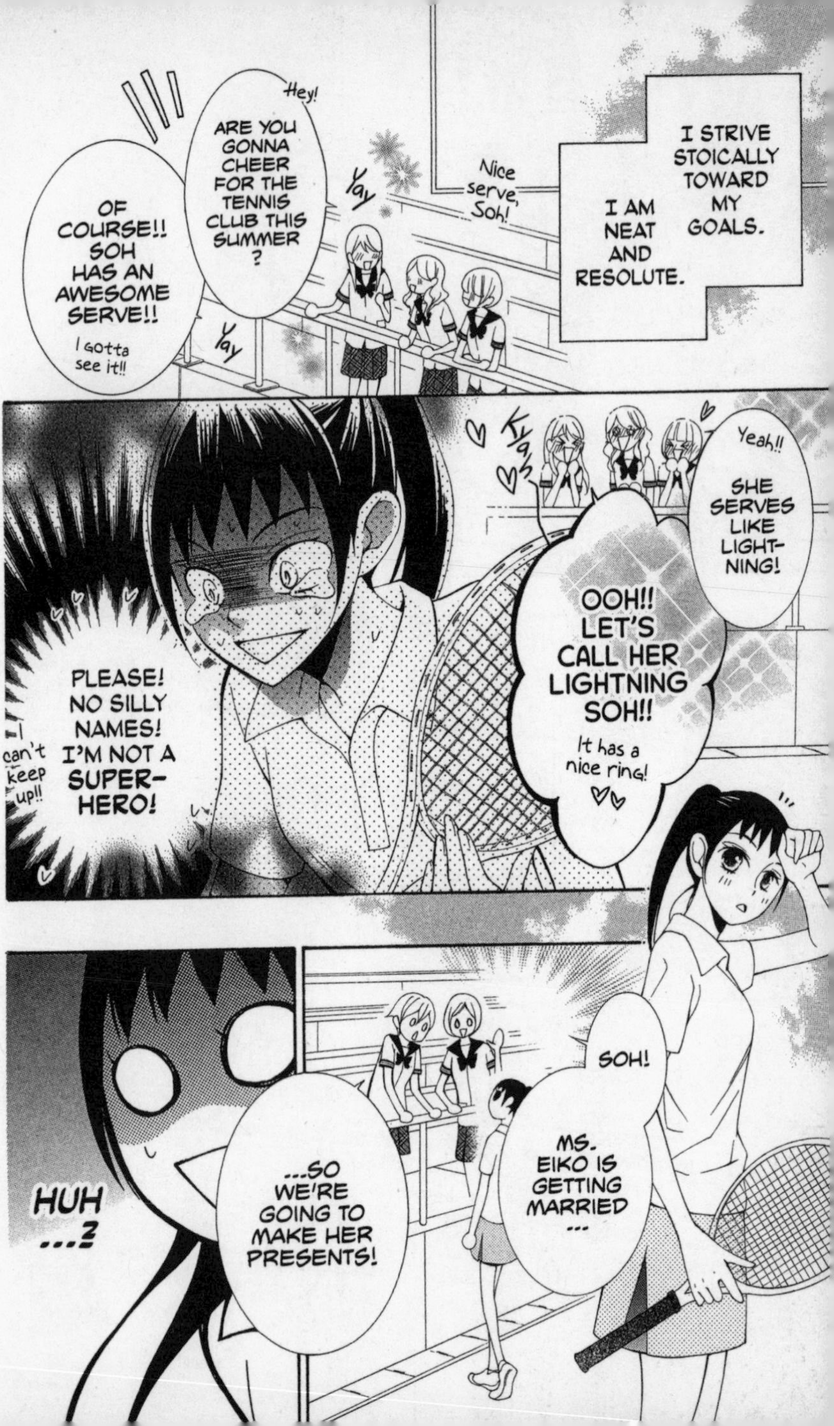
I STRIVE STOICALLY TOWARD MY GOALS.
I AM NEAT AND RESOLUTE.
Nice serve, Soh!
Yay
Hey!
ARE YOU GONNA CHEER FOR THE TENNIS CLUB THIS SUMMER?
Yay
OF COURSE!! SOH HAS AN AWESOME SERVE!!
I gotta see it!!
Yeah!!
SHE SERVES LIKE LIGHT-NING!
Kyah
OOH!! LET'S CALL HER LIGHTNING SOH!!
It has a nice ring!
PLEASE! NO SILLY NAMES! I'M NOT A SUPER-HERO!
I can't keep up!!
SOH!
MS. EIKO IS GETTING MARRIED...
...SO WE'RE GOING TO MAKE HER PRESENTS!
HUH...?

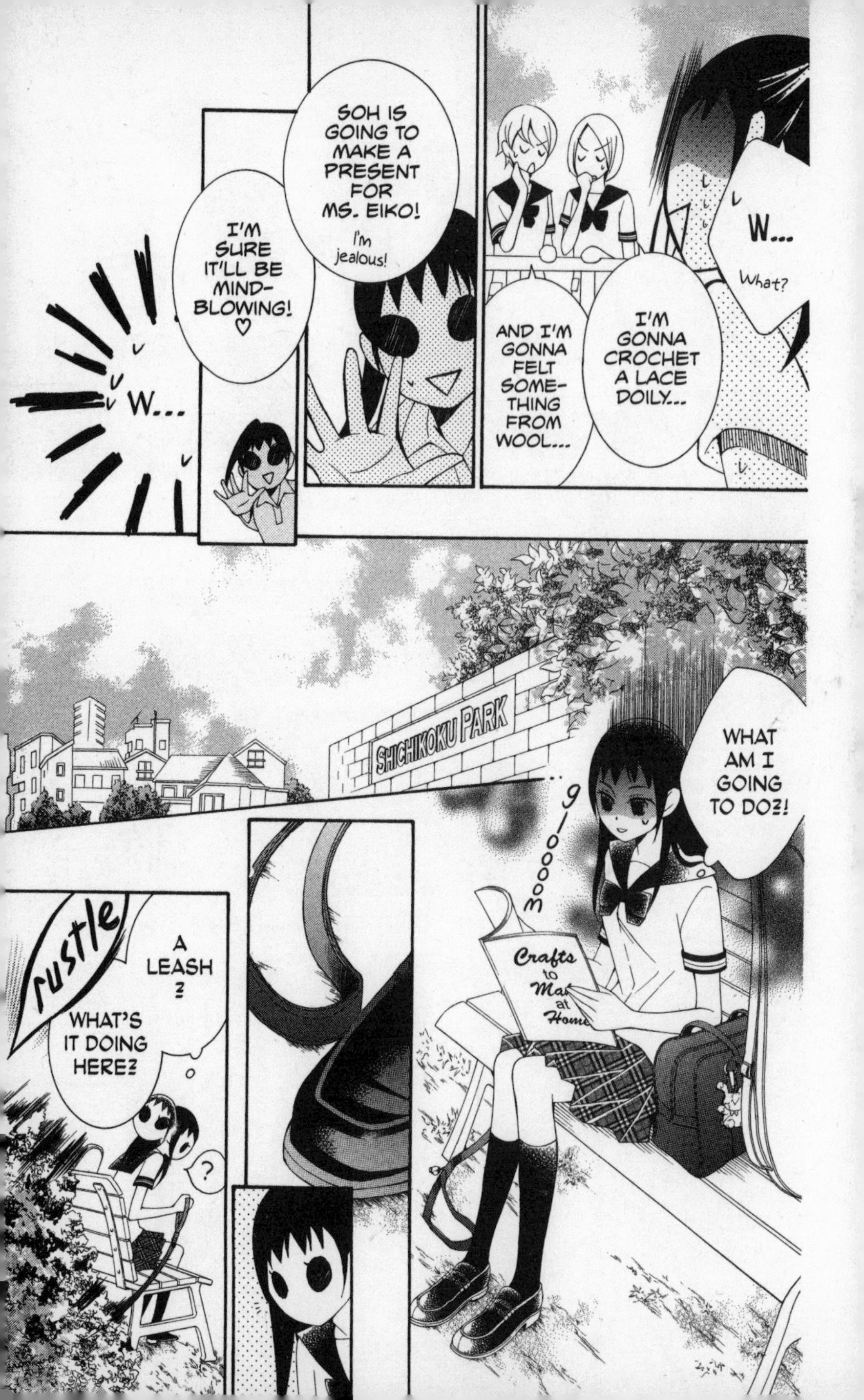
W...
What?
I'M GONNA CROCHET A LACE DOILY...
AND I'M GONNA FELT SOMETHING FROM WOOL...
SOH IS GOING TO MAKE A PRESENT FOR MS. EIKO!
I'm jealous!
I'M SURE IT'LL BE MIND-BLOWING! ♡
W...
SHICHIKOKU PARK
WHAT AM I GOING TO DO?!
gloooom
Crafts to Ma... at Home
rustle
A LEASH?
WHAT'S IT DOING HERE?
?

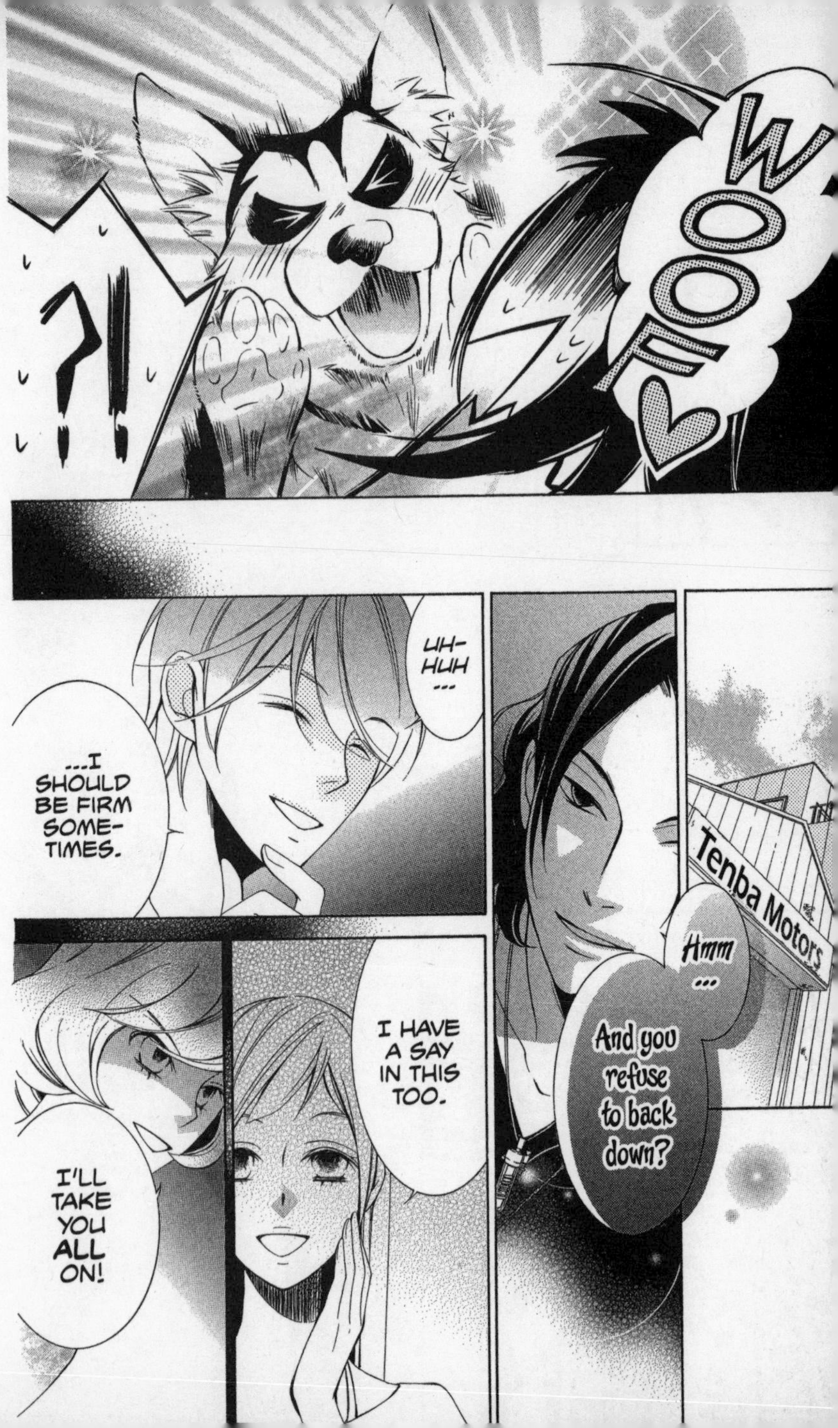
WOOF♥
?!!
Tenba Motors
Hmm...
And you refuse to back down?
UH-HUH...
...I SHOULD BE FIRM SOME-TIMES.
I HAVE A SAY IN THIS TOO.
I'LL TAKE YOU ALL ON!

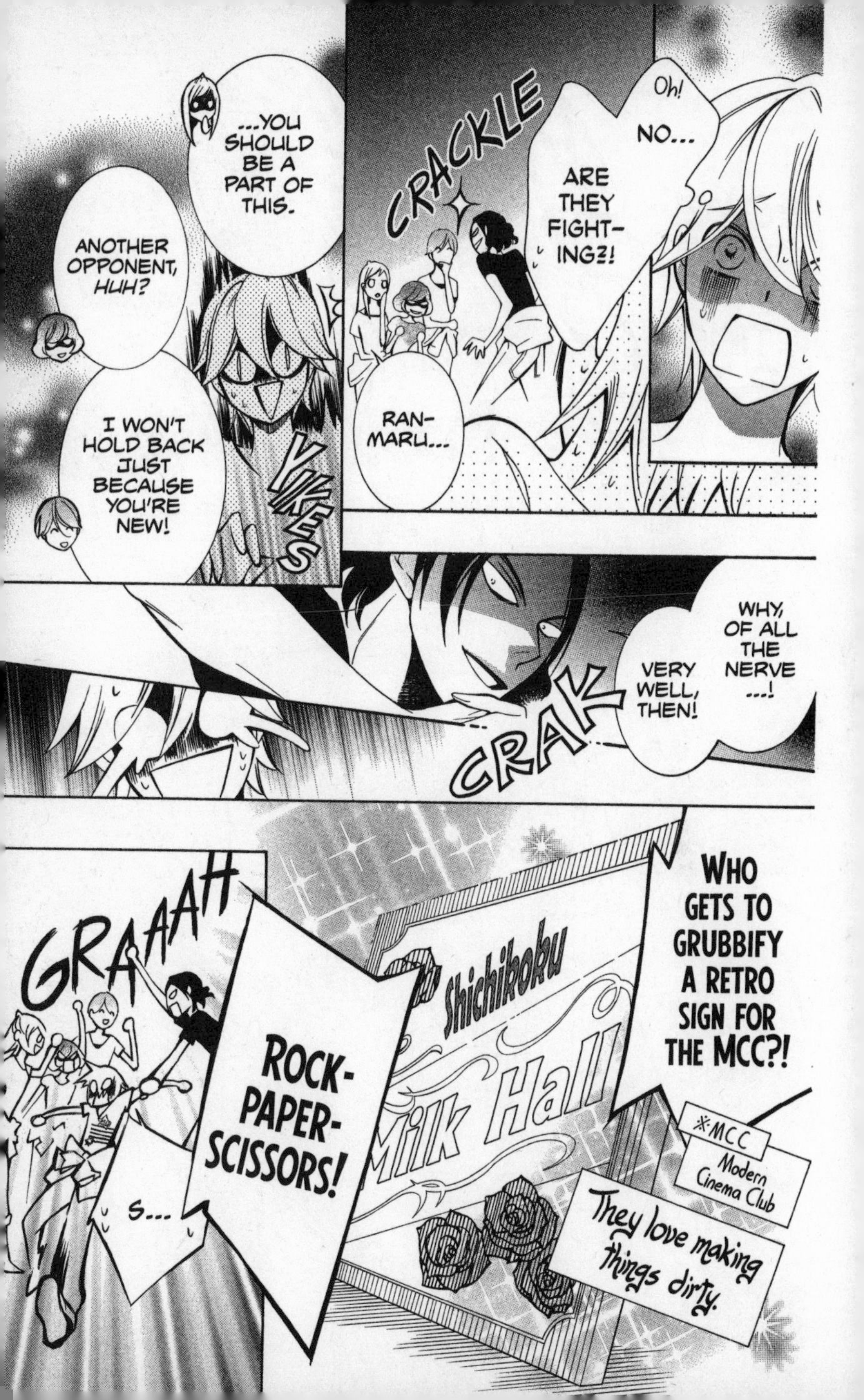
Oh!
NO...
ARE THEY FIGHTING?!
CRACKLE
RAN-MARU...
...YOU SHOULD BE A PART OF THIS.
ANOTHER OPPONENT, HUH?
YIKES
I WON'T HOLD BACK JUST BECAUSE YOU'RE NEW!
WHY, OF ALL THE NERVE...!
VERY WELL, THEN!
CRAK
WHO GETS TO GRUBBIFY A RETRO SIGN FOR THE MCC?!
※MCC
Modern Cinema Club
They love making things dirty.
Shichibroku
Milk Hall
ROCK-PAPER-SCISSORS!
S...
GRAAAH

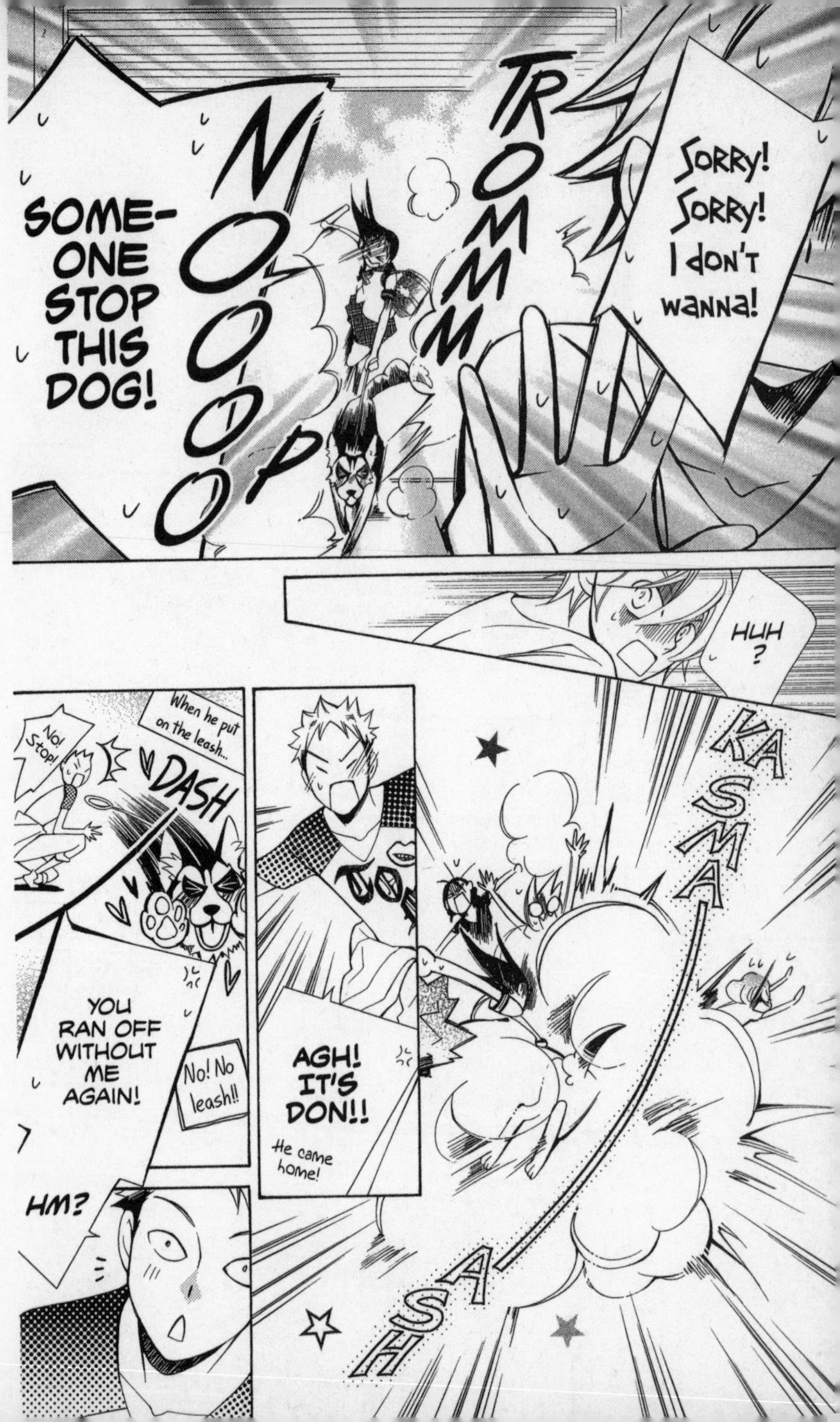
Sorry! Sorry! I don't wanna!
TROMMM
NOOOOOO
SOME-ONE STOP THIS DOG!
HUH?
KASMA
ASH
AGH! IT'S DON!!
He came home!
When he put on the leash...
No! Stop!
DASH
YOU RAN OFF WITHOUT ME AGAIN!
No! No leash!!
HM?

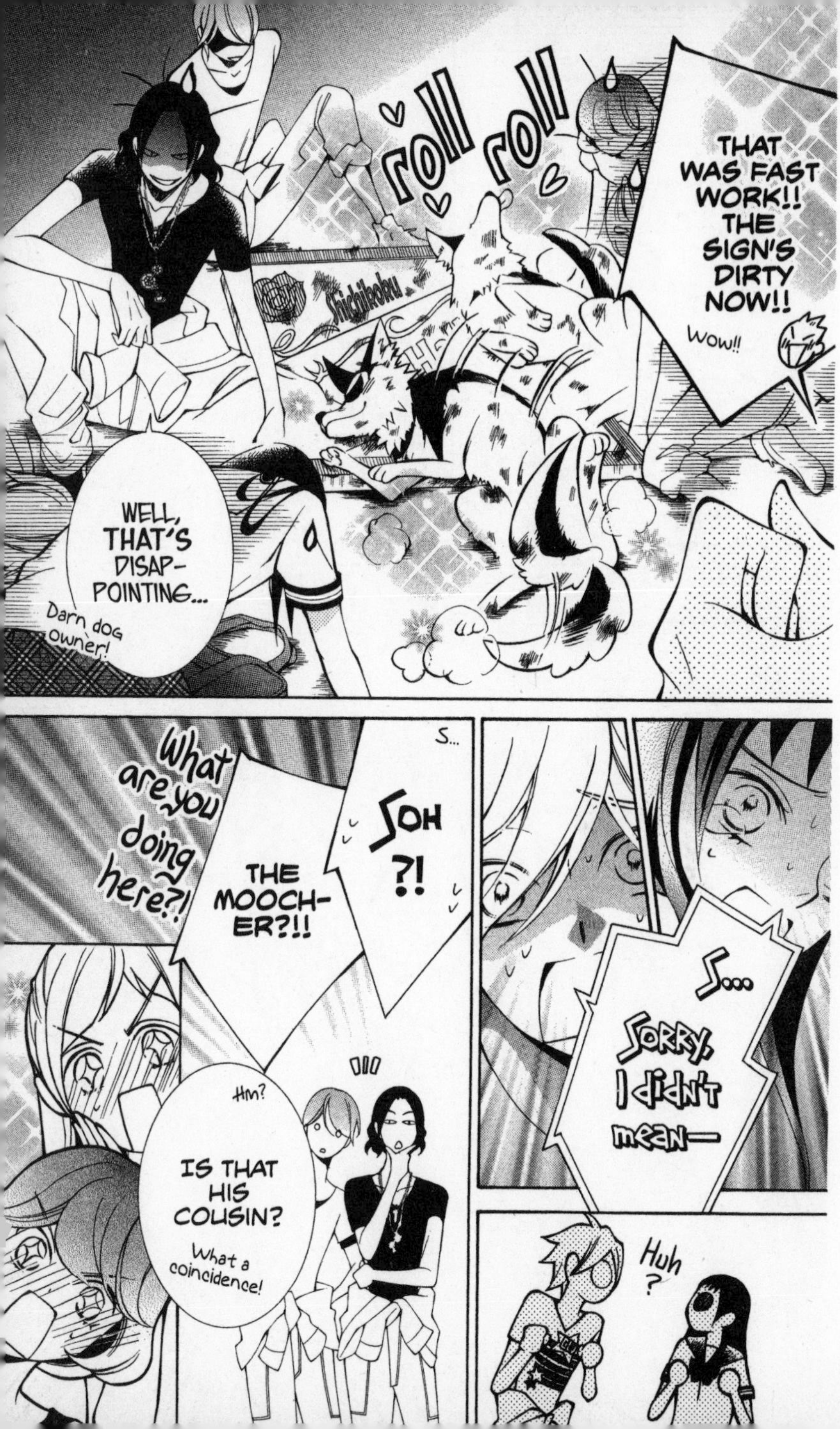

THAT WAS FAST WORK!! THE SIGN'S DIRTY NOW!!
Wow!!
roll roll
Shichikoku
WELL, THAT'S DISAPPOINTING...
Darn dog owner!
S...
SORRY, I didn't mean—
S...
SOH ?!
THE MOOCHER?!!
What are you doing here?!
Hm?
IS THAT HIS COUSIN?
What a coincidence!
Huh ?

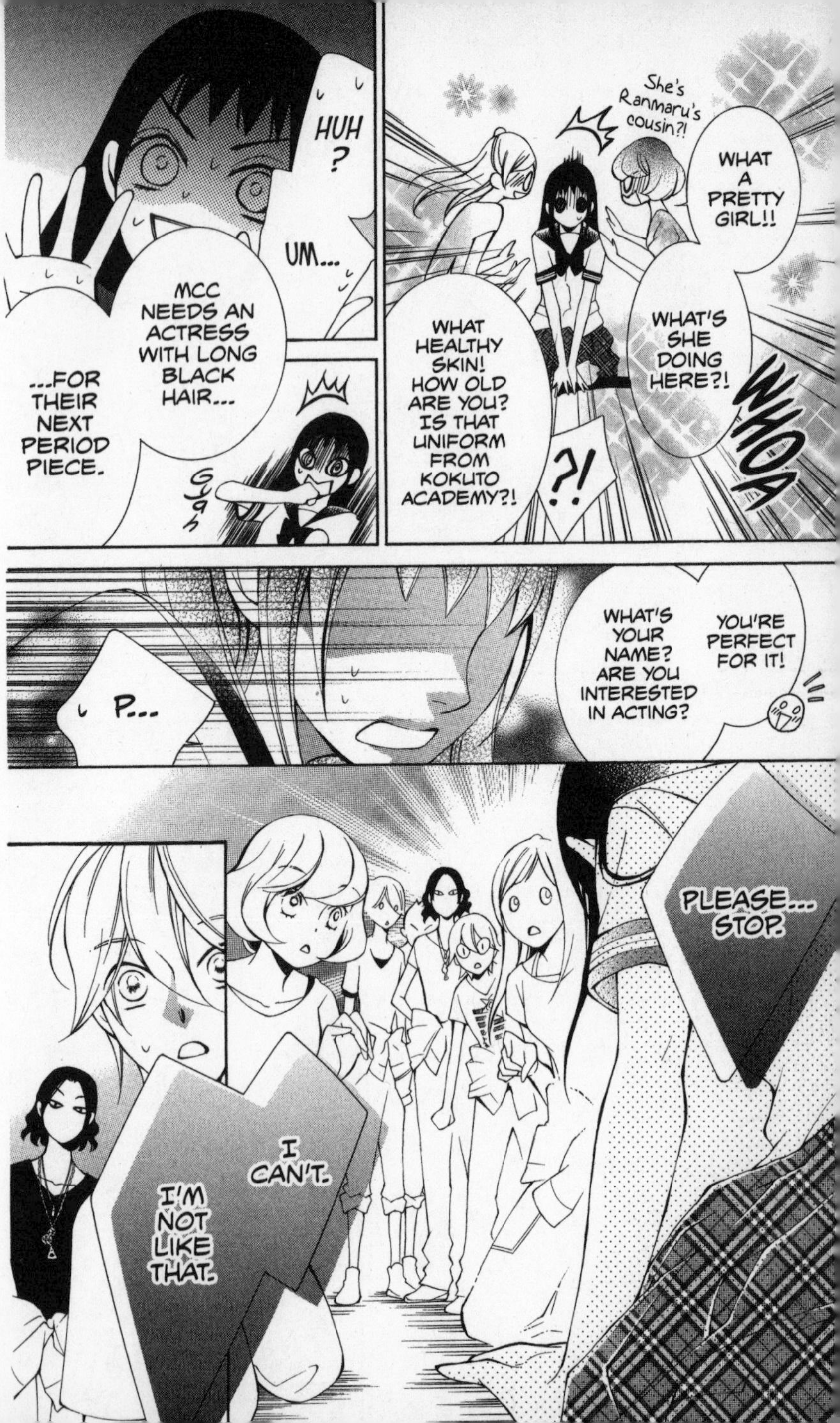
She's Ranmaru's cousin?!
WHAT A PRETTY GIRL!!
WHAT'S SHE DOING HERE?!
WHOA
WHAT HEALTHY SKIN! HOW OLD ARE YOU? IS THAT UNIFORM FROM KOKUTO ACADEMY?!
?!
HUH?
UM...
MCC NEEDS AN ACTRESS WITH LONG BLACK HAIR...
...FOR THEIR NEXT PERIOD PIECE.
Gyah
YOU'RE PERFECT FOR IT!
WHAT'S YOUR NAME? ARE YOU INTERESTED IN ACTING?
P...
PLEASE... STOP.
I CAN'T.
I'M NOT LIKE THAT.

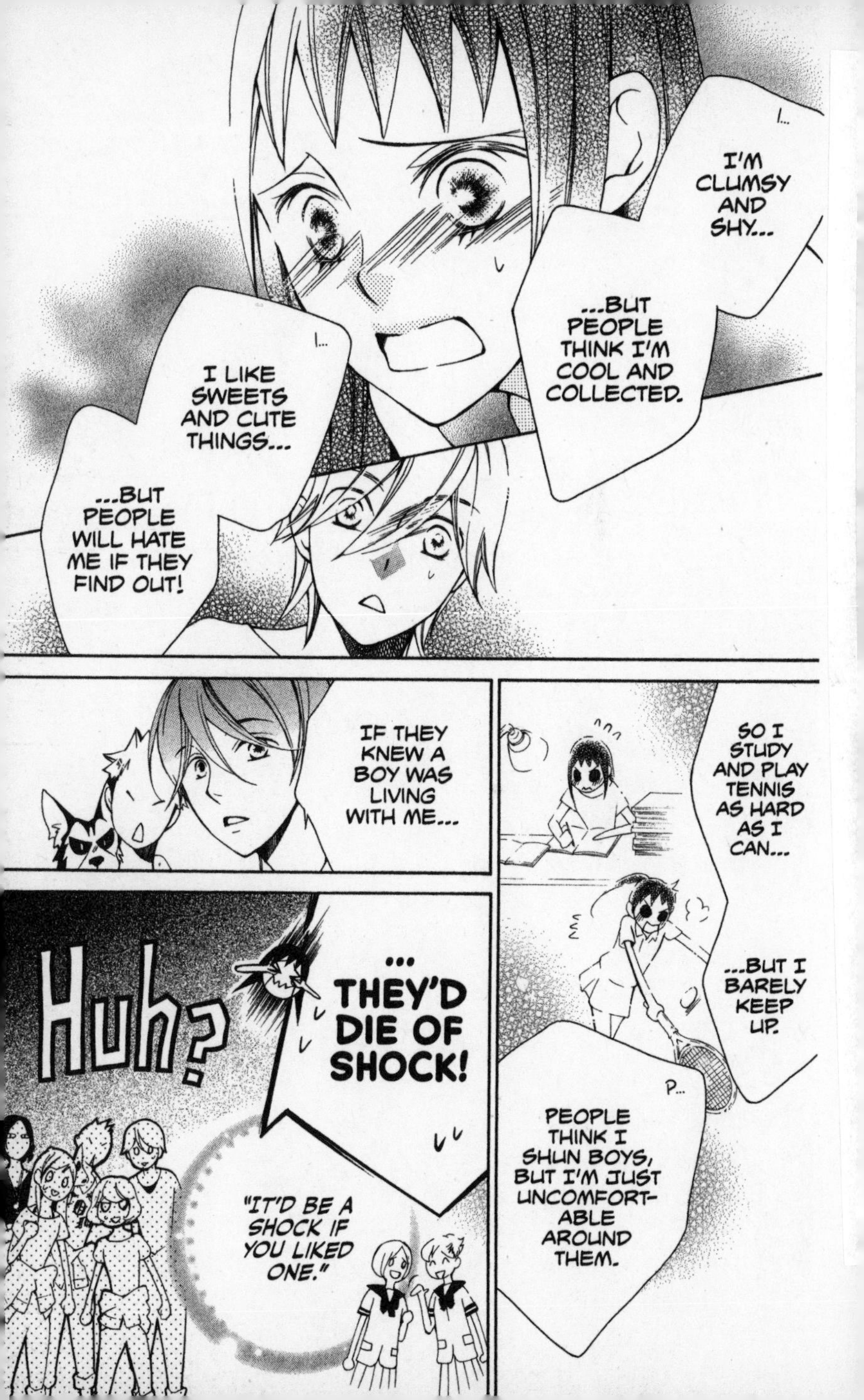
I...
I'M CLUMSY AND SHY...
...BUT PEOPLE THINK I'M COOL AND COLLECTED.
I...
I LIKE SWEETS AND CUTE THINGS...
...BUT PEOPLE WILL HATE ME IF THEY FIND OUT!
SO I STUDY AND PLAY TENNIS AS HARD AS I CAN...
...BUT I BARELY KEEP UP.
P...
PEOPLE THINK I SHUN BOYS, BUT I'M JUST UNCOMFORT-ABLE AROUND THEM.
IF THEY KNEW A BOY WAS LIVING WITH ME...
...THEY'D DIE OF SHOCK!
Huh?
"IT'D BE A SHOCK IF YOU LIKED ONE."

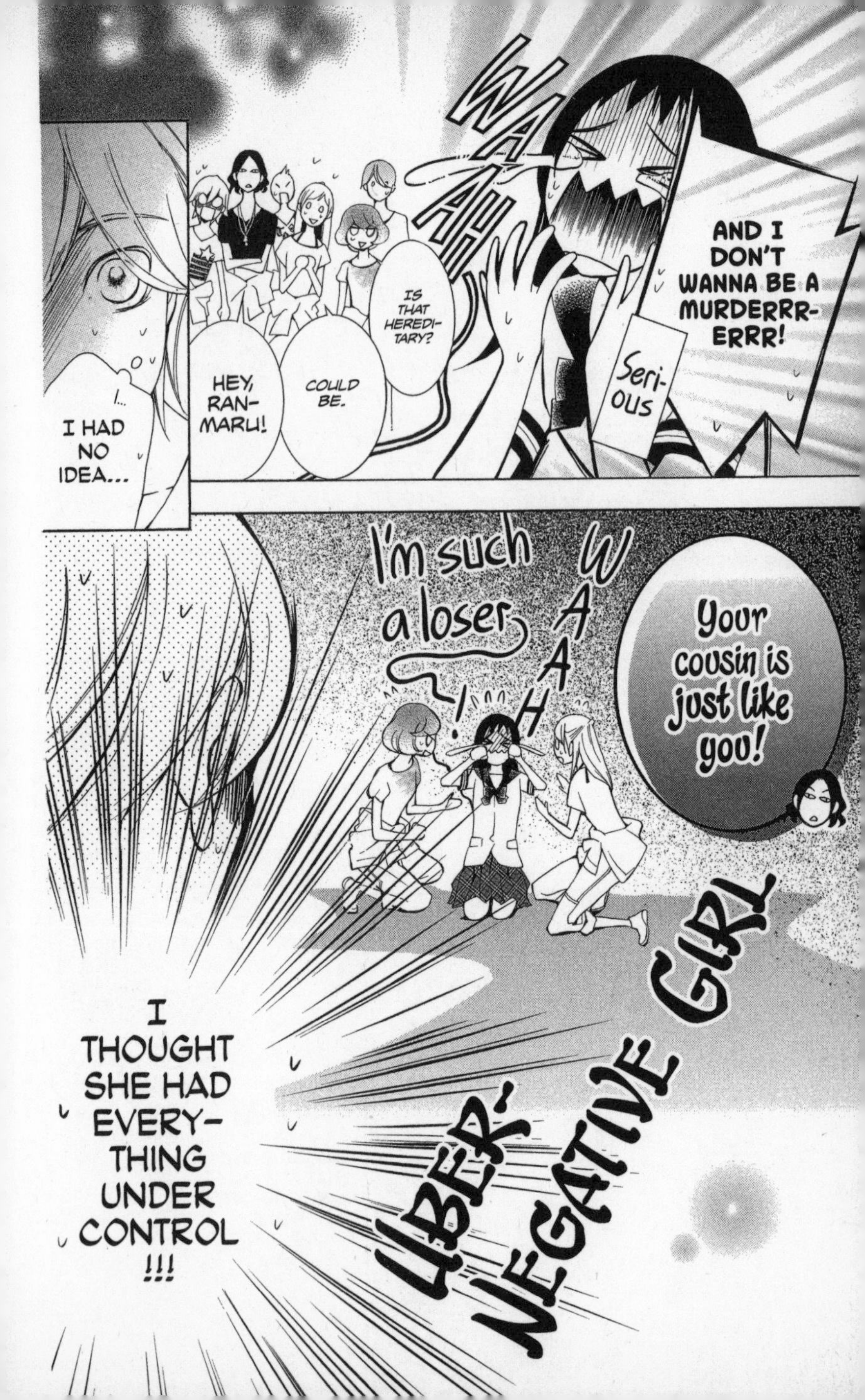
WAAAH
AND I DON'T WANNA BE A MURDERRR-ERRR!
Seri-ous
IS THAT HEREDI-TARY?
COULD BE.
HEY, RAN-MARU!
I... I HAD NO IDEA...
Your cousin is just like you!
WAAH
I'm such a loser!
UBER-NEGATIVE GIRL
I THOUGHT SHE HAD EVERY-THING UNDER CONTROL !!!

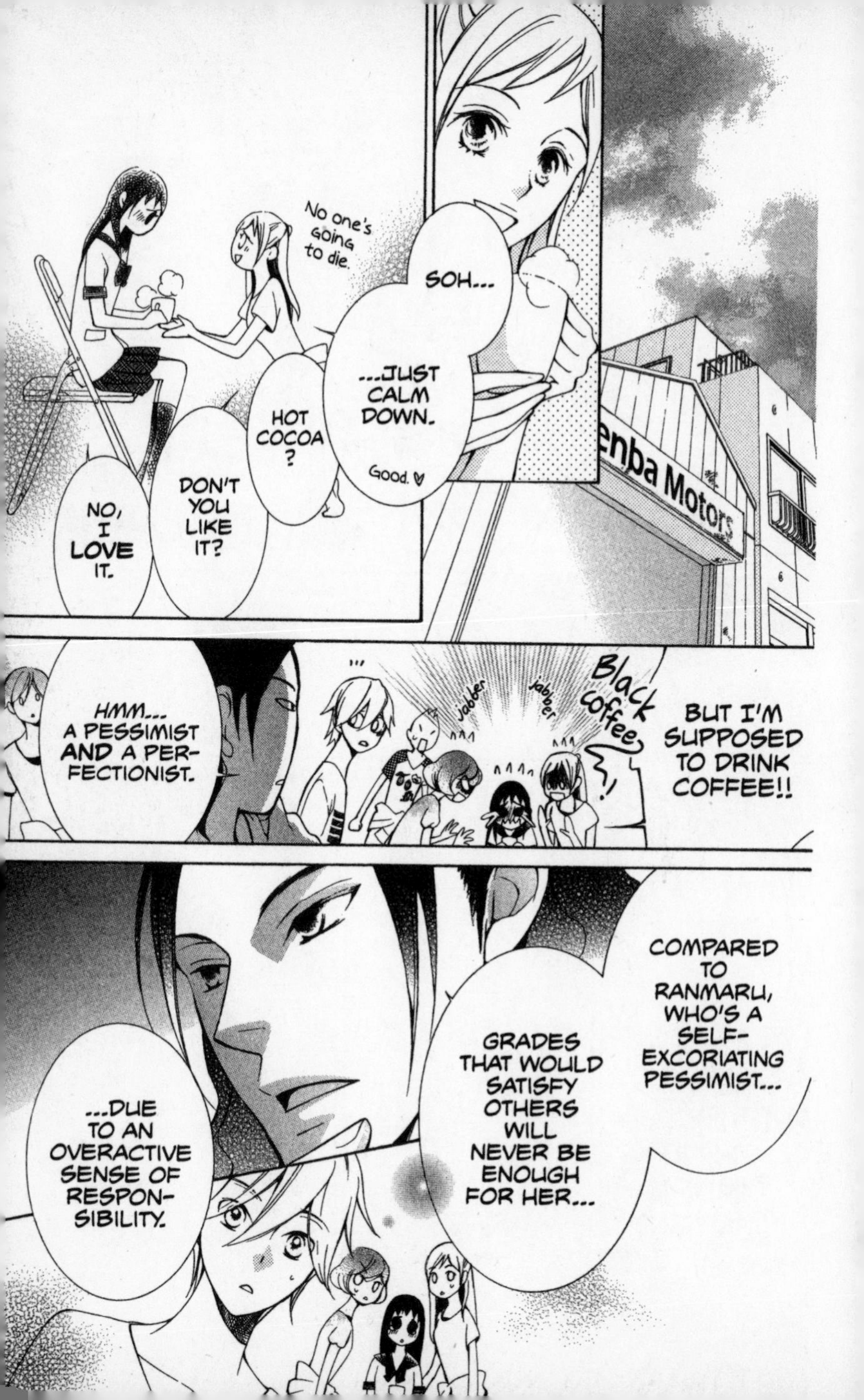
enba Motors
SOH...
...JUST CALM DOWN.
Good. ♥
No one's going to die.
HOT COCOA?
DON'T YOU LIKE IT?
NO, I LOVE IT.
BUT I'M SUPPOSED TO DRINK COFFEE!!
Black coffee
jabber
jabber
HMM... A PESSIMIST AND A PERFECTIONIST.
COMPARED TO RANMARU, WHO'S A SELF-EXCORIATING PESSIMIST...
GRADES THAT WOULD SATISFY OTHERS WILL NEVER BE ENOUGH FOR HER...
...DUE TO AN OVERACTIVE SENSE OF RESPONSIBILITY.

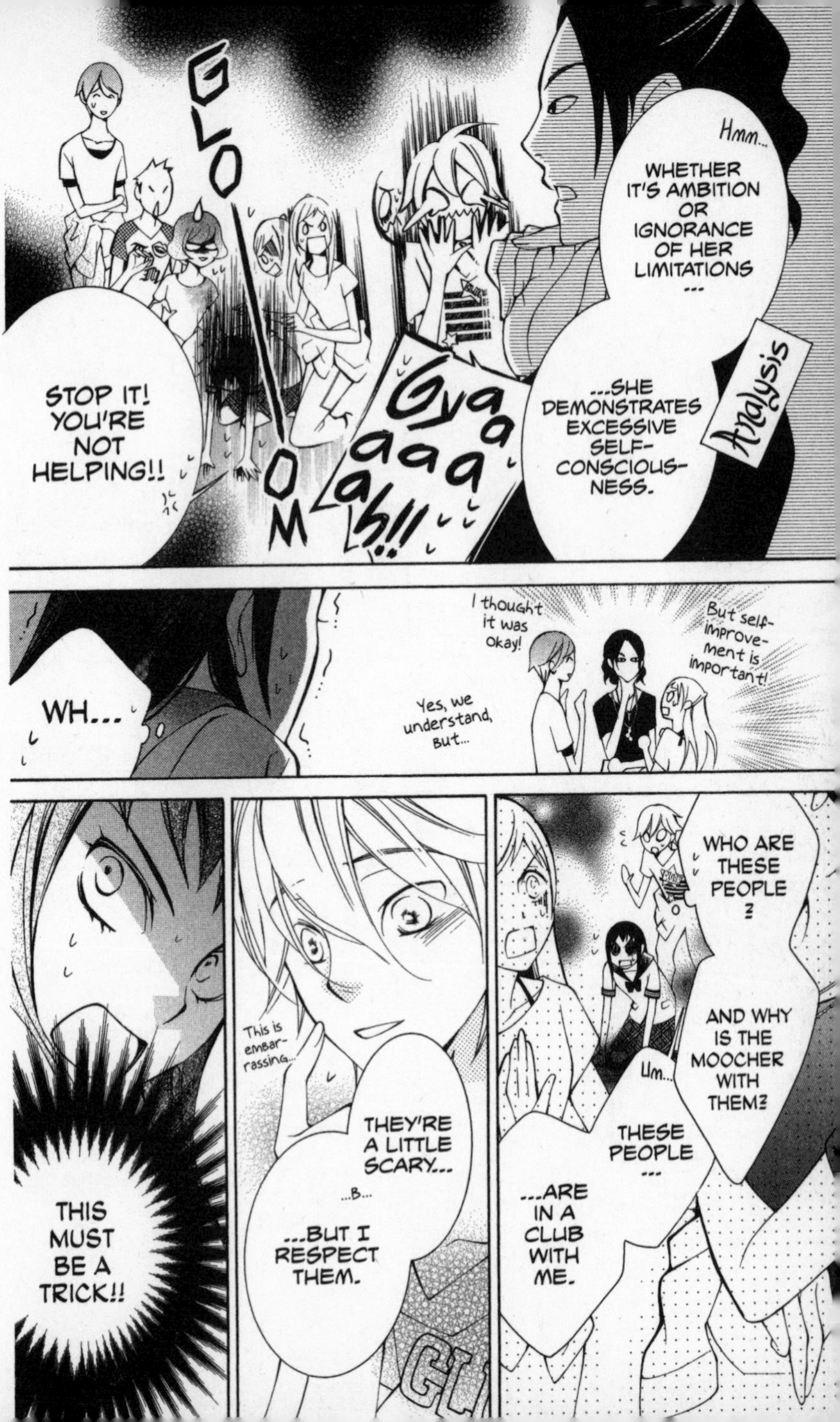
Hmm...
WHETHER IT'S AMBITION OR IGNORANCE OF HER LIMITATIONS...
Analysis
...SHE DEMONSTRATES EXCESSIVE SELF-CONSCIOUSNESS.
Gyaaaaaah!!
GLOOM
STOP IT! YOU'RE NOT HELPING!!
But self-improvement is important!
I thought it was okay!
Yes, we understand, but...
WH...
WHO ARE THESE PEOPLE?
AND WHY IS THE MOOCHER WITH THEM?
Um...
THESE PEOPLE...
...ARE IN A CLUB WITH ME.
This is embarrassing...
THEY'RE A LITTLE SCARY...
...B...
...BUT I RESPECT THEM.
THIS MUST BE A TRICK!!

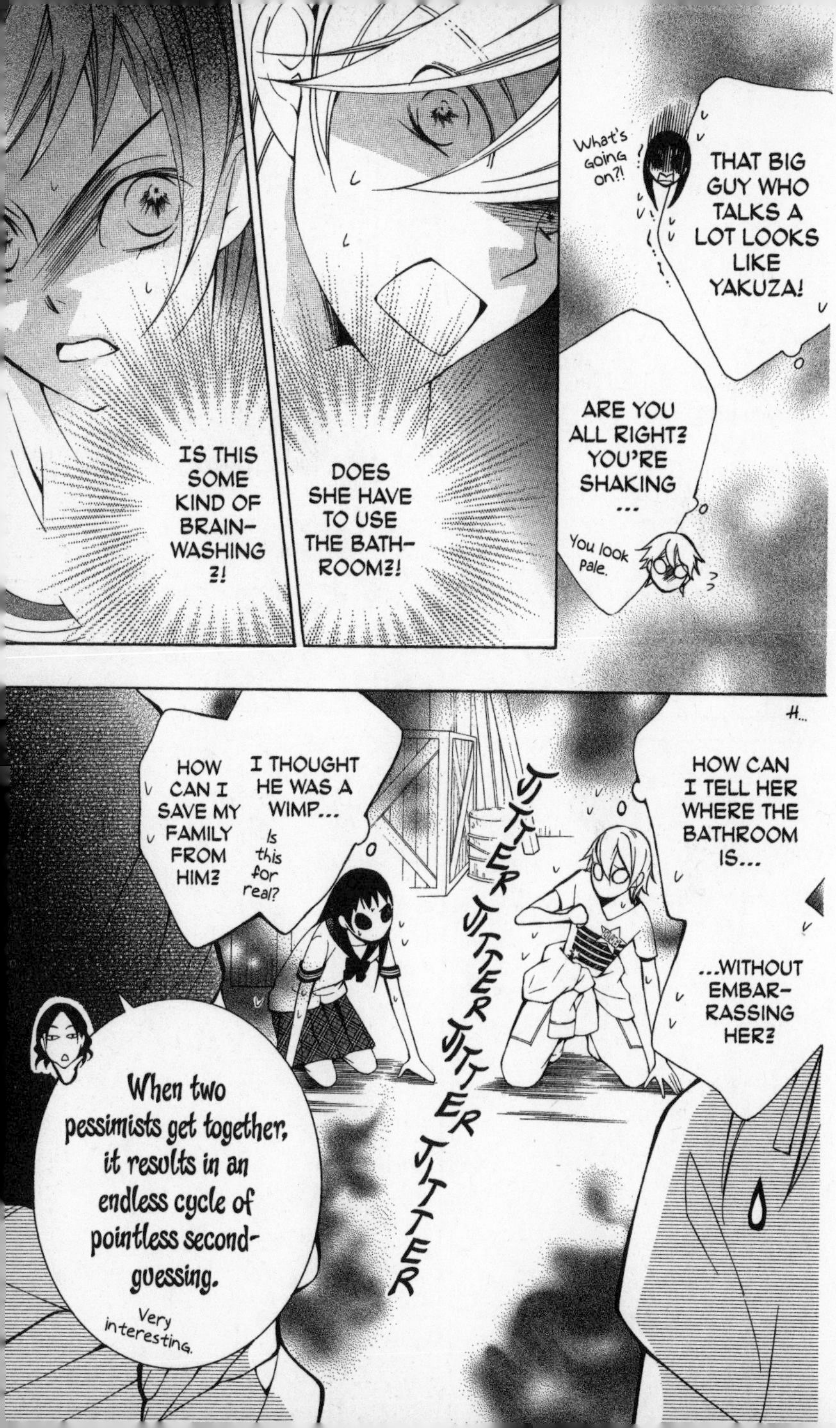
THAT BIG GUY WHO TALKS A LOT LOOKS LIKE YAKUZA!
What's going on?!
ARE YOU ALL RIGHT? YOU'RE SHAKING...
You look pale.
DOES SHE HAVE TO USE THE BATHROOM?!
IS THIS SOME KIND OF BRAIN-WASHING?!
H...
HOW CAN I TELL HER WHERE THE BATHROOM IS...
...WITHOUT EMBAR-RASSING HER?
JITTER JITTER JITTER JITTER
I THOUGHT HE WAS A WIMP...
Is this for real?
HOW CAN I SAVE MY FAMILY FROM HIM?
When two pessimists get together, it results in an endless cycle of pointless second-guessing.
Very interesting.

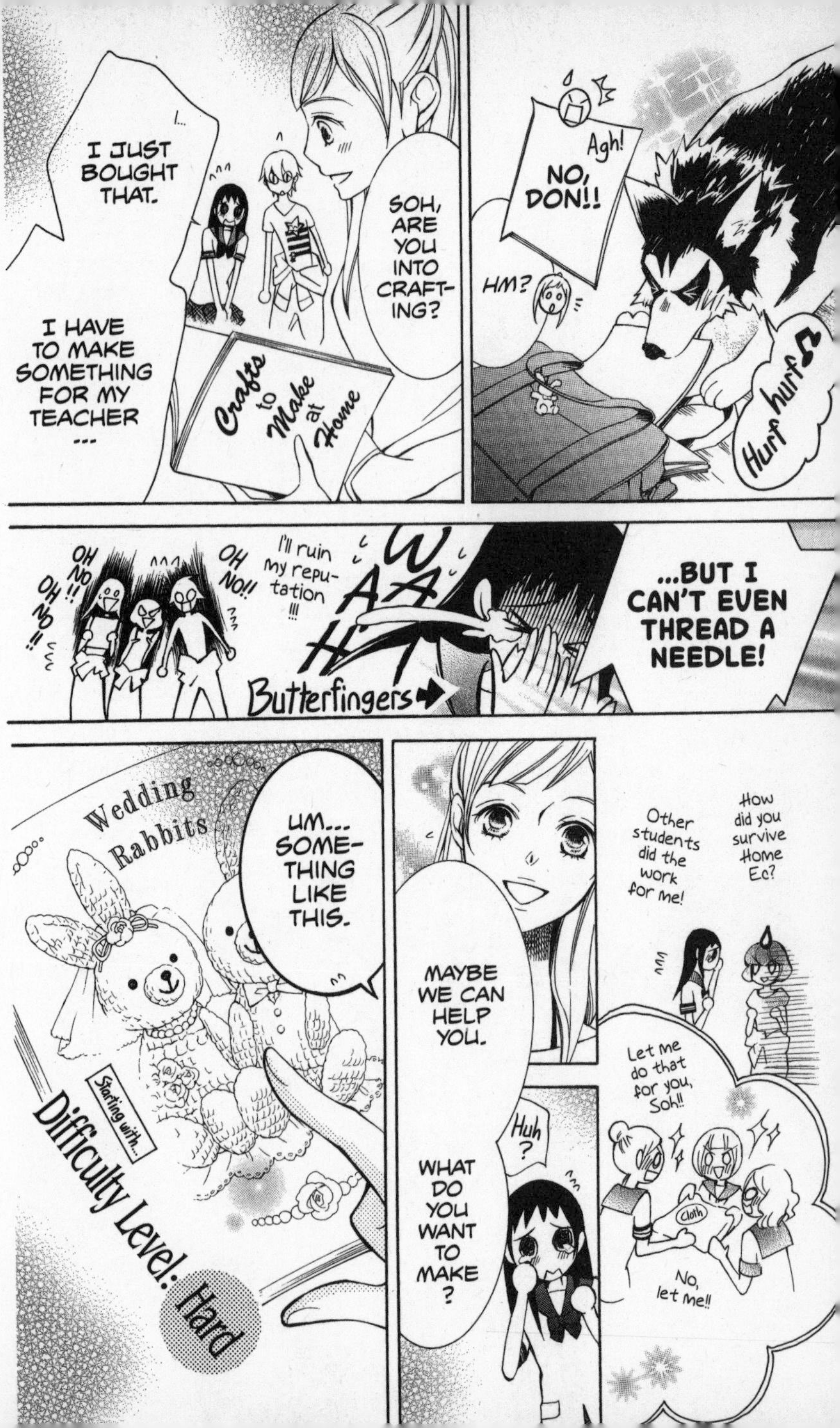
Agh!
NO, DON!!
HM?
Hurf hurf♫
SOH, ARE YOU INTO CRAFTING?
I...
I JUST BOUGHT THAT.
I HAVE TO MAKE SOMETHING FOR MY TEACHER...
Crafts to Make at Home
...BUT I CAN'T EVEN THREAD A NEEDLE!
WAAH
Butterfingers
I'll ruin my reputation!!!
OH NO!!
OH NO!!
OH NO!!
How did you survive Home Ec?
Other students did the work for me!
MAYBE WE CAN HELP YOU.
Let me do that for you, Soh!!
Cloth
No, let me!!
Huh?
WHAT DO YOU WANT TO MAKE?
UM... SOMETHING LIKE THIS.
Wedding Rabbits
Starting with...
Difficulty Level: Hard

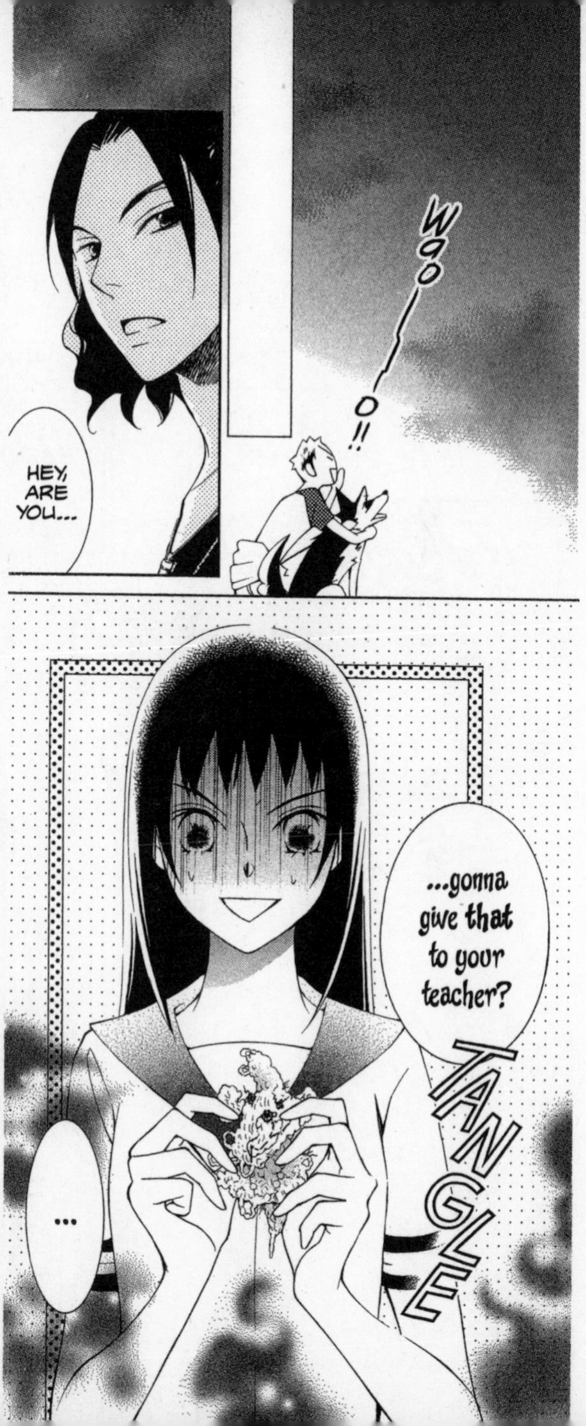
WOO-----O!!
HEY, ARE YOU...
...gonna give that to your teacher?
TANGLE
...

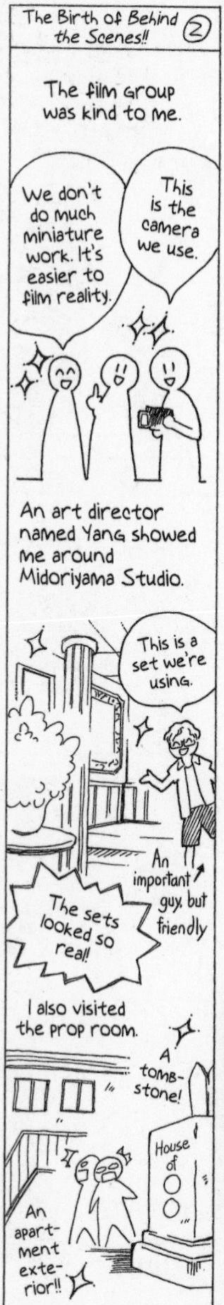
The Birth of Behind the Scenes!! 2
The film group was kind to me.
This is the camera we use.
We don't do much miniature work. It's easier to film reality.
An art director named Yang showed me around Midoriyama Studio.
This is a set we're using.
An important guy, but friendly
The sets looked so real!
I also visited the prop room.
A tombstone!
House of ○○
An apartment exterior!!

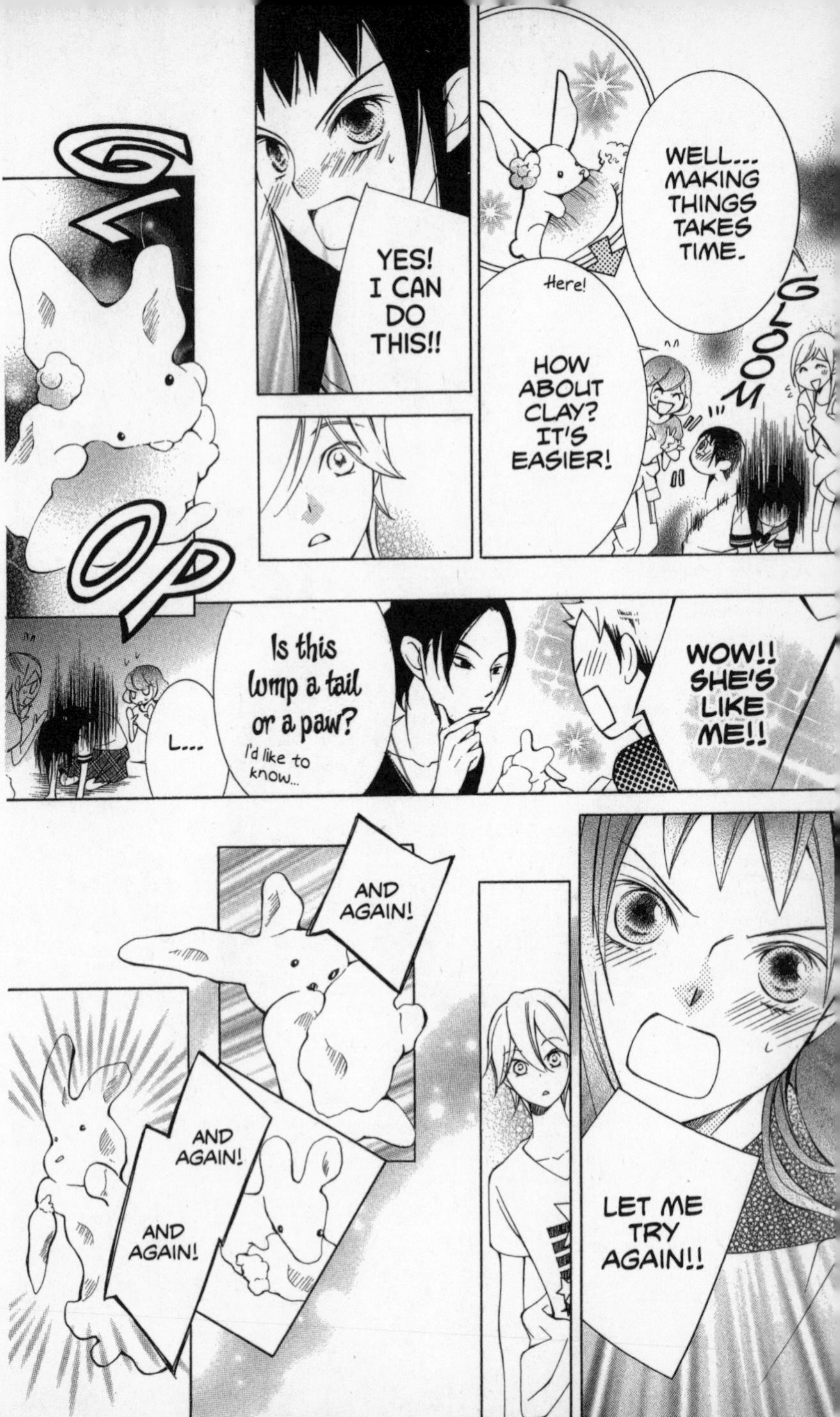
WELL... MAKING THINGS TAKES TIME.
GLOOM
Here!
HOW ABOUT CLAY? IT'S EASIER!
YES! I CAN DO THIS!!
GLOP
WOW!! SHE'S LIKE ME!!
Is this lump a tail or a paw?
I'd like to know...
L...
LET ME TRY AGAIN!!
AND AGAIN!
AND AGAIN!
AND AGAIN!

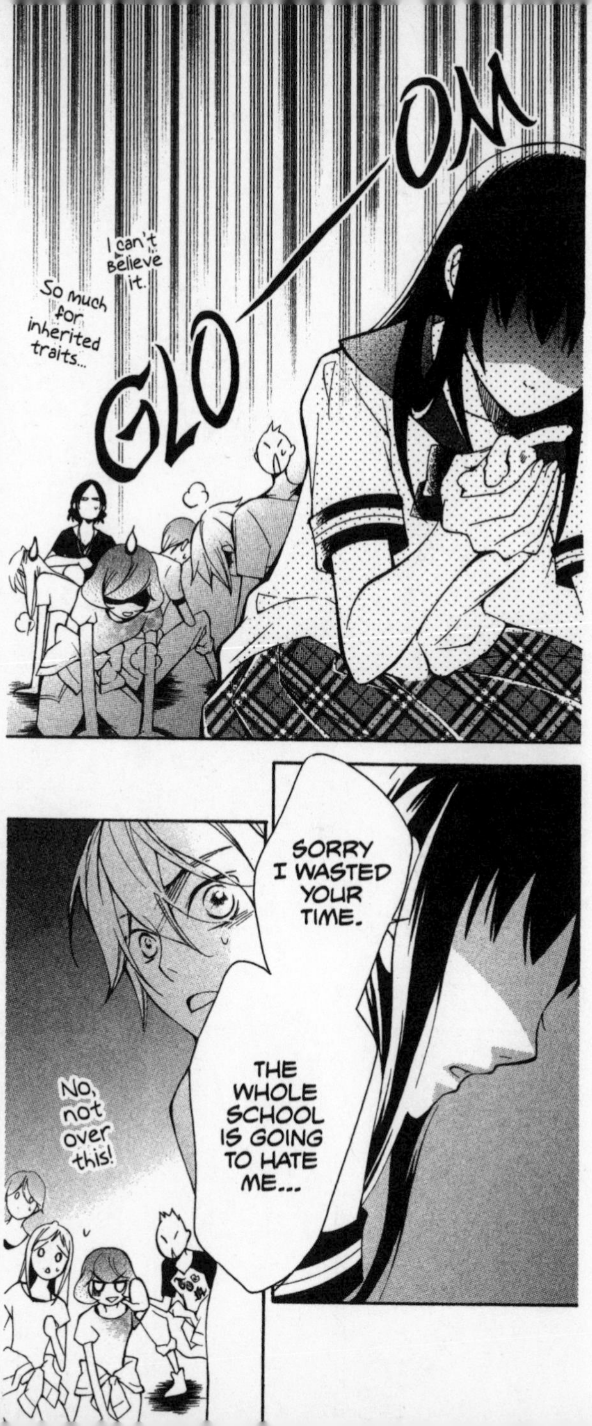
GLO—OM
I can't believe it.
So much for inherited traits...
SORRY I WASTED YOUR TIME.
THE WHOLE SCHOOL IS GOING TO HATE ME...
No, not over this!

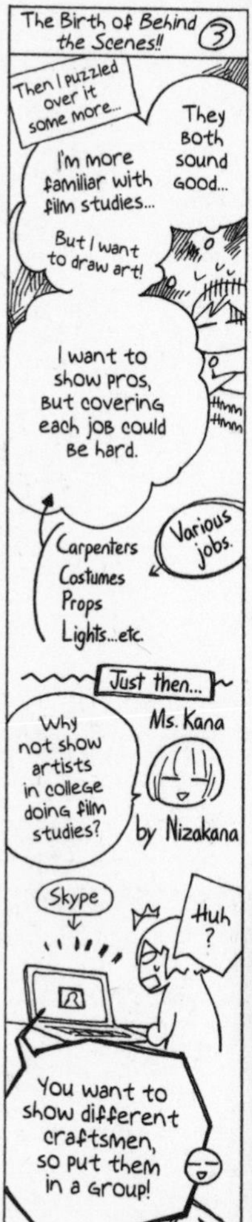
The Birth of Behind the Scenes!! 3
Then I puzzled over it some more...
They both sound good...
I'm more familiar with film studies...
But I want to draw art!
I want to show pros, but covering each job could be hard.
Hmm Hmm
Various jobs.
Carpenters
Costumes
Props
Lights...etc.
Just then...
Why not show artists in college doing film studies?
Ms. Kana
by Nizakana
Skype
Huh?
You want to show different craftsmen, so put them in a group!
Eureka!
Why didn't I think of that?
I owe this manga to Ms. Kana!

She really helped me out!

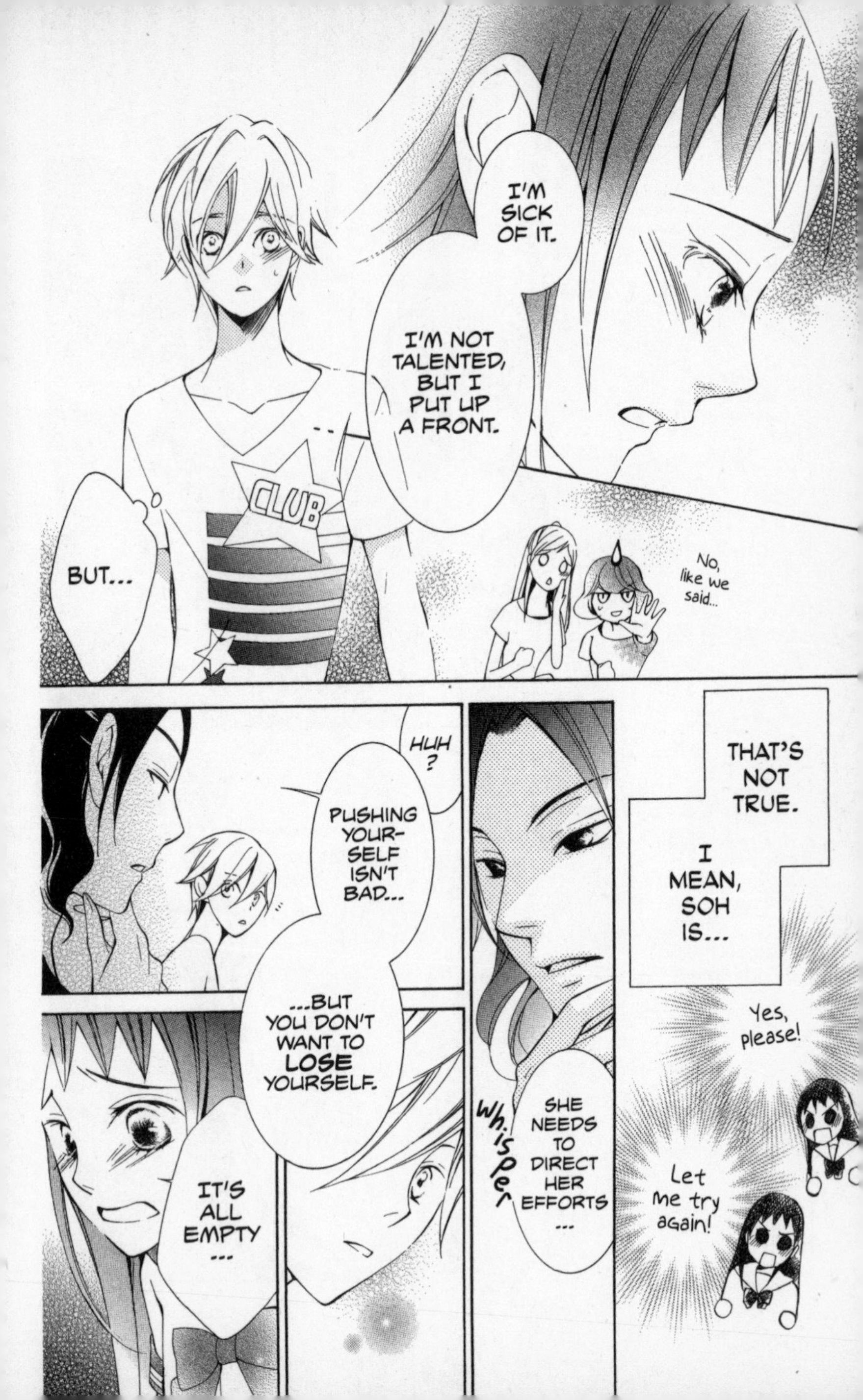

I'M SICK OF IT.
I'M NOT TALENTED, BUT I PUT UP A FRONT.
No, like we said...
BUT...
THAT'S NOT TRUE.
I MEAN, SOH IS...
Yes, please!
Let me try again!
Whisper
SHE NEEDS TO DIRECT HER EFFORTS...
HUH?
PUSHING YOURSELF ISN'T BAD...
...BUT YOU DON'T WANT TO LOSE YOURSELF.
IT'S ALL EMPTY...

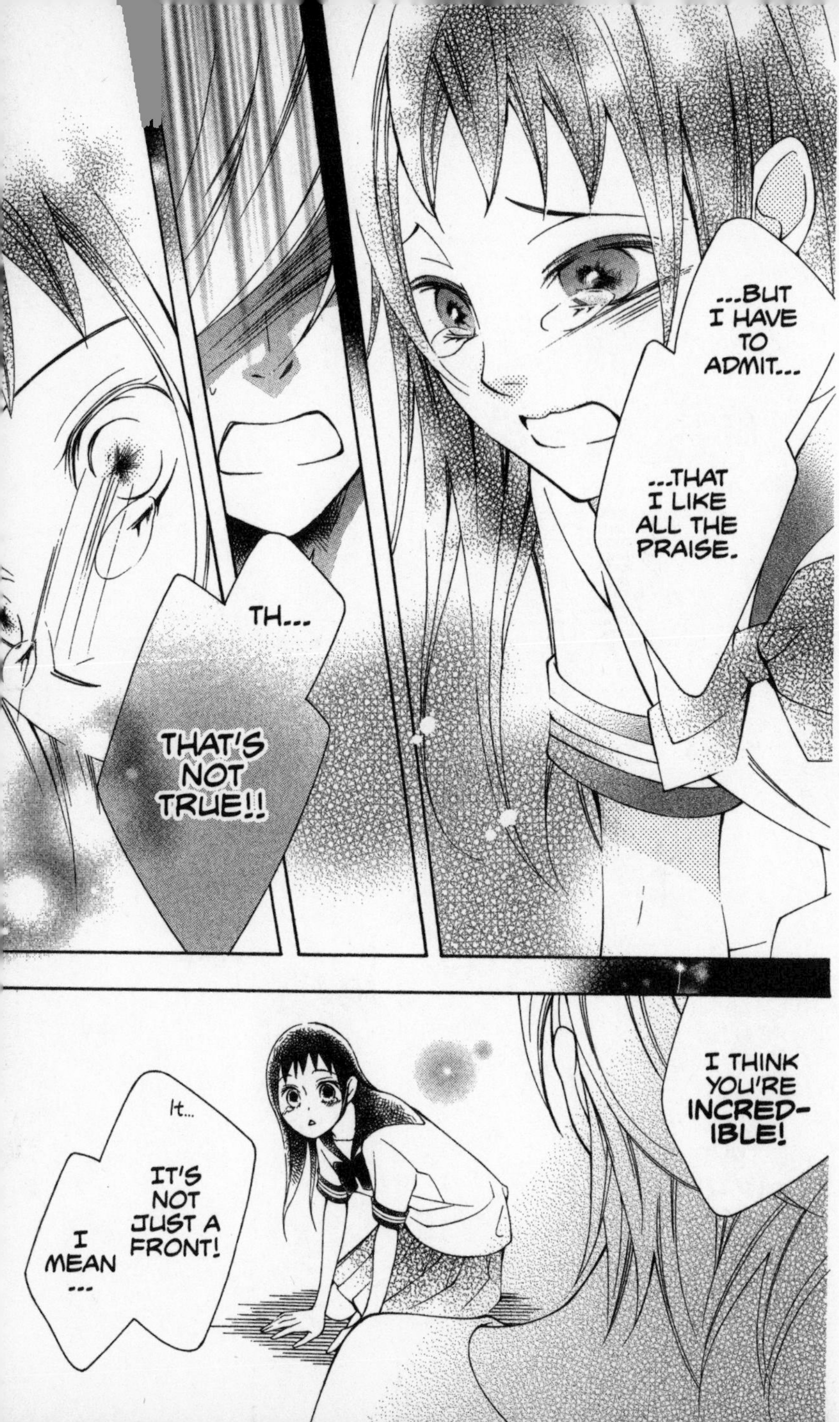
...BUT I HAVE TO ADMIT...
...THAT I LIKE ALL THE PRAISE.
TH...
THAT'S NOT TRUE!!
I THINK YOU'RE INCRED-IBLE!
It...
IT'S NOT JUST A FRONT!
I MEAN ...

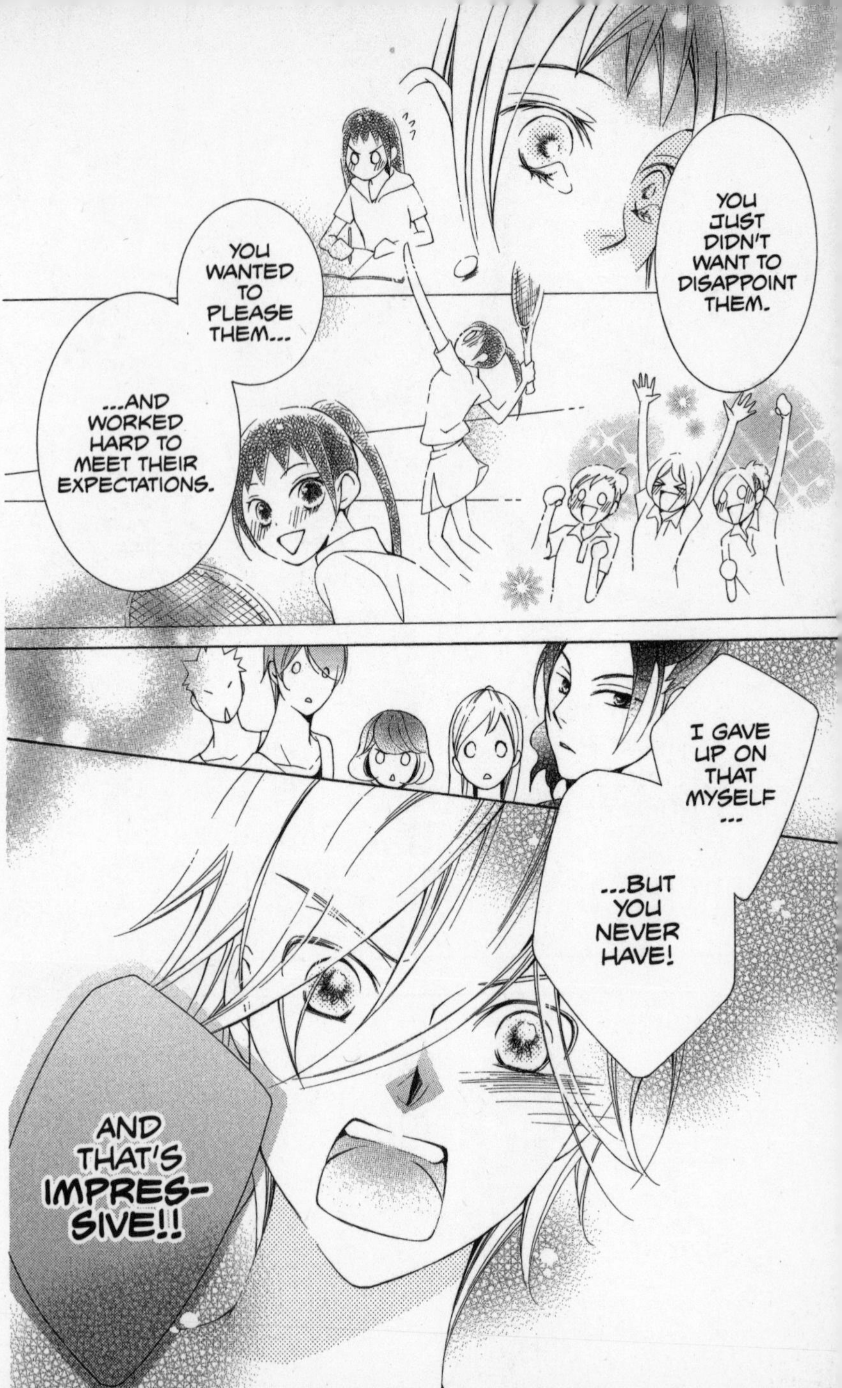
YOU JUST DIDN'T WANT TO DISAPPOINT THEM.
YOU WANTED TO PLEASE THEM...
...AND WORKED HARD TO MEET THEIR EXPECTATIONS.
I GAVE UP ON THAT MYSELF...
...BUT YOU NEVER HAVE!
AND THAT'S IMPRES-SIVE!!

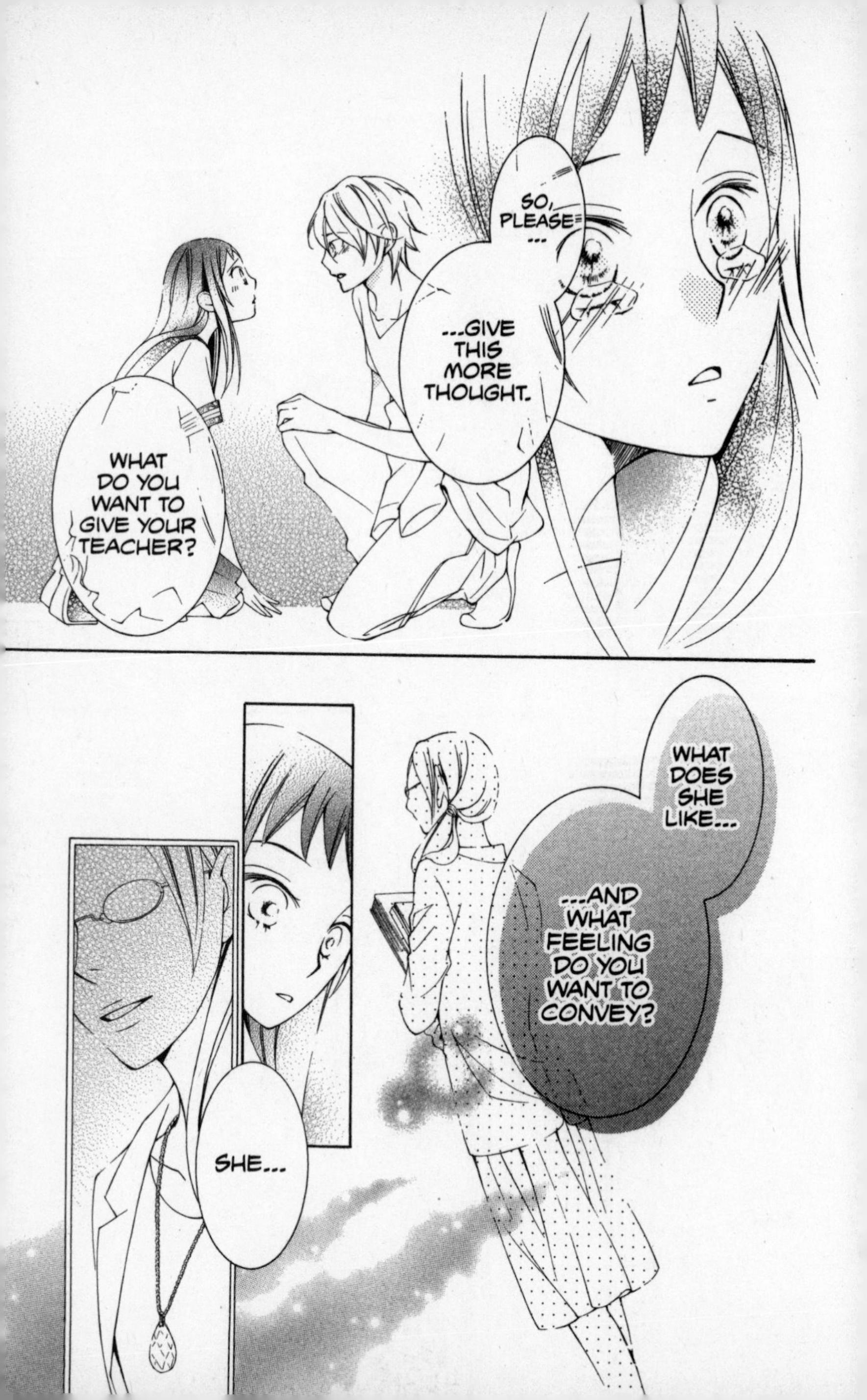
SO, PLEASE...
...GIVE THIS MORE THOUGHT.
WHAT DO YOU WANT TO GIVE YOUR TEACHER?
WHAT DOES SHE LIKE...
...AND WHAT FEELING DO YOU WANT TO CONVEY?
SHE...

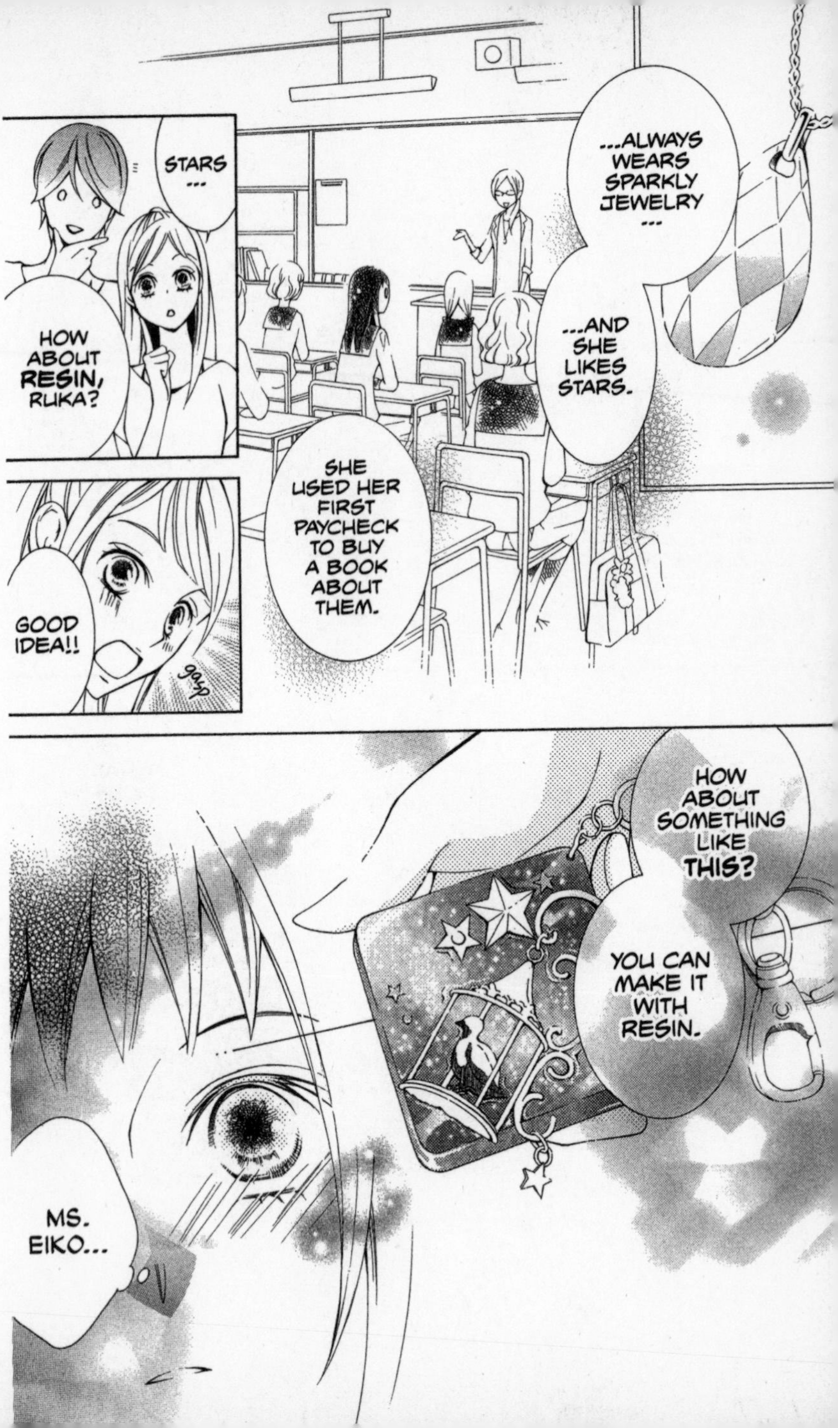
...ALWAYS WEARS SPARKLY JEWELRY...
...AND SHE LIKES STARS.
SHE USED HER FIRST PAYCHECK TO BUY A BOOK ABOUT THEM.
STARS...
HOW ABOUT RESIN, RUKA?
GOOD IDEA!!
gasp
HOW ABOUT SOMETHING LIKE THIS?
YOU CAN MAKE IT WITH RESIN.
MS. EIKO...

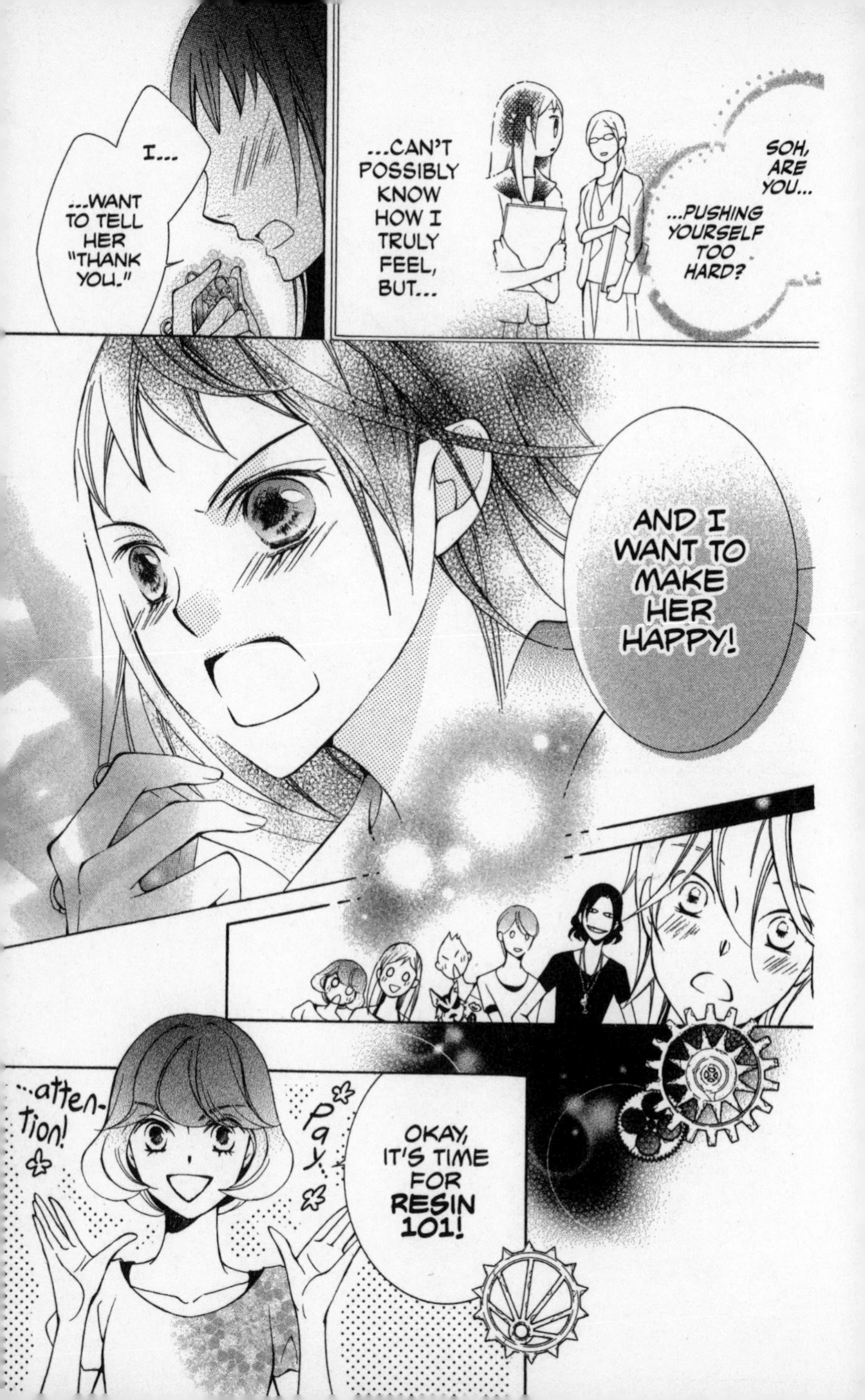
SOH, ARE YOU...
...PUSHING YOURSELF TOO HARD?
...CAN'T POSSIBLY KNOW HOW I TRULY FEEL, BUT...
I...
...WANT TO TELL HER "THANK YOU."
AND I WANT TO MAKE HER HAPPY!
OKAY, IT'S TIME FOR RESIN 101!
Pay...
...atten-tion!

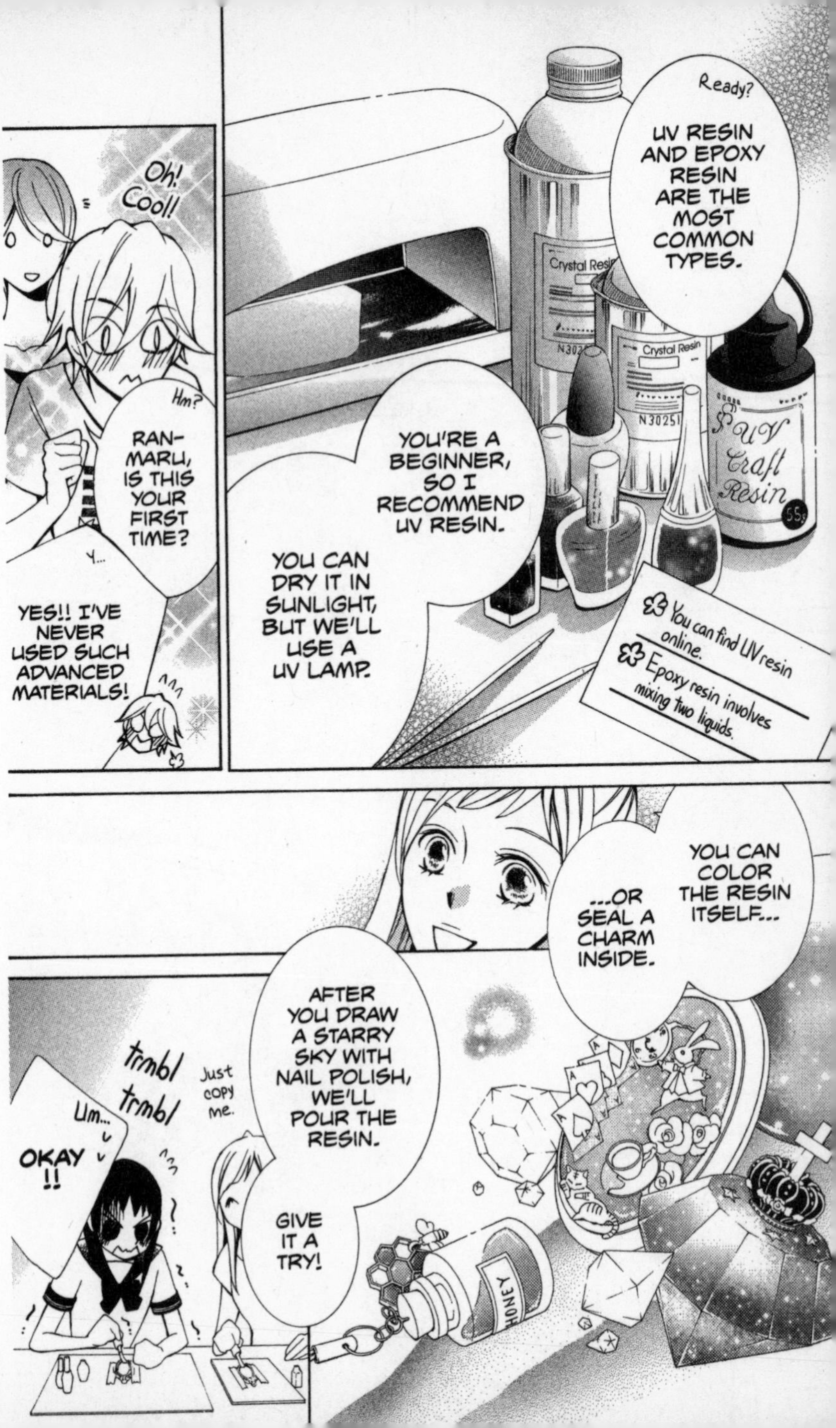
Ready?
UV RESIN AND EPOXY RESIN ARE THE MOST COMMON TYPES.
Crystal Resin
N30251
UV Craft Resin
55g
YOU'RE A BEGINNER, SO I RECOMMEND UV RESIN.
YOU CAN DRY IT IN SUNLIGHT, BUT WE'LL USE A UV LAMP.
You can find UV resin online.
Epoxy resin involves mixing two liquids.
Oh! Cool!
Hm?
RAN-MARU, IS THIS YOUR FIRST TIME?
Y...
YES!! I'VE NEVER USED SUCH ADVANCED MATERIALS!
YOU CAN COLOR THE RESIN ITSELF...
...OR SEAL A CHARM INSIDE.
AFTER YOU DRAW A STARRY SKY WITH NAIL POLISH, WE'LL POUR THE RESIN.
HONEY
GIVE IT A TRY!
Just copy me.
trmbl trmbl
Um...
OKAY!!

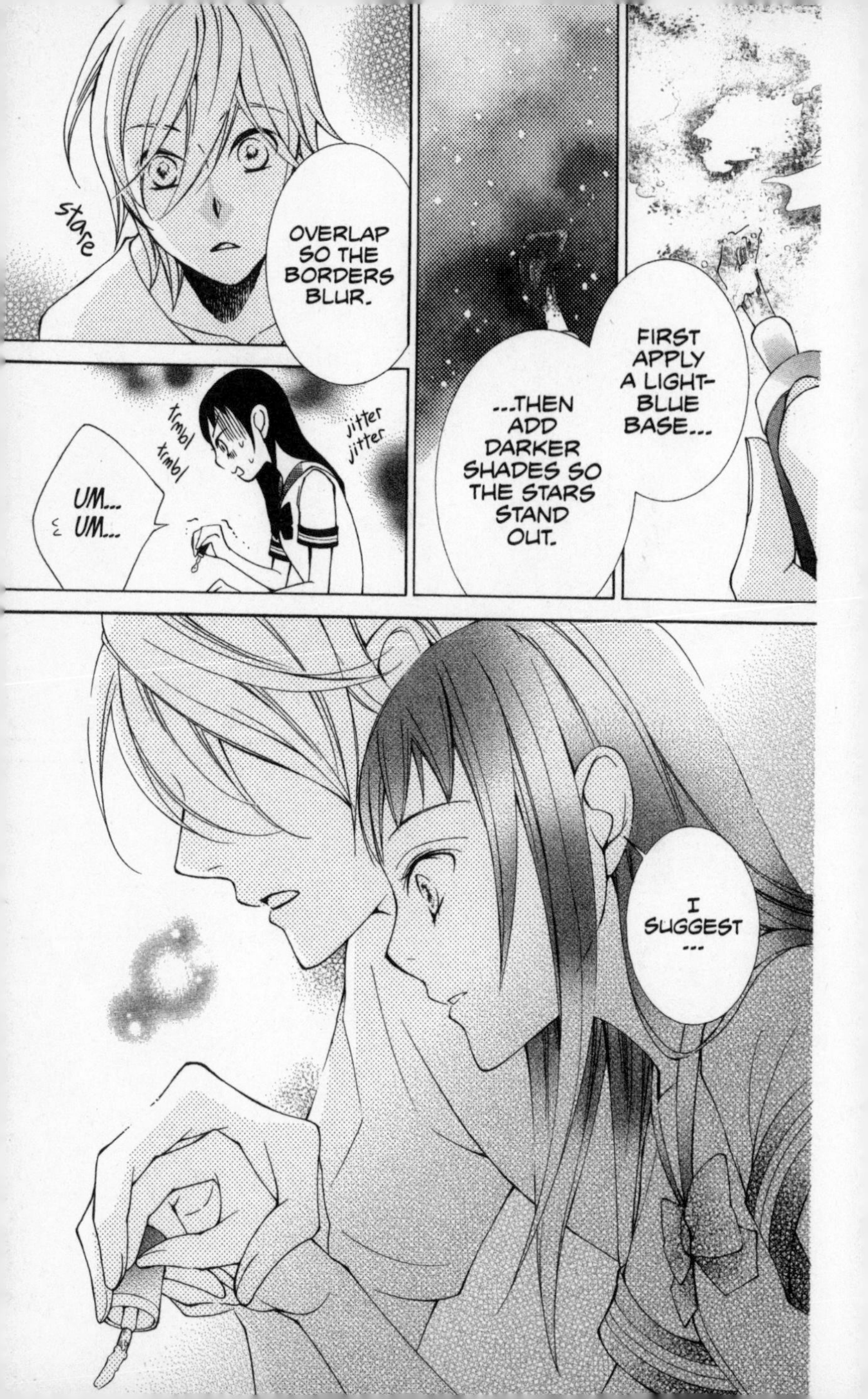
FIRST APPLY A LIGHT-BLUE BASE...
...THEN ADD DARKER SHADES SO THE STARS STAND OUT.
OVERLAP SO THE BORDERS BLUR.
stare
jitter jitter
trmbl trmbl
UM... UM...
I SUGGEST ...

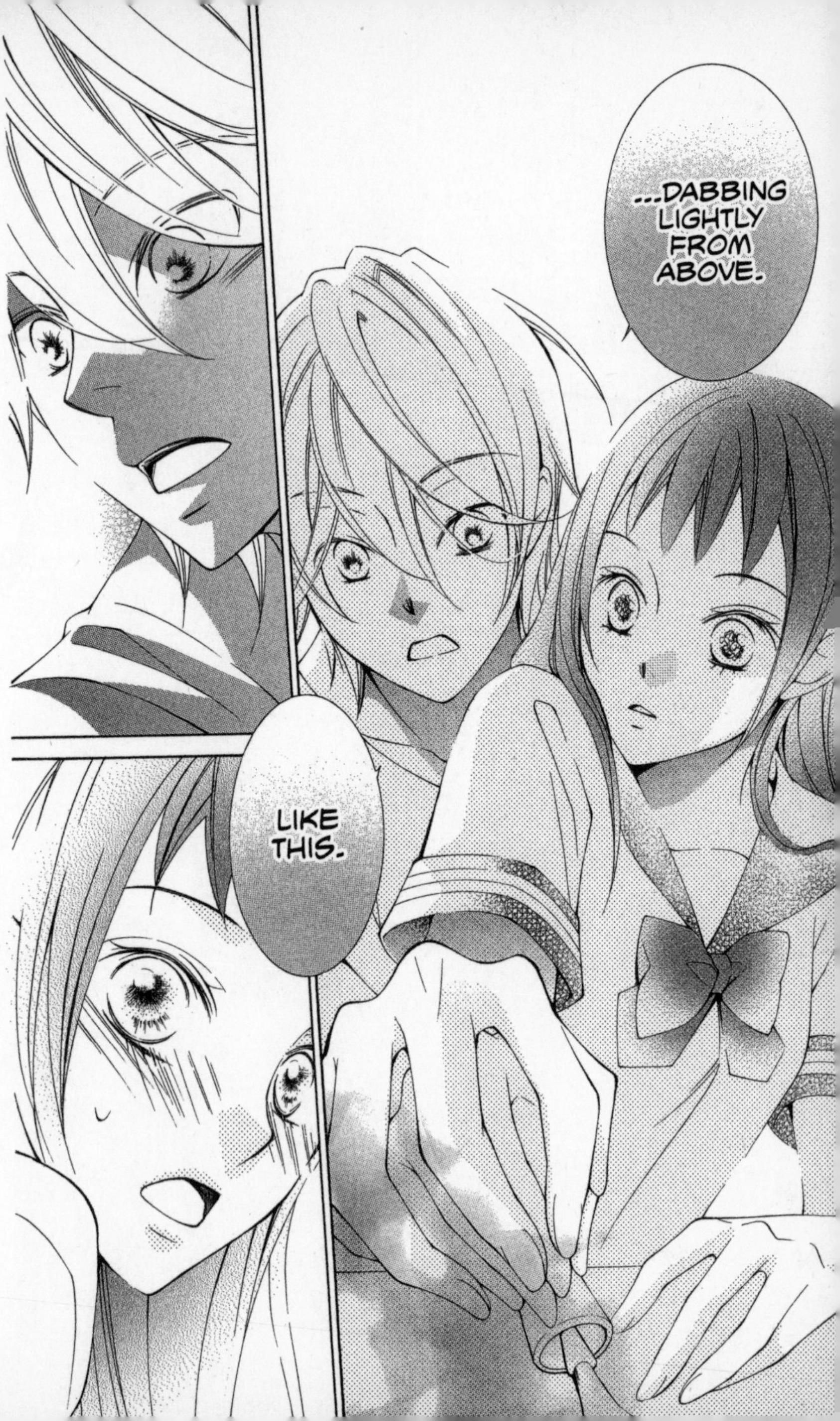
...DABBING LIGHTLY FROM ABOVE.
LIKE THIS.

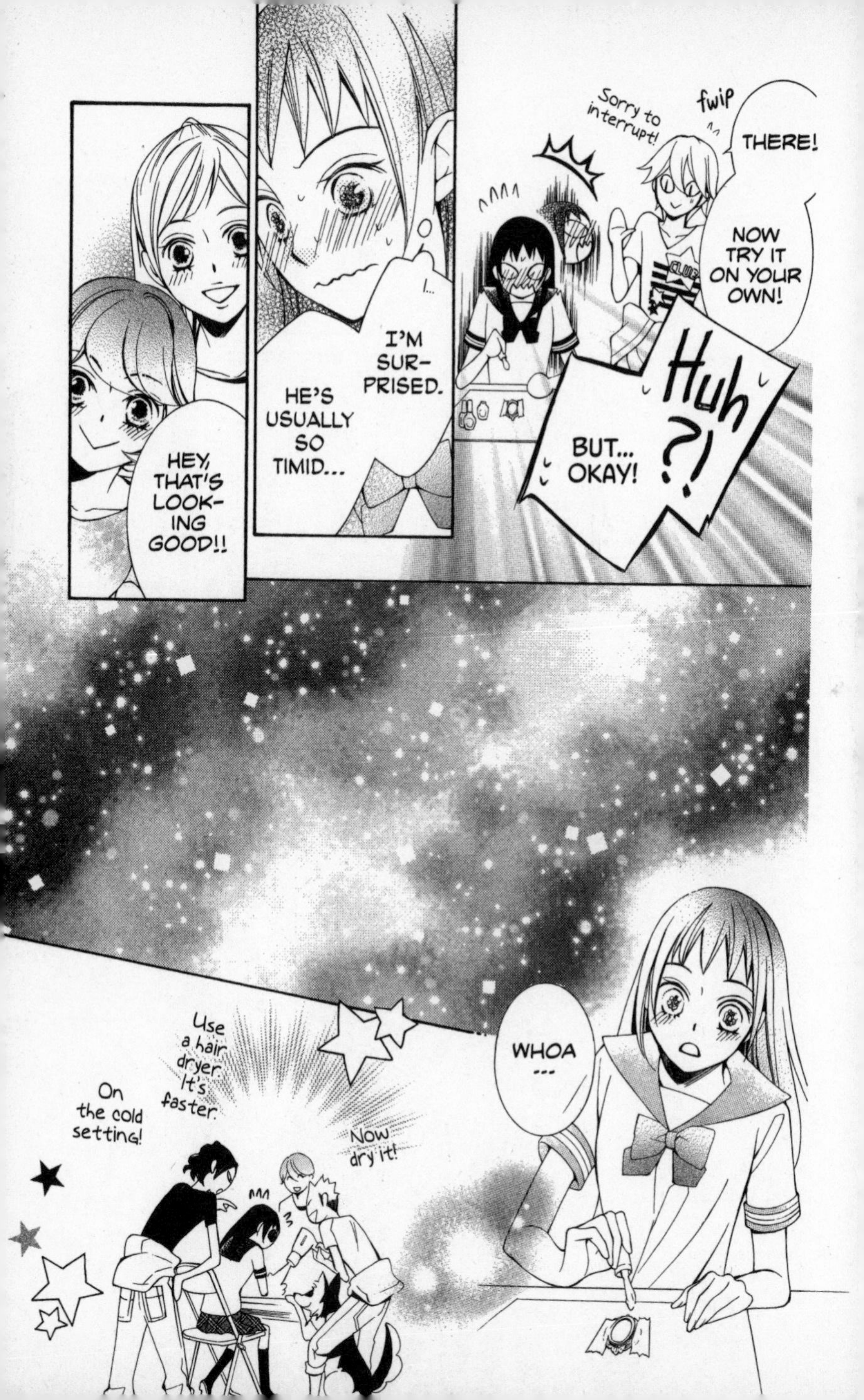
THERE!
fwip
Sorry to interrupt!
NOW TRY IT ON YOUR OWN!
Huh?!
BUT... OKAY!
I...
I'M SURPRISED.
HE'S USUALLY SO TIMID...
HEY, THAT'S LOOKING GOOD!!
WHOA...
Now dry it!
Use a hair dryer. It's faster.
On the cold setting!

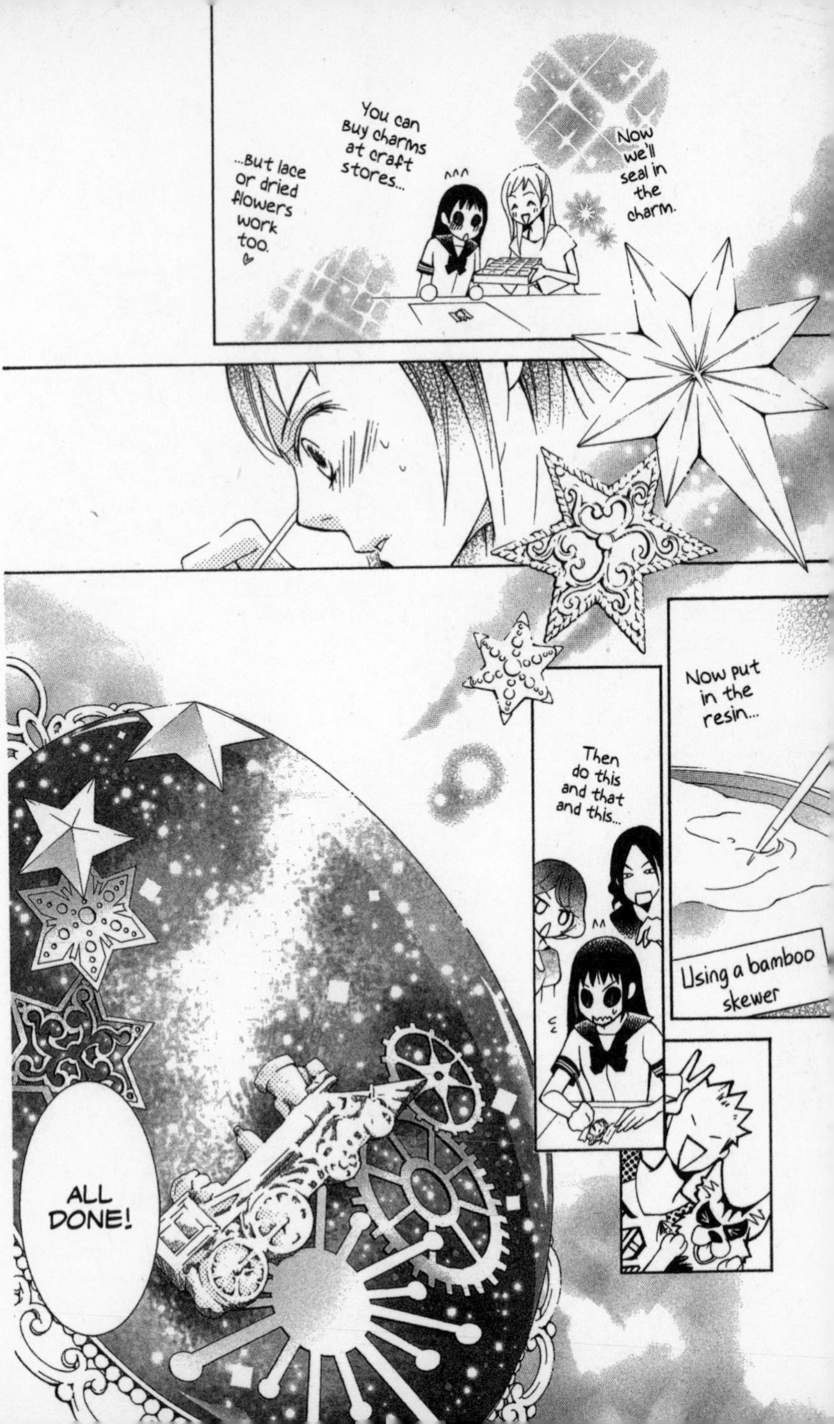

Now we'll seal in the charm.
You can buy charms at craft stores...
...But lace or dried flowers work too.
Now put in the resin...
Using a bamboo skewer
Then do this and that and this...
ALL DONE!

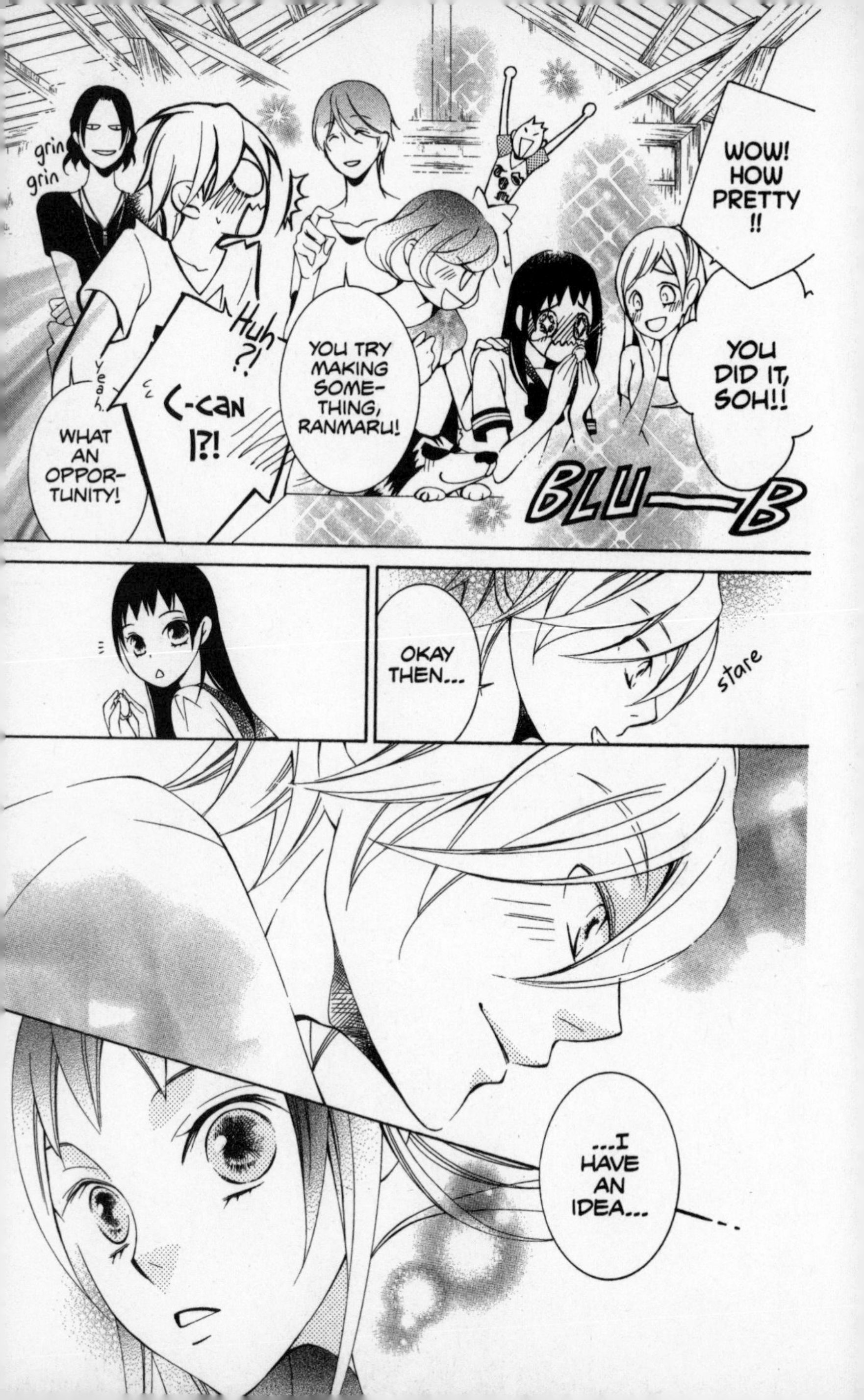
WOW! HOW PRETTY!!
YOU DID IT, SOH!!
BLU—B
YOU TRY MAKING SOME-THING, RANMARU!
Huh?!
I-CAN I?!
grin grin
yeah.
WHAT AN OPPOR-TUNITY!
stare
OKAY THEN...
...I HAVE AN IDEA...

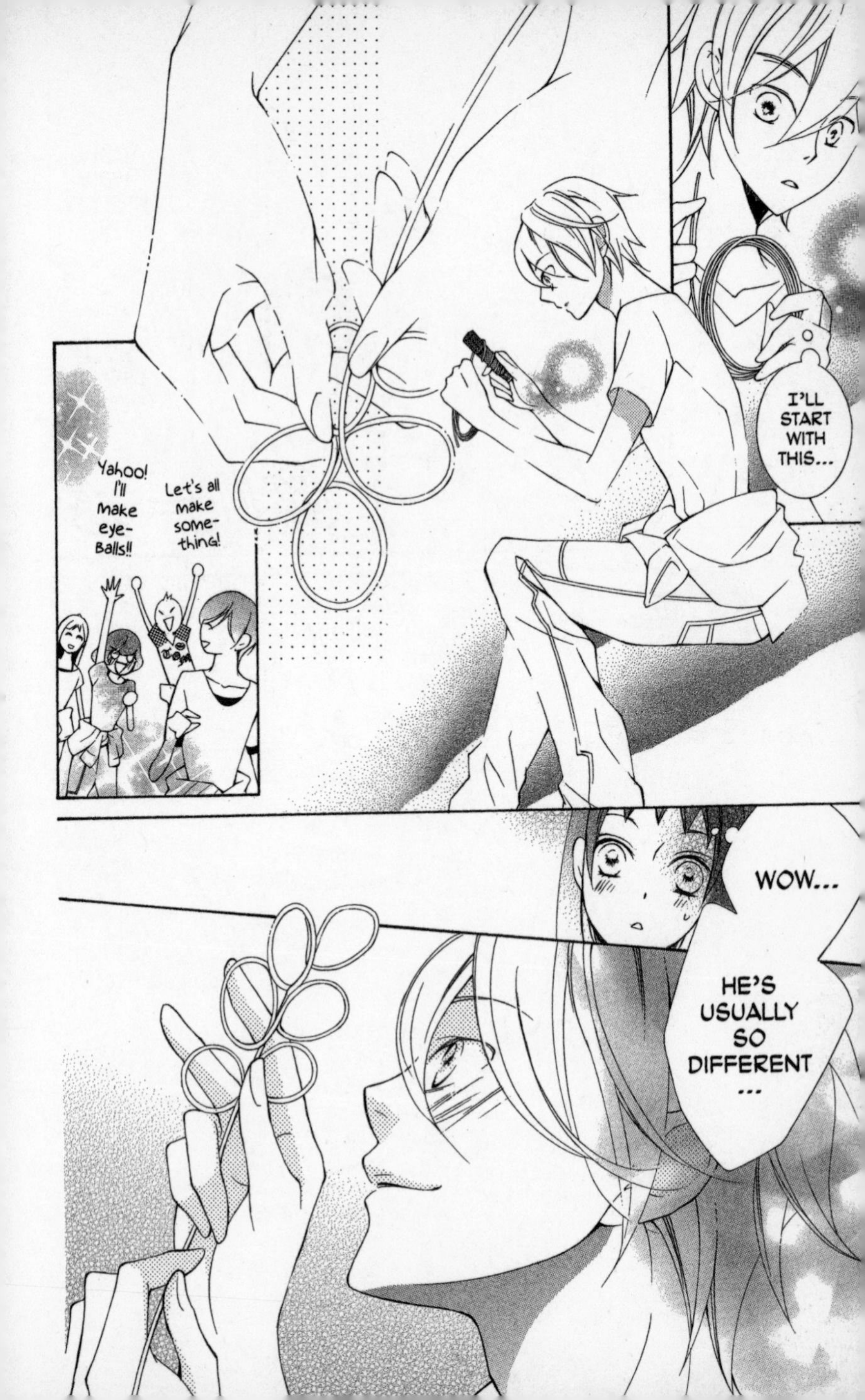
I'LL START WITH THIS...
Let's all make some-thing!
Yahoo! I'll make eye-Balls!!
WOW...
HE'S USUALLY SO DIFFERENT ...

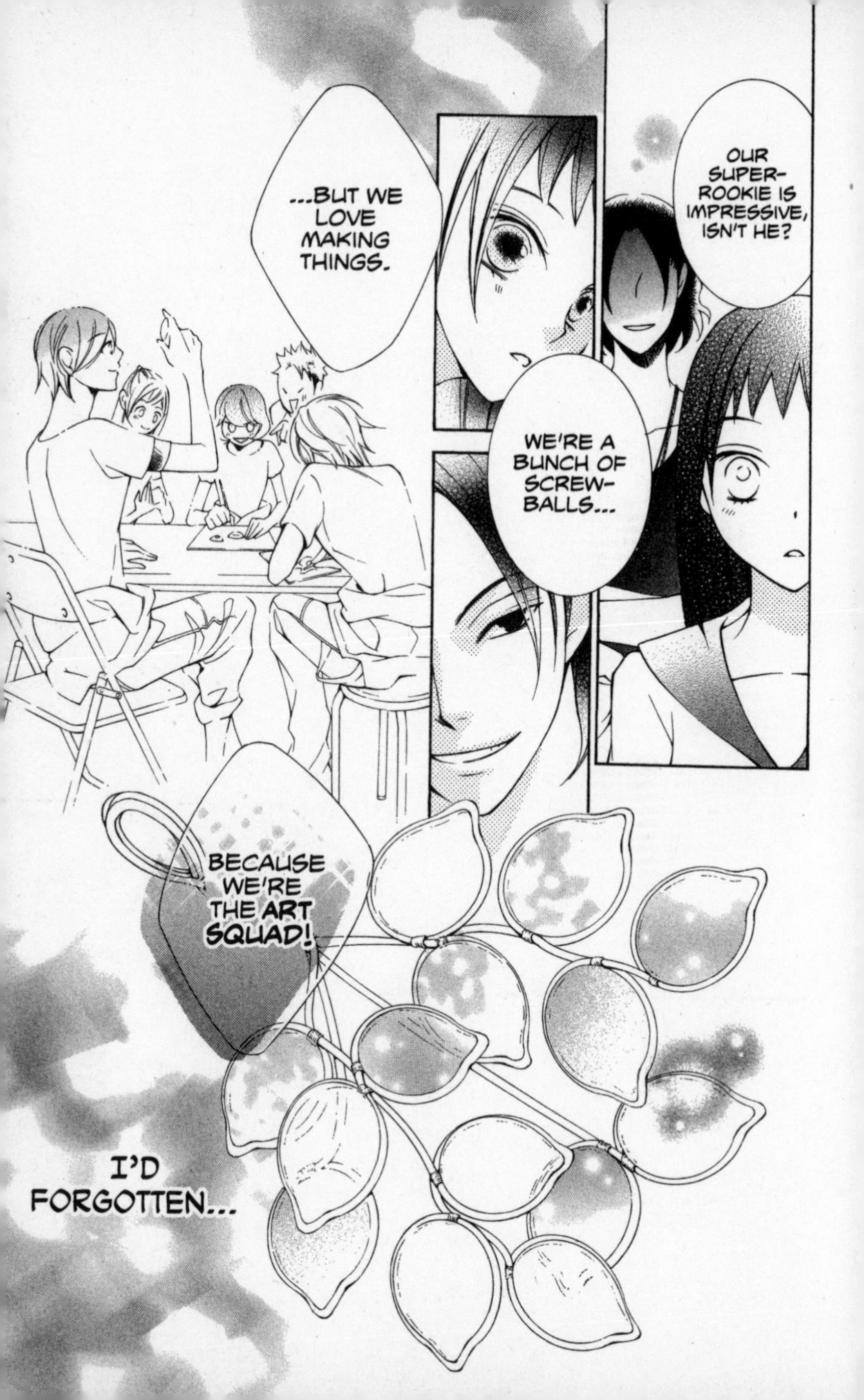
OUR SUPER-ROOKIE IS IMPRESSIVE, ISN'T HE?
WE'RE A BUNCH OF SCREW-BALLS...
...BUT WE LOVE MAKING THINGS.
BECAUSE WE'RE THE ART SQUAD!
I'D FORGOTTEN...

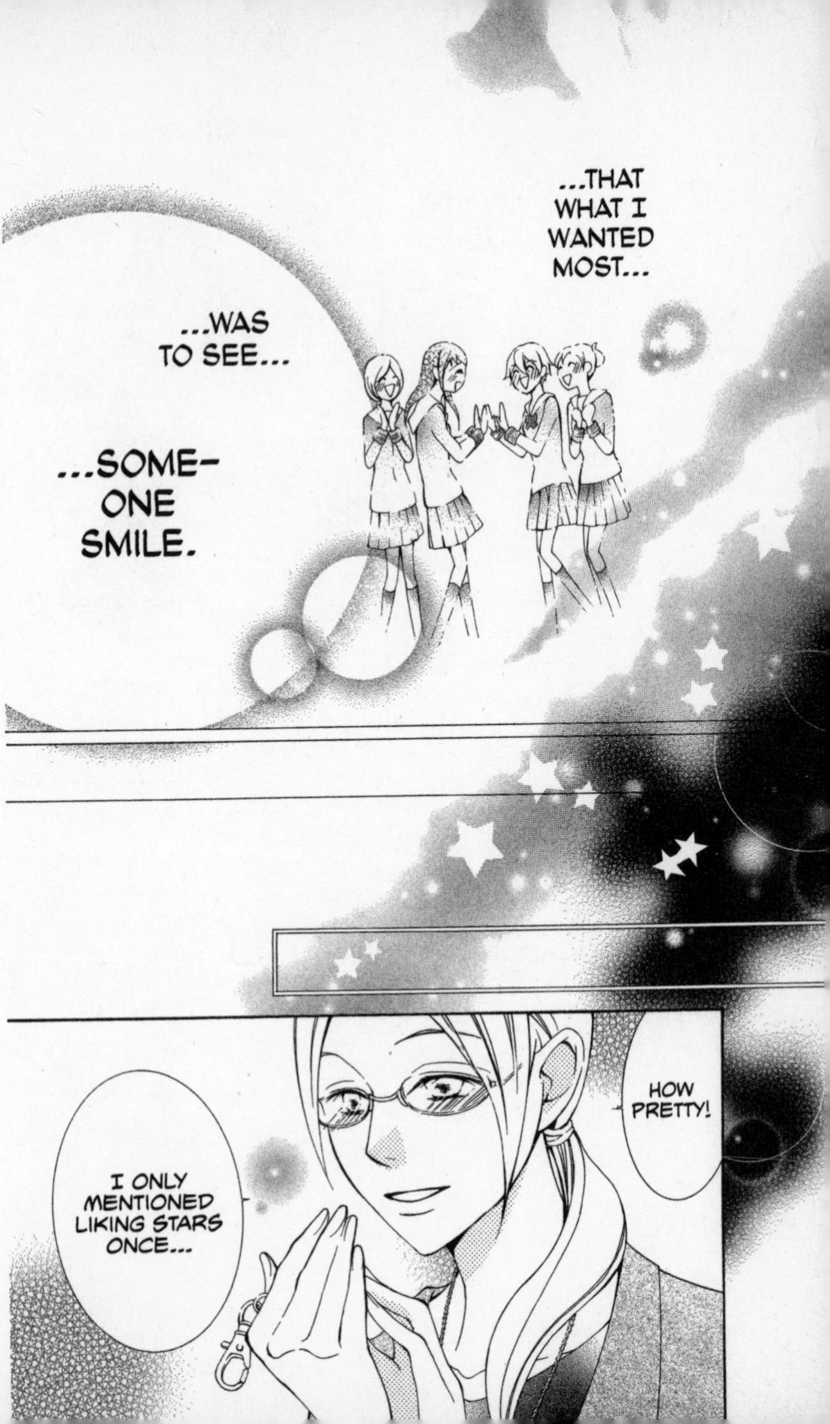
...THAT WHAT I WANTED MOST...
...WAS TO SEE...
...SOME-ONE SMILE.
HOW PRETTY!
I ONLY MENTIONED LIKING STARS ONCE...

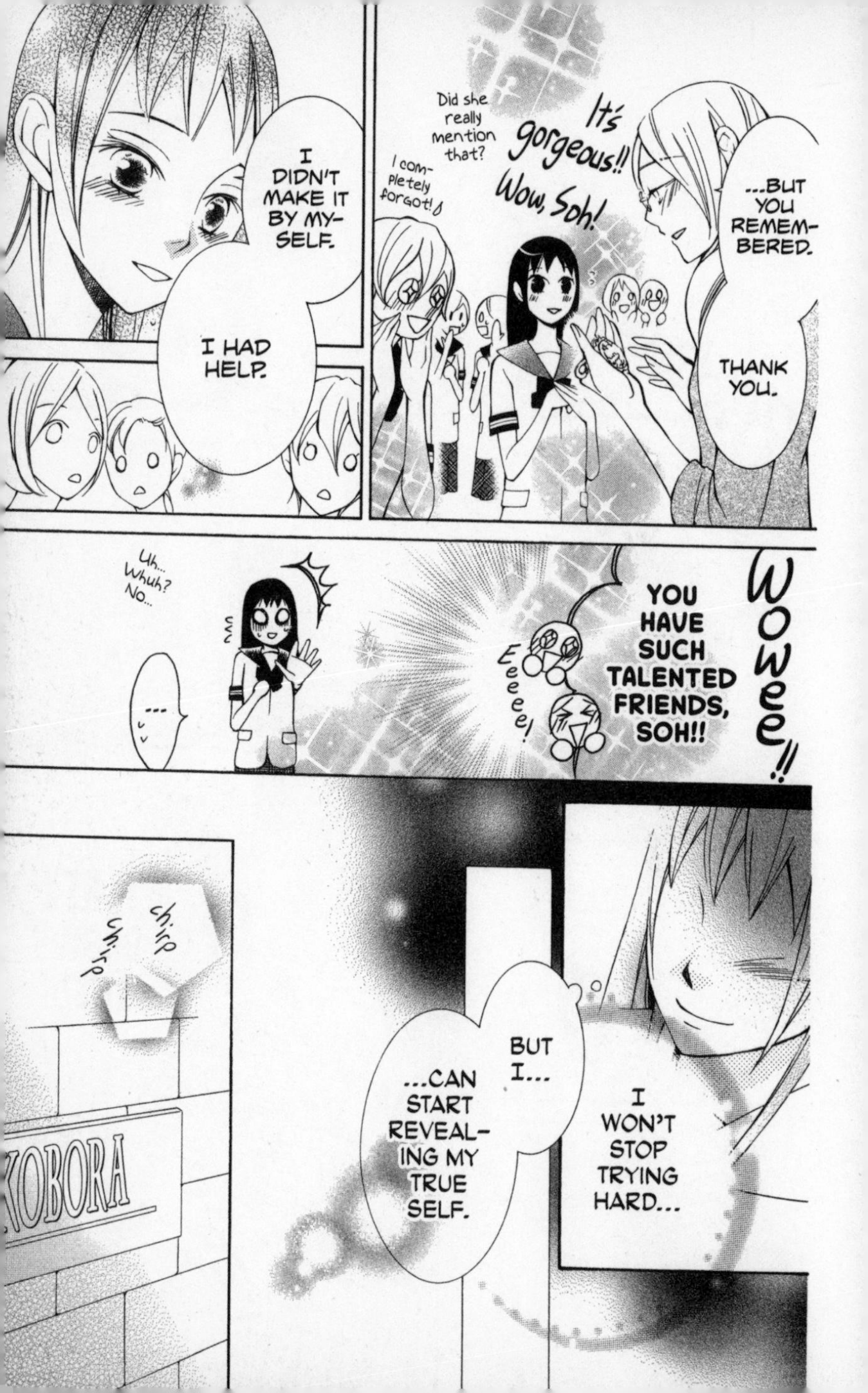
...BUT YOU REMEMBERED.
THANK YOU.
It's gorgeous!! Wow, Soh!
Did she really mention that?
I completely forgot! ♪
I DIDN'T MAKE IT BY MYSELF.
I HAD HELP.
Wowee!!
YOU HAVE SUCH TALENTED FRIENDS, SOH!!
Eeeee!
Uh... Whuh? No...
...
I WON'T STOP TRYING HARD...
BUT I...
...CAN START REVEALING MY TRUE SELF.
chirp chirp
KOBORA

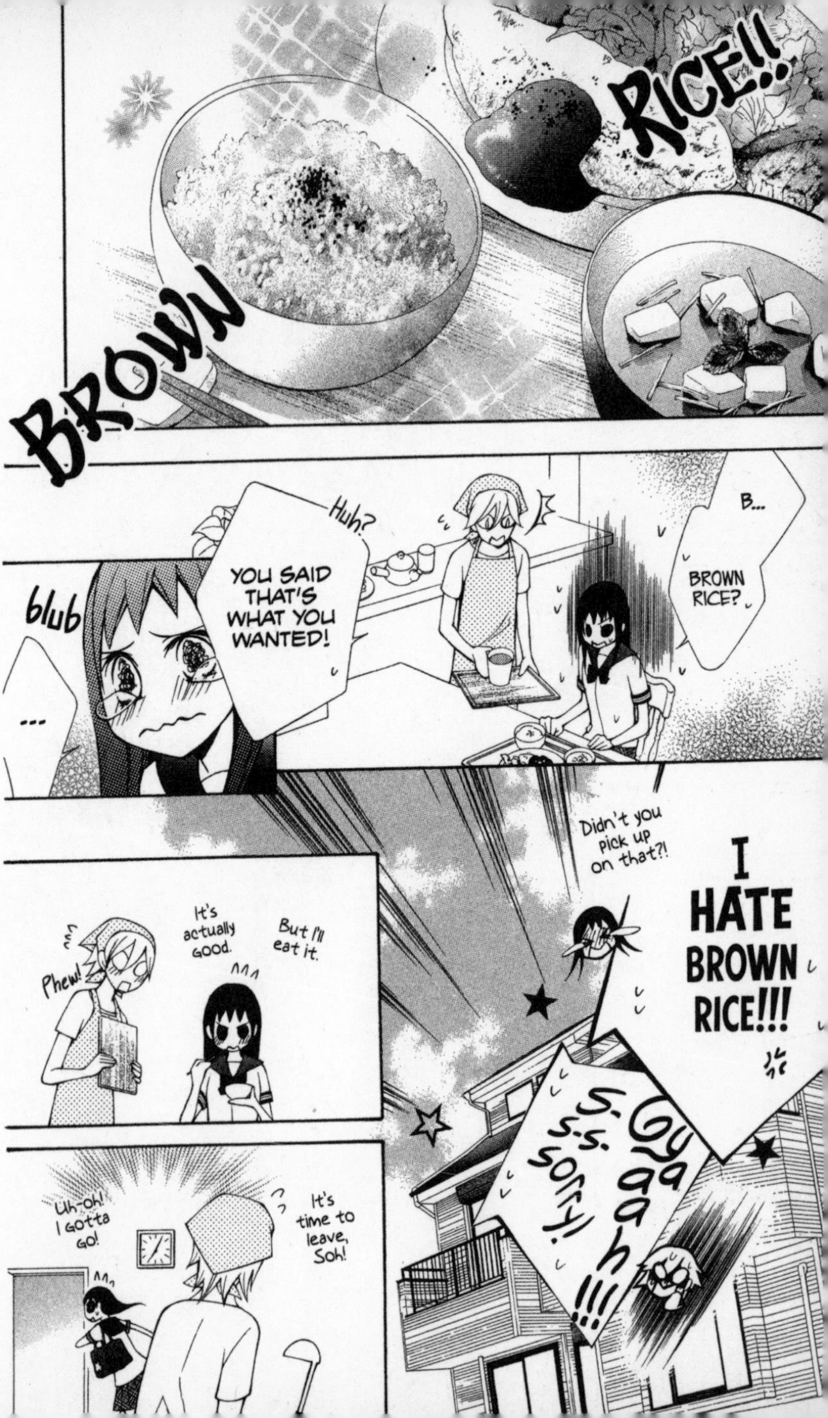
BROWN RICE!!
B...
BROWN RICE?
Huh?
YOU SAID THAT'S WHAT YOU WANTED!
blub
...
I HATE BROWN RICE!!!
Didn't you pick up on that?!
Gyaaah!!!
S-S-S-sorry!
It's actually good.
But I'll eat it.
Phew!
It's time to leave, Soh!
Uh-oh! I gotta go!

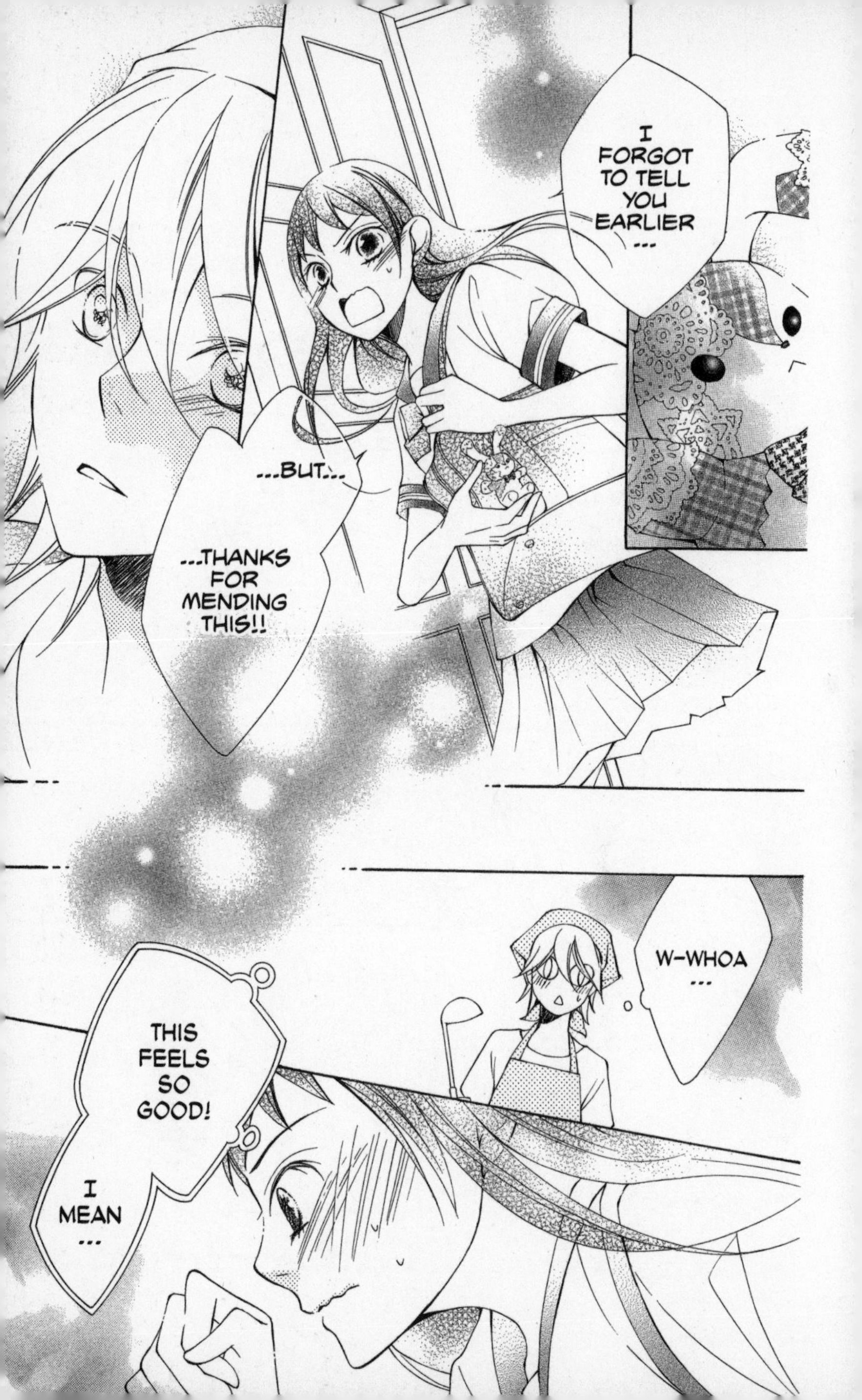
I FORGOT TO TELL YOU EARLIER...
...BUT...
...THANKS FOR MENDING THIS!!
W-WHOA...
THIS FEELS SO GOOD!
I MEAN...

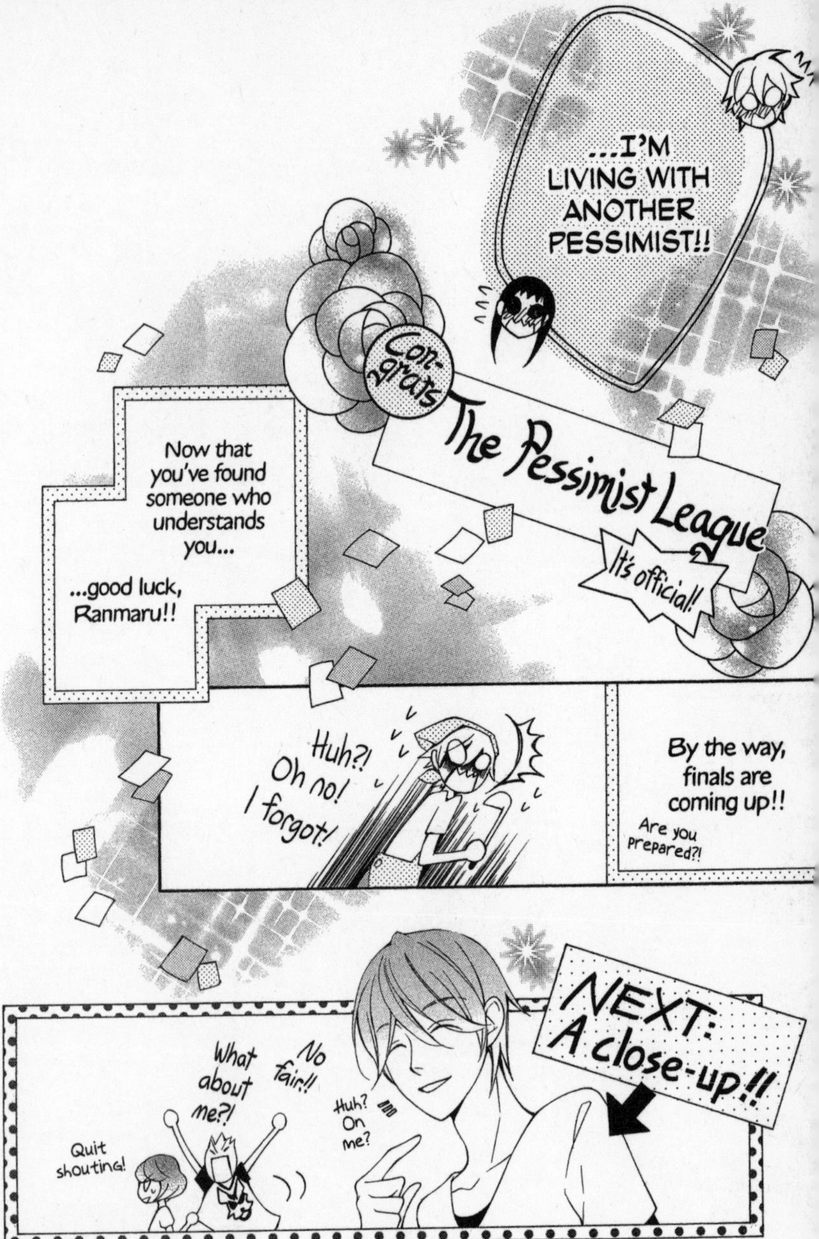

...I'M LIVING WITH ANOTHER PESSIMIST!!
Congrats
The Pessimist League
It's official!
Now that you've found someone who understands you...
...good luck, Ranmaru!!
By the way, finals are coming up!!
Are you prepared?!
Huh?! Oh no! I forgot!
NEXT: A close-up!!
Huh? On me?
No fair!!
What about me?!
Quit shouting!

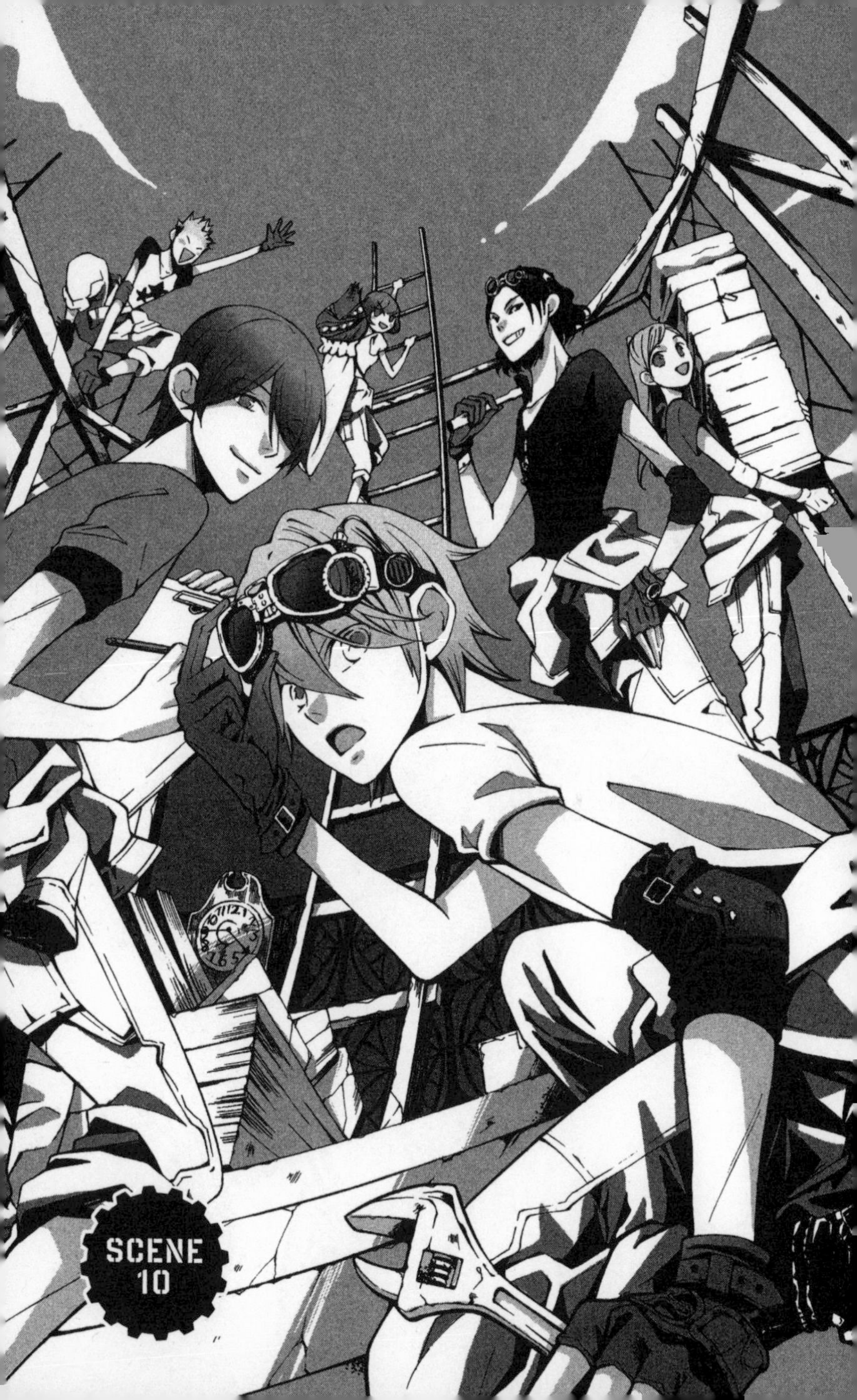
SCENE
10

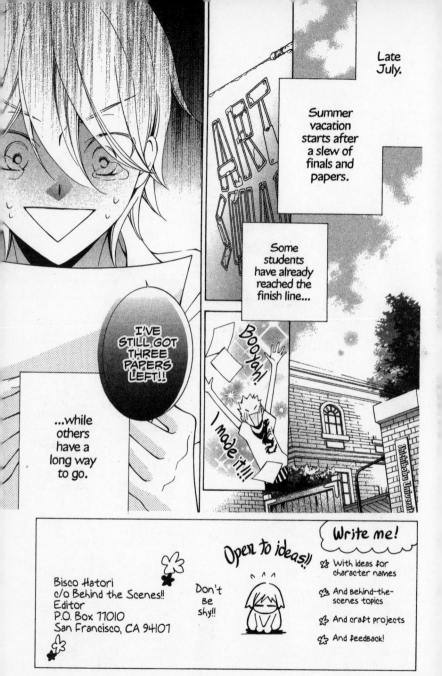

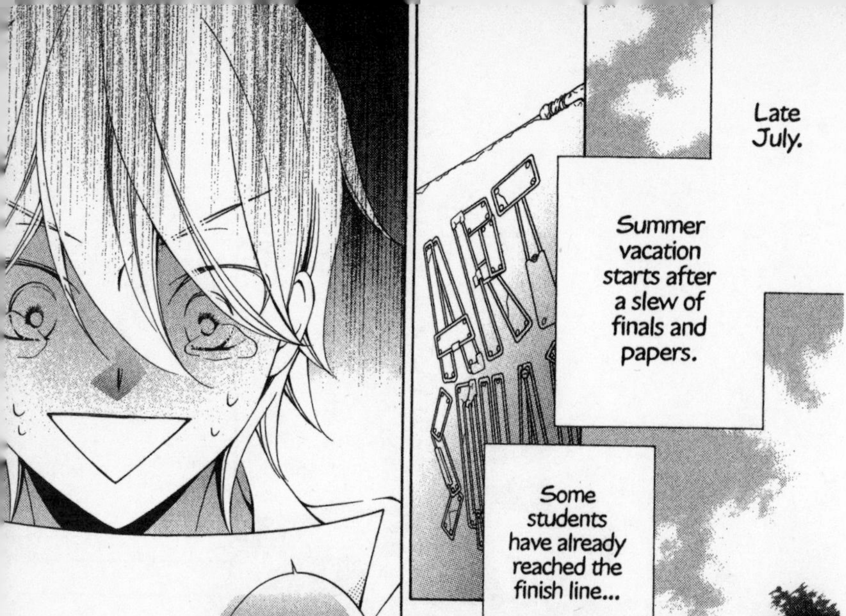
Late July.
Summer vacation starts after a slew of finals and papers.
Some students have already reached the finish line...
Booyah!
I made it!!!
I'VE STILL GOT THREE PAPERS LEFT!!
...while others have a long way to go.

Write me!

Open to ideas!!

With ideas for character names

And behind-the-scenes topics

And craft projects

And feedback!

Don't be shy!!

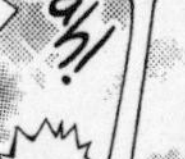

Bisco Hatori
c/o Behind the Scenes!! Editor
P.O. Box 77010
San Francisco, CA 94107

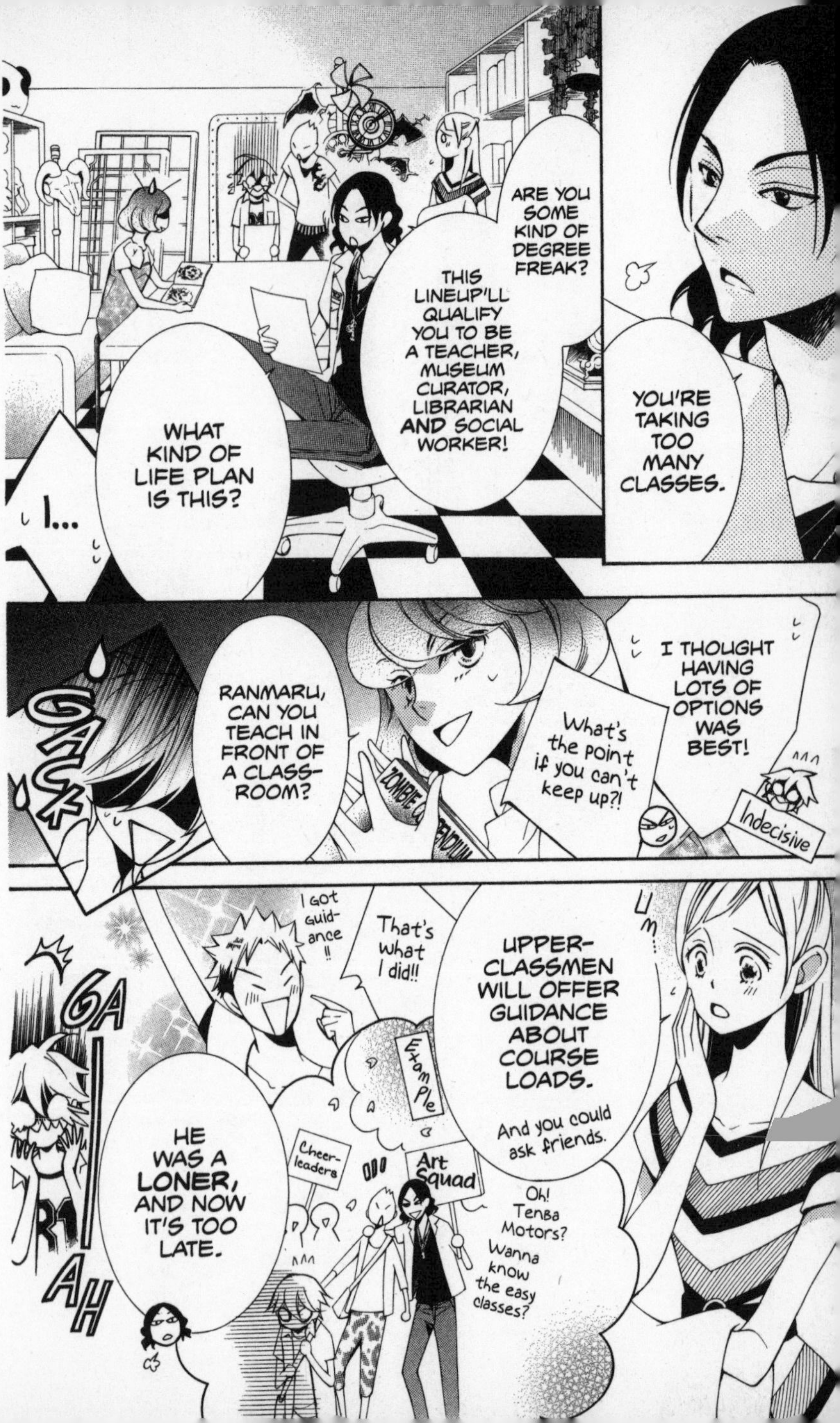
YOU'RE TAKING TOO MANY CLASSES.
ARE YOU SOME KIND OF DEGREE FREAK?
THIS LINEUP'LL QUALIFY YOU TO BE A TEACHER, MUSEUM CURATOR, LIBRARIAN AND SOCIAL WORKER!
WHAT KIND OF LIFE PLAN IS THIS?
I...
I THOUGHT HAVING LOTS OF OPTIONS WAS BEST!
Indecisive
What's the point if you can't keep up?!
RANMARU, CAN YOU TEACH IN FRONT OF A CLASS-ROOM?
GACK
UM...
UPPER-CLASSMEN WILL OFFER GUIDANCE ABOUT COURSE LOADS.
And you could ask friends.
Oh! Tenba Motors? Wanna know the easy classes?
That's what I did!!
I got guid-ance!!
Example
Art Squad
Cheer-leaders
HE WAS A LONER, AND NOW IT'S TOO LATE.
GAAH

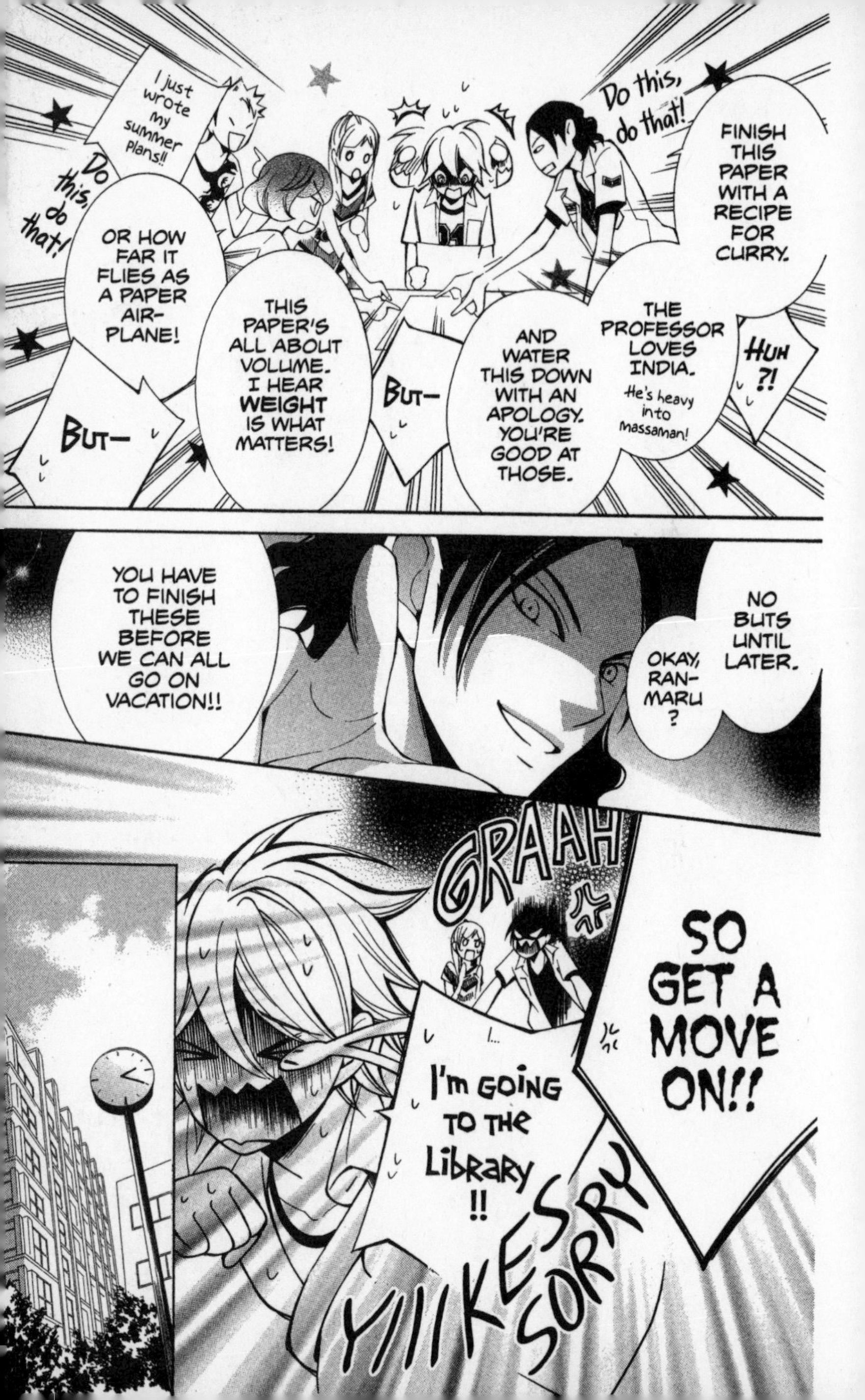
Do this, do that!
FINISH THIS PAPER WITH A RECIPE FOR CURRY.
HUH ?!
THE PROFESSOR LOVES INDIA.
He's heavy into Massaman!
AND WATER THIS DOWN WITH AN APOLOGY. YOU'RE GOOD AT THOSE.
BUT—
THIS PAPER'S ALL ABOUT VOLUME. I HEAR WEIGHT IS WHAT MATTERS!
I just wrote my summer plans!!
Do this, do that!
OR HOW FAR IT FLIES AS A PAPER AIR-PLANE!
BUT—
NO BUTS UNTIL LATER.
OKAY, RAN-MARU?
YOU HAVE TO FINISH THESE BEFORE WE CAN ALL GO ON VACATION!!
GRAAH
SO GET A MOVE ON!!
I...
I'm GOING TO THE Library!!
SORRY
YIIKES

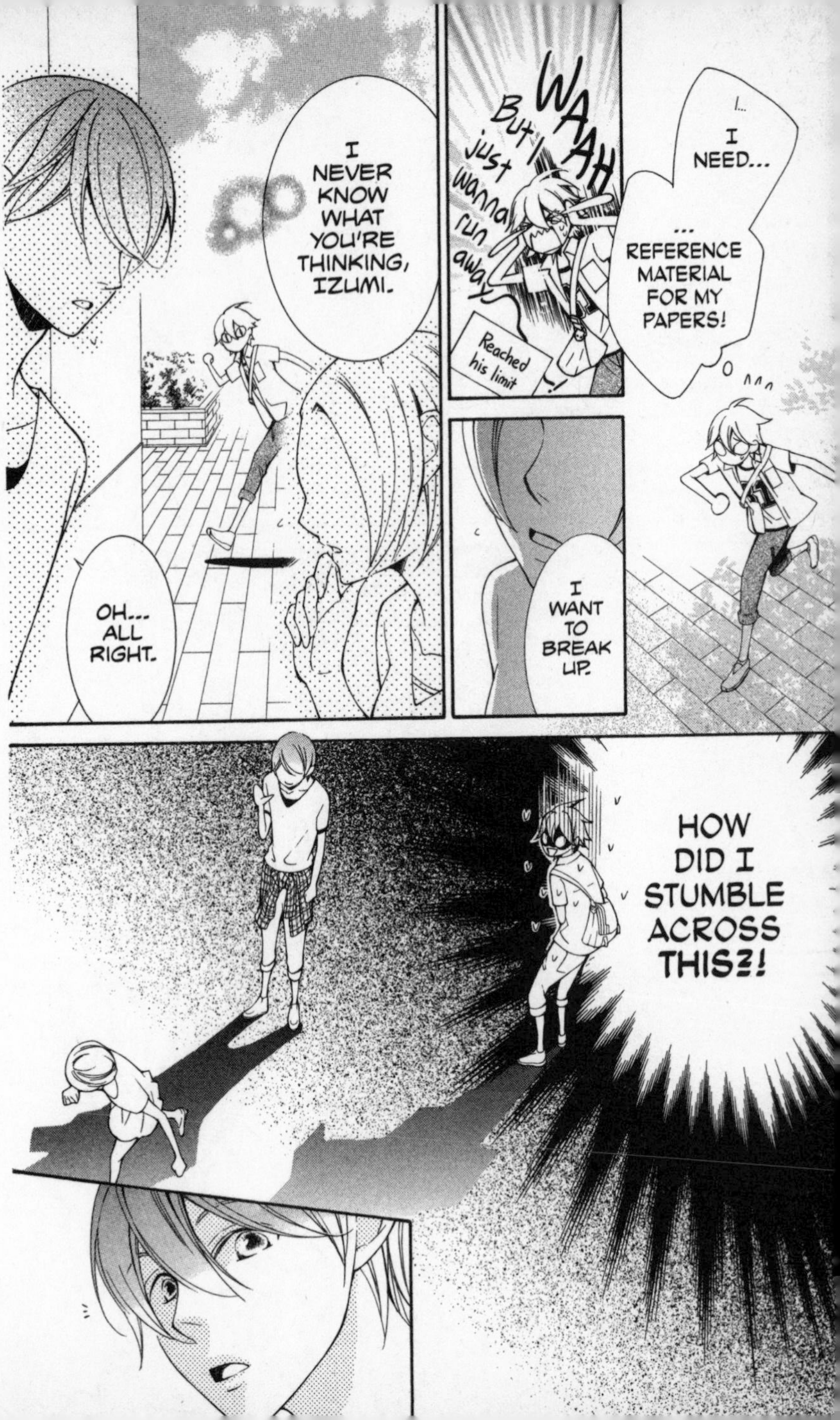
I...
I NEED...
...REFERENCE MATERIAL FOR MY PAPERS!
WAAAH
But I just wanna run away
Reached his limit
I WANT TO BREAK UP.
I NEVER KNOW WHAT YOU'RE THINKING, IZUMI.
OH... ALL RIGHT.
HOW DID I STUMBLE ACROSS THIS?!

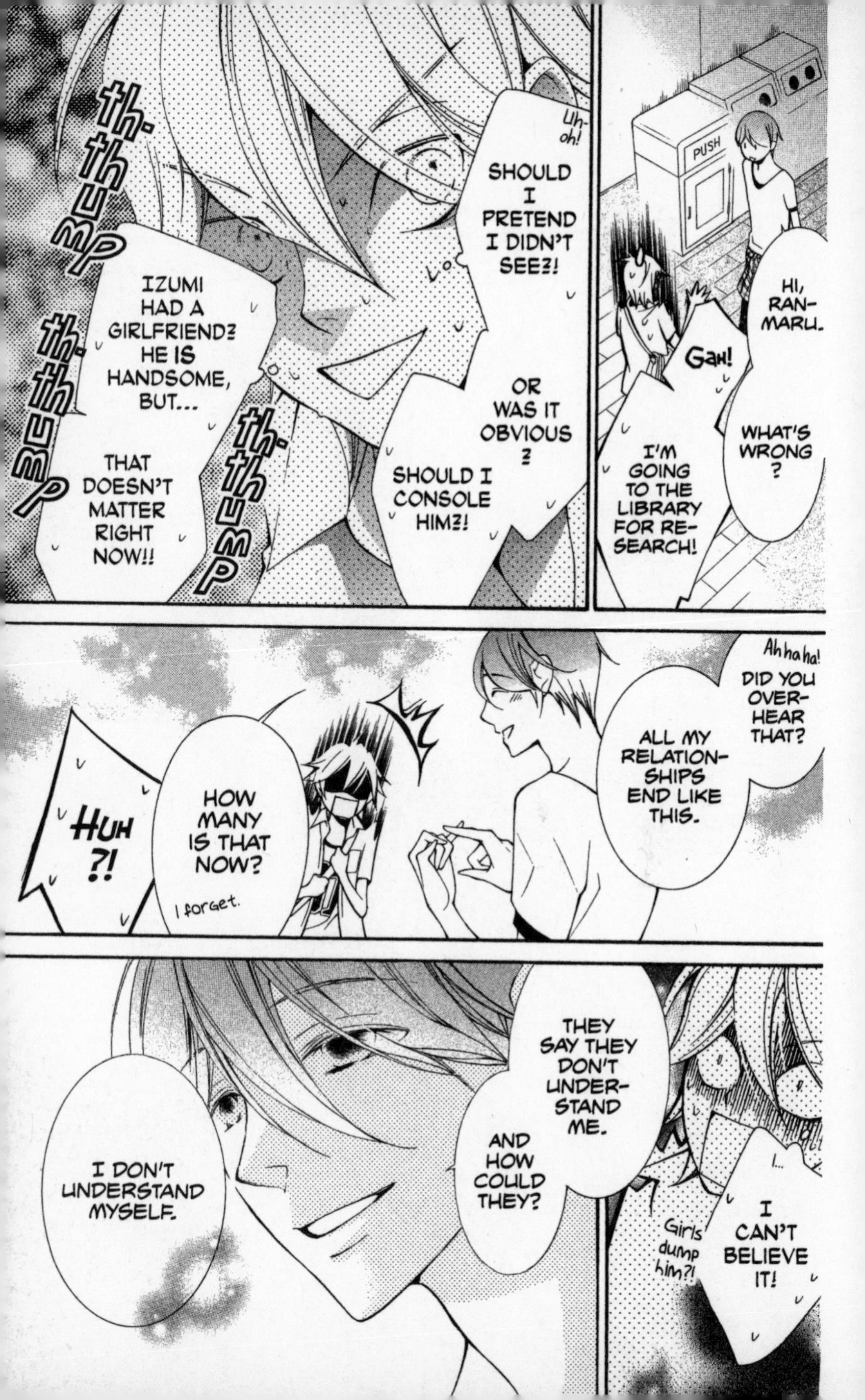

HI, RAN-MARU.
GAH!
WHAT'S WRONG?
I'M GOING TO THE LIBRARY FOR RE-SEARCH!
Uh-oh!
SHOULD I PRETEND I DIDN'T SEE?!
OR WAS IT OBVIOUS?
SHOULD I CONSOLE HIM?!
th-th-thump
IZUMI HAD A GIRLFRIEND? HE IS HANDSOME, BUT...
THAT DOESN'T MATTER RIGHT NOW!!
th-th-thump
Ahhaha!
DID YOU OVER-HEAR THAT?
ALL MY RELATION-SHIPS END LIKE THIS.
HOW MANY IS THAT NOW?
I forget.
HUH?!
I...
I CAN'T BELIEVE IT!
Girls dump him?!
THEY SAY THEY DON'T UNDER-STAND ME.
AND HOW COULD THEY?
I DON'T UNDERSTAND MYSELF.

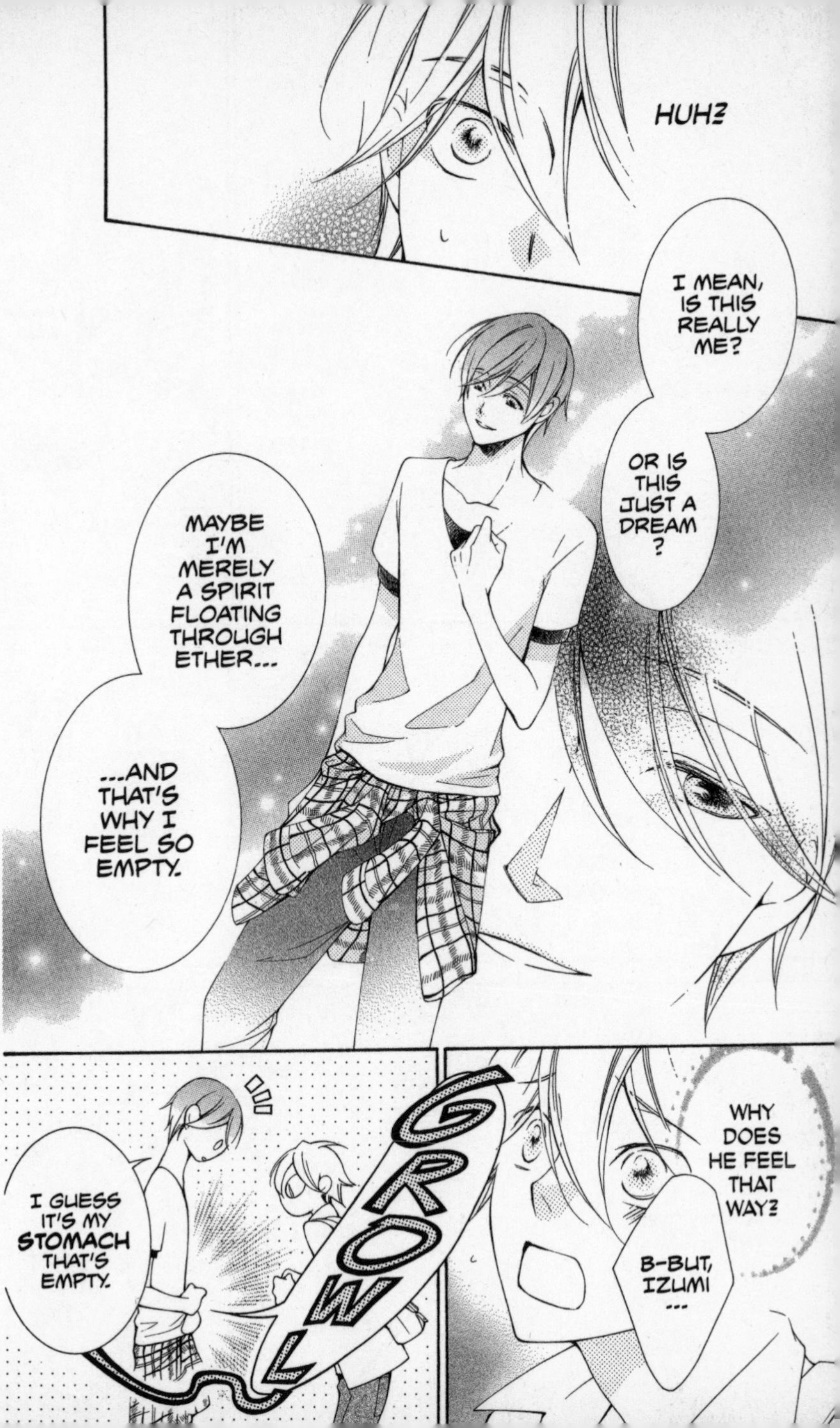
HUH?
I MEAN, IS THIS REALLY ME?
OR IS THIS JUST A DREAM?
MAYBE I'M MERELY A SPIRIT FLOATING THROUGH ETHER...
...AND THAT'S WHY I FEEL SO EMPTY.
WHY DOES HE FEEL THAT WAY?
B-BUT, IZUMI ...
GROWL
I GUESS IT'S MY STOMACH THAT'S EMPTY.

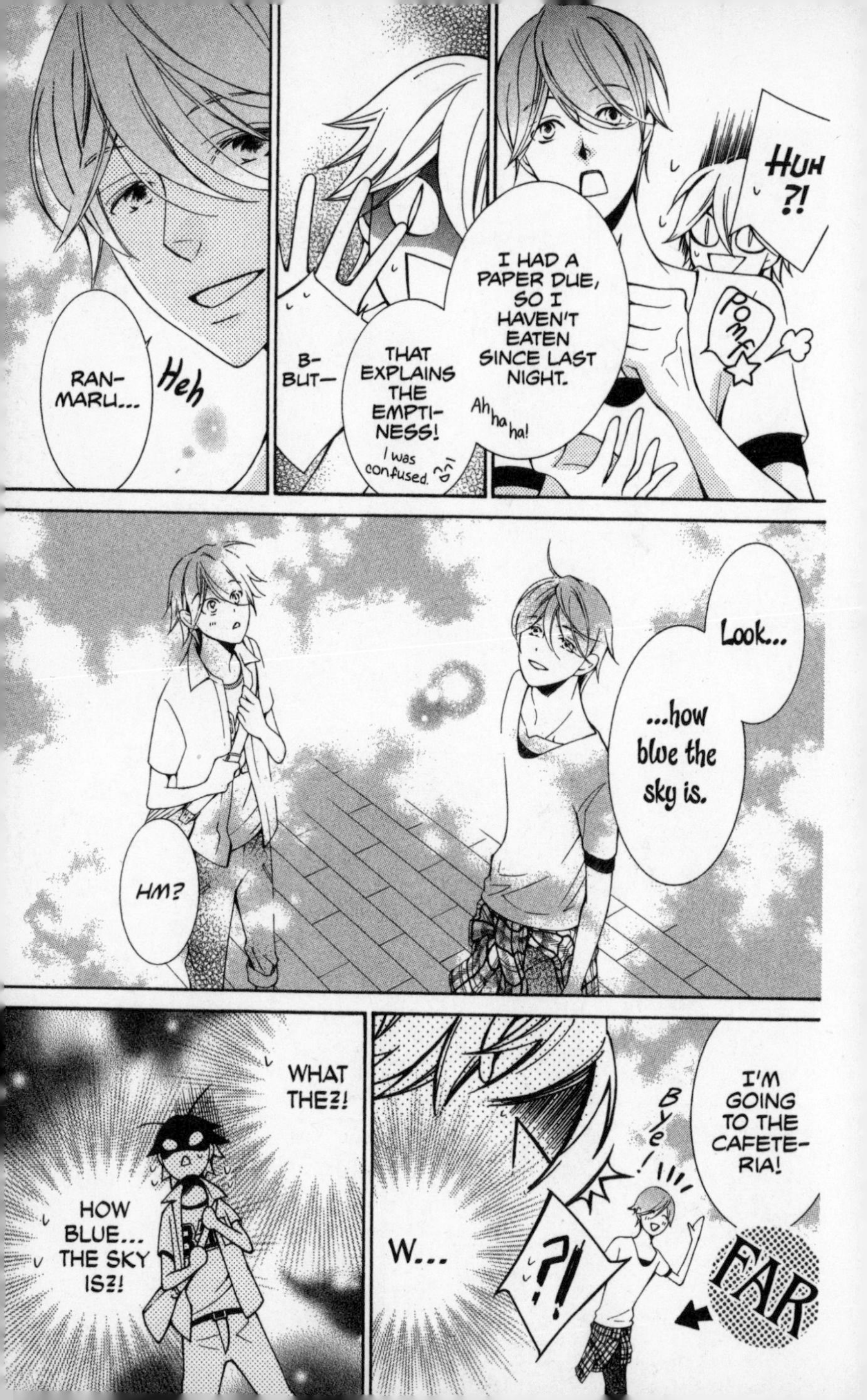
HUH ?!
POMF☆
I HAD A PAPER DUE, SO I HAVEN'T EATEN SINCE LAST NIGHT.
Ah ha ha!
THAT EXPLAINS THE EMPTINESS!
I was confused.
B-BUT—
Heh
RAN-MARU...
Look...
...how blue the sky is.
HM?
I'M GOING TO THE CAFETERIA!
Bye!
FAR
?!
W...
WHAT THE?!
HOW BLUE... THE SKY IS?!

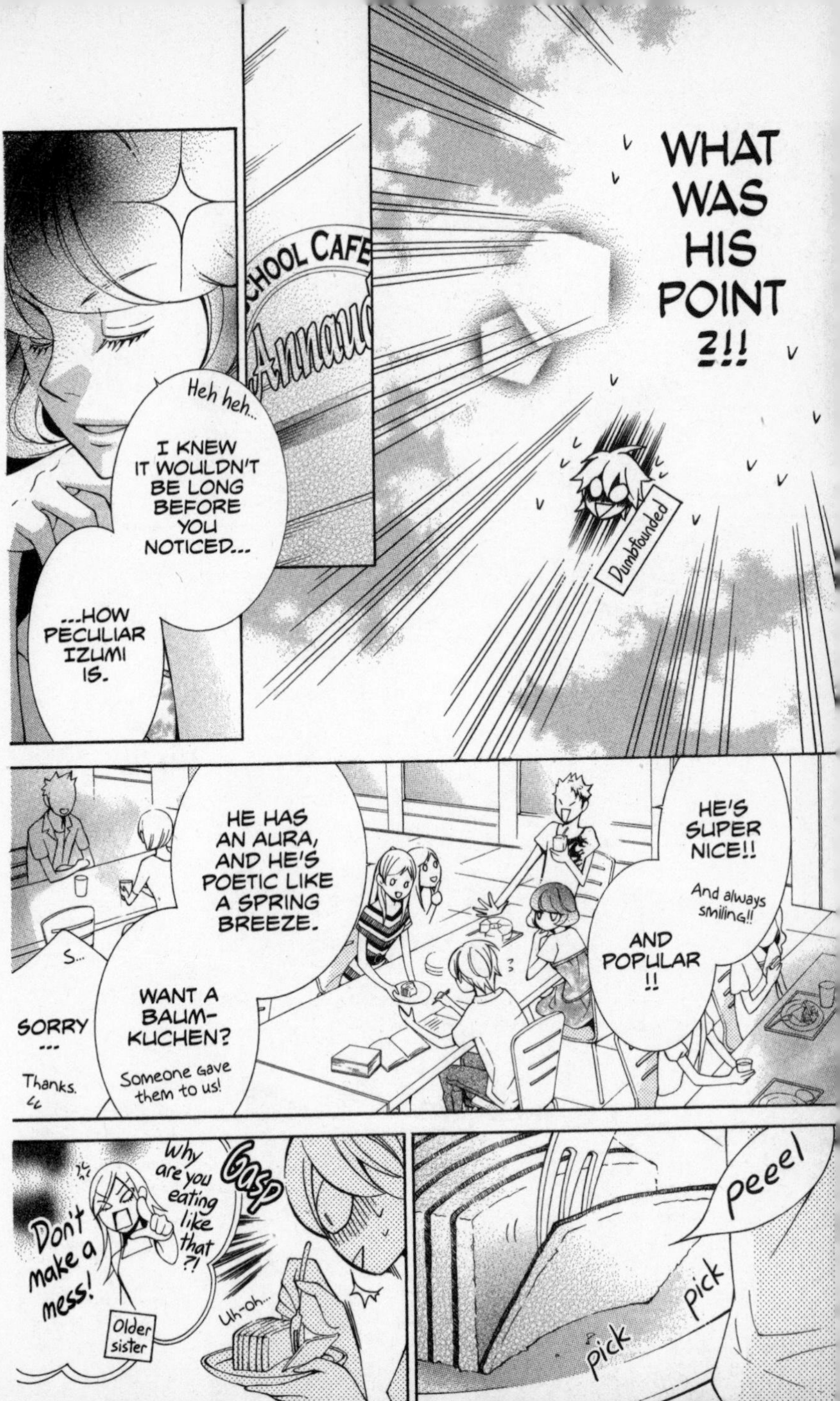
WHAT WAS HIS POINT ?!!
Dumbfounded
SCHOOL CAFE
Heh heh...
I KNEW IT WOULDN'T BE LONG BEFORE YOU NOTICED...
...HOW PECULIAR IZUMI IS.
HE'S SUPER NICE!!
And always smiling!!
AND POPULAR !!
HE HAS AN AURA, AND HE'S POETIC LIKE A SPRING BREEZE.
WANT A BAUM-KUCHEN?
Someone gave them to us!
S...
SORRY...
Thanks.
peeel
pick pick
pick
Gasp
Why are you eating like that?!
Don't make a mess!
Older sister
Uh-oh...

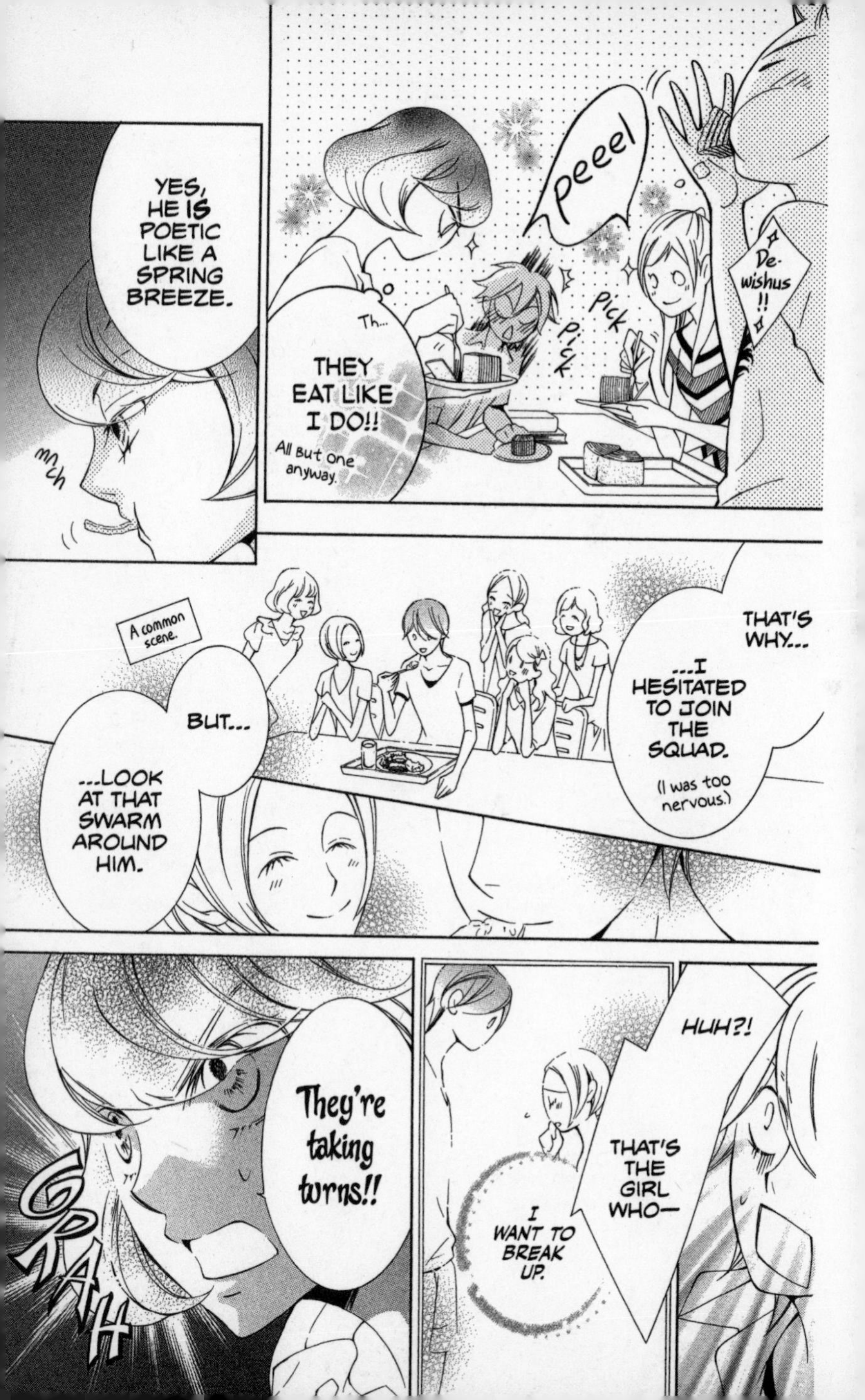
De-wishus!!
peeel
pick pick pick
Th...
THEY EAT LIKE I DO!!
All but one anyway.
YES, HE IS POETIC LIKE A SPRING BREEZE.
mnch
THAT'S WHY...
...I HESITATED TO JOIN THE SQUAD.
(I was too nervous.)
A common scene.
BUT...
...LOOK AT THAT SWARM AROUND HIM.
HUH?!
THAT'S THE GIRL WHO—
I WANT TO BREAK UP.
They're taking turns!!
GRAH

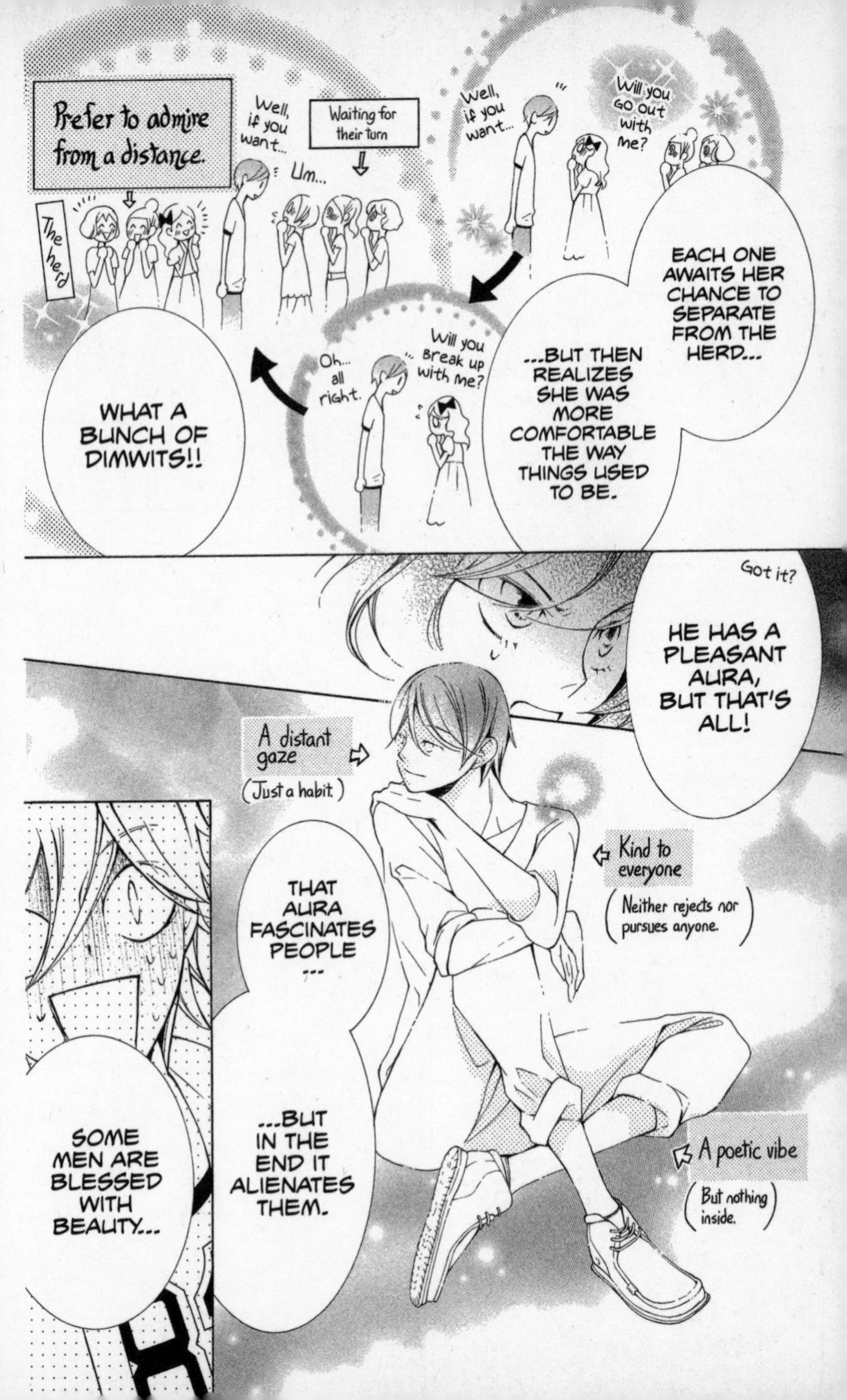
Will you go out with me?
Well, if you want...
EACH ONE AWAITS HER CHANCE TO SEPARATE FROM THE HERD...
...BUT THEN REALIZES SHE WAS MORE COMFORTABLE THE WAY THINGS USED TO BE.
Will you break up with me?
Oh... all right.
Waiting for their turn
Um...
Well, if you want...
Prefer to admire from a distance.
The herd
WHAT A BUNCH OF DIMWITS!!
Got it?
HE HAS A PLEASANT AURA, BUT THAT'S ALL!
Kind to everyone
(Neither rejects nor pursues anyone.)
A distant gaze
(Just a habit.)
THAT AURA FASCINATES PEOPLE...
...BUT IN THE END IT ALIENATES THEM.
A poetic vibe
(But nothing inside.)
SOME MEN ARE BLESSED WITH BEAUTY...

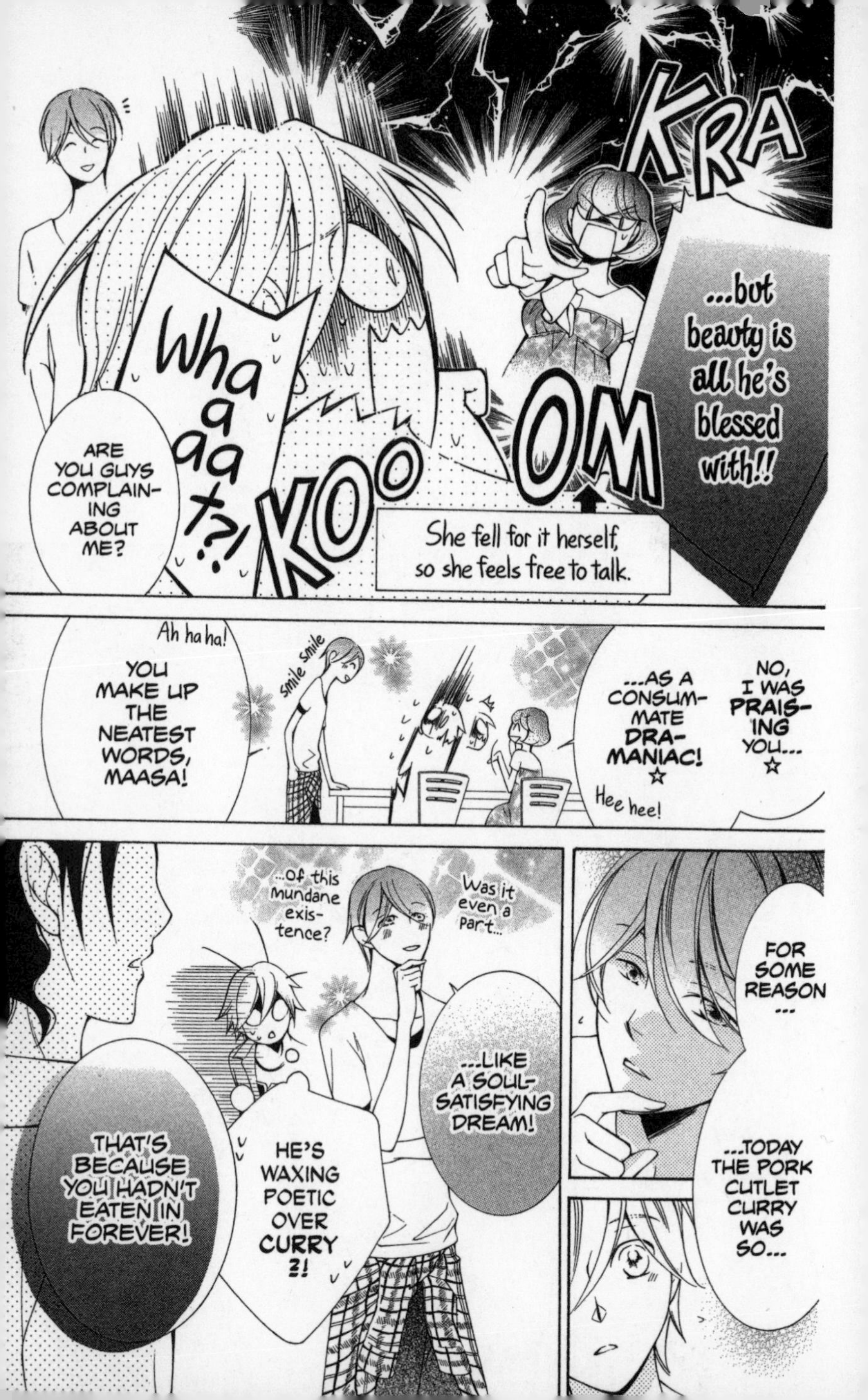
KRA
...but beauty is all he's blessed with!!
KOOOM
She fell for it herself, so she feels free to talk.
Whaaaat?!
ARE YOU GUYS COMPLAIN-ING ABOUT ME?
NO, I WAS PRAIS-ING YOU... ☆
...AS A CONSUM-MATE DRA-MANIAC! ☆
Hee hee!
smile smile
Ah ha ha!
YOU MAKE UP THE NEATEST WORDS, MAASA!
FOR SOME REASON...
...TODAY THE PORK CUTLET CURRY WAS SO...
Was it even a part...
...of this mundane exis-tence?
...LIKE A SOUL-SATISFYING DREAM!
HE'S WAXING POETIC OVER CURRY?!
THAT'S BECAUSE YOU HADN'T EATEN IN FOREVER!

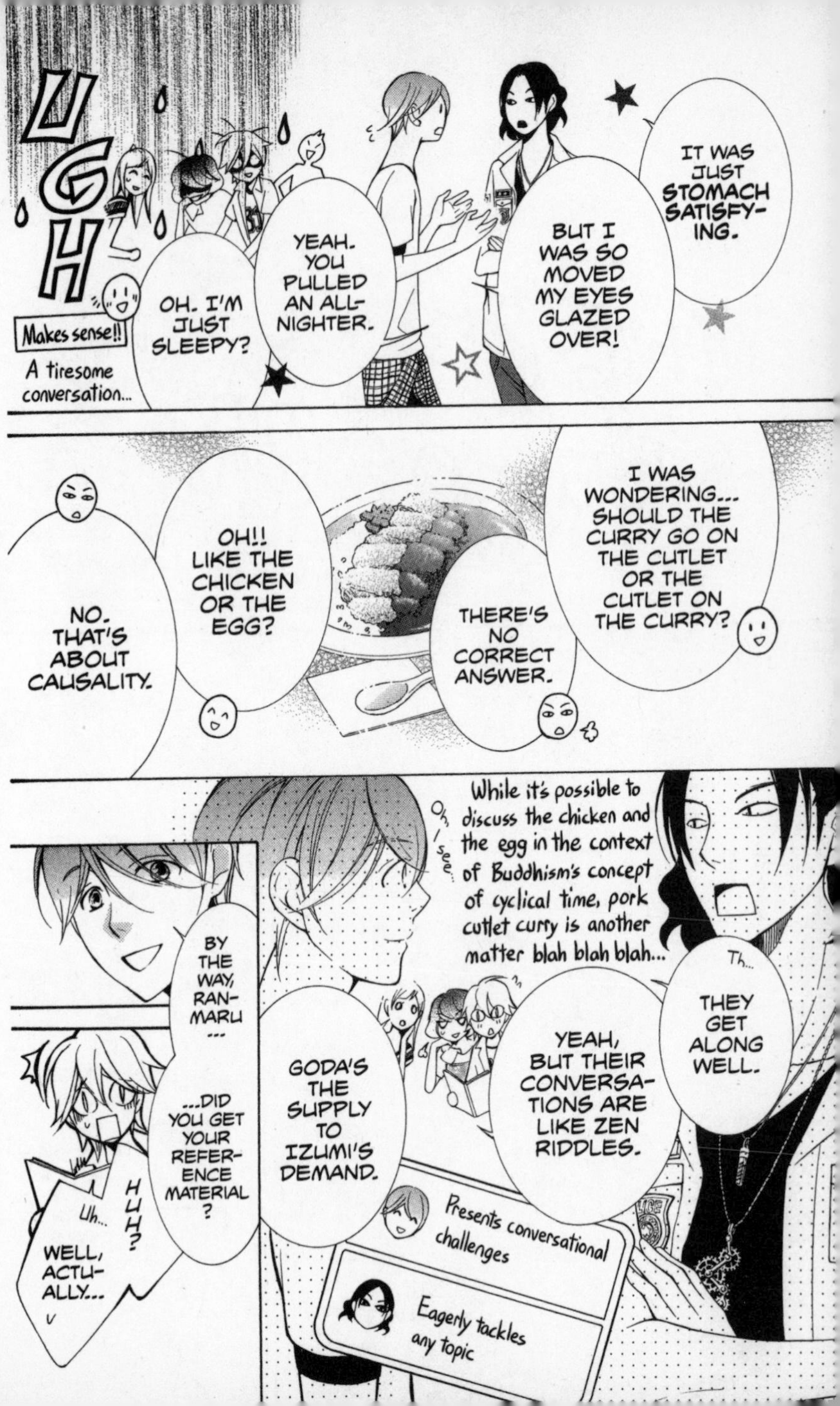
IT WAS JUST STOMACH SATISFYING.
BUT I WAS SO MOVED MY EYES GLAZED OVER!
YEAH. YOU PULLED AN ALL-NIGHTER.
OH. I'M JUST SLEEPY?
UGH
Makes sense!!
A tiresome conversation...
I WAS WONDERING... SHOULD THE CURRY GO ON THE CUTLET OR THE CUTLET ON THE CURRY?
THERE'S NO CORRECT ANSWER.
OH!! LIKE THE CHICKEN OR THE EGG?
NO. THAT'S ABOUT CAUSALITY.
While it's possible to discuss the chicken and the egg in the context of Buddhism's concept of cyclical time, pork cutlet curry is another matter blah blah blah...
Oh, I see...
Th...
THEY GET ALONG WELL.
YEAH, BUT THEIR CONVERSATIONS ARE LIKE ZEN RIDDLES.
GODA'S THE SUPPLY TO IZUMI'S DEMAND.
Presents conversational challenges
Eagerly tackles any topic
BY THE WAY, RANMARU...
...DID YOU GET YOUR REFERENCE MATERIAL?
HUH?
Uh...
WELL, ACTUALLY...

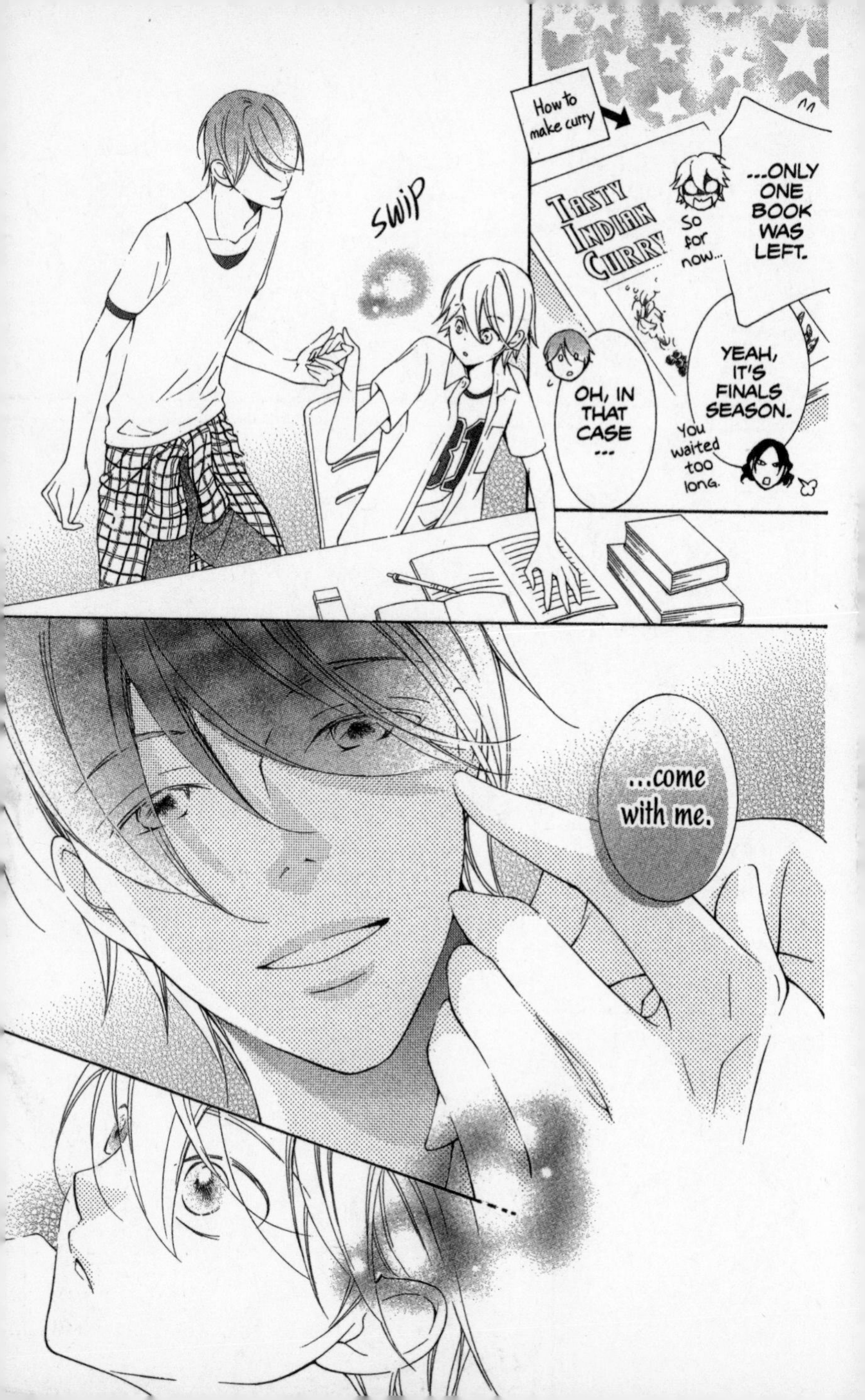
How to make curry
TASTY INDIAN CURRY
...ONLY ONE BOOK WAS LEFT.
So for now...
YEAH, IT'S FINALS SEASON.
You waited too long.
OH, IN THAT CASE ...
SWIP
...come with me.
...

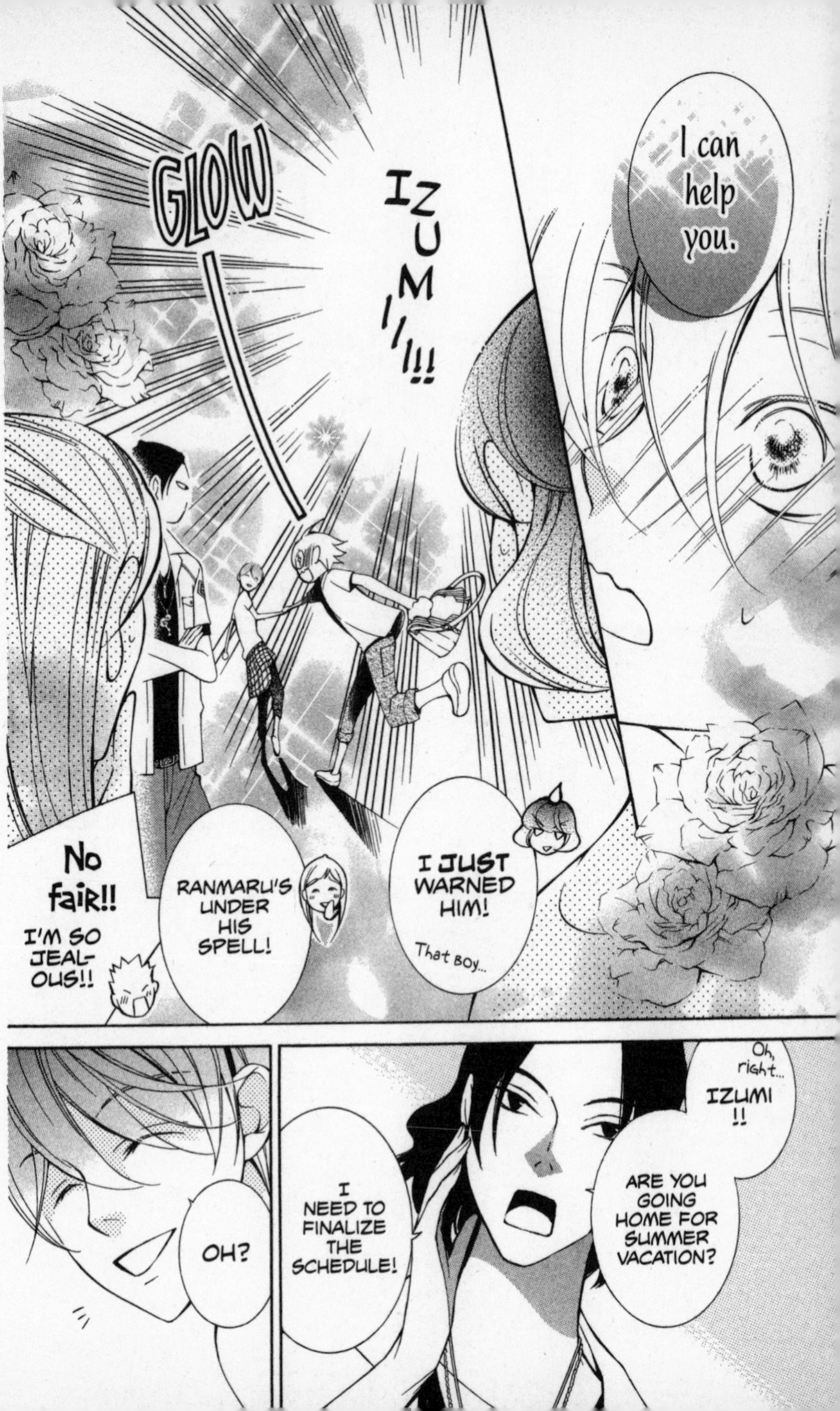
I can help you.
IZUMIII!!!
GLOW
I JUST WARNED HIM!
That boy...
RANMARU'S UNDER HIS SPELL!
No fair!!
I'M SO JEAL-OUS!!
Oh, right...
IZUMI!!
ARE YOU GOING HOME FOR SUMMER VACATION?
I NEED TO FINALIZE THE SCHEDULE!
OH?

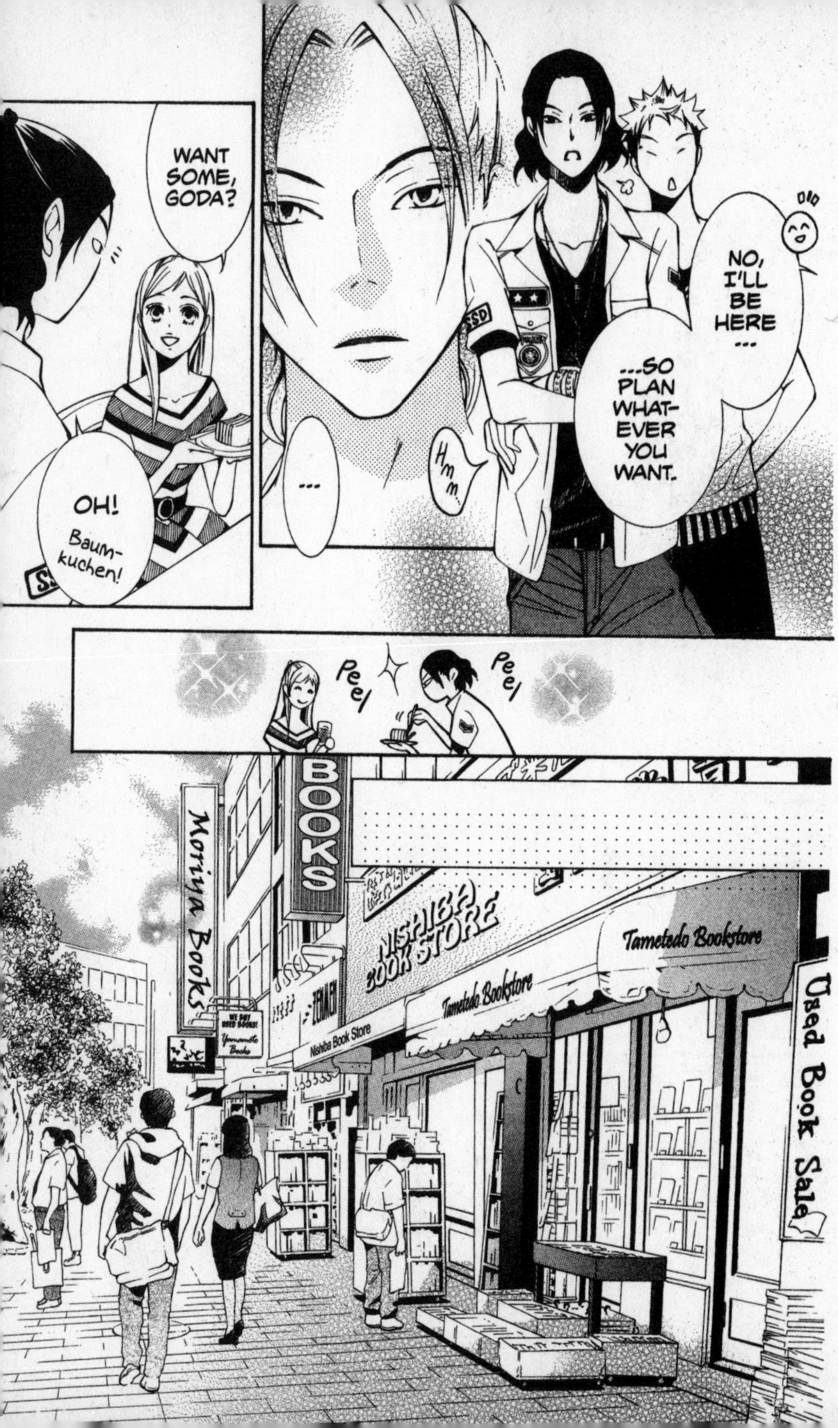

NO, I'LL BE HERE...
...SO PLAN WHATEVER YOU WANT.
Hmm...
...
WANT SOME, GODA?
OH! Baumkuchen!
Peel
Peel
Used Book Sale
Tametedo Bookstore
Tametedo Bookstore
NISHIBA BOOK STORE
BOOKS
Nishiba Book Store
Moriya Books
WE BUY USED BOOKS! Yamamoto Books

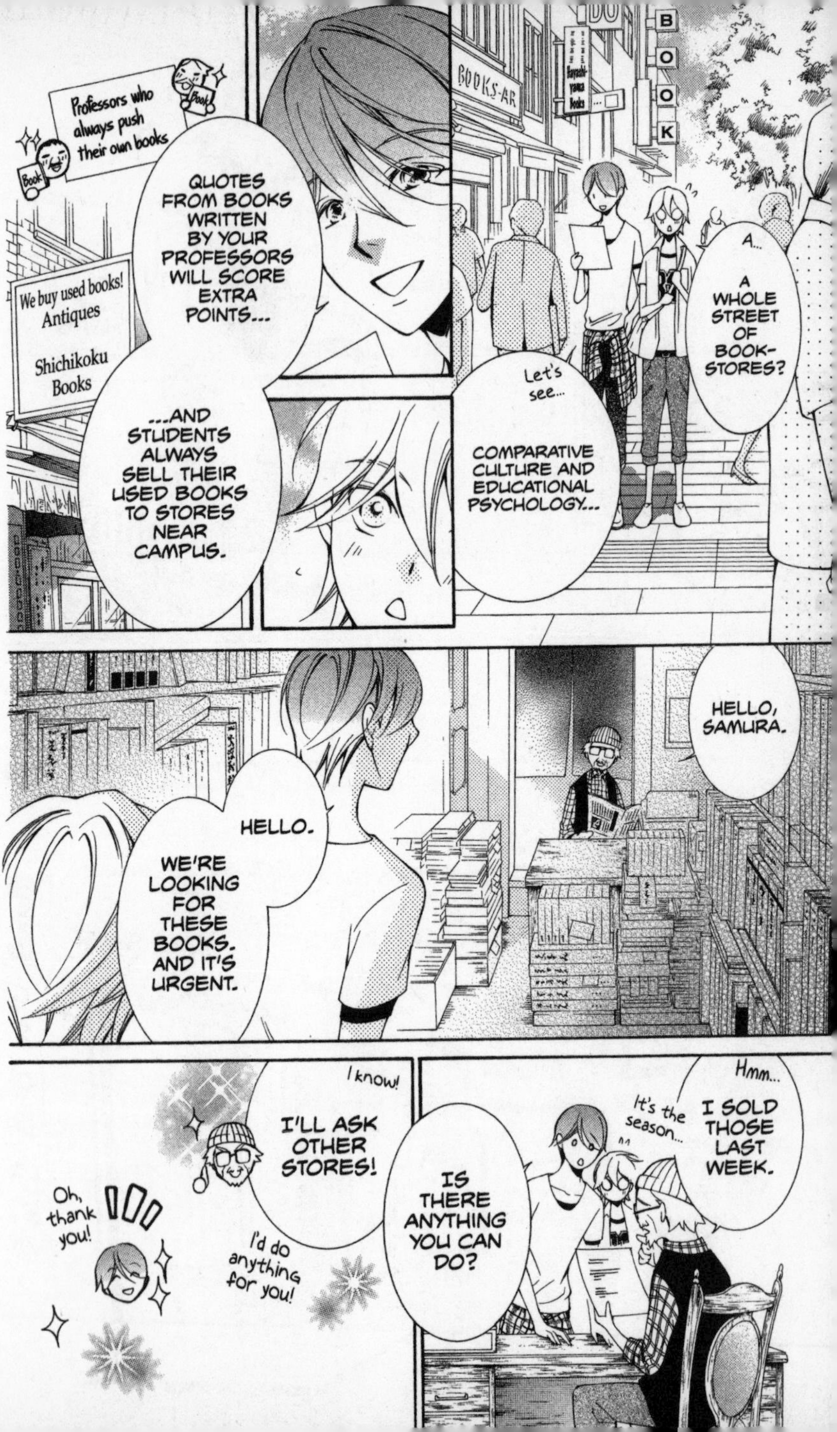
BOOK
BOOKS-AR
Hayashi-yama Books
A...
A WHOLE STREET OF BOOK-STORES?
Let's see...
COMPARATIVE CULTURE AND EDUCATIONAL PSYCHOLOGY...
QUOTES FROM BOOKS WRITTEN BY YOUR PROFESSORS WILL SCORE EXTRA POINTS...
...AND STUDENTS ALWAYS SELL THEIR USED BOOKS TO STORES NEAR CAMPUS.
Professors who always push their own books
Book
Book
We buy used books! Antiques
Shichikoku Books
HELLO, SAMURA.
HELLO.
WE'RE LOOKING FOR THESE BOOKS. AND IT'S URGENT.
Hmm...
I SOLD THOSE LAST WEEK.
It's the season...
IS THERE ANYTHING YOU CAN DO?
I know!
I'LL ASK OTHER STORES!
Oh, thank you!
I'd do anything for you!

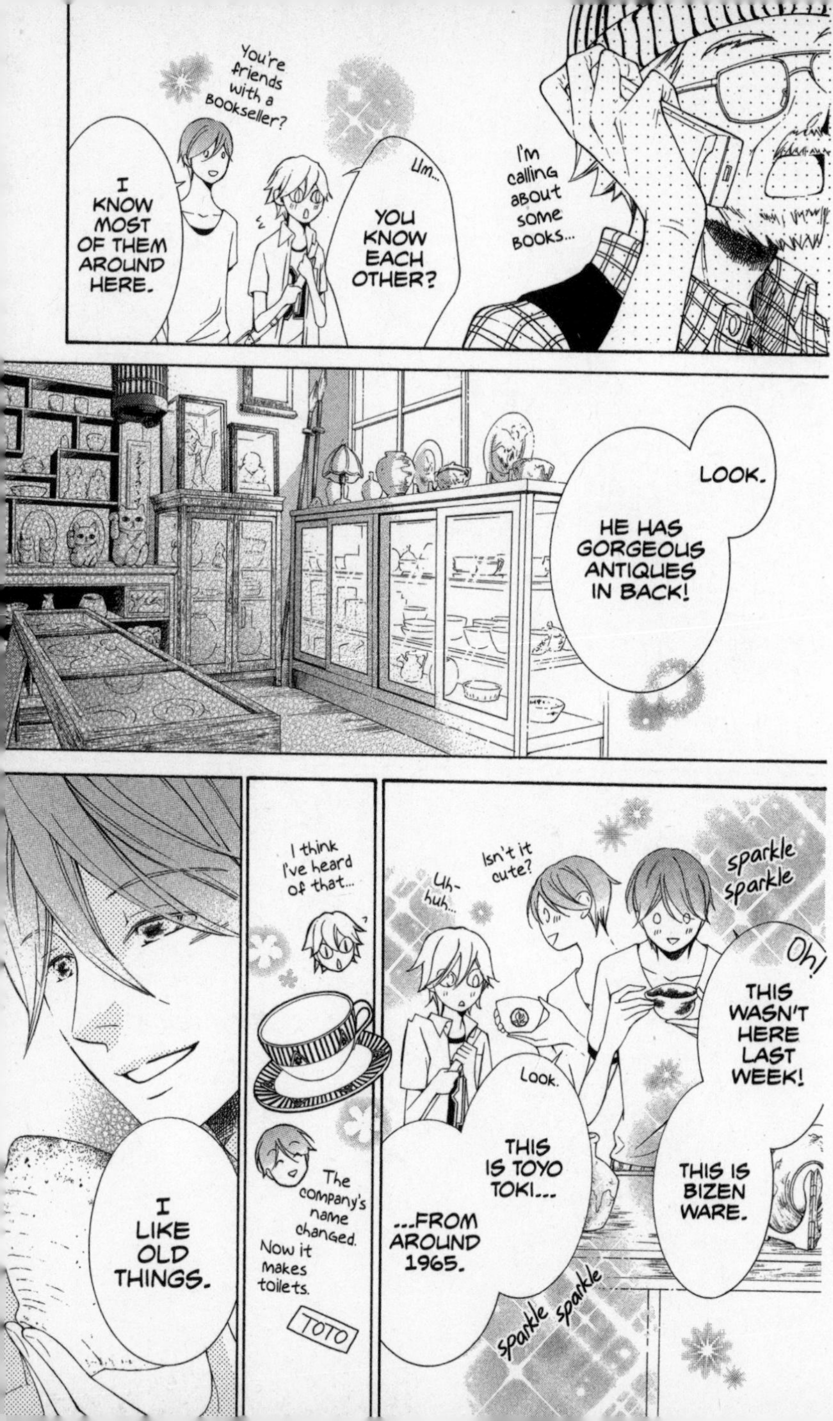
I'm calling about some books...
Um... YOU KNOW EACH OTHER?
You're friends with a Bookseller?
I KNOW MOST OF THEM AROUND HERE.
LOOK. HE HAS GORGEOUS ANTIQUES IN BACK!
sparkle sparkle
Oh! THIS WASN'T HERE LAST WEEK!
Isn't it cute?
Uh-huh...
THIS IS BIZEN WARE.
Look. THIS IS TOYO TOKI...
...FROM AROUND 1965.
sparkle sparkle
I think I've heard of that...
The company's name changed. Now it makes toilets.
TOTO
I LIKE OLD THINGS.

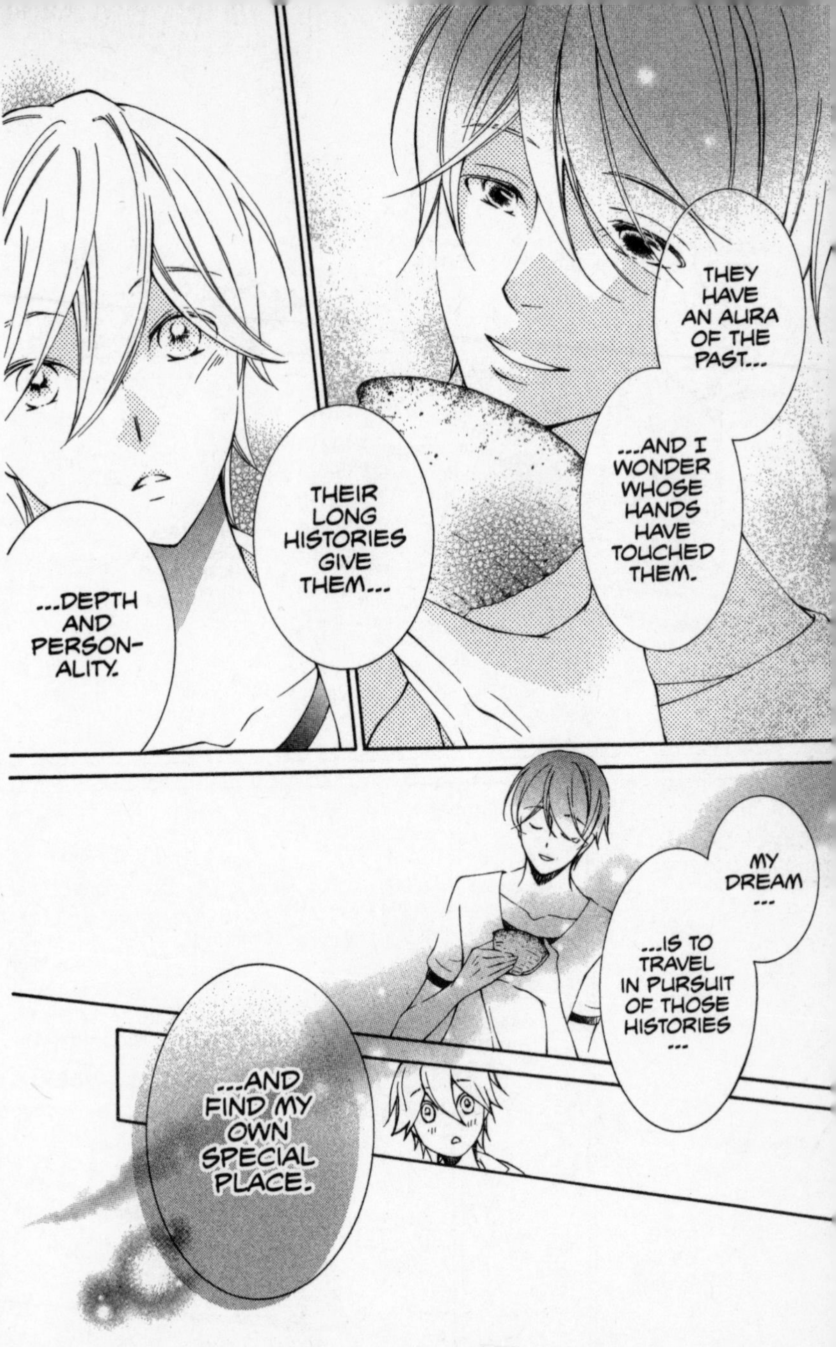
THEY HAVE AN AURA OF THE PAST...
...AND I WONDER WHOSE HANDS HAVE TOUCHED THEM.
THEIR LONG HISTORIES GIVE THEM...
...DEPTH AND PERSON-ALITY.
MY DREAM...
...IS TO TRAVEL IN PURSUIT OF THOSE HISTORIES...
...AND FIND MY OWN SPECIAL PLACE.

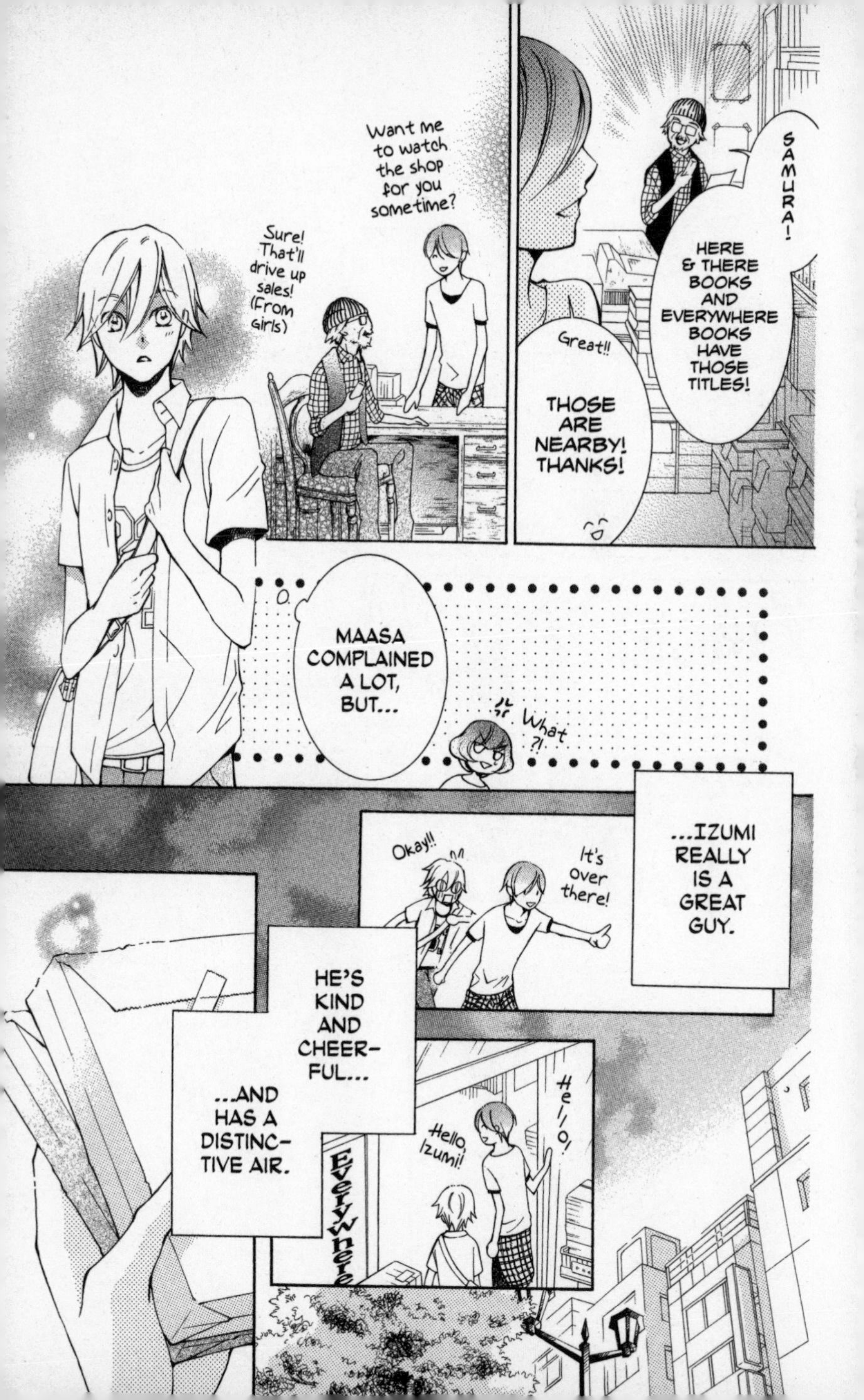
SAMURA!
HERE & THERE BOOKS AND EVERYWHERE BOOKS HAVE THOSE TITLES!
Great!!
THOSE ARE NEARBY! THANKS!
Want me to watch the shop for you sometime?
Sure! That'll drive up sales! (From girls)
MAASA COMPLAINED A LOT, BUT...
What?!
...IZUMI REALLY IS A GREAT GUY.
It's over there!
Okay!!
HE'S KIND AND CHEER-FUL...
...AND HAS A DISTINC-TIVE AIR.
Hello!
Hello, Izumi!
Everywhere

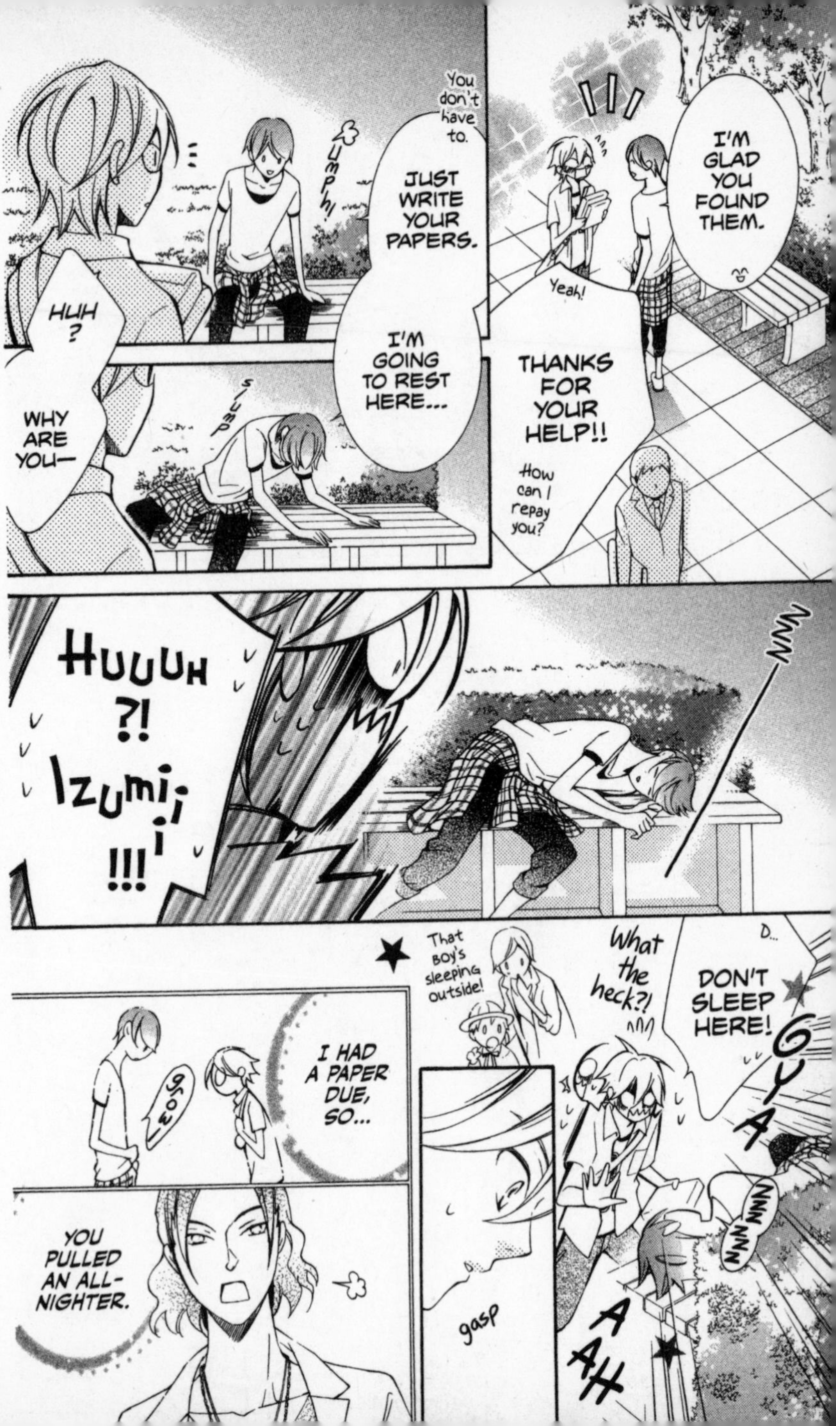
I'M GLAD YOU FOUND THEM.
Yeah!
THANKS FOR YOUR HELP!!
How can I repay you?
You don't have to.
HUMPH!
JUST WRITE YOUR PAPERS.
I'M GOING TO REST HERE...
SLUMP
HUH?
WHY ARE YOU—
NNN
HUUUH?! Izumiiii!!!
That boy's sleeping outside!
What the heck?!
D...
DON'T SLEEP HERE!
GYAA
NNN NNN
AAH
gasp
growl
I HAD A PAPER DUE, SO...
YOU PULLED AN ALL-NIGHTER.

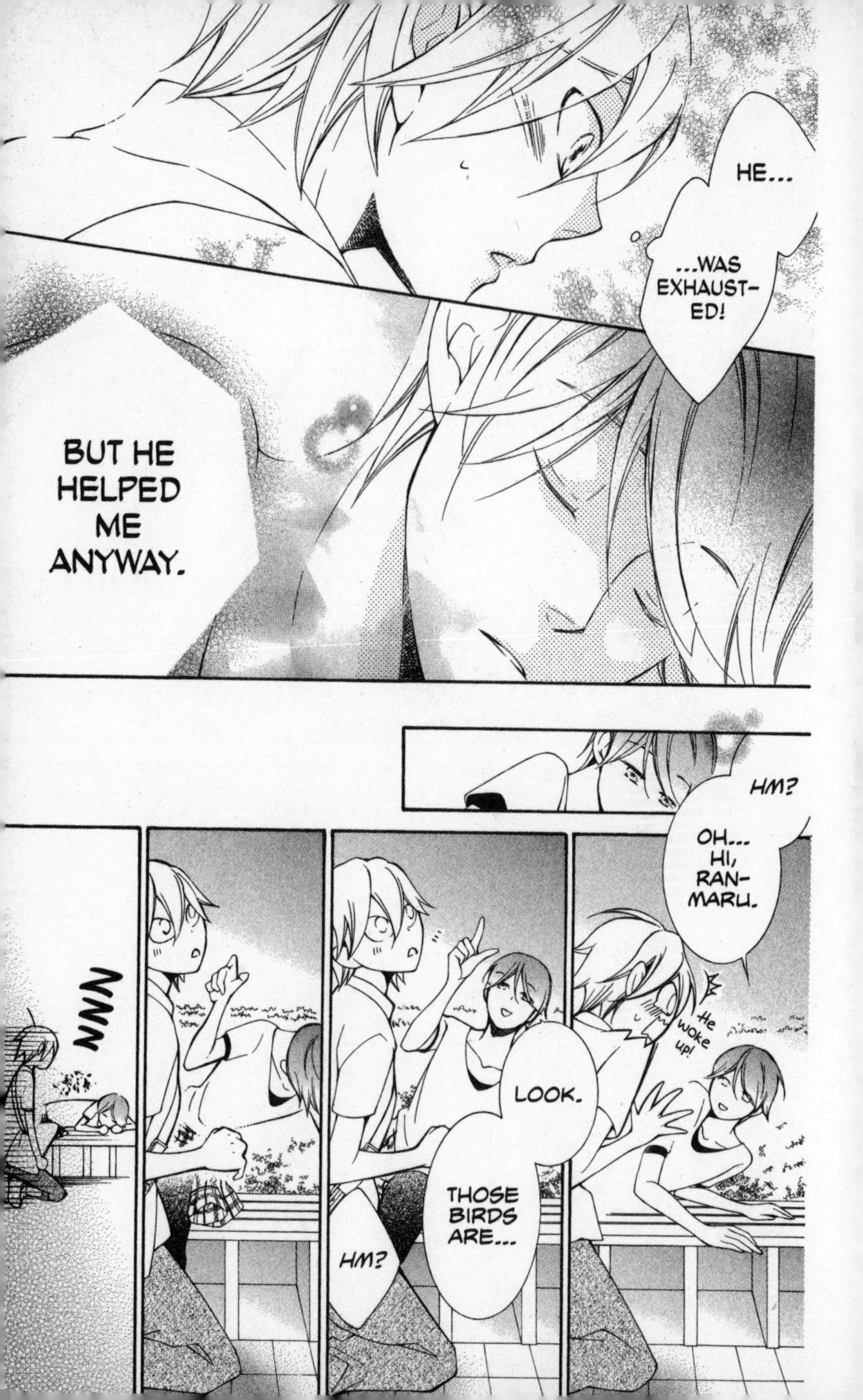
HE...
...WAS EXHAUSTED!
BUT HE HELPED ME ANYWAY.
HM?
OH... HI, RANMARU.
He woke up!
LOOK.
THOSE BIRDS ARE...
HM?
NNN

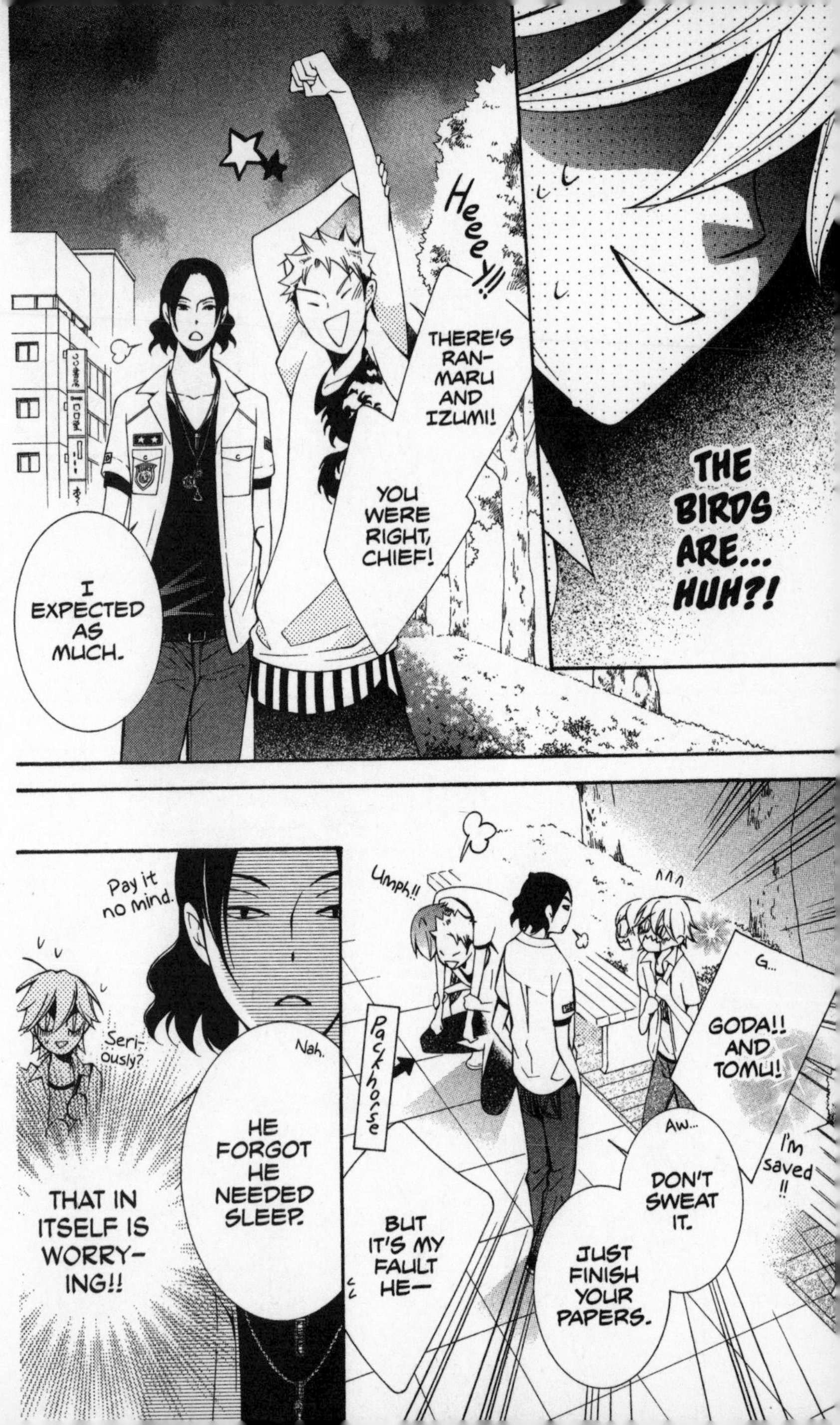
THE BIRDS ARE... HUH?!
Heeey!!
THERE'S RANMARU AND IZUMI!
YOU WERE RIGHT, CHIEF!
I EXPECTED AS MUCH.
G...
GODA!! AND TOMU!
I'm saved!!
Umph!!
Packhorse
Aw...
DON'T SWEAT IT.
JUST FINISH YOUR PAPERS.
BUT IT'S MY FAULT HE—
Pay it no mind.
Nah.
HE FORGOT HE NEEDED SLEEP.
Seriously?
THAT IN ITSELF IS WORRYING!!

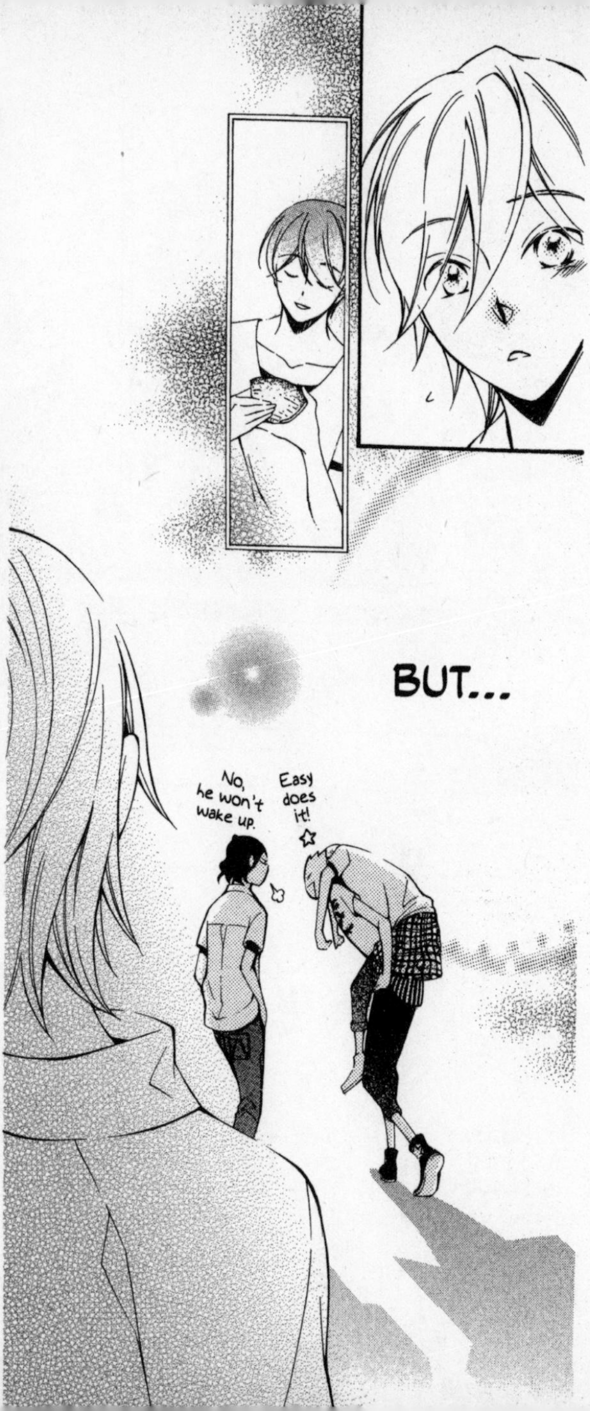
BUT...
Easy does it!
No, he won't wake up.

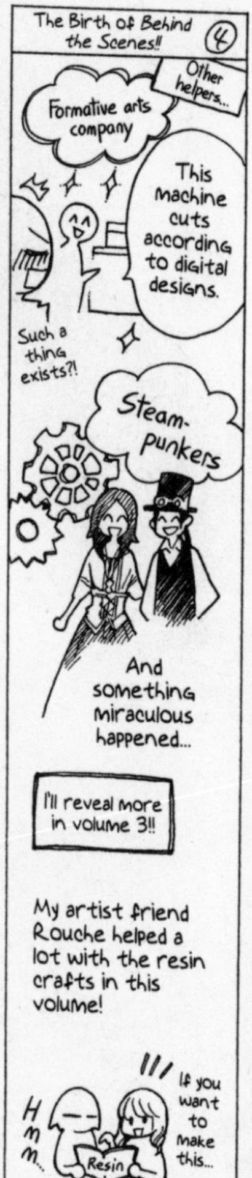
The Birth of Behind the Scenes!! 4
Other helpers...
Formative arts company
This machine cuts according to digital designs.
Such a thing exists?!
Steam-punkers
And something miraculous happened...
I'll reveal more in volume 3!!
My artist friend Rouche helped a lot with the resin crafts in this volume!
If you want to make this...
Resin
Hmm...
She sent me a video!
Gyah! How help-ful!
Rouche participates in events and runs an online shop.

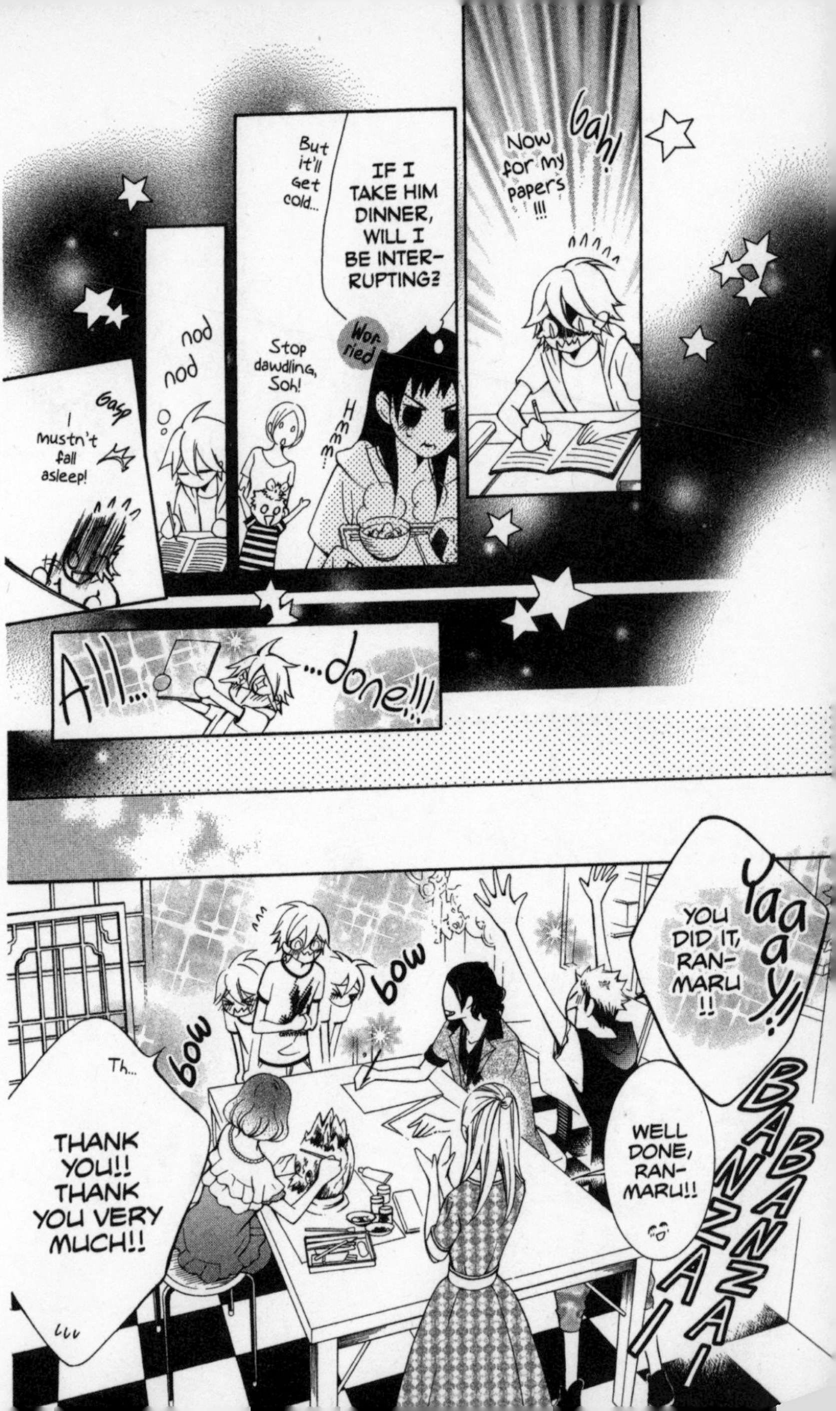
Bah!
Now for my papers!!!
IF I TAKE HIM DINNER, WILL I BE INTERRUPTING?
But it'll get cold...
Worried
Hmm...
Stop dawdling, Soh!
nod
nod
Gasp
I mustn't fall asleep!
All...
...done!!!
Yaaay!!
YOU DID IT, RAN-MARU!!
BANZAI
BANZAI
WELL DONE, RAN-MARU!!
bow
bow
Th...
THANK YOU!! THANK YOU VERY MUCH!!

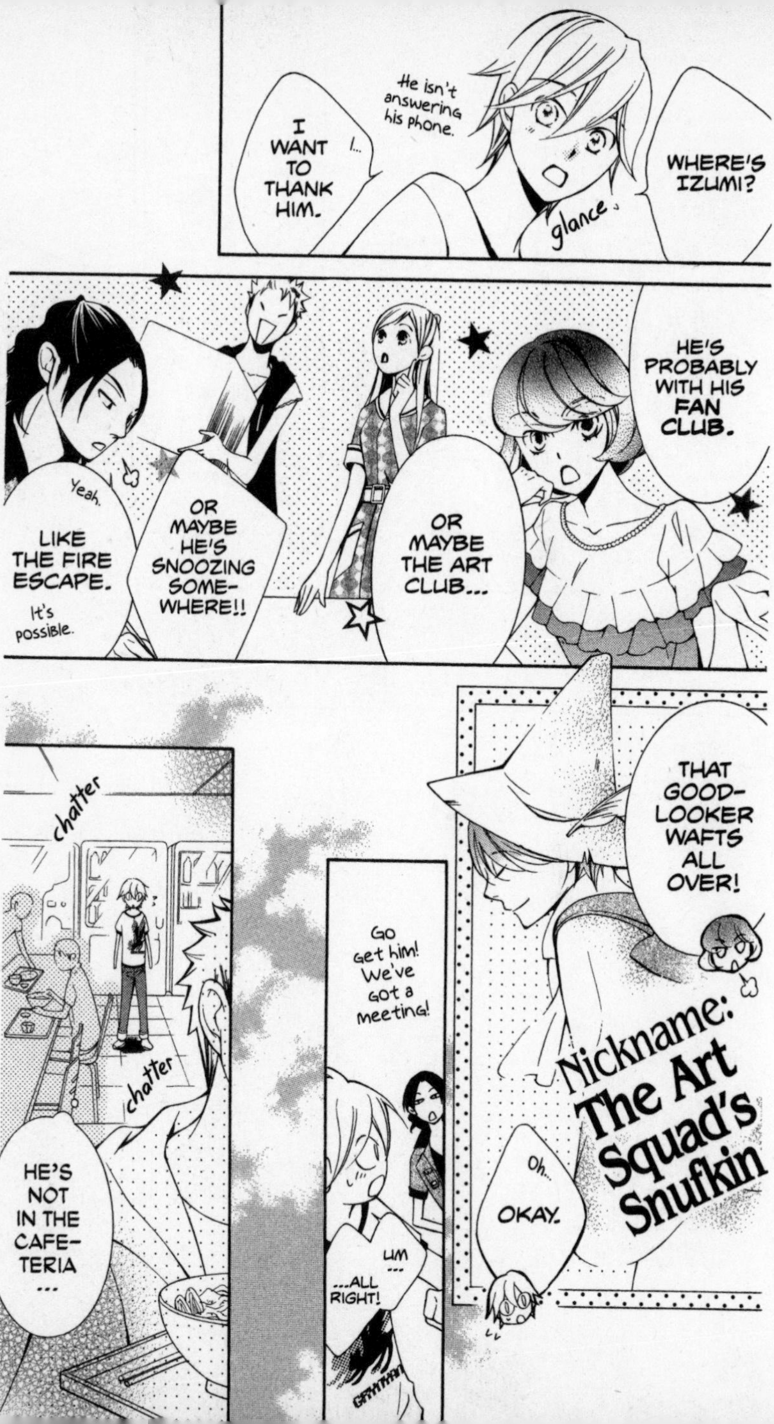
WHERE'S IZUMI?
glance
He isn't answering his phone.
I...
I WANT TO THANK HIM.
HE'S PROBABLY WITH HIS FAN CLUB.
OR MAYBE THE ART CLUB...
OR MAYBE HE'S SNOOZING SOME-WHERE!!
Yeah.
LIKE THE FIRE ESCAPE.
It's possible.
THAT GOOD-LOOKER WAFTS ALL OVER!
Nickname: The Art Squad's Snufkin
Oh...
OKAY.
Go get him! We've got a meeting!
UM...
...ALL RIGHT!
chatter
chatter
HE'S NOT IN THE CAFE-TERIA...

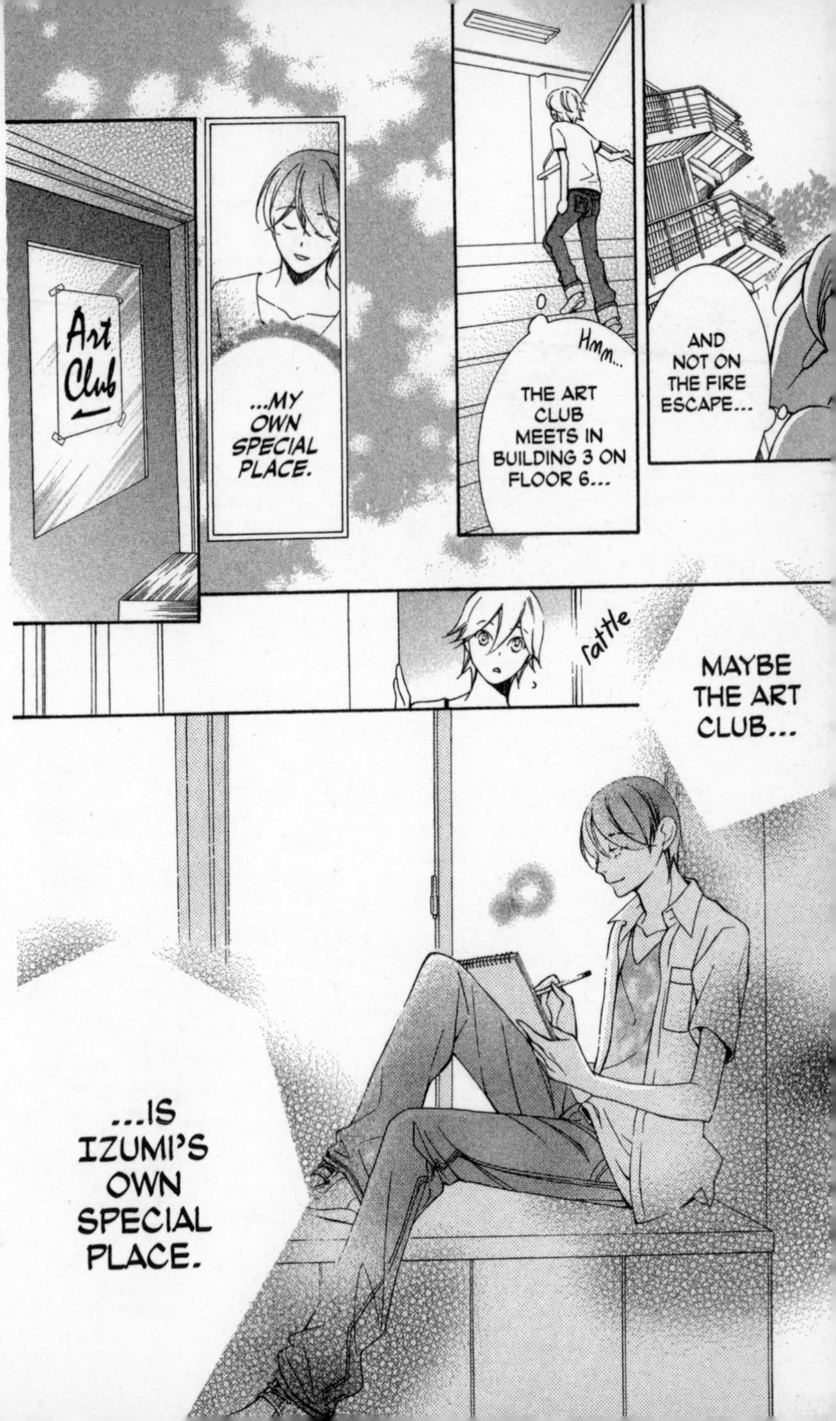
AND NOT ON THE FIRE ESCAPE...
Hmm...
THE ART CLUB MEETS IN BUILDING 3 ON FLOOR 6...
...MY OWN SPECIAL PLACE.
Art Club
rattle
MAYBE THE ART CLUB...
...IS IZUMI'S OWN SPECIAL PLACE.

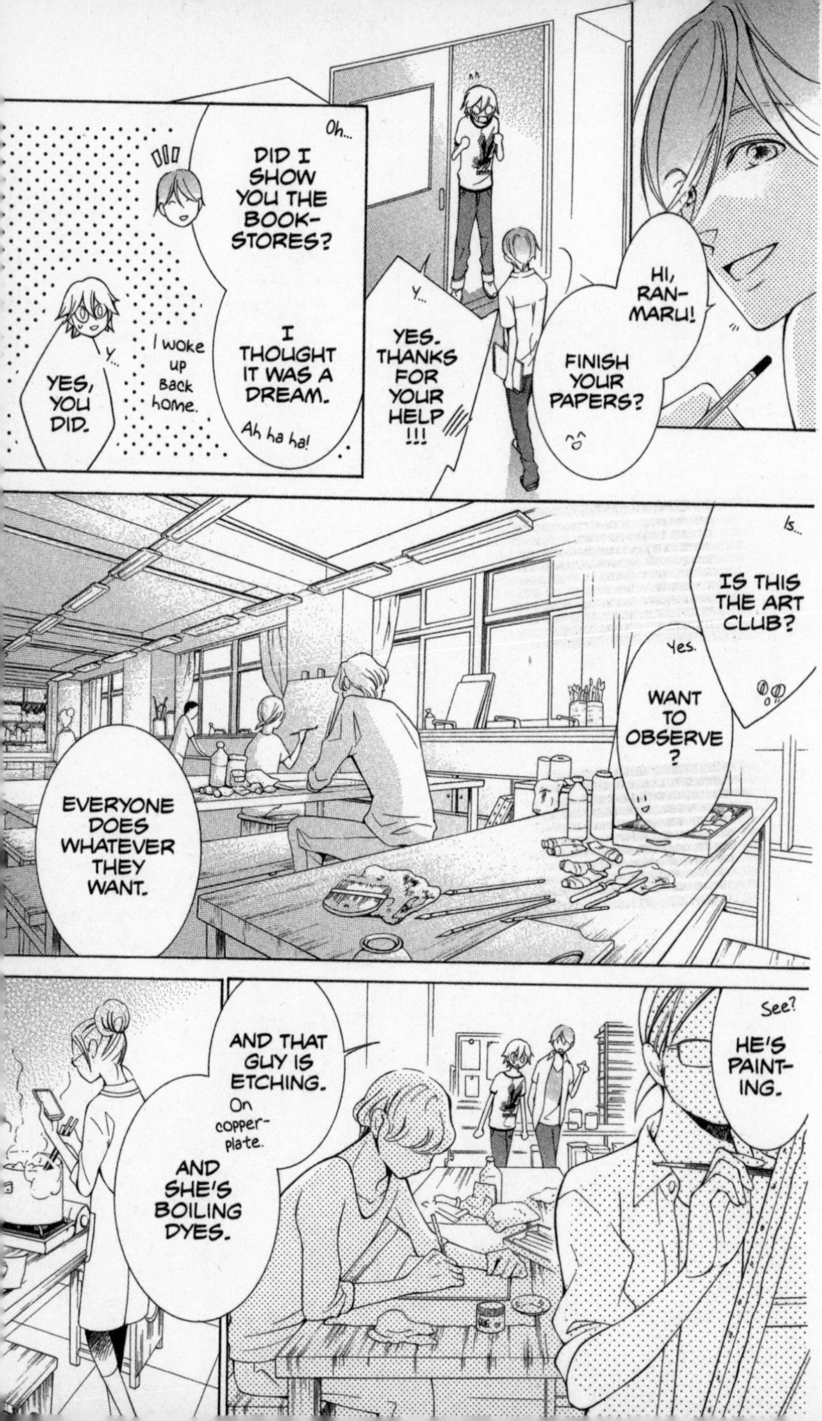
HI, RAN-MARU!
FINISH YOUR PAPERS?
Y...
YES. THANKS FOR YOUR HELP!!!
Oh...
DID I SHOW YOU THE BOOK-STORES?
I THOUGHT IT WAS A DREAM.
Ah ha ha!
I woke up Back home.
Y...
YES, YOU DID.
Is...
IS THIS THE ART CLUB?
Yes.
WANT TO OBSERVE?
EVERYONE DOES WHATEVER THEY WANT.
See?
HE'S PAINT-ING.
AND THAT GUY IS ETCHING.
On copper-plate.
AND SHE'S BOILING DYES.

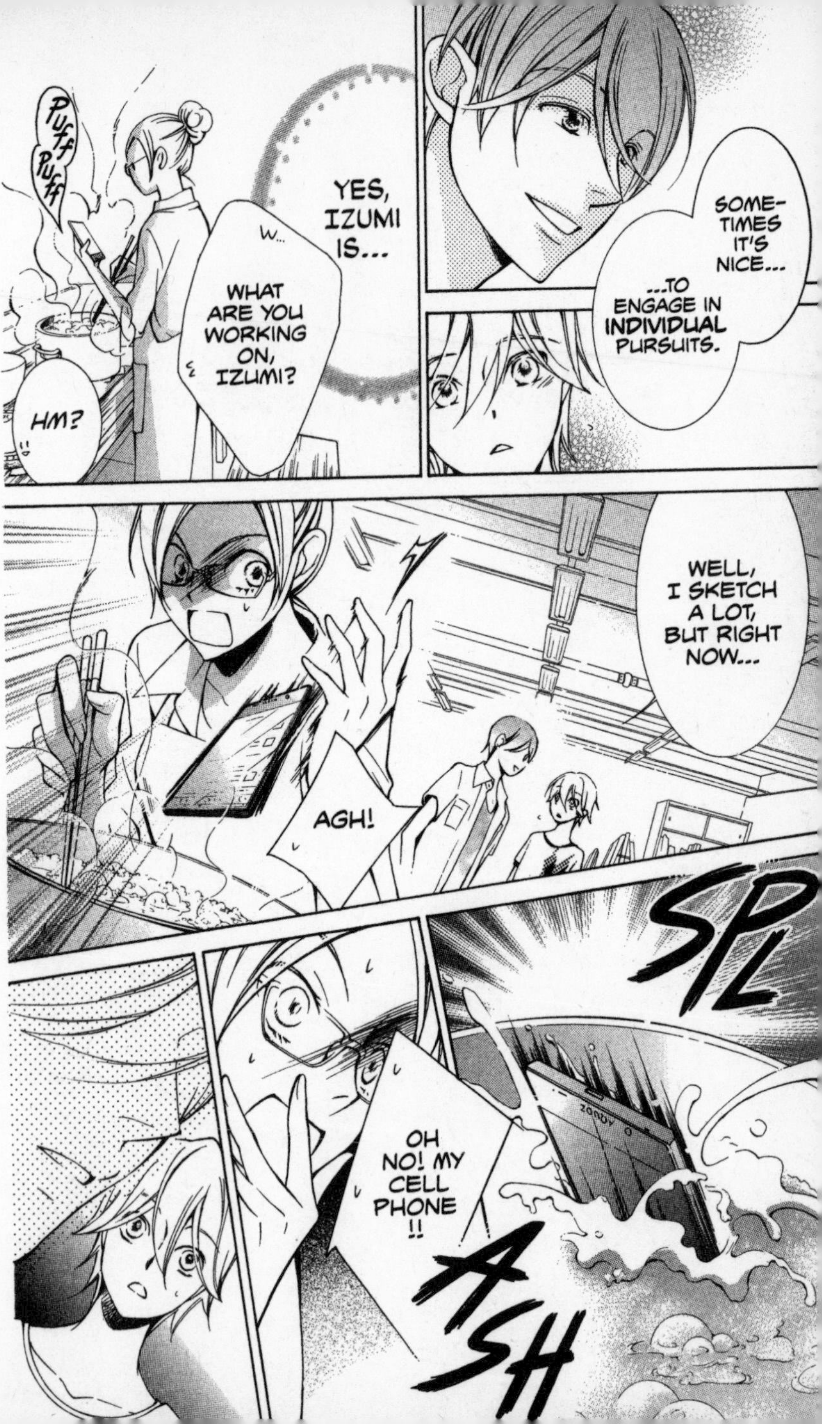

SOME-TIMES IT'S NICE...
...TO ENGAGE IN INDIVIDUAL PURSUITS.
YES, IZUMI IS...
W... WHAT ARE YOU WORKING ON, IZUMI?
Puff Puff
HM?
WELL, I SKETCH A LOT, BUT RIGHT NOW...
AGH!
SPLASH
OH NO! MY CELL PHONE!!

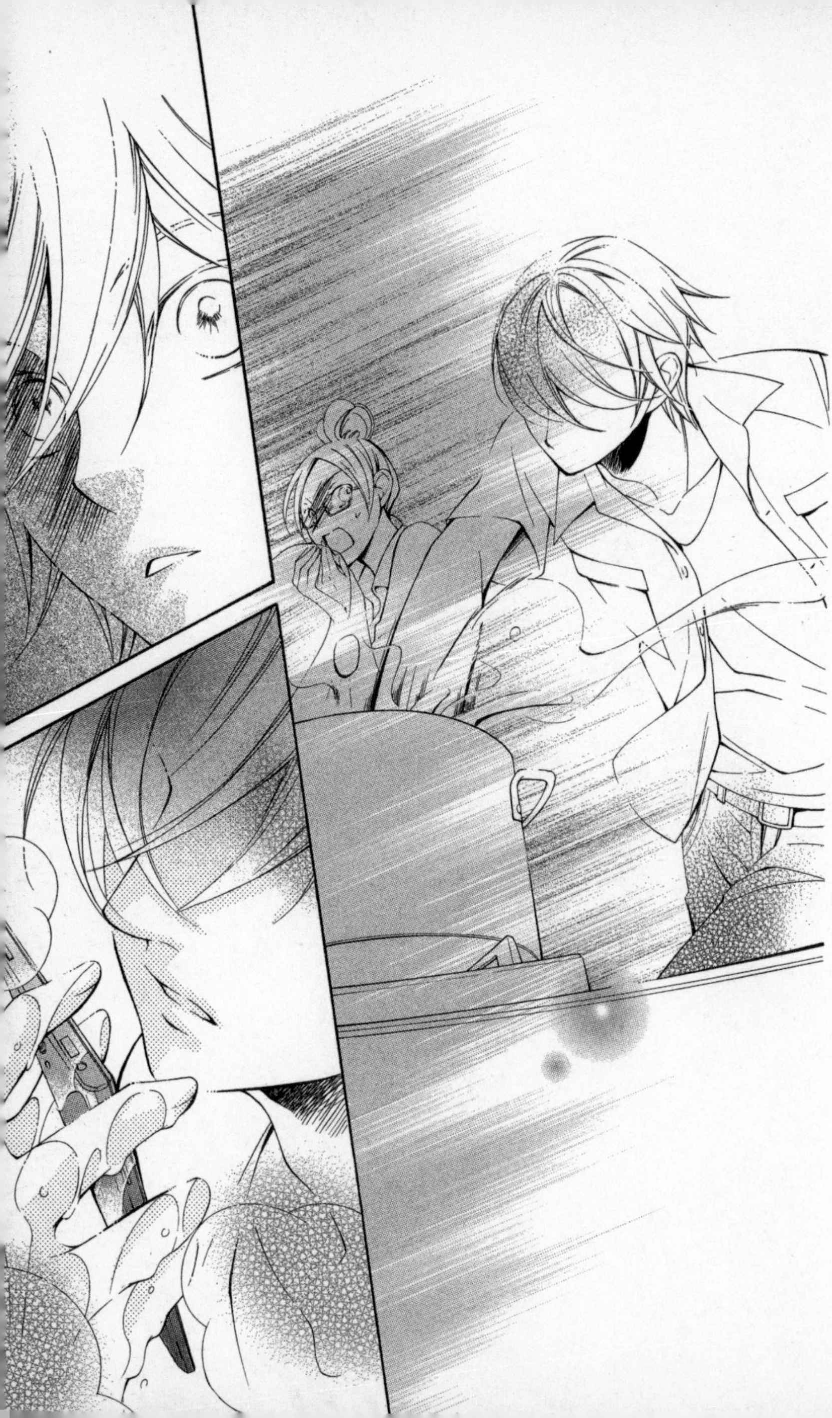

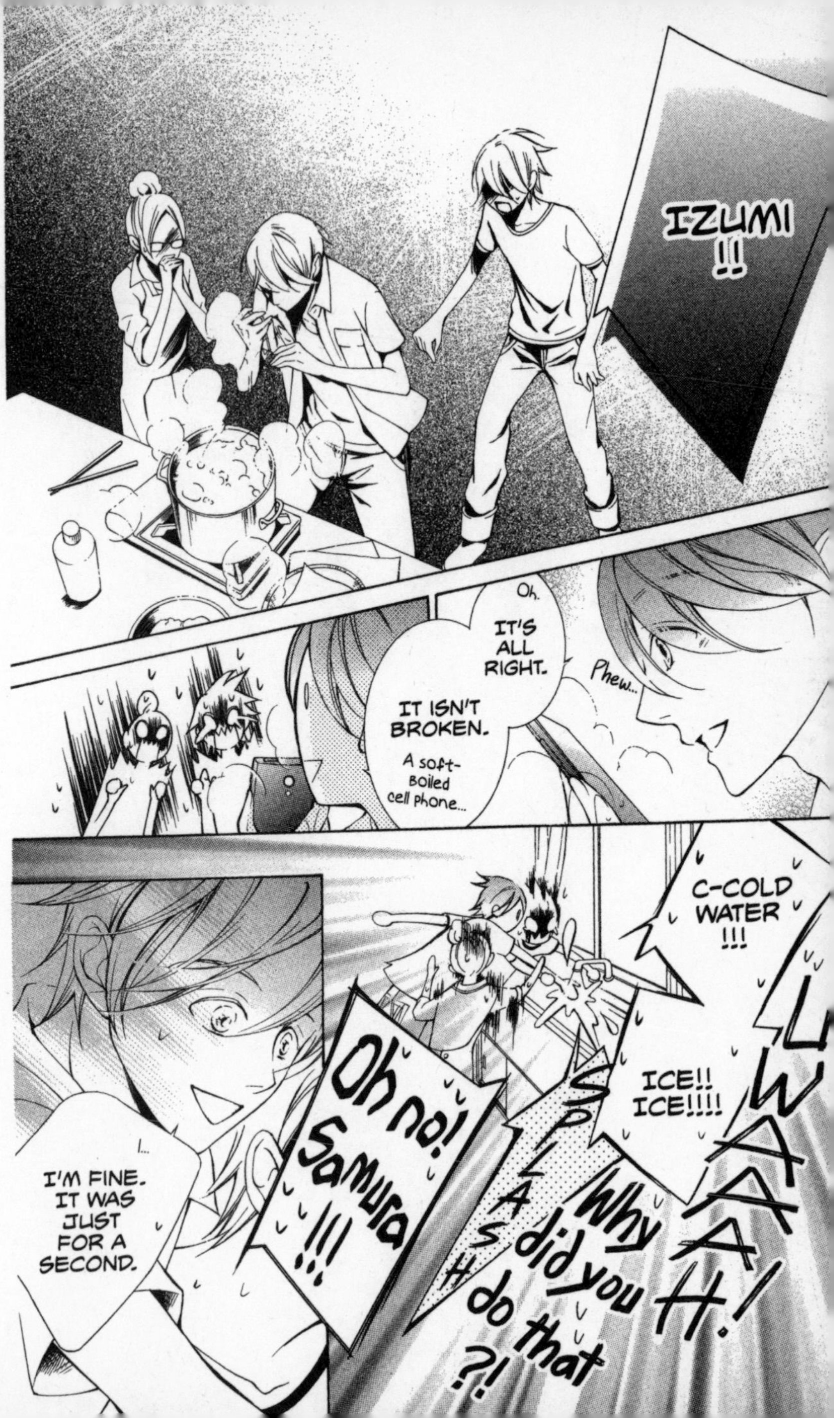
IZUMI !!
Oh.
IT'S ALL RIGHT.
IT ISN'T BROKEN.
Phew...
A soft-boiled cell phone...
C-COLD WATER !!!
UWAAAH!
ICE!! ICE!!!!
SPLASH
Why did you do that ?!
Oh no! Samura !!!
I...
I'M FINE. IT WAS JUST FOR A SECOND.

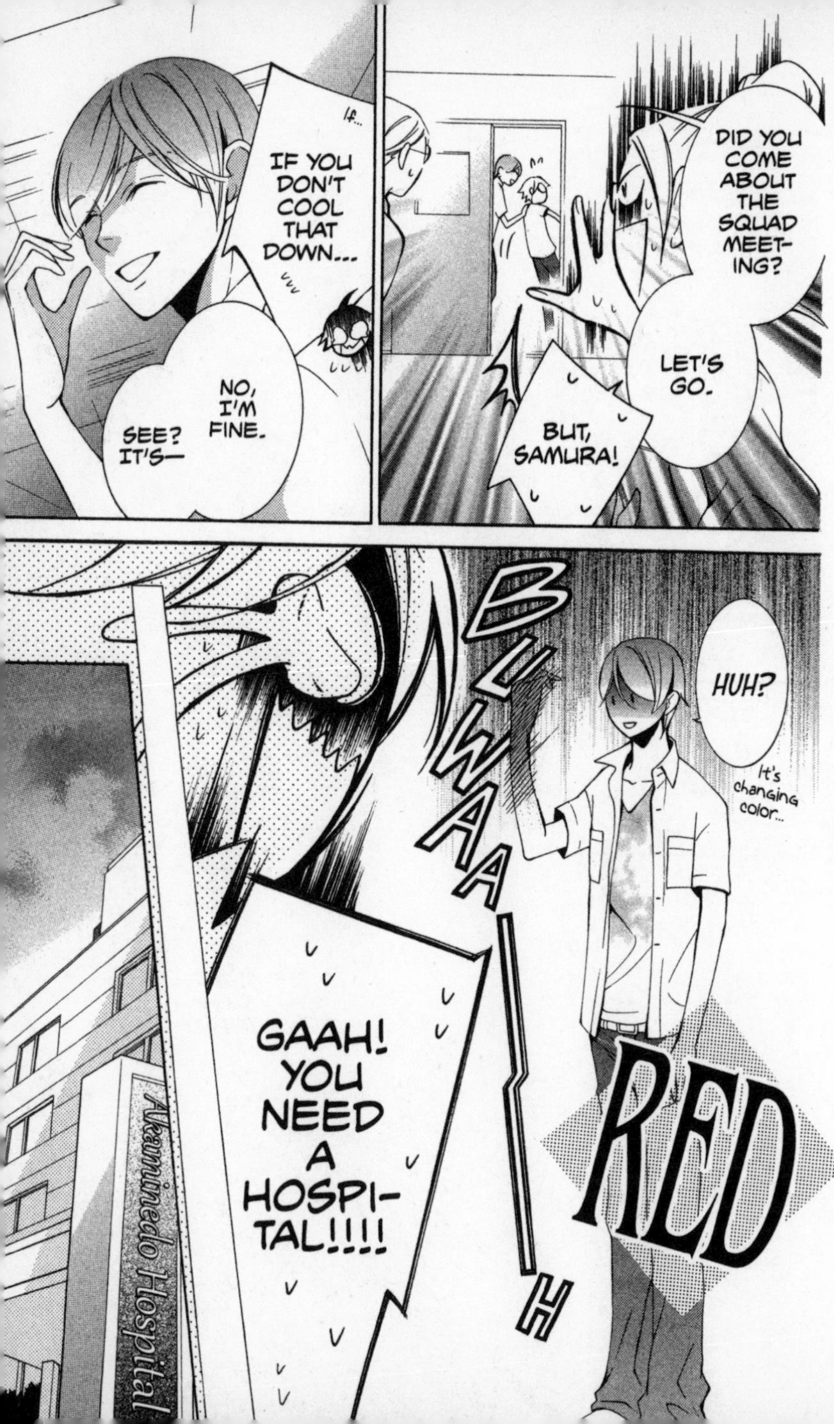

DID YOU COME ABOUT THE SQUAD MEETING?
LET'S GO.
BUT, SAMURA!
If...
IF YOU DON'T COOL THAT DOWN...
NO, I'M FINE.
SEE? IT'S—
HUH?
It's changing color...
RED
BLWAAAH
GAAH! YOU NEED A HOSPITAL!!!!
Akaminedo Hospital

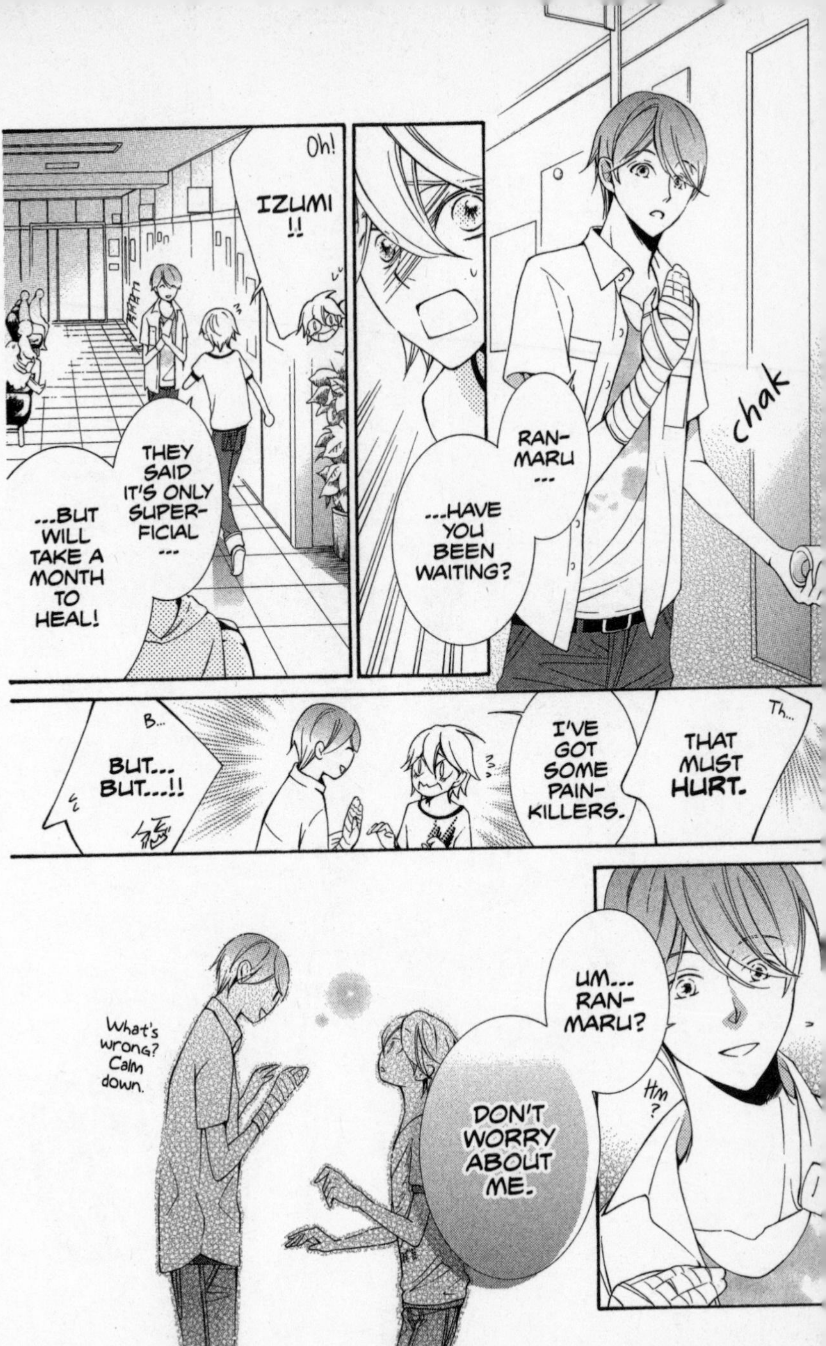
chak
RAN-MARU...
...HAVE YOU BEEN WAITING?
Oh!
IZUMI!!
THEY SAID IT'S ONLY SUPER-FICIAL...
...BUT WILL TAKE A MONTH TO HEAL!
Th...
THAT MUST HURT.
I'VE GOT SOME PAIN-KILLERS.
B...
BUT... BUT...!!
UM... RAN-MARU?
Hm?
DON'T WORRY ABOUT ME.
What's wrong? Calm down.

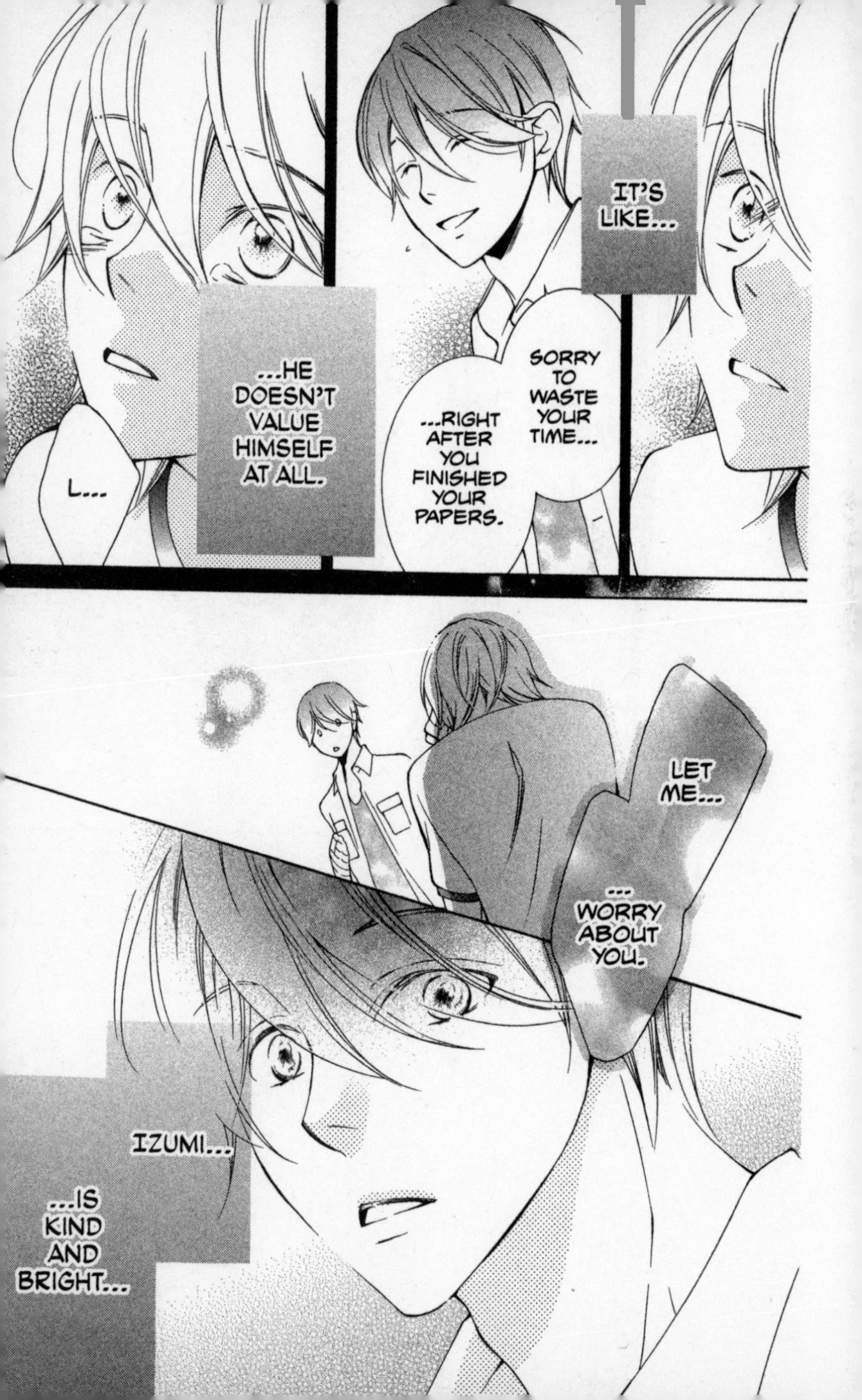
IT'S LIKE...
SORRY TO WASTE YOUR TIME...
...RIGHT AFTER YOU FINISHED YOUR PAPERS.
...HE DOESN'T VALUE HIMSELF AT ALL.
L...
LET ME...
...WORRY ABOUT YOU.
IZUMI...
...IS KIND AND BRIGHT...

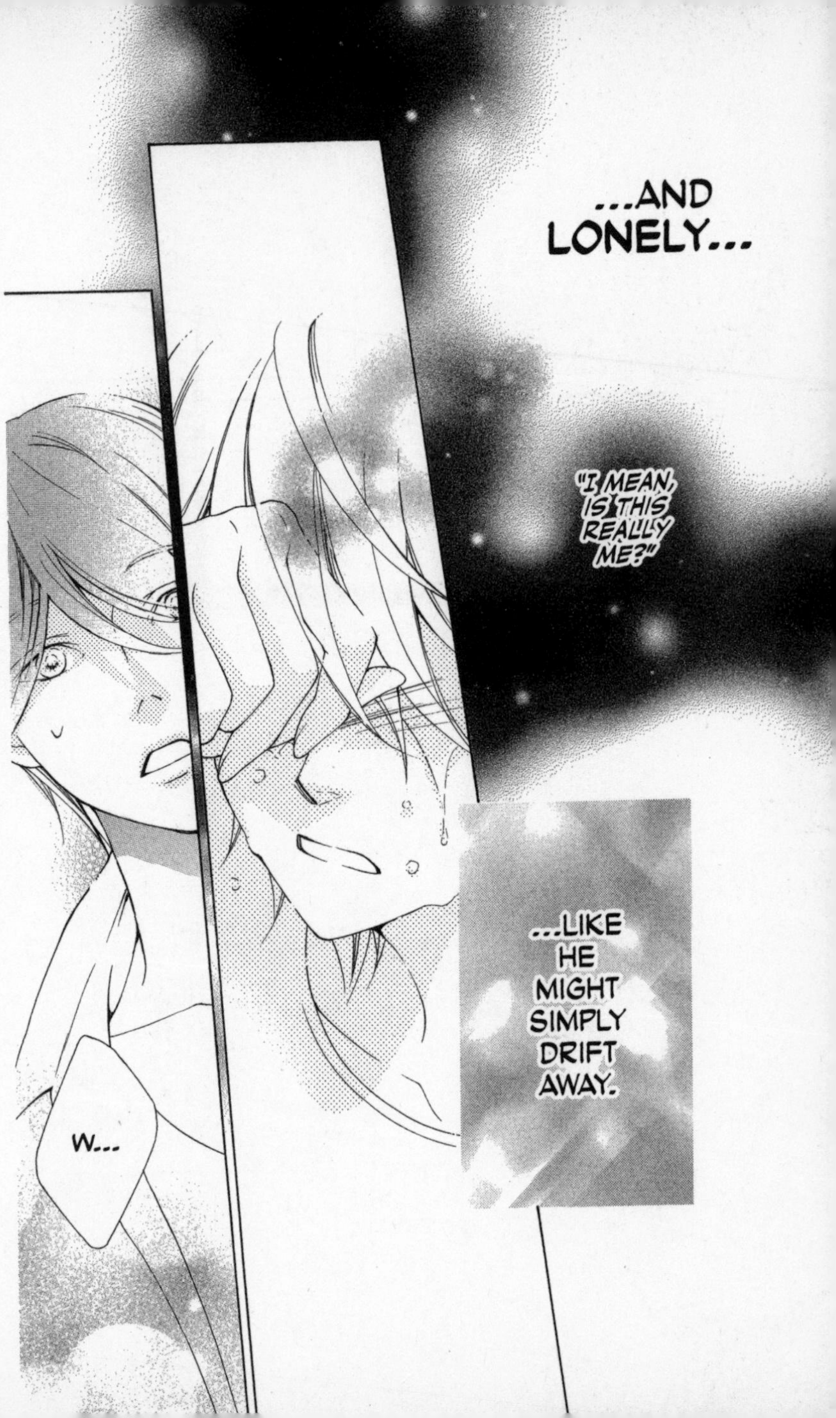
...AND LONELY...
"I MEAN, IS THIS REALLY ME?"
...LIKE HE MIGHT SIMPLY DRIFT AWAY.
W...

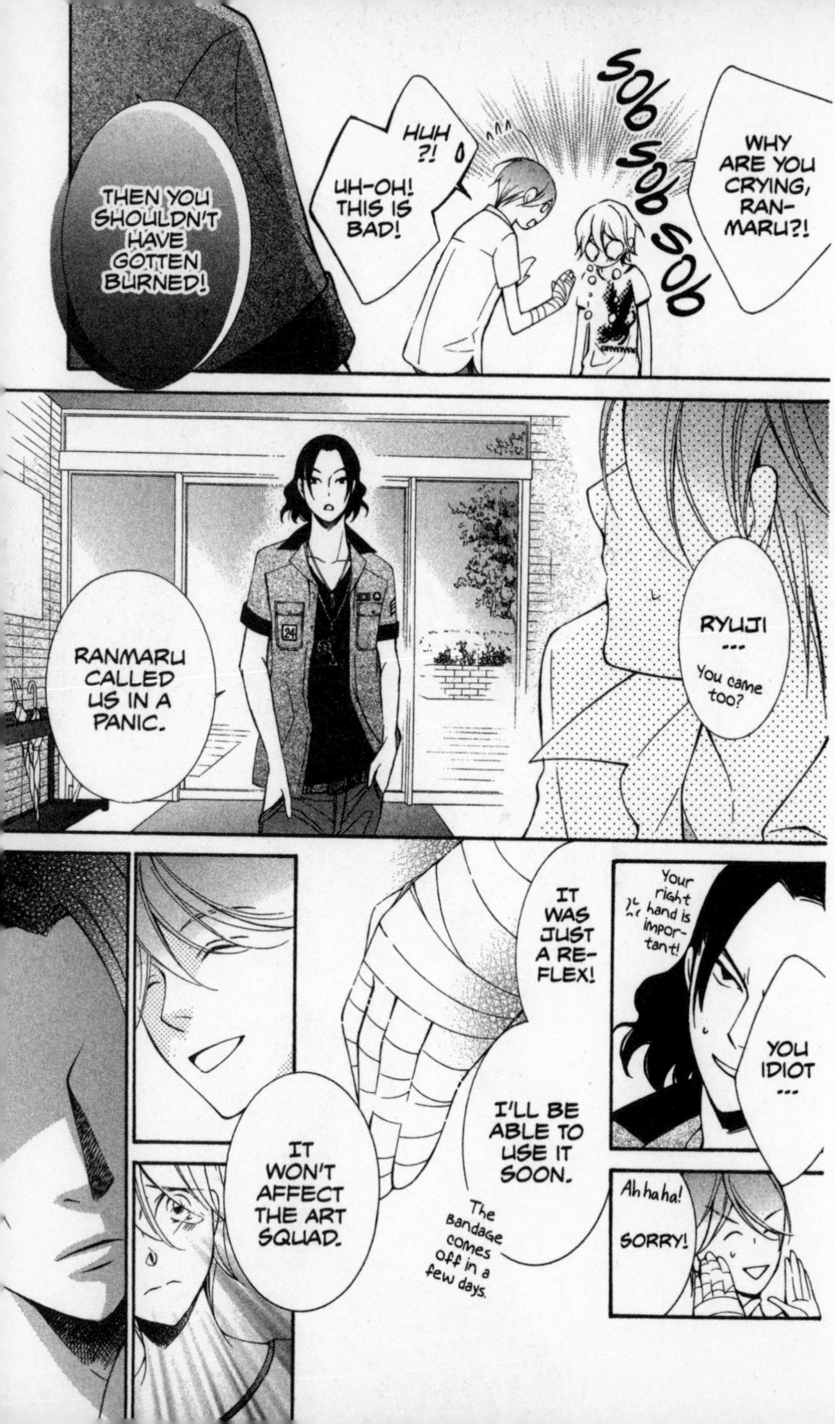
WHY ARE YOU CRYING, RAN-MARU?!
SOB SOB SOB
HUH ?!
UH-OH! THIS IS BAD!
THEN YOU SHOULDN'T HAVE GOTTEN BURNED!
RYUJI...
You came too?
RANMARU CALLED US IN A PANIC.
Your right hand is impor-tant!
YOU IDIOT...
Ahhaha!
SORRY!
IT WAS JUST A RE-FLEX!
I'LL BE ABLE TO USE IT SOON.
The bandage comes off in a few days.
IT WON'T AFFECT THE ART SQUAD.

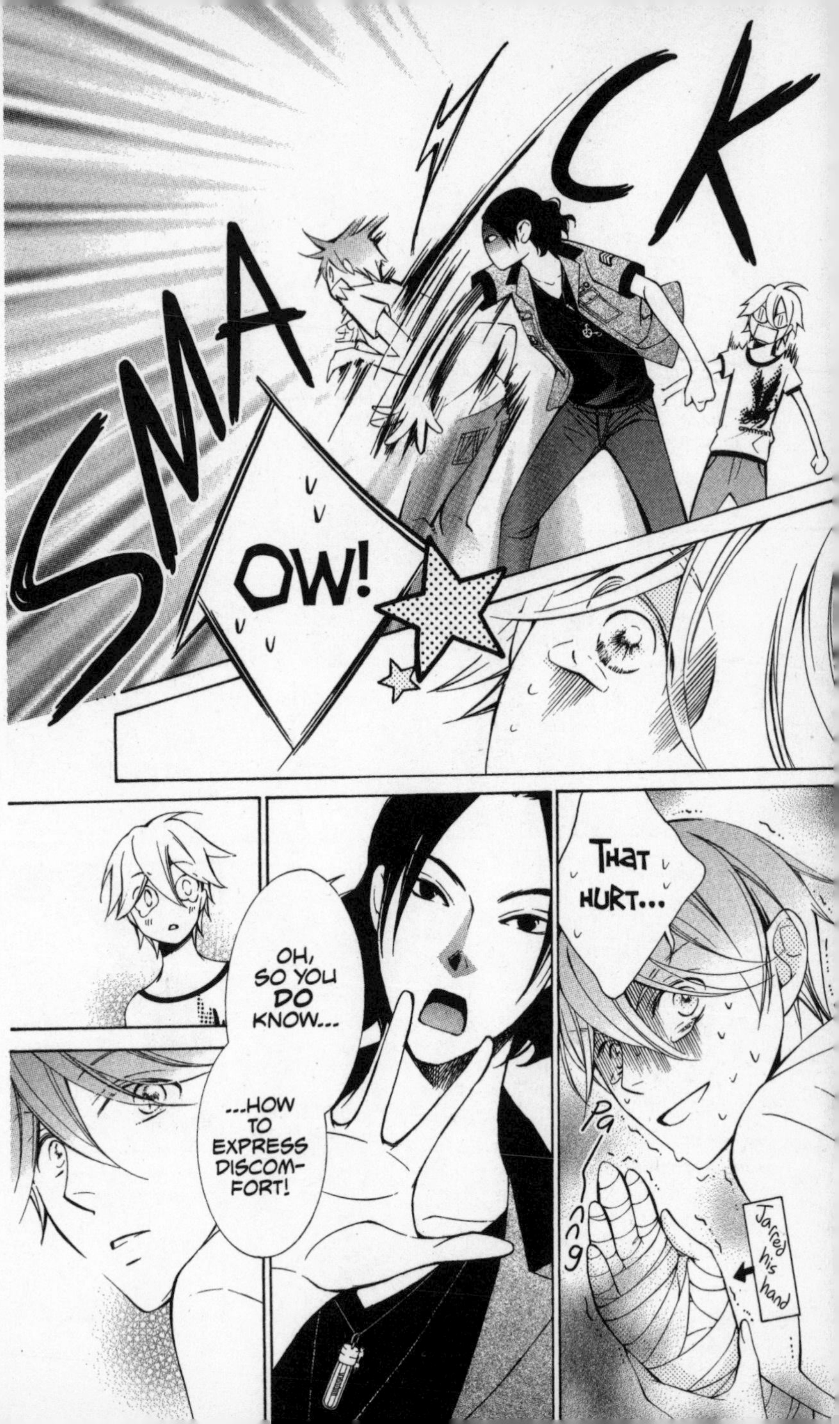
SMACK
OW!
THAT HURT...
Jarred his hand
OH, SO YOU DO KNOW...
...HOW TO EXPRESS DISCOMFORT!

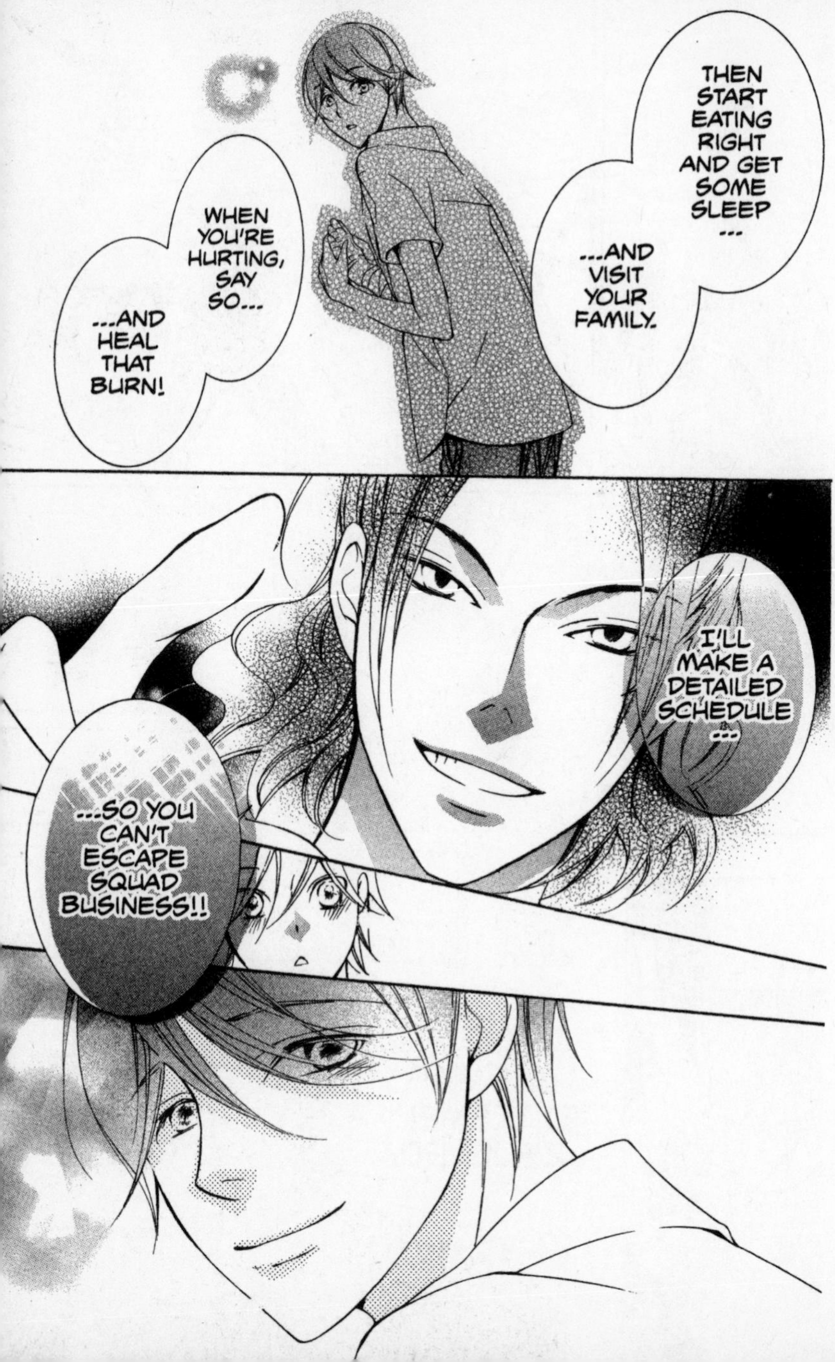
THEN START EATING RIGHT AND GET SOME SLEEP...
...AND VISIT YOUR FAMILY.
WHEN YOU'RE HURTING, SAY SO...
...AND HEAL THAT BURN!
I'LL MAKE A DETAILED SCHEDULE...
...SO YOU CAN'T ESCAPE SQUAD BUSINESS!!

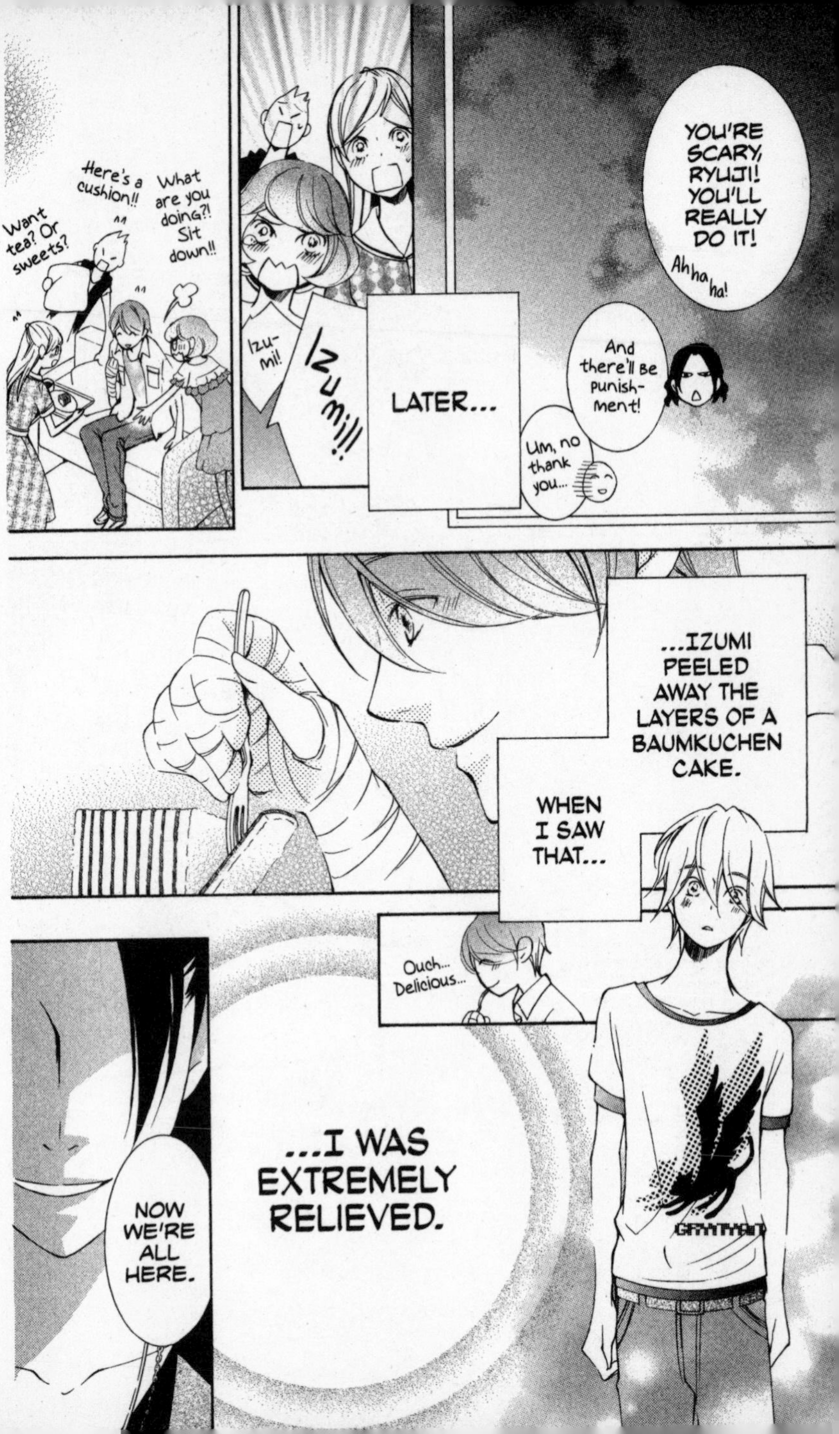
YOU'RE SCARY, RYUJI! YOU'LL REALLY DO IT!
Ahhaha!
And there'll be punishment!
Um, no thank you...
LATER...
IZUMI!!
Izu-mi!
What are you doing?! Sit down!!
Here's a cushion!!
Want tea? Or sweets?
...IZUMI PEELED AWAY THE LAYERS OF A BAUMKUCHEN CAKE.
WHEN I SAW THAT...
Ouch... Delicious...
...I WAS EXTREMELY RELIEVED.
NOW WE'RE ALL HERE.

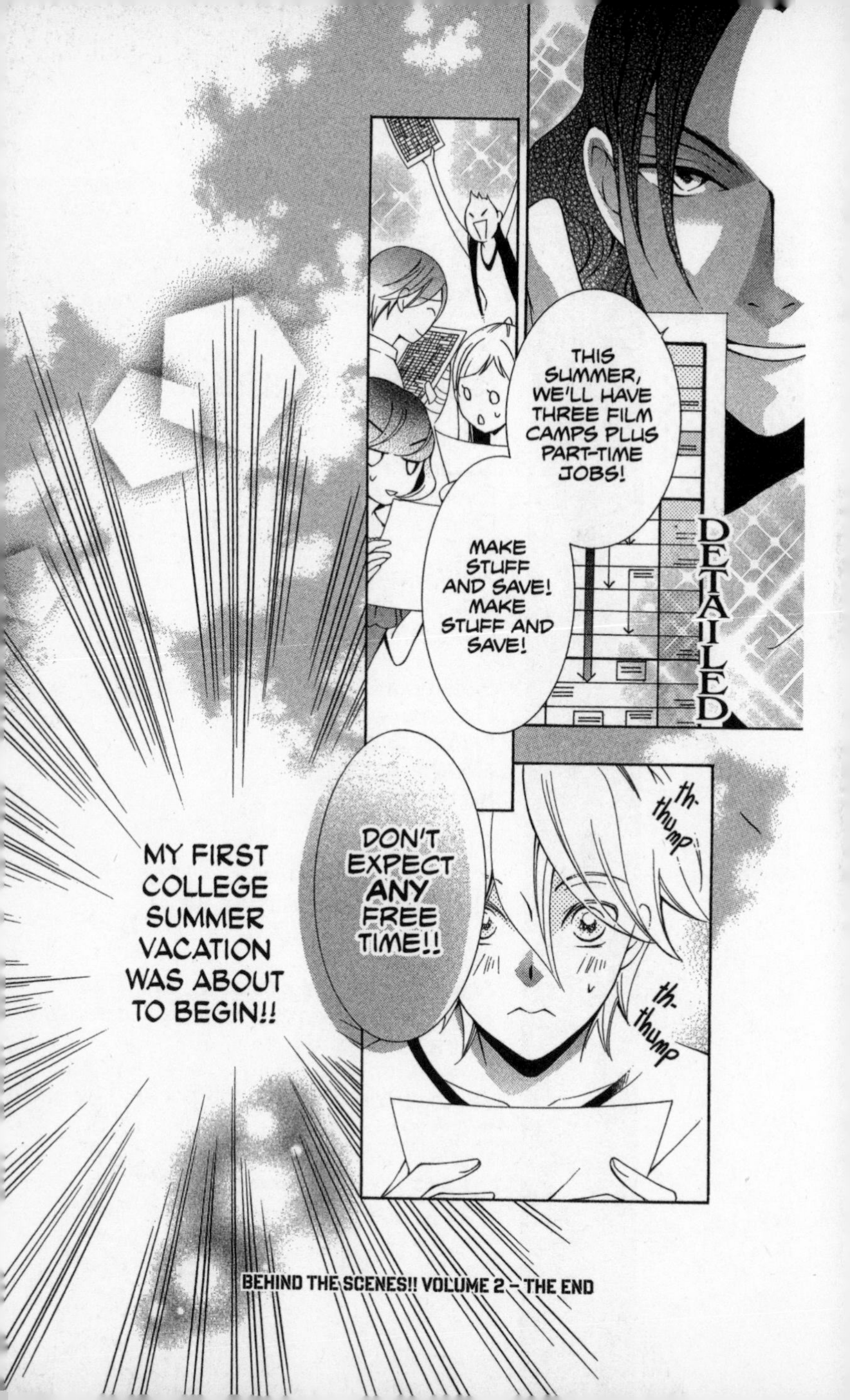
THIS SUMMER, WE'LL HAVE THREE FILM CAMPS PLUS PART-TIME JOBS!
DETAILED
MAKE STUFF AND SAVE! MAKE STUFF AND SAVE!
th-thump
DON'T EXPECT ANY FREE TIME!!
th-thump
MY FIRST COLLEGE SUMMER VACATION WAS ABOUT TO BEGIN!!
BEHIND THE SCENES!! VOLUME 2 – THE END

Special Thanks!!

Ms. O
Nakamura-sama
Everyone on the editorial staff
Everyone involved in publishing this book

YANG-sama
Yasuhito Tachibana-sama
Namiko Yokota-sama

Steampunk Jewelry Forêt-sama
Rodemu-sama
Nafumi Sasaki-sama
Rouche-sama
Kana-sama

Staff:
Yui Natsuki, Aya Aomura, Umeko, Yutori
Hizakura, Shizuru Onda, Keiko

Assistants:
Namiki-sama, Kakeda-sama, Shii Tsuno-
kawa, Tadano-sama, Midori Shiino-sama,
Akira Kono-sama

All the people reading this book!

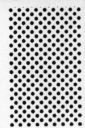

2015

GLOSSARY

Page 14, panel 3: Otaku
An *otaku* is a collector or hobbyist, and the term is similar to "nerd" or "geek."

Page 83, panel 3: Yukhoe
Korean tartar made with raw, seasoned chopped beef or organ meats.

Page 103, panel 5: Taiyaki
Fish-shaped cakes, usually filled with sweet bean paste.

Page 163, panel 3: Bizen ware
One of the oldest Japanese pottery traditions, which began in the Heian period. Bizen ware has a reddish-brown color.

Page 171, panel 3: Snufkin
A character from the Finnish series *Moomin*. Snufkin is a cool wanderer.

AUTHOR BIO

I enjoy talking with people who make things. People who are always thinking about their next project have a low-key way of speaking that also somehow has a feeling of forward momentum—and I love it!

-Bisco Hatori

Bisco Hatori made her manga debut with *Isshun kan no Romance* (A Moment of Romance) in *LaLa DX* magazine. The comedy *Ouran High School Host Club* was her breakout hit and was published in English by VIZ Media. Her other works include *Detarame Mousouryoku Opera* (Sloppy Vaporous Opera), *Petite Pêche!* and the vampire romance *Millennium Snow*, which was also published in English by VIZ Media.

Behind the Scenes!!

VOLUME 2

Shojo Beat Edition

STORY AND ART BY Bisco Hatori

English Translation & Adaptation/John Werry
Touch-Up Art & Lettering/Sabrina Heep
Design/ Izumi Evers
Editor/Pancha Diaz

Urakata!! by Bisco Hatori
© Bisco Hatori 2015
All rights reserved.
First published in Japan in 2015 by HAKUSENSHA, Inc., Tokyo.
English language translation rights arranged with HAKUSENSHA, Inc.,
Tokyo.

Printed in the U.S.A.

Published by VIZ Media, LLC
P.O. Box 77010
San Francisco, CA 94107

10 9 8 7 6 5 4 3 2 1
First printing, July 2016

www.viz.com

www.shojobeat.com

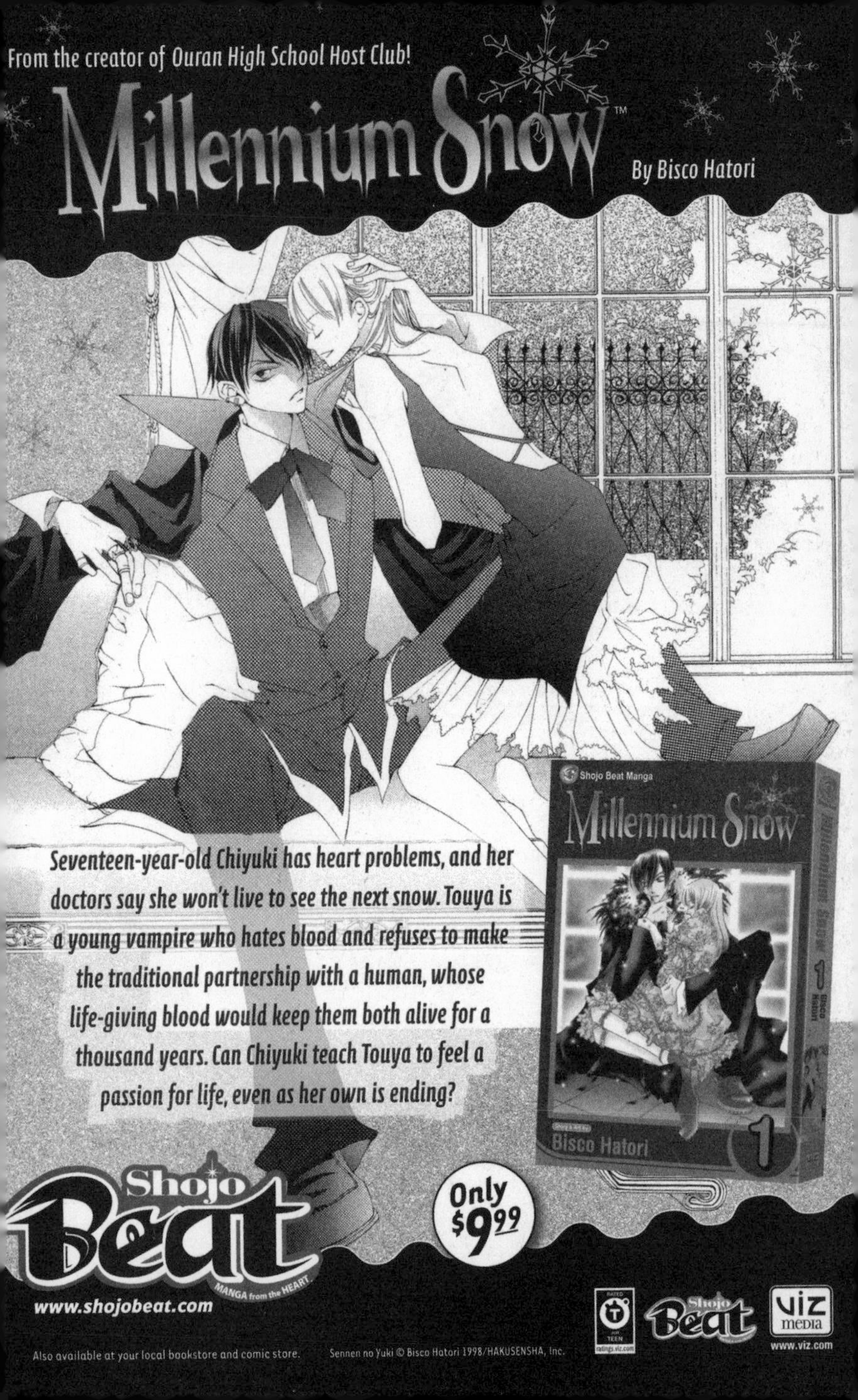
From the creator of Ouran High School Host Club!
Millennium Snow™
By Bisco Hatori
Shojo Beat Manga
Millennium Snow
1
Bisco Hatori
Seventeen-year-old Chiyuki has heart problems, and her doctors say she won't live to see the next snow. Touya is a young vampire who hates blood and refuses to make the traditional partnership with a human, whose life-giving blood would keep them both alive for a thousand years. Can Chiyuki teach Touya to feel a passion for life, even as her own is ending?
Shojo Beat
MANGA from the HEART
Only $9.99
www.shojobeat.com
RATED T TEEN
Shojo Beat
VIZ media
www.viz.com
Also available at your local bookstore and comic store.
Sennen no Yuki © Bisco Hatori 1998/HAKUSENSHA, Inc.

YOU MAY BE READING THE WRONG WAY!

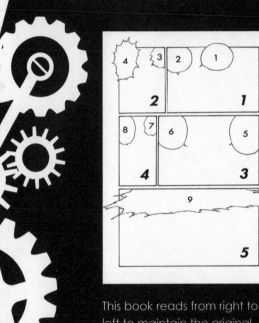

This book reads from right to left to maintain the original presentation and art of the Japanese edition, so action, sound effects and word balloons are reversed. This diagram shows how to follow the panels. Turn to the other side of the book to begin.